FROM DISTANT DAYS

MYTHS, TALES, AND POETRY OF ANCIENT MESOPOTAMIA

Benjamin R. Foster

CDL Press
Bethesda, Maryland

Library of Congress Cataloging-in-Publication Data

Foster, Benjamin R. (Benjamin Read)
    From distant days : myths, tales, and poetry of ancient
Mesopotamia / Benjamin R. Foster
        p.   cm.
    ISBN 1-883053-09-9
    1. Assyro-Babylonian literature — Translations into English.
I. Title.
PJ3953.F67   1995
892'.1—dc20   94-48817
                                                          CIP

The preparation of the contents of this volume was made possible by a grant from the Translations Program of the National Endowment for the Humanities, an independent Federal agency.

Copyright © 1995 by Benjamin R. Foster. All rights reserved. This book may not be reproduced, in whole or in part, in any form (beyond that copying permitted by Sections 107 and 108 of the U. S. Copyright Law and except by reviewers for the public press), without written permission from the publisher, CDL Press, P.O. Box 34454, Bethesda, MD 20827.

Designed by Karen Polinger Foster and Elizabeth Lyons.

Cover: Akkadian literary tablets from the Yale Babylonian Collection, reproduced by permission. Cover photo by Daniel Lopez, Yale Audio Visual Center.

ISBN 1-883053-09-9

Contents

Preface   vii
Introduction   1

I. GODS AND THEIR DEEDS

Epic of Creation   9
Story of the Flood   52
When Ishtar Went to the Netherworld   78
How Nergal Became King of the Netherworld   85
How Adapa Lost Immortality   97
Etana, the King without an Heir   102
Anzu, the Bird Who Stole Destiny   115
How Erra Wrecked the World   132

II. KINGS AND THEIR DEEDS

Legends of Sargon of Akkad   165
Legend of Naram-Sin   171
Tukulti-Ninurta Epic   178
Nebuchadnezzar and Marduk   197
Tiglath-Pileser and the Beasts   206
The King of Justice   208

III. DIVINE SPEECH

Prophecies   213
Letters from Gods   214
Marduk Prophecy   215
Oracles to Assyrian Kings   218

IV. Hymns and Prayers

INDIVIDUAL PRAYERS

To Adad	221
To Dumuzi	222
To Ea	223
To Ea, Shamash, and Marduk	224
To Family Ghosts	227
To Girra	228
To Gula	229
To Ishtar	238
To Marduk	247
To Nabu	249
To Nusku	252
To Shamash	254
To a Personal God	267
To Any God	269

ROYAL PRAYERS

Coronation Prayer for Assyrian Kings	272
Prayer at the Gods' Repast	273
Assurnasirpal I, on Occasion of Illness	274
Sargon II, for His New City	278
Assurbanipal, Pious Scholar	282
Nebuchadnezzar II, for His Public Works	283
Nabonidus, for His Public Works	285

DIVINERS' PRAYERS

The Cedar	288
The Sacrificial Gazelle	291
The Sacrificial Lamb	291
Will Ur-Utu be Alive and Well?	292

LETTER PRAYERS

Kussulu to the Moon God	293
Ur-Nanshe to Ninsianna	294
Apil-Adad to "God My Father"	294

V. Sorrow and Suffering

Dialogue between a Man and His God	295
Poem of the Righteous Sufferer	298
A Sufferer's Salvation	314
The Babylonian Theodicy	316
Lament for a City	324
Who Has Not Sinned?	326
The Piteous Sufferer	328
Elegy for a Woman Dead in Childbirth	329

VI. Love and Sex

Love Charms	331
Against Arousal	341
Love Lyrics of Rim-Sin	342
Love Lyrics of Nabu and Tashmetu	344
Love Lyrics of Ishtar of Babylon	347
Ishtar Will Not Tire	349
Ishtar at the Tavern	350
The Faithful Lover	351

VII. Stories and Humor

At the Cleaners	355
The Poor Man of Nippur	357
Why Do You Curse Me?	363
The Jester	365
The Gilgamesh Letter	368
The Dialogue of Pessimism	370
Against a Bleating Goat	373
The Dog's Boast	374
Land for the Birds	375

VIII. Wisdom

Counsels of Wisdom	377
Proverbs and Sayings	381
Proverbs from Letters	389
Advice to a Prince	391

IX. Magic Spells

Birth and Childhood	393
Against Lamashtu	400
Against Demons, Phantoms, Ghosts	406
Against Disease and Discomfort	410
Professional and Business Life	422
Against Witchcraft and Sorcery	425
The World Around	429

Glossary of Proper Names	433

Preface

This book is a selection, rearrangement, and abridgment of *Before the Muses, An Anthology of Akkadian Literature* (Bethesda, MD: CDL Press, 1993). Readers who wish to learn more about these compositions or who want to read further in Akkadian literature are referred to the larger work. Several texts have been included in this volume that are not in *Before the Muses*. Of these, the Mari prophecies are drawn from J.-M. Durand, *Archives Épistolaires de Mari* I/1 (Paris, 1988), nos. 213, 214 (Annunitum); 197, 209 (Dagan); 192 (Ishtar of Nineveh, with W. Yuhong, *Nouvelles Assyriologiques Brèves et Utilitaires* 1994 no. 38); and 194 (Shamash). Land for the Birds is drawn from T. Kwasman and S. Parpola, *Legal Transactions of the Royal Court of Nineveh* Part I (Helsinki, 1991), no. 288, with collation by J. Scurlock, *Nouvelles Assyriologiques Brèves et Utilitaires* 1993 no. 17.

For significant improvements made here to translations from *Before the Muses*, I am indebted to M. Dietrich in J. C. de Moor et al., ed., *Verse in Ancient Near Eastern Prose* (Neukirchen, 1993), 41-67 (A Sufferer's Salvation); A. R. George in *Iraq* 55 (1993), 63-75 (At the Cleaners, The Poor Man of Nippur, Why Do You Curse Me?), plus improvements to The Cedar communicated privately; W. L. Moran in *The Journal of the Ancient Near Eastern Society* 22 (1993), 113-120 (Kussulu to the Moon-God); N. Veldhuis, *A Cow of Sin* (Groningen, 1991) (Sin and the Cow). I have taken this occasion to make minor revisions and corrections throughout.

I am indebted to the contributions of many scholars in my preparation of these translations; my detailed acknowledgments are found throughout *Before the Muses* and apply to this volume as well. I thank Karen Polinger Foster for her assistance.

The line numbers used here refer in most cases to the English text, not to ancient manuscripts. Square brackets indicate gaps in the original manuscripts, parentheses explanatory additions by the translator, and three dots obscure words or phrases. Material set off by < > indicates a presumed omission by an ancient scribe.

INTRODUCTION

Akkadian refers to a Semitic language spoken and written in Babylonia and Assyria from about 2500 B.C. to the beginning of the Christian era. Akkadian literature is preserved on clay tablets discovered in the ruins of Mesopotamian palaces, temples, and private houses from throughout this long period of time. Since the decipherment of Akkadian about 1850, scholars have labored to piece together and understand this long-forgotten literature. The result has been the recovery of stories, poems, and artful expression a thousand years older than Homer or the Bible. This means that an important chapter can now be written for the beginnings of world literature.

The reader will need to accept certain challenges in confronting texts rescued from the obscurity of a dead civilization. The tablets on which these compositions were written are usually broken or incomplete, so that words, sentences, and entire episodes may be lost. Fortunately, additional pieces of these texts frequently come to light in archaeological excavations and in museum collections. Furthermore, the Akkadian language is still not so well understood as are other ancient languages, such as Greek or Hebrew, so that uncertainties may remain as to the meaning of words or entire passages. Texts may have different editions, versions, or variants from different places and times, so that in some instances the translations perforce combine different versions for the sake of clarity. Despite these problems, enormous progress has been made in understanding this ancient literary tradition. Reconstruction of Mesopotamian civilization and its literature is a rapidly evolving discipline and holds much promise for the future.

Akkadian literature often deals with subjects unfamiliar to the modern reader. The first nine texts chosen here are extended narratives having for their subject the gods of a polytheistic world—their relations to one another, to the cosmos, and to the human race. One major theme is their rivalry: how one god achieves supremacy over others. Another significant theme is the unequal relationship between the gods and the human race. Human beings were created to serve the gods, to feed and house them, and to relieve them of any need to work. Humans are destined to die, whereas the gods live forever. Moreover, humans can never be certain that their actions, however well-intentioned, are pleasing or even acceptable to the gods, who may punish, neglect, or destroy their subjects for no apparent or weighty reason. Therefore justice and equity are not inherent in creation, although favored by some gods, such as the sun, but must be worked out by humans themselves. The gods may lie, cheat, steal, and deceive each other, the very actions that human beings may be punished for. These possibilities make for a certain drama in the universe, if at the same time for a certain moral bleakness.

A second important subject of Akkadian literature is kingship and the deeds of kings. Kings could be heroes, vainglorious or admirable. They could journey to distant places on exciting quests, win wars, and make their names famous throughout history. They could protect their subjects from harm and punish or kill their enemies. Kings could safeguard community institutions or the rites and property of the gods. They could promote economic well-being and justice, protect the disadvantaged, and win the fickle favor of the gods for their land. Kings' successes, failures, wealth, and suffering were deemed grander and more worthy of story-telling than those of lesser people. So too their limitations and absurdities were more dramatic, their births and deaths more solemn in their significance than those of ordinary mortals.

For many readers, stories about gods and kings may seem narrative strategies for a culture that assigned little artistic value to the present or to empirically recognizable experience. This judgment is supported by the absence of narrative features familiar to the modern reader: a sense of place and a sense of the passage of time. Yet for other readers these compositions preserve ancient religious belief or mythology, as well as political ideology about rulers and how they should act and be regarded by their subjects. Nor need one of these perspectives exclude the other. Indeed, the social and cultural context of most Akkadian literature is unknown, so the significance of these texts for their ancient audiences can only be guessed.

Akkadian preserves a large body of material purporting to be the speech of gods. The earliest documents are reports in letters found at Mari in Syria, dating to the first quarter of the second millennium B.C. These record the speech of ecstatics, often consisting of warnings and advice to the king, and so are referred to as "prophecy," humans speaking on behalf of the gods. Divine speech could also occur in written form, either in the form of a letter from a god or in the form of a literary discourse, as in the Marduk Prophecy. From the first millennium B.C. come divine oracles to Assyrian kings. These resemble the Mari prophecies in theme and tone, but are preserved in collections written out in literary fashion. They may in some instances have been vouchsafed to the king directly, rather than through ecstatics or prophets.

Akkadian devotional expression embraces aspects of hymn, prayer, and magic. Hymns celebrate deities' attributes and praise their power, importance, and concern for humanity. Prayers ask for help and relief from sorrow and suffering. Since sickness and misfortune were often seen as divine punishment, some prayers acknowledge guilt or probe the reasons for a deity's anger, at the same time seeking to placate it. Some hymns and prayers incorporate magical language that was of its own power supposed to avert harm portended for the suppliant.

Within this large and diverse body of expression are important subgroups, such as prayers in the names of ruling kings. These prayers were sometimes composed in connection with official matters, such as the construction of buildings, whereas others were purely personal. Another group of prayers reflects the needs of professional people, especially diviners. Divination was the leading Mesopotamian science and intellectual endeavor. For the diviner, every event and phenomenon held potential significance for humanity if the signs could be interpreted correctly. One branch of divination depended on observations, such as eclipses, the negative portents of which could be averted by prayer and ritual. Another branch elicited responses to specific questions by posing the question to a god of divination and then by examining the entrails of a sacrificial animal to interpret the marks and configurations as positive or negative replies. Diviners prayed for unambiguous signs and the expertise to read them correctly. Another group of prayers was composed in letter form, addressed to a deity and deposited in a temple for the god to read and act upon. These could be written by private individuals or rulers. Examples of both types are presented here.

Some Akkadian literature may be grouped on the basis of theme. For example, the relationship between suffering and justice is explored in several important compositions: why do good people suffer and wicked prosper? Are the gods really interested in fairness and justice? Sometimes pain, destruction, and death appear random in a world supposedly ordered by superior intelligences. Unhappiness can take many other forms in Akkadian literature, for example, illness, poverty, defeat, the death of a young mother.

Love and sex are important themes as well. Magic spells were used to attract desire and enhance sexual activity. One spell here presented seeks to suppress the onset of desire. Some poems celebrate marriage, sometimes in a ritual or cultic setting. Others reflect casual or commercial sex. One satirizes the pathetic devotion of unequal love.

Readers of Akkadian enjoyed stories, jokes, parody, and other light literary entertainment. This could be crude and scatological, or academic, or in the style of a folktale, subtle or absurd. These compositions depend for effect on breaking taboos, exaggeration, and reversing expectations. They often draw on situations of everyday life in a ridiculous way.

Wisdom refers to proverbs, advice, and observations on how to achieve satisfaction, success, and a clearer understanding of morality and proper behavior. The examples chosen here are drawn from school books, collections of ancient lore, and letters of advice quoting traditional wisdom. These themes are developed in other literary contexts as well, such as the Great Hymn to Shamash, which includes a section on integrity in business and commerce, or in the legend of the king Naram-Sin who, in his impetuous arrogance, ignored the advice of the gods as seen through divination and so risked his life and reign.

Magic spells are concerned with personal and social needs, ills, and anxieties. Some are intended to help successful childbirth or to quiet fretful babies. Others seek to protect infants and toddlers from harm, personified as the demon Lamashtu, who invaded the home to hurt, steal, or kill children. Many spells confront personified evil such as devils or phantoms. Demons were a third state of being, between gods and humans. They could include the wraiths of humans who were not buried properly or who were cheated of a normal fruitful life, so returned to harass others out of envy. Some spells combat disease and discomfort. Others are for use in situations such as lawsuits, loss of property, or for professional and social advancement. Some ward off black magic and witchcraft, others natural phenomena such as mad dogs or troublesome insects. The hopes, wishes, and fears expressed in them reveal human psychology of millennia ago.

Turning to consideration of how writers of Akkadian expressed their ideas, the reader is at a disadvantage because much of their literary art is invisible in translation. Certain important narrative strategies and rhetorical figures can, however, be appreciated to some extent, of which one of the most characteristic is parallelism.

Parallelism refers to repeated reformulation of the same message such that subsequent statements of it restate, expand, complete, contrast, make more specific, complement, or carry further the first statement. The following example is a simple case of this:

> Sing of a goddess, most awe-inspiring goddess,
> Let her be praised, mistress of people,
> > greatest of the Igigi-igods.
> Sing of Ishtar, most awe-inspiring goddess,
> Let her be praised, mistress of women,
> > greatest of the Igigi-gods.

The parallelism is developed in each half line of poetry. At first a goddess is praised; then in the third line her name replaces the general term. Likewise, "people" is rendered more specific by "women," since particular needs of women are alluded to later in the poem. Otherwise the couplets are identical.

Here is a second, somewhat more complex example, still within four lines of poetry:

> My slave cursed me openly in the assembly (of gentlefolk),
> My slave girl defamed me before the mob.
> An acquaintance would see me and make himself scarce,
> My family set me down as an outsider.

In this case, parallelism is used to convey all possible instances. The first two lines include male and female, citizens and slaves, upper class and lower class: all members of society. The theme of denunciation by inferiors is developed in the second pair of lines by moving to people of equal social status, then to blood relations. The lower classes slander him, his equals avoid him, his intimates renounce him. The first two lines depend on acts of speech, the second on physical actions. More subtle aspects of the parallelism include manipulation of syntax. Here the subject of each sentence is set at the beginning of each successive line for extra emphasis, an uncommon pattern in Akkadian poetry. Furthermore, the subjects are ranked in successive lines from least to most intimate. Some contrasts are left to the reader to infer. For example, cursing in the first line suggests denouncing a person to the gods, while defaming in the next implies denouncing in human society. This is therefore another instance of expressing totality by use of inclusive contrasts. Note in addition that in the third line the acquaintances distance themselves from the sufferer, removing themselves from his circle, while in the fourth the family unites to exclude him from their circle, thereby distancing him. The reader sensitive to possibilities of parallelism can appreciate directly one of the fundamental devices in the Akkadian poetic repertory.

Another important device in Akkadian literature is use of repetition. Whereas parallelism usually implies reformulation of a thought in different words, repetition implies restatement in the same words, or with only slight changes, such as grammatical person. Extensive use of repetition in Akkadian narrative shows it to be a favored device of story telling. Repetition lengthens narrative to allow development of details and injection of subordinate material that might otherwise burden a continuous poetic narrative too heavily.

Repetition was also to achieve specific narrative effects, especially in dramatic scenes. An example is the assault on the chief god's household by the striking gods in the Story of the Flood, Tablet I lines 71ff. The narrator emphasizes the major turns of events by continued repetition of short sets of lines in staccato fashion:

> Enlil made ready to speak
> And said to his vizier Nusku,
> "Nusku, bar your gate,
> "Get your weapons and stand before me."
> Nusku barred his gate,
> Got his weapons and stood before Enlil.
> Nusku made ready to speak,
> And said to the warrior Enlil,
> "My lord, your face is (gone pale as) tamarisk,
> "Your own offspring! Why did you fear?
> "My lord, your face is (gone pale as) tamarisk,
> "Your own offspring! Why did you fear?"

When negotiations begin between the two sides in Tablet I lines 117ff., the repetitions involve much larger blocks of text, suggesting a more leisurely pace of events.

This style of narrative is carried to extremes in the Epic of Creation, where in the beginning of the poem speeches are repeated within speeches, suggesting the sluggishness and ineffectiveness of the older gods. As soon as the youthful Marduk receives his charge and is off to battle, action is narrated with scarcely a repetition until the defeat of Tiamat. The last part of the poem is one long speech, but with no repetition, for Marduk's speech is effective and creative.

Close attention to this technique will greatly enhance the reader's appreciation of Akkadian narrative compositions.

Not all Akkadian literature relies on these devices. Magic spells, for example, often have a pungent directness and use simple poetic techniques familiar to the modern reader from nursery rhymes or commercial jingles. Despite their simplicity, they can speak to the reader directly from the dark, private recesses of human fears and needs.

Akkadian prayers, in contrast, tend to follow conventional patterns and draw on a limited repertory of figures. In structure, for example, they often open with an invocation to the god, with terms of praise, then turn to the suppliant's suffering, and next offer to praise the divinity's power if the suffering is relieved. Sometimes there are requests for intervention by a divine spouse and assertions that other gods will be pleased with favorable action. The examples chosen here are particularly fine ones of their type or offer interesting individual features.

As in any literature, individual authors are found who experiment with traditional forms and techniques. The Great Hymn to Shamash, for example, combines various disparate compositions in different styles, presumably by different authors, into one complex whole. The author of How Erra Wrecked the World experimented with narrative voice, alternating an omniscient narrator with first and second person narration by the two principal characters.

Readers may observe differences in style by contrasting the first tablet of the Story of the Flood with the first tablet of the Epic of Creation or with the highly refined parallelism of the Poem of the Righteous Sufferer. Some differences in style are attributable to the fashions of different periods, as the Story of the Flood poem is probably 500 years older than the Epic of Creation, whereas the Poem of the Righteous Sufferer probably was composed sometime between these two.

The reader may also note interdependencies. The Epic of Creation, for example, was perhaps modeled on a version of Anzu, the Bird Who Stole Destiny. The passage at the end of How Erra Wrecked the World that claims that its text was approved by Erra may be modeled on the similar passage at the end of the Epic of Creation that claims it was approved by Marduk. Certain motifs and figures such as similes may recur in different hymns and prayers. This implies that the texts are not isolated compositions but belong to a larger cultural texture of which we can perceive only fragments and traces.

Readers who approach these works as they would modern fiction, seeking dramatic development of a story, character growth, a sense of time and place, probability and verisimilitude, ending with resolution of a conflict, are therefore urged to discard their familiar arsenal of expectations. Readers who seek these texts in terms closer to the intentions of those who composed them will discover the pleasure and uncertainty of venturing into a wholly different world of artistic expression.

I
GODS AND THEIR DEEDS

Epic of Creation

The Epic of Creation celebrates the exaltation of the Babylonian god Marduk to supreme deity of the Mesopotamian pantheon after he had saved the gods from attack by Tiamat, the ocean. The poem ascribes to Marduk reorganization of the universe, with Babylon at the center of it, and inspiration for the creation of mankind in order to sustain the gods. It offers an explanation of various names it assigns to Marduk. This poem should not be considered "the" Mesopotamian creation story; rather, it is the individual work of a poet who viewed Babylon as the center of the universe, and Marduk, god of Babylon, as head of the pantheon. This message was not lost on contemporary readers, for, in some Assyrian versions of the poem, Assur was substituted for Marduk. Therefore this poem can be read as a document of Babylonian nationalism. It may be a product of Babylonian nationalistic revival at the time of Nebuchadnezzar I (twelfth century B.C.), though there is no firm evidence for its date of composition. To judge from its language and content, the poem dates to the latter part of the second millennium B.C.

Some modern scholars have used this text as a Babylonian explanation for the necessity of absolute rule. According to them, it portrays an evolution of political authority from an assembly of equals working out policy to an absolute monarch proclaiming policy. In their view, the text can be read as a metaphor for the evolution of Mesopotamian political institutions from a reconstructed local assembly of elders to absolute kingship claiming divine sanction on a regional or international scale. The catalyst for this change is portrayed as outside threat calling for a resolute war leader. The leader demanded, as his terms for leadership, absolute obedience, even when the threat of war was removed.

As the poet portrays this, the gods willingly surrender their power in return for perpetual safety and maintenance. For the latter purpose mankind is created. The rebellious human spirit, as seen in the Story of the Flood, has no place in this poem, where the highest good for man is to discover and understand his place in the divinely ordered universe.

The poem is a work of great complexity and abounds with conceptual and philological problems. There are still many obscure passages and words. A predilection for certain types of words and constructions, together with the overarching scheme of the poem, suggests the work of a single author. Though naturally there are variants in the manuscript tradition, there is no reason to suppose that the fundamental content of the work has been altered by successive generations, as has sometimes been suggested, just as there is no reason to elevate this composition to a greater authority than it deserves. It was esteemed highly in the first half of the first millennium B.C, as witnessed by the numerous copies that have turned up in both Assyria and Babylonia, by the preparation of an ancient commentary to the names of Marduk (Tablet VII), and by the ritual use of the composition in the Babylonian new year's festival as stated in late sources. It was quoted or referred to in other texts about Marduk.

The least accessible part of the text for the modern reader will be the passage dealing with the names of Marduk, as it exemplifies techniques of Mesopotamian explanatory philology. The names are explained or translated, where their etymology seemed transparent, and then expounded in other ways through assigning further significance to elements within the name.

The poem begins and ends with concepts of naming. The poet evidently considers naming both an act of creation and an explanation of something already brought into being. For the poet, the name, properly understood, discloses the significance of the created thing. Semantic and phonological analysis of names could lead to understanding of the things named. Names, for this poet, are a text to be read by the informed, and bear the same intimate and revealing relationship to what they signify as this text does to the events it narrates. In a remarkable passage at the end, the poet presents his text as the capstone of creation in that it was bearer of creation's significance to mankind.

The poetry of the Epic of Creation shows command of a wide range of traditional poetic techniques and profound learning. A contrast between speech and action is drawn in the first four tablets, in that speech, characteristic of the old order of the gods, can run to considerable length and repetition. A hint of circularity is provided by the concentrically arranged rehearsals of the narrative; by the climax of Tablet III speech occurs within speech within speech within speech. This device is favored in traditional tale-telling as a narrative frame and as a demonstration of virtuosity, but it is seldom developed to such an extent in Akkadian literature (though compare Anzu, the Bird Who Stole Destiny, on which the Epic of Creation may have been modeled). By contrast, the speech and action characteristic of the new order of the gods under Marduk are narrated rapidly, with a minimum of repetition. The last part of the poem is one continuing speech, explaining and celebrating Marduk's fifty names.

Tablet I

(Before anything was, mother ocean [Tiamat] and fresh water(?) [Apsu] mingled to produce the first of a series of pairs of gods. The descendants, with their boisterous behavior, stir Tiamat and Apsu. Although Tiamat bears it in good part, Apsu wishes to kill the offspring. The father is urged on by his counsellor. Apsu's intentions are foiled by Ea, who kills him and restrains his counsellor. He founds his home in Apsu, the watery domain represented by the slain primeval father, and dwells there with his wife.)

When on high no name was given to heaven,	(1)
Nor below was the netherworld called by name,	
Primeval Apsu was their progenitor,	
And matrix-Tiamat[1] was she who bore them all,	
They were mingling their waters together,	(5)
No cane brake was intertwined nor thicket matted close.[2]	
When no gods at all had been brought forth,	
None called by names, none destinies ordained,	
Then were the gods formed within the(se two).	
Lahmu and Lahamu[3] were brought forth,	
were called by name.	(10)
When they had waxed great, had grown up tall,	
Anshar and Kishar[4] were formed, greater than they,	
They grew lengthy of days, added years to years.	
Anu their firstborn was like his forebears,	
Anshar made Anu, his offspring, his equal.	(15)
Then Anu begot in his image Nudimmud,[5]	
Nudimmud was he who dominated(?) his forebears:	
Profound in wisdom, acute of sense, he was massively strong,	
Much mightier than his grandfather Anshar,	
No rival had he among the gods his brethren.	(20)
The divine brethren banded together,	
Confusing Tiamat as they moved about in their stir,	

1. Tiamat is the name of the ocean; Apsu is generally taken to refer to fresh water.
2. That is, nothing divided or covered the waters.
3. Primeval deities.
4. Anshar and Kishar are the circle or horizon of heaven and earth. Anshar was later used by Assyrian scholars as a way of referring to Assur, thus giving him primacy over Marduk.
5. Another name for Ea, god of wisdom.

Roiling the vitals of Tiamat,
By their uproar distressing the interior of the Divine Abode.[1]
Apsu could not reduce their clamor, (25)
But Tiamat was silent before them.
Their actions were noisome to her,
Their behavior was offensive, (but) she was indulgent.
Thereupon Apsu, begetter of the great gods,
Summoned Mummu[2] his vizier, saying to him, (30)
"Mummu, vizier who contents me,
"Come, let us go to Tiamat."
They went, took their places facing Tiamat,
They took counsel concerning the gods their offspring.
Apsu made ready to speak, (35)
Saying to her, Tiamat, in a loud voice,
"Their behavior is noisome to me!
"By day I have no rest, at night I do not sleep!
"I wish to put an end to their behavior, to do away with it!
"Let silence reign that we may sleep." (40)
When Tiamat had heard this,
She grew angry and cried out to her spouse,
She cried out bitterly, outraged that she stood alone,
(For) he had urged evil upon her,
"What? Shall we put an end to what we formed? (45)
"Their behavior may be most noisome,
    but we should bear it in good part."
It was Mummu who answered, counselling Apsu,
The vizier was not receptive to the counsel of his creatrix,[3]
"Put an end here and now, father, to their troublesome ways!
"By day you should have rest, at night you should sleep." (50)
Apsu was delighted with him, he beamed.
On account of the evils he plotted against the gods his children,
He embraced Mummu, around his neck,

---

1. Andurna, a cosmic locality, perhaps an abode of the gods.
2. Mummu is used in line 4 as a common noun referring to Tiamat ("matrix"), preparing for the wordplay in line 48.
3. Play on words between Mummu-Tiamat and Mummu the vizier.

He sat on his knees so he could kiss him.[1]
Whatever they plotted between them, (55)
Was repeated to the gods their offspring.
The gods heard it as they stirred about,
They were stunned, they sat down in silence.
Surpassing in wisdom, ingenious, resourceful,
Ea was aware of all, discerned their stratagem. (60)
He fashioned it, he established it, a master plan,
He made it artful, his superb magic spell.
He recited it and brought (him) to rest in the waters,[2]
He put him in deep slumber, he was fast asleep,
He made Apsu sleep, he was drenched with slumber, (65)
Mummu the advisor was drowsy with languor.
He untied his sash, he stripped off his tiara,
He took away his aura, he himself put it on.
He tied up Apsu, he killed him,
Mummu he bound, he locked him securely. (70)
He founded his dwelling upon Apsu,
He secured Mummu, held (him) firm by a leadrope.
After Ea had captured and vanquished his foes,
Had won the victory over his opponents,
In his chamber, in profound quiet, he rested. (75)
He called it "Apsu," which he assigned sanctuaries.
He established therein his chamber,
Ea and Damkina his wife dwelt there in splendor.

(Birth and childhood of the hero Marduk, who is born with full strength. He is given the four winds by his grandfather.)

In the cella of destinies, the abode of designs,
The most capable, the sage of the gods, the Lord was begotten, (80)
In the midst of Apsu Marduk was formed,
In the midst of holy Apsu was Marduk formed!
Ea his father begot him,
Damkina his mother was confined with him.

---

1. As interpreted here, Apsu bends down to kiss Mummu, so is presumably taller.
2. Variant: "on the waters."

He suckled at the breasts of goddesses, (85)
The attendant who raised him endowed him well with glories.
His body was magnificent, fiery his glance,
He was a hero at birth, he was a mighty one from the beginning!
When Anu his grandfather saw him,
He was happy, he beamed, his heart was filled with joy. (90)
He perfected him, so that his divinity was strange,
He was much greater, he surpassed them in every way.
His members were fashioned with cunning
    beyond comprehension,
Impossible to conceive, too difficult to visualize:
Fourfold his vision, fourfold his hearing, (95)
When he moved his lips a fire broke out.
Formidable[1] his fourfold perception,
And his eyes, in like number, saw in every direction.
He was tallest of the gods, surpassing in form,
His limbs enormous, he was surpassing at birth. (100)
"The son Utu, the son Utu,[2]
"The son, the sun, the sunlight of the gods!"
He wore (on his body) the auras of ten gods,
    had (them) wrapped around his head too,
Fifty glories[3] were heaped upon him.
Anu formed and produced the four winds, (105)
He put them in his hand, "Let my son play!"[4]
He fashioned dust, he made a storm bear it up,
He caused a wave and it roiled Tiamat,
Tiamat was roiled, churning day and night,
The gods, finding no rest, bore the brunt of each wind. (110)

---

1. "Formidable" is an attempt to render a pun in the original between *rabû* "great" and *erbu* "four."
2. A series of interlingual puns on son and sun, only one level of which can be rendered in English. The cuneiform signs used to write the name Marduk, AMAR.UD, are here construed as *māru* "son" and Utu "sun."
3. Marduk has fifty names in this text. In a late god list, Marduk was assigned the number 50. Perhaps this was done so that Marduk could replace Enlil (also number 50) as head of the pantheon.
4. Or: "My son, let them whirl."

(Tiamat is stirred to action by the angry gods.)

They plotted evil in their hearts,
They said to Tiamat their mother,
"When he killed Apsu your husband,
"You did nothing to save him but sat by, silent.
"Now he has made four terrible winds, (115)
"They are roiling your vitals so we cannot sleep.
"You had no care for Apsu your husband,
"As for Mummu, who was captured, you remained aloof.
"You are [no mo]ther, you churn back and forth, confused.
"As for us, who cannot lie down to rest,
    you do not love us! (120)
"Our ... [   ], our eyes are pinched,
"Lift this unremitting yoke, let us sleep!
"[Rai]se a [storm], give them what they deserve,
"[Ma]ke a [tempest], turn them into nothingness."
When Tiamat [heard] these words, they pleased her, (125)
"[As y]ou have counselled, we will make a tempest,[1]
"[We will] the gods within it,
"(For) they have been adopting [wicked ways]
    against the gods [thei]r parents."
[They clo]sed ranks and drew up at Tiamat's side,
Angry, scheming, never lying down night and day, (130)
[Ma]king warfare, rumbling, raging,
Convening in assembly, that they might start hostilities.
Mother Hubur[2] who can form everything,
Added countless invincible weapons,
    gave birth to monster serpents,
Pointed of fang, with merciless incisors(?), (135)
She filled their bodies with venom for blood.
Fierce dragons she clad with glories,
Causing them to bear auras like gods, (saying)
"Whoever sees them shall collapse from weakness!

---

1. Or: "monsters," but this would leave the reference in line 127 unclear.
2. Another epithet of Mummu-Tiamat.

"Wherever their bodies make onslaught,
    they shall not turn back!" (140)
She deployed serpents, dragons, and hairy hero-men,
Lion monsters, lion men, scorpion men,
Mighty demons, fish men, bull men,
Bearing unsparing arms, fearing no battle.
Her commands were absolute, no one opposed them, (145)
Eleven indeed on this wise she crea[ted].[1]
From among the gods her offspring,
    who composed her assembly,
She raised up Qingu[2] from among them,
    it was he she made greatest!
Leadership of the army, command of the assembly,
Arming, contact, advance of the melee, (150)
Wardenship of the (spoils?) of battle,
(All) she entrusted to him, made him sit on the dais.
"I cast your spell. I make you the greatest in the assembly
    of the gods,
"Kingship of all the gods I put in your power.
"You are the greatest, my husband, you are illustrious, (155)
"Your command shall always be greatest,
    over all the Anunna-gods."
She gave him the tablet of destinies,[3]
    had him hold it to his chest, (saying)
"As for you, your command will not be changed,
    your utterance will be eternal.
"Now that Qingu is the highest and has taken [supremacy],
"And has [ordained] destinies for his divine children, (160)
"Whatever you (gods) say shall cause fire to [subside],[4]
"Your concentrated venom shall make the mighty one yield."

1. This number was reached by adding the "monster serpents" of 134, the "fierce dragons" of 137, and the nine creatures of 141-143.
2. A male deity about whom little otherwise is known.
3. The tablet of destinies, though not a clearly defined concept in Mesopotamian tradition, was sometimes considered to be in the netherworld and was presumably inscribed with a person's destiny and day of death. In the Anzu story, on which this episode is based, the tablet gave the power to control divine spheres of responsibility and thus universal authority.
4. Contrast Tablet I line 96.

Tablet II

(Tiamat's preparations are known to Ea, who, in apparent despair, goes to Anshar, king of the gods. The relevant passages of Tablet I are repeated verbatim. Anshar is horror-stricken; he blames Ea for what has occurred. Since Ea started the trouble, he must find a solution to it. This accords well with Ea's plans for his son.)

    Tiamat assembled her creatures, (1)
    Drew up for battle against the gods her brood.
    Thereafter Tiamat, more than(?) Apsu, was become an evildoer.[1]
    She informed Ea that she was ready for battle.
    When Ea heard this, (5)
    He was struck dumb with horror and sat stock still.
    After he had thought and his distress had calmed,
    He made straight his way to Anshar his grandfather.
    He came in before his grandfather, Anshar,
    All that Tiamat plotted he recounted to him, (10)
    "My father, Tiamat our mother has grown angry with us,
    "She has convened an assembly, furious with rage.
    "All the gods rallied around her,
    "Even those you created are going over to her side,
    "They are massing around her, ready at Tiamat's side. (15)
    "Angry, scheming, never lying down night and day,
    "Making warfare, rumbling, raging,
    "Convening in assembly, that they might start hostilities.
    "Mother Hubur, who can form everything,
    "Added countless invincible weapons,
        gave birth to monster serpents, (20)
    "Pointed of fang, with merciless incisors(?),
    "She filled their bodies with venom for blood.
    "Fierce dragons she clad with glories,
    "Causing them to bear auras like gods, (saying)
        'Whoever sees them shall collapse from weakness! (25)
        'Wherever their bodies make onslaught,
            they shall not turn back!'

---

1. One could also understand "on account of Apsu" or "against Apsu" (in that case now the domain of Ea).

"She deployed serpents, dragons, and hairy hero-men,
"Lion monsters, lion men, scorpion men,
"Mighty demons, fish men, bull men,
"Bearing unsparing arms, fearing no battle. (30)
"Her commands were absolute, no one opposed them,
"Eleven indeed on this wise she created.
"From among the gods her offspring,
    who composed her assembly,
"She raised up Qingu from among them,
    it was he she made greatest!
"Leadership of the army, command of the assembly, (35)
"Arming, contact, advance of the melee,
"Wardenship of the (spoils?) of battle,
"(All) she entrusted to him, made him sit on the dais.

  'I cast your spell. I make you the greatest in the assembly
    of the gods,
  'Kingship of all the gods I put in your power. (40)
  'You are the greatest, my husband, you are illustrious.
  'Your command shall always be greatest,
    over all the Anunna-gods.'

"She gave him the tablet of destinies,
    had him hold it to his chest, (saying)

  'As for you, your command will not be changed, your
    utterance will be eternal.
  'Now that Qingu is the highest
    and has taken [supremacy], (45)
  'And has [ordained] destinies for his divine children,
  'Whatever you (gods) say shall cause fire to [subside],
  'Your concentrated venom shall make the mighty one yield.'"

(Anshar flies into a passion at Ea, blaming him for what has transpired. Ea defends himself by pointing out the necessity for Apsu's murder. Anshar thereupon orders Ea to subdue Tiamat. Ea is unable to do so, so Anshar sends out Anu, who is likewise unable. This situation was no doubt anticipated by Ea, who is waiting to produce his favorite son from the wings. This provides the opportunity for Marduk to take his place and to make his great demand.)

[When Anshar heard] the speech, he was deeply distressed,
He cried out "Woe!"; he bit his lips, (50)
His spirits were angry, his mind was uneasy,
His cries to Ea his offspring grew choked,
"My son, you yourself were instigator of battle!
"Do you bear the consequences of your own handiwork!
"You went forth and killed Apsu, (55)
"So Tiamat, whom you have enraged,
    where is one who can face her?"
The sage counsellor, wise prince,
Producer of wisdom, divine Nudimmud,
Answered his father Anshar gently,
With soothing words, calming speech, (60)
"My father, inscrutable, ordainer of destinies,
"Who has power to create and destroy,
"O Anshar, inscrutable, ordainer of destinies,
"Who has power to create and destroy,
"I will declare my thoughts to you, relent for a moment, (65)
"Recall in your heart that I made a good plan.
"Before I undertook to kill Apsu,
"Who had foreseen what is happening now?
"Ere I was the one who moved quickly to snuff out his life,
"I indeed, for it was I who destroyed him, [wh]at was there? (70)
When Anshar heard this, it pleased him,
He calmed down, saying to Ea,
"Your deeds are worthy of a god,
"You can(?) [   ] a fierce, irresistible stroke,
"Ea, your deeds are worthy of a god, (75)
"You can(?) [   ] a fierce, irresistible stroke,
"Go then to Tiamat, sub[due] her onslaught,
"May her anger [be pacified] by [your] magic spell."
When he heard the command [of his father] A[nshar],
He set off, making straight his way, (80)
Ea went to seek out Tiamat's stratagem.
He stopped, horror-stricken, then turned back.
He came before Anshar the sovereign,
He beseeched him with entreaties, saying,

"[My father], Tiamat has carried her actions beyond me, (85)
"I sought out her course, but my spell cannot counter it.
"Her strength is enormous, she is utterly terrifying,
"She is reinforced with a host, none can come out against her.
"Her challenge was in no way reduced but overwhelmed me,
"I became afraid at her clamor, I turned back. (90)
"My father, do not despair, send another to her,
"A woman's force may be very great, but it cannot match a man's.
"Do you scatter her ranks, thwart her intentions,
"Before she lays her hands on all of us."
Anshar was shouting, in a passion, (95)
To Anu his son he said these words,
"Stalwart son, valiant warrior,
"Whose strength is enormous, whose onslaught is irresistible,
"Hurry, take a stand before Tiamat,
"Soothe her feelings, let her heart be eased. (100)
"If she will not listen to what you say,
"Say something by way of entreaty to her, so that she be pacified."
When he heard what his father Anshar said,
He set off, [made str]aight his way,
Anu went to seek out Tiamat's stratagem. (105)
He stopped, horror-stricken, then turned back.
He came before [Ansha]r, [his father who begot him],
He beseeched him with entreaties, s[aying],
"My father, Tiamat has carried her actions beyond me,
"I sought out her course, but my s[pell cannot counter it]. (110)
"Her strength is enormous, she is utterly terrifying,
"She is reinforced with a host, none can [come out against] her.
"Her challenge was in no way reduced, but overwhelmed me.
"I became afraid at her clamor, I turned back.
"My father, do not despair, send another to her, (115)
"A woman's strength may be very great,
    but it cannot match a man's.
"Do you scatter her ranks, thwart her intentions,
"Before she lays her hands on all of us."
Anshar fell silent, gazing at the ground,
Nodding towards Ea, he shook his head. (120)

The Igigi-gods and Anunna-gods were all assembled,
With lips closed tight, they sat in silence.
Would no god go out [at his] command?
Against Tiamat would none go as [he] ordered?
Then Anshar, father of the great gods, (125)
His heart was angry, he [would not summon] anyone!

(Ea summons Marduk privately and informs him that his hour is now come. He enjoins him to present himself respectfully before his great-grandfather as a volunteer in time of crisis. Ea does not explicitly advise Marduk what price to set on his services, as the poet makes that come from the heart of Marduk himself. Marduk is warmly received by the elder gods and his offer to be champion is willingly accepted. Now Marduk offers his terms: if he is to save all the gods, he is to become their supreme, unquestioned leader, always.)

The mighty firstborn, champion of his father,
Hastener to battle, the warrior Marduk
Did Ea summon to his secret place,
Told him his secret words,[1] (130)
"O Marduk, think, heed your father,
"You are my son who can relieve his heart!
"Draw nigh, approach Anshar,
"Make ready to speak. He was angry,
    seeing you he will be calm."
The Lord was delighted at his father's words, (135)
He drew near and waited upon Anshar.
When Anshar saw him, his heart was filled with joyful feelings,
He kissed his lips, he banished his gloom.
"My father, let not your lips be silent but speak,
"Let me go, let me accomplish your heart's desire. (140)
"[O Anshar], let not your lips be silent but speak,
"Let me go, let me accomplish your heart's desire!
"What man is it who has sent forth his battle against you?"
"[My son], Tiamat, a woman,
    comes out against you to arms."
"[My father], creator, rejoice and be glad, (145)

---

1. Uncertain. While this could be a reference to magic words, it could as well refer to Marduk's demand, 155-162.

"Soon you will trample the neck of Tiamat.
"[Anshar], creator, rejoice and be glad,
"Soon you will trample [the neck] of Tiamat!"
"[Go], son, knower of all wisdom,
"Bring Tiamat to rest with your sacral spell.   (150)
"Make straight, quickly, with the storm chariot,
"Let it not veer from its [course], turn (it) back!"
The Lord was delighted at his grandfather's words,
His heart was overjoyed as he said to his grandfather,
"Lord of the gods, of the destiny of the great gods,   (155)
"If indeed I am to champion you,
"Subdue Tiamat and save your lives,
"Convene the assembly, nominate me for supreme destiny!
"Take your places in the Assembly Place of the Gods,[1]
         all of you, in joyful mood.
"When I speak, let me ordain destinies instead of you.   (160)
"Let nothing that I shall bring about be altered,
"Nor what I say be revoked or changed."

Tablet III

(Anshar convokes the gods for this purpose, commissioning his vizier, Gaga, to wait upon Lahmu and Lahamu to tell them the story of Tiamat's threat and Marduk's offer. Lahmu and Lahamu are terrified. They and the other gods convene, eat and drink liberally, and in the festive mood of a reunion, they surrender their authority to Marduk.)

Anshar made ready to speak,   (1)
Saying to Gaga his vizier these words,
"Gaga, vizier who contents me,
"Let it be you that I send off towards Lahmu and Lahamu.
"You know how [to find a way], you can make a fine speech.   (5)
"Send over to my presence the gods my ancestors,
"Let them bring all the gods before me.
"Let them converse, sit down at a feast,
"On produce of the field let them feed, imbibe of the vine.

---

1. Ubshu-ukkenna, a cosmic locality, called "abode of counsel."

"Let them ordain destiny for Marduk, their champion. (10)
"Be off, Gaga, wait upon them,
"All that I tell you, repeat to them:

'It is Anshar your son who has ordered me to come,
'He has bade me speak in full the command of his heart,
'To wit: (15)

"Tiamat our mother has grown angry with us,
"She has convened an assembly, furious with rage.
"All the gods rallied around her,
"Even those you created are going over to her side.
"They are massing around her, ready at Tiamat's side. (20)
"Angry, scheming, never lying down night and day,
"Making warfare, rumbling, raging,
"Convening in assembly, that they might start hostilities.
"Mother Hubur, who can form everything,
"Added countless invincible weapons,
    gave birth to monster serpents, (25)
"Pointed of fang, with merciless incisors(?),
"She filled their bodies with venom for blood.
"Fierce dragons she clad with glories,
"Causing them to bear auras like gods, (saying)

'Whoever sees them shall collapse from weakness! (30)
'Wherever their bodies make onslaught,
    they shall not turn back.'

"She deployed serpents, dragons, and hairy hero-men,
"Lion monsters, lion men, scorpion men,
"Mighty demons, fish men, bull men,
"Bearing unsparing arms, fearing no battle. (35)
"Her commands were absolute, no one opposed them.
"Eleven indeed on this wise she created.
"From among the gods her offspring,
    who composed her assembly,
"She raised up Qingu from among them,
    it was he she made greatest!
"Leadership of the army, command of the assembly, (40)
"Arming, contact, advance of the melee,

"Wardenship of the (spoils?) of battle:
"All she entrusted to him, made him sit on the dais.

   'I cast your spell, I make you the greatest
      in the assembly of the gods,
   'Kingship of all the gods I put in your power. (45)
   'You are greatest, my husband, you are illustrious,
   'Your command shall always be greatest,
      over all the Anunna-gods.'

"She gave him the tablet of destinies,
   had him hold it to his chest, (saying)

   'As for you, your command will not be changed,
      your utterance will be eternal.
   'Now that Qingu is the highest and has
      taken over [supremacy], (50)
   'And has [ordained] destinies for his divine children,
   'Whatever you (gods) say shall cause fire to [subside],
   'Your concentrated venom shall make
      the mighty one yield.'

"I sent Anu, he could not confront her,
"Nudimmud was afraid and turned back. (55)
"Marduk came forward,
   the sage of the gods, your son,
"He has resolved to go against Tiamat.
"When he spoke, he said to me,

   'If indeed I am to champion you,
   'Subdue Tiamat and save your lives, (60)
   'Convene the assembly,
      nominate me for supreme destiny!
   'Take your places in the Assembly Place
      of the Gods, all of you, in joyful mood,
   'When I speak, let me ordain destinies instead of you.
   'Let nothing that I shall bring about be altered,
   'Nor what I say be revoked or changed.' (65)

"Come quickly to me,
   straightaway ordain him your destinies,

"Let him go and confront your powerful enemy."
Gaga went and made straight his way
Towards Lahmu and Lahamu the gods his ancestors.
He prostrated, kissed the ground before them. (70)
He stood up straight and said to them,
"It is Anshar your son who has ordered me to come,
"He has bade me speak in full the command of his heart:

'Tiamat our mother has grown angry with us,
'She has convened an assembly, furious with rage. (75)
'All the gods rallied around her,
'Even those you created are going over to her side.
'They are massing around her, ready at Tiamat's side.
'Angry, scheming, never lying down night and day,
'Making warfare, rumbling, raging, (80)
'Convening in assembly, that they might start hostilities.
'Mother Hubur, who can form everything,
'Added countless invincible weapons,
 gave birth to monster serpents,
'Pointed of fang, with merciless incisors(?),
'She filled their bodies with venom for blood. (85)
'Fierce dragons she clad with glories,
'Causing them to bear auras like gods, (saying)

"Whoever sees them shall collapse from weakness!
"Wherever their bodies make onslaught
 they shall not turn back!"

'She deployed serpents, dragons, and hairy hero-men, (90)
'Lion monsters, lion men, scorpion men,
'Mighty demons, fish men, bull men,
'Bearing unsparing arms, fearing no battle.
'Her commands were absolute, no one opposed them.
'Eleven indeed on this wise she created! (95)
'From among the gods her offspring
 who composed her assembly,
'She raised up Qingu from among them,
 it was he she made greatest!
'Leadership of the army, command of the assembly,

'Arming, contact, advance of the melee,
'Division of the (spoils?) of battle: (100)
'(All) she entrusted to him, made him sit on the dais.

> "I cast your spell and make you the greatest
>   in the assembly of the gods,
> "Kingship of all the gods I put in your power.
> "You shall be the greatest, you are my only spouse,
> "Your name shall always be greatest,
>   over all the Anunna-gods." (105)

'She gave him the tablet of destinies, had him
    hold it to his chest, (saying)

> "As for you, your command will not be changed,
>   your utterance will be eternal.
> "Now that Qingu is the highest
>   and has taken over [supremacy],
> "And has [ordained] destinies for his divine children,
> "Whatever you (gods) say
>   shall cause fire to [subside], (110)
> "Your concentrated venom will make
>   the mighty one yield."

'I sent Anu, he could not confront her,
'Nudimmud was afraid and turned back.
'Marduk came forward, the sage of the gods, your son,
'He has resolved to go against Tiamat. (115)
'When he spoke, he said to me,

> "If indeed I am to champion you,
> "Subdue Tiamat and save your lives,
> "Convene the assembly,
>   nominate me for supreme destiny!
> "In the Assembly Place of the Gods
>   take your places, all of you, in joyful mood. (120)
> "When I speak, let me ordain destinies instead of you.
> "Let nothing that I shall bring about be altered,
> "Nor what I say be revoked or changed."

'Hurry to me, straightaway ordain him your destinies,

"'Let him go and confront your powerful enemy.'" (125)

When Lahmu and Lahamu heard, they cried aloud,
All of the Igigi-gods wailed bitterly,
"What (is our) hostility,
    that she has taken a[ct]ion (against) us?[1]
"We scarcely know what Tiamat might do!"
They swarmed together and came. (130)
All the great gods, ordainers of [destinies],
Came before Anshar and were filled with [joy].
One kissed the other in the assembly [ ],
They conversed, sat down at a feast,
On produce of the field they fed, imbibed of the vine, (135)
With sweet liquor they made their gullets run,
They felt good from drinking the beer.
Most carefree, their spirits rose,
To Marduk their champion they ordained destiny.

Tablet IV

(Marduk takes the throne and is hailed by all the gods in a coronation ceremony. Proof is administered of his supremacy. He is hailed as king, is given the trappings of royalty, chooses his weapons, and sets forth on his quest.)

They set out for him a princely dais, (1)
He took his place before his fathers for sovereignty.
"You are the most important among the great gods,
"Your destiny is unrivalled, your command is supreme.
"O Marduk, you are the most important among the great gods, (5)
"Your destiny is unrivalled, your command is supreme!
"Henceforth your command cannot be changed,
"To raise high, to bring low, this shall be your power.
"Your command shall be truth, your word shall not be wrong.
"Not one of the gods shall go beyond the limits you set. (10)
"Support is wanted for the gods' sanctuaries,
"Wherever their shrines shall be, your own shall be established.

---

1. Or, "Why be opposed?" The second half of the line is problematic.

"O Marduk, you are our champion,
"We bestow upon you kingship of all and everything.
"Take your place in the assembly, your word shall be supreme. (15)
"May your weapon never strike wide but dispatch your foes.
"O Lord, spare his life who trusts in you,
"But the god who has taken up evil, snuff out his life!"
They set up among them a certain constellation,
To Marduk their firstborn said they (these words), (20)
"Your destiny, O Lord, shall be foremost of the gods',
"Command destruction or creation, they shall take place.
"At your word the constellation shall be destroyed,
"Command again, the constellation shall be intact."
He commanded and at his word the constellation was destroyed, (25)
He commanded again and the constellation was created anew.
When the gods his fathers saw what he had commanded,
Joyfully they hailed, "Marduk is king!"
They bestowed in full measure scepter, throne, and staff,
They gave him unopposable weaponry that vanquishes enemies. (30)
"Go, cut off the life of Tiamat,
"Let the winds bear her blood away as glad tidings!"
The gods, his fathers, ordained the Lord's destiny,
On the path to success and authority did they set him marching.
He made the bow, appointed it his weapon, (35)
He mounted the arrow, set it on the string.
He took up the mace, held it in his right hand,
Bow and quiver he slung on his arm.
Thunderbolts he set before his face,
With raging fire he covered his body. (40)
Then he made a net to enclose Tiamat within,
He deployed the four winds that none of her might escape:
South Wind, North Wind, East Wind, West Wind,
Gift of his grandfather Anu;[1] he fastened the net at his side.
He made ill wind, whirlwind, cyclone, (45)

---

1. The gift refers to the four winds (see Tablet I lines 105-106), not the net. The original has an elaborate poetic structure that cannot be reproduced clearly in translation. "At his side" could also mean "on his arm."

Four-ways wind, seven-ways wind, destructive wind,
  irresistible wind:
He released the winds which he had made, the seven of them,
Mounting in readiness behind him to roil inside Tiamat.
Then the Lord raised the Deluge, his great weapon.
He mounted the terrible chariot,
  the unopposable Storm Demon, (50)
He hitched to it the four-steed team, he tied them at his side:[1]
"Slaughterer," "Merciless," "Overwhelmer," "Soaring."
Their lips are curled back, their teeth bear venom,
They know not fatigue, they are trained to trample down.
He stationed at his right gruesome battle and strife, (55)
At his left the fray that overthrows all formations.
He was garbed in a ghastly armored garment,
On his head he was covered with terrifying auras.
The Lord made straight and pursued his way,
Toward raging Tiamat he set his face. (60)
He was holding a spell ready upon his lips,
A plant, antidote to venom, he was grasping in his hand.
At that moment the gods were stirring, stirring about him,
The gods his fathers were stirring about him,
  the gods stirring about him.

(Marduk approaches for battle while the gods hover fearfully near him. He is temporarily discomfited by the sight of the enemy. Tiamat intimates that Marduk's support is disloyal. Ignoring Qingu, he challenges her to single combat and indicts her for the contemplated murder of her own children. Stung to a fury, Tiamat herself advances for battle. Marduk kills her, destroys her forces, takes the tablet of destinies, and puts it on himself.)

The Lord drew near, to find out the intent(?) of Tiamat, (65)
He was looking for the stratagem of Qingu her spouse.
As he looked, his tactic turned to confusion,
His reason was overthrown, his actions panicky,
And as for the gods his allies, who went at his side,

---

1. Apparently the ends of the reins, normally held by an attendant, are here strapped to him, to keep both hands free for fighting. Balancing in a chariot with weapons in both hands and guiding a four-steed team by the belt is, of course, a heroic feat of the first order.

When they saw the valiant vanguard, their sight failed them. (70)
Tiamat cast her spell pointblank,
Falsehood, lies she held ready on her lips.
"... lord, the gods rise against you,
"They assembled [where] they are, (but) are they on your side?"[1]
The Lord [raised] the Deluge, his great weapon, (75)
To Tiamat, who acted conciliatory,[2] sent he (this word),
"Why outwardly do you assume a friendly attitude,
"While your heart is plotting to open attack?
"Children cried out as their parents were deceitful,
"And you, their own mother, spurned all natural feeling.[3] (80)
"You named Qingu to be spouse for you,
"Though he had no right to be, you set him up for chief god.
"You attempted wicked deeds against Anshar,
    sovereign of the gods,
"And you have perpetrated your evil against the gods my fathers.
"Though main force is drawn up,
    though these your weapons are in array, (85)
"Come within range, let us duel, you and I!"
When Tiamat heard this,
She was beside herself, she turned into a maniac.
Tiamat shrieked loud, in a passion,
Her frame shook all over, down to the ground. (90)
He was reciting the incantation, casting his spell,
While the gods of battle were whetting their blades.
Tiamat and Marduk, sage of the gods, drew close for battle,
They locked in single combat, joining for the fray.
The Lord spread out his net, encircled her, (95)
The ill wind he had held behind him he released in her face.
Tiamat opened her mouth to swallow,
He thrust in the ill wind so she could not close her lips.

---

1. Uncertain. Tiamat evidently tells Marduk that the gods he is championing are actually disloyal to him.
2. Or: "who was furious."
3. The precise significance of Marduk's remarks is not clear. While he may refer to Tiamat's natural goodwill towards her children (Tablet I lines 28, 46), it seems more likely that he refers to her insinuation that he had best beware the loyalty of those he championed.

The raging winds bloated her belly,
Her insides were stopped up, she gaped her mouth wide. (100)
He shot off the arrow, it broke open her belly,
It cut to her innards, it pierced the heart.
He subdued her and snuffed out her life,
He flung down her carcass, he took his stand upon it.
After the vanguard had slain Tiamat, (105)
He scattered her forces, he dispersed her host.
As for the gods her allies, who had come to her aid,
They trembled, terrified, they ran in all directions,
They tried to make a way out(?) to save their[1] lives,
There was no escaping the grasp that held (them)! (110)
He drew them in and smashed their weapons.
They were cast in the net and sat in a heap,
They were heaped up in the corners, full of woe,
They were bearing his punishment, to prison confined.
As for the eleven creatures, the ones adorned with glories, (115)
And the demonic horde(?), which all went at her side,
He put on lead ropes, he bound their arms.
He trampled them under, together with their belligerence.
As for Qingu, who was trying to be great among them,
He captured him and reckoned him among the doomed. (120)
He took away from him the tablet of destinies
    that he had no right to,
He sealed it with a seal and affixed it to his chest.

(Splitting Tiamat's corpse in half, Marduk uses one piece to create the heavens. Her blood is borne off by the wind as evidence of her death. Marduk makes Esharra, an abode in heaven, as a counterpart of Apsu.)

Having captured his enemies and triumphed,
Having shown the mighty(?) foe subservient(?),[2]
Having fully achieved Anshar's victory over his enemies, (125)
Valiant Marduk having attained what Nudimmud desired,
He made firm his hold over the captured gods,

---

1. Text has "his life."
2. This may refer to a triumphal parade.

Then turned back to Tiamat whom he had captured.
The Lord trampled upon the frame of Tiamat,
With his merciless mace he crushed her skull. (130)
He cut open the arteries of her blood,
He let the North Wind bear (it) away as glad tidings.
When his fathers saw, they rejoiced and were glad,
They brought him gifts and presents.
He calmed down. Then the Lord was inspecting her carcass, (135)
That he might divide(?) the monstrous lump
    and fashion artful things.
He split her in two, like a fish for drying,
Half of her he set up and made as a cover, (like) heaven.[1]
He stretched out the hide and assigned watchmen,
And ordered them not to let her waters escape. (140)
He crossed heaven and inspected (its) sacred places,[2]
He made a counterpart of Apsu,
    the dwelling of Nudimmud.
The Lord measured the construction of Apsu,
The Great Sanctuary, its likeness, he founded, Esharra.[3]
The Great Sanctuary, Esharra, which he built, (is) heaven,[4] (145)
He made Ea, Enlil, and Anu dwell in their holy places.

Tablet V

(Marduk organizes the stars and planets and marks off years. He establishes his own planet, called Nebiru, as a marker for all the others in their motion. He regulates the moon, sun, weather, and subterranean waters. He links the various parts of the cosmos.)

He made the position(s) for the great gods, (1)
He established (in) constellations the stars, their counterparts.
He marked the year, described its boundaries,[5]

---

1. That is, he made a cover to the watery deep that served as a "sky" for it.
2. Marduk models his new home after Apsu, the domain of Ea.
3. Esharra means "The House of Totality," the domain of Enlil. See Tablet IV line 145, V line 120, VI line 66.
4. Or, perhaps, "(is in) heaven."
5. That is, laid out the ecliptic?

He set up twelve months of three stars each.[1]
After he had patterned the days of the year, (5)
He fixed the position of Nebiru to mark the (stars') relationships.[2]
Lest any make an error or go astray,
He established the position(s) of Enlil and Ea in relation to it.[3]
He opened up gates on both (sides of her) ribs,
He made strong bolts to left and right. (10)
In her liver he established the zenith.
He made the moon appear, entrusted (to him) the night.
He assigned to him the crown jewel of nighttime
    to mark the day (of the month):
"Every month, without ceasing, start off with the (crescent) disk.
"At the beginning of the month, waxing over the land, (15)
"You shine with horns to mark six days,
"At the seventh day, the disk as [ha]lf.
"At the fifteenth day, you shall be in opposition,
    at the midpoint of each [month].
"When the sun f[ac]es you from the horizon of heaven,
"Wane at the same pace and form in reverse. (20)
"At the day of di[sappeara]nce, approach the sun's course,
"On the [ ] of the thirtieth day, you shall be in conjunction
    with the sun a second time.
"I d[efined?] the celestial signs, proceed on their path,
"[ ] approach each other and render (oracular) judgment.
"The sun shall [ ] ..., killing, oppression (25)
"[ ] me."
W[hen he]
The val[iant]
The sun [ ]
In [ ] (30)
"Let [ ]
"[ ]
"Let there arise no [ ]

---

1. Babylonian astrolabes assign three stars to each month; here Marduk is portrayed as creating this pattern.
2. Refers to the daily rotation of the stars.
3. "It" refers to Nebiru, apparently in relation to the equator.

"Let there be [   ]
"In [   ]   (35)
"Da[ily   ]."
After [he had   ]
[   ]
He ma[de   ]
One year [   ]   (40)
At New Year [   ]
(Another) year [   ]
"Let [   ]
"The doorbolt of sunrise [ ]."
After he had as[signed   ],   (45)
[And fixed] the watches of night and day,
[   ] the foam of Tiamat,
Marduk created [   ]
He compacted (the foam) into c[louds] and made (them) billow.
To raise the wind, to cause rainfall,   (50)
To make mists steam, to pile up her spittle (as snow?),
He assigned to himself, put under his control.
He set down her head and piled [ ]¹ upon it,
He opened underground springs, a flood was let flow(?).
From her eyes he undammed the Euphr[ates] and Tigris,   (55)
He stopped up her nostrils, he left ...
He heaped up high-peaked mo[unt]ains from(?) her dugs.
He drilled through her waterholes to carry off the catchwater.
He coiled up her tail and tied it as(?) "The Great Bond."²
[   ] Apsu beneath, at his feet.   (60)
He set her crotch as the brace of heaven,
He set [half of] her as a roof, he established the netherworld.
[t]ask, he caused the oceans to surge within her.
[He spre]ad his net, let all (within) escape,
He formed the ... [ ] of heaven and netherworld,   (65)
Tightening their bond [ ] ...

---

1. On the basis of Tablet VII line 70 one may restore "mountain" here, but this is not assured.
2. That is, the link that holds heaven and the world below together.

(Marduk distributes trophies, parades his defeated enemies, and is celebrated as a returning hero.)

    After he had designed his prerogatives
        and devised his responsibilities,
    He founded (their) [sanc]tuaries, entrusted (those) to Ea.
    [The tablet] of destinies, which he took from Qingu
        and brought away,
    As the foremost gift he took away, he presented (it) to Anu.   (70)
    The [   ] of battle,
        which dangled and fluttered about (in the net),
    [ ] he led before his fathers.
    [And as for] the eleven creatures which Tiamat created ...
    He smashed their [wea]pons, he tied them to his feet.
    He made images [of them] and set them up
        at the [Gate of] Apsu: (75)
    "Lest ever after they be forgotten, let this be the sign."
    When [the gods] saw, they rejoiced and were glad,
    Lahmu, Lahamu, and all his fathers.
    Anshar [embra]ced him,
        proclaimed (his) salutation (to be) "king."
    [A]nu, Enlil, and Ea gave him gifts,   (80)
    [ ] Damkina his mother made cries of joy over him,
    She(?) made his face glow with (cries of) "Good ...!"[1]
    To Usmu,[2] who brought (Damkina's) gift at the glad tidings,
    [He en]trusted the ministry of Apsu and care of the sanctuaries.
    All the Igigi-gods together prostrated before him,   (85)
    [And] the Anunna-gods, all there are, were doing him homage,
    The whole of them joined together to pay him reverence,
    [Before him] they stood, they prostrated, "This is the king!"

(Marduk cleans himself and dons his insignia. The gods swear allegiance to him; he undertakes to maintain them.)

    [After] his fathers had celebrated him in due measure,

---

1. This is evidently a congratulatory exclamation, with a play on Damkina and *dumqu* ("good").
2. Advisor or messenger god to Ea, a Janus-like figure with a double head.

[   ] covered with the dust of battle.   (90)
[   ] ...
With cedar [oil] and [ ] he anoi[nted] his body,
He clothed himself in [his] princely [gar]ment,
The kingly aura, the awe-inspiring tiara.
He picked up the mace, he held it in his right hand,   (95)
[   ] he held in his left hand.
[   ]
[   ] he made firm at his feet.
He set over [   ]
The staff of success and authority [he hung] at his side. (100)
After he [had put on] the aura of [his kingship],
His netted sack, the Apsu [ ] awesomeness.
He was seated like [   ]
In [his] throne room [   ]
In his cella [   ]   (105)
The gods, all there are, [   ]
Lahmu and Lahamu [   ]
Made ready to speak and [said to] the Igigi-gods,
"Formerly [Mar]duk was 'our beloved son',
"Now he is your king, pay heed to his command."   (110)
Next all of them spoke and said,
"'Lugaldimmerankia' is his name, trust in him!"
When they had given kingship over to Marduk,
They said to him expressions of good will and obedience,
"Henceforth you shall be provider for our sanctuaries,   (115)
"Whatever you shall command, we will do."

(Marduk creates Babylon as the terrestrial counterpart of Esharra, abode of the gods in heaven. The gods are to repose there during their earthly sojourns.)

Marduk made ready to speak and said
(These) words to the gods his fathers,
"Above Apsu, the azure dwelling,
"Opposite Esharra, which I built above you,   (120)
"Below the sacred places, whose grounding I made firm,
"A house I shall build, my favorite abode.

"Within it I shall establish its holy place,
"I shall appoint my (holy) chambers,
    I shall establish my kingship.
"When you go up from Apsu to assembly, (125)
"Let your stopping places be there to receive you.[1]
"When you come down from heaven to [assembly],
"Let your stopping places be there to receive all of you.
"I shall call [its] name [Babylon], Abode of the Great Gods,
"We shall all hold fe[stival]s with[in] it." (130)
When the gods his fathers heard what he commanded,
They ... [   ]
"Over all things which your hands have created,
"Who has [authority, save for you]?
"Over the earth that you have created, (135)
"Who has [authority, save for] you?
"Babylon, to which you have given name,
"Make our [stopping place] there forever.
"Let them[2] bring us our daily portions,
"[   ] our [   ]." (140)
"Whosoever shall [ ] our task which we [ ],
"In his place [ ] his toil [ ]."
[Marduk] rejoiced [   ]
The gods [   ] ... them.
... [ ] them li[ght]. (145)
He opened [ ] ... [ ]

        (two lines fragmentary)

The gods prostrated before him, saying,
To Lugaldimmeran[ki]a, their lord, they [said], (150)
"Formerly [we called you] 'The Lord, [our beloved] son,'
"Now 'Our King' ... [shall be your name],
"He whose [sacral] sp[ell] saved [our lives],
"[au]ra, ma[ce], and ne[t],

---

1. That is, when the gods or their cult images travel in Babylonia, they can find accommodation in specific chambers of the Babylonian temples.
2. Who "they" refers to is disputed. It may refer to the defeated gods, it may be impersonal, or it may refer proleptically to the Babylonians.

"[Ea? ev]ery [sk]ill. (155)
"Let him make the plans, we ... [ ]."

Tablet VI

(The rebellious gods are offered a general pardon if they will produce their leader. They produce Qingu, claiming that he started the war. He is sacrificed, and his blood is used to make a human being; compare Story of the Flood Tablet I lines 218ff.)

When [Mar]duk heard the speech of the gods, (1)
He was resolving to make artful things:
He would tell his idea[1] to Ea,
What he thought of in his heart he proposes,
"I shall compact blood, I shall cause bones to be, (5)
"I shall make stand a human being, let "Man" be its name.
"I shall create humankind,
"They shall bear the gods' burden that those may rest.[2]
"I shall artfully double the ways of the gods:
"Let them be honored as one but divided in twain."[3] (10)
Ea answered him, saying these words,
He told him a plan to let the gods rest,[4]
"Let one, their brother, be given to me,
"Let him be destroyed so that people can be fashioned.
"Let the great gods convene in assembly, (15)
"Let the guilty one be given up that they may abide."
Marduk convened the great gods in assembly,
He spoke to them magnanimously as he gave the command,
The gods heeded his utterance,
As the king spoke to the Anunna-gods (these) words, (20)

1. Literally: "his utterance," but to judge from the context, the utterance is so far purely internal.
2. From the necessity of providing for themselves.
3. A reference to two main divisions of the Mesopotamian pantheon, Anunna-gods and Igigi-gods, or to the supernal and infernal deities (compare Tablet VI lines 39ff.).
4. The text assigns Marduk primacy in the creation of man by giving him the "idea," since Mesopotamian tradition, established centuries before this text was written, agreed that Ea/Enki had been the actual creator, along with the Mother Goddess.

"Let your first reply be the truth!
"Do you speak with me truthful words!
"Who was it that made war,
"Suborned Tiamat and drew up for battle?
"Let him be given over to me, the one who made war, (25)
"I shall make him bear his punishment, you shall be released."
The Igigi, the great gods answered him,
To Lugaldimmerankia, sovereign of all the gods, their lord,
"It was Qingu who made war,
"Suborned Tiamat and drew up for battle." (30)
They bound and held him before Ea,
They imposed the punishment on him and shed his blood.
From his blood he made mankind,
He imposed the burden of the gods and exempted the gods.
After Ea the wise had made mankind, (35)
They imposed the burden of the gods on them!
That deed is beyond comprehension,
By the artifices of Marduk did Nudimmud create!

(Marduk divides the gods of heaven and netherworld. The gods build Esagila, Marduk's temple in Babylon.)

Marduk the king divided the gods,
The Anunna-gods, all of them, above and below, (40)
He assigned to Anu for duty at his command.
He set three hundred in heaven for (their) duty,
A like number he designated for the ways of the netherworld:
He made six hundred dwell in heaven and netherworld.
After he had given all the commands, (45)
And had divided the shares of the Anunna-gods
    of heaven and netherworld,
The Anunna-gods made ready to speak,
To Marduk their lord they said,
"Now, Lord, you who have liberated us,
"What courtesy may we do you? (50)
"We will make a shrine, which is to be called by name

"'Chamber that shall be Our Stopping Place',
    we shall find rest therein.
"We shall lay out the shrine, let us set up its emplacement,
"When we come thither (to visit you), we shall find rest therein."
When Marduk heard this, (55)
His features glowed brightly, like the day,
"Then make Babylon the task that you requested,
"Let its brickwork be formed, build high the shrine."
The Anunna-gods set to with hoes,
One (full) year they made its bricks. (60)
When the second year came,
They raised up Esagila, the counterpart of Apsu,
They built the high ziggurat of (counterpart-)Apsu,
For Anu-Enlil-Ea[1] they founded his house and dwelling.
Majestically he took his seat before them, (65)
Its pinnacles were facing toward the base of Esharra.
After they had done the work of Esagila,
All the Anunna-gods devised their own shrines.

(The gods come to the new temple for a celebration. After a feast, they take their places to ordain destinies.)

The three hundred Igigi-gods of heaven
    and the six hundred of Apsu all convened.
The Lord, in the Highest Shrine,
    which they built as his dwelling, (70)
Seated the gods his fathers for a banquet,
"This is Babylon, your place of dwelling.
"Take your pleasure there, seat yourselves in its delights!"
The great gods sat down,
They set out cups, they sat down at the feast. (75)
After they had taken their enjoyment inside it,
And in awe-inspiring Esagila had conducted the offering,
All the orders and designs had been made permanent,

---

1. The three divine names together may here be taken as a syncretism for Marduk; compare Tablet VII lines 136, 140.

All the gods had divided the stations
    of heaven and netherworld,
The fifty great gods took their thrones, (80)
The seven gods of destinies were confirmed forever
    for rendering judgment.

(Marduk's bow becomes a constellation.)

The Lord took the bow, his weapon, and set it before them,
The gods his fathers looked upon the net he had made.
They saw how artfully the bow was fashioned,
His fathers were praising what he had brought to pass. (85)
Anu raised (it), speaking to the assembly of the gods,
He kissed the bow, "This be my daughter!"
He named the bow, these are its names:
"'Longwood' shall be the first, 'Conqueror' shall be the second."
The third name, 'Bow Star', he made visible in heaven, (90)
He established its position with respect to the gods his brethren.

(Marduk is made supreme god. Anshar gives him a second name, Asalluhi. Anshar explains Marduk's role among gods and men with respect to this second name.)

After Anu had ordained the destinies of the bow,
He set out the royal throne
    which stood highest among the gods,
Anu had him sit there, in the assembly of the gods.
Then the great gods convened, (95)
They made Marduk's destiny highest, they prostrated themselves.
They laid upon themselves a curse (if they broke the oath),
With water and oil they swore, they touched their throats.[1]
They granted him exercise of kingship over the gods,
They established him forever for
    lordship of heaven and netherworld. (100)
Anshar gave him an additional name, Asalluhi,
"When he speaks, we shall all do obeisance,
"At his command the gods shall pay heed.
"His word shall be supreme above and below,

---

1. A symbolic slashing gesture meaning that they may die if they break the oath.

"The son, our champion, shall be the highest. (105)
"His lordship shall be supreme, he shall have no rival,
"He shall be the shepherd of the black-headed folk,[1] his creatures.
"They shall tell of his ways, without forgetting, in the future.
"He shall establish for his fathers great food offerings,
"He shall provide for them,
    he shall take care of their sanctuaries. (110)
"He shall cause incense burners to be savored,
    he shall make their chambers rejoice.
"He shall make on earth the counterpart
    of what he brought to pass in heaven,
"He shall appoint the black-headed folk to serve him.
"Let the subject peoples be mindful
    that their gods should be invoked,
"At his command let them heed their goddess(es). (115)
"Let their gods, their goddesses be brought food offerings,
"Let (these) not be forgotten, let them sustain their gods.
"Let their holy places be apparent(?),
    let them build their sanctuaries.[2]
"Let the black-headed folk be divided as to gods,
"(But) by whatever name we call him, let him be our god.[3] (120)

(Beginning of the explanation of Marduk's fifty names. Names 1-9 are those borne by Marduk prior to this point in the narrative. Each of them is correlated with crucial points in the narrative as follows: (1) his birth, (2-3) his creation of the human race to provide for the gods, (4) his terrible anger but his willingness to spare the rebellious gods, (5) his proclamation by the gods as supreme among them, (6) his organization of the cosmos, (7) his saving the gods from danger, (8) his sparing the gods who fought on the side of Tiamat, but his killing of Tiamat and Qingu, and (9) his enabling the gods to proceed with the rest of what is narrated.)

---

1. The Mesopotamians.
2. The holy places show forth their own qualities of holiness so that mankind builds shrines there.
3. That is, Marduk is to be the one god of all the gods, no matter how many gods mankind may serve.

"Let us pronounce his fifty names,
"That his ways shall be (thereby) manifest, his deeds likewise(?):
    (1) MARDUK!
"Who, from his birth, was named by his forefather Anu,
"Establisher of pasture and watering place,
    who enriches (their) stables,
"Who by his Deluge weapon subdued the stealthy ones, (125)
"Who saved the gods his forefathers from danger.
"He is indeed the Son, the Sun, the most radiant of the gods,
"They shall walk in his brilliant light forever.
"On the people whom he made,
    creatures with the breath of life,
"He imposed the gods' burden, that those be released. (130)
"Creation, destruction, absolution, punishment:
"Each shall be at his command, these shall gaze upon him.
"(2) MARUKKA shall he be,
    the god who created them (mankind),
"Who granted (thereby) the Anunna-gods contentment,
    who let the Igigi-gods rest.
"(3) MARUTUKKU shall be the trust of his land,
    city and people, (135)
"The people shall praise him forever.
"(4) MERSHAKUSHU, angry but deliberative,
    furious but relenting,
"Deep is his heart, all encompassing his feelings.
"(5) LUGALDIMMERANKIA is his name
    which we all pronounced,
"Whose commands we exalted above those
    of the gods his fathers. (140)
"He shall be 'Lord of All the Gods of Heaven and Netherworld',
The king at whose revelations the gods above and below
    stand in dread.
"(6) NADE-LUGALDIMMERANKIA
    is the name we invoked, instructor of all the gods,
"Who founded for us dwellings out of danger
    in heaven and netherworld,
"And who divided the stations for the Igigi and Anunna-gods. (145)

"At his name the gods shall tremble and quake
  in (their) dwellings.
"(7) ASALLUHI is that name of his which Anu,
  his father, pronounced.
"He is the light of the gods, the mighty leader,
"Who, according to his name, is protective spirit
  of god and land,
"And who in mighty single combat
  saved our dwellings from harm. (150)
"Asalluhi they named secondly (8) NAMTILA,
  god who maintains life,
"Who, according to his nature, repaired the shattered gods,
"The lord who revived the moribund gods by his sacral spell,
"Let us praise the destroyer of the wayward foes!
"Asalluhi, whose name was called thirdly (9) NAMRU, (155)
"The pure god who purifies our ways."
Anshar, Lahmu, and Lahamu named three each of his names,
They said to the gods their sons,
"We have named three each of his names,
"Do you, as we have, invoke his names." (160)
Joyfully the gods heeded their command,
As they took counsel in the Assembly Place of the Gods,
"The valiant son, our champion,
"Our provider, we will exalt his name!"
They sat down in their assembly to name (his) destinies, (165)
In all their rites they invoked of him a name.

Tablet VII

(Deals with Marduk's three Asaru-names [10-12], his five Tutu-names [13-17], his six Shazu-names [18-23], his four Enbilulu-names [24-27], his two Sirsir-names [28-29]. Some of these reflect Marduk's role as a vegetation deity.)

"(10) ASARI, bestower of cultivation, who established surveys, (1)
"Creator of grain and fibrous plants,
  who causes vegetation to sprout,

"(11) ASARALIM, who is honored in the house of counsel,
    whose counsel excels,
"Whom the gods heed, without fear,
"(12) ASARALIMNUNNA, the honored one,
    light of the father who begot [him],   (5)
"Who implements the decrees of Anu, Enlil, Ea, and Ninshiku.
"He is their provider who assigns their portions,
"Who increases abundance of the field for the land.
"(13) TUTU is [he] who effected their restoration,
"He shall purify their shrines that they may be at rest,   (10)
"He shall devise the spell that the gods may be calm.
"Should they rise in anger, they shall turn [back].
"He shall be supreme in the assembly of the gods his [fathers],
"No one among the gods shall [make himself equal] to him.
"Tutu is (14) ZIUKKENNA, life of [his] masses,   (15)
"Who established the holy heavens for the gods,
"Who took control of where they went, assigned their stations,
"He shall not be forgotten by teeming mankind,
    [let them hold fast to] his [deeds].
"Tutu they called thirdly (15) ZIKU, who maintains purity,
"God of the fair breeze,
    lord who hears and accedes (to prayers),   (20)
"Producer of riches and wealth, who establishes abundance,
"Who turned all our want to plenty,
"Whose fair breeze we caught whiff of in our great danger,
"Let them ever speak of his exaltation, let them sing his praises!
"Tutu let teeming mankind magnify fourthly as (16) AGAKU, (25)
"Lord of the sacral spell, reviver of the moribund,
"Who had mercy on the vanquished gods,
"Who removed the yoke imposed on the gods, his enemies,
"Who, to free them, created mankind,
"The merciful, whose power is to revive.   (30)
"Word of him shall endure, not to be forgotten,
"In the mouth of the black-headed folk,
    whom his hands have created.
"Tutu, fifthly, is (17) TUKU,
    his sacral spell shall ever be on their lips,

"Who with his sacral spell uprooted all the evil ones.
"(18) SHAZU, who knows the heart of the gods,
    who was examining the inside, (35)
"Lest he allow evildoers to escape from him,
"Who established the assembly of the gods,
    who contented them,
"Who subdued the unsubmissive,
    their (the gods') broad [pro]tection,
"Who administers justice, uproots twisted testimony,
"In whose place falsehood and truth are distinguished. (40)
"Shazu they shall praise secondly as (19) ZISI,
    who silenced those who rose (against him),
"Who banished paralyzing fear from the body
    of the gods his fathers,
"Shazu is, thirdly, (20) SUHRIM,
    who uprooted all enemies with the weapon,
"Who thwarted their plots, turned them into nothingness,
"Who snuffed out all wicked ones,
    as many as came against him. (45)
"The gods shall ever be joyful in the assembly!
"Shazu is, fourthly, (21) SUHGURIM,
    who ensured obedience for the gods his fathers,
"Who uprooted the enemy, destroyed their offspring,
"Who thwarted their maneuvers, excepting none of them.
"His name shall be invoked and spoken in the land! (50)
"Shazu later generations shall tradite fifthly as (22) ZAHRIM,
"Who destroyed all adversaries, all the disobedient,
"Who brought all the fugitive gods into their sanctuaries.
"This his name shall be the truth!
"To Shazu, moreover, they shall render all honor sixthly as
    (23) ZAHGURIM, (55)
"He it is who destroyed all foes in battle.
"(24) ENBILULU, lord who made them flourish, is he,
"The mighty one named by them, who instituted offerings,
"Who established grazing and watering places for the land,
"Who opened channels, apportioned abundant waters. (60)

"Enbilulu they shall [invoke] secondly as (25) EPADUN,
    lord of open country and flood(?),
"Irrigator of heaven and earth, former of furrows,
    who formed the sacred(?) plowland in the steppe,
"Who regulated dike and ditch,
    who delimited the plowed land.
"Enbilulu they shall praise thirdly as (26) ENBILULU-GUGAL,
    irrigator of the watercourses of the gods,
"Lord of abundance, plenty, high yields, (65)
"Producer of wealth, enricher of all the inhabited world,
"Bestower of grain, who causes barley to appear.
"Enbilulu is (27) HEGAL,
    who heaps up abundance for the ... peoples,
"Who rains prosperity over the wide earth,
    who makes vegetation flourish.
"(28) SIRSIR, who heaped up the mountain(s) above Tiamat, (70)
"Who ravaged the corpse of Ocean with [his] weapon,
"Ruler of the land, their faithful shepherd,
"To whom have been granted the cultivated field,
    the subsistence field, the furrow,
"Who crossed vast Tiamat back and forth in his wrath,
"Spanning her like a bridge at the place of single combat.[1] (75)
"Sirsir they named secondly (29) MALAH, let it remain so,
"Tiamat is his vessel and he the boatman.

(The remaining names are treated singly or in groups, beginning with the defeat of Tiamat and ascending to his proclamation as lord of the universe. Whereas his earlier names referred to his innate nature, his later ones commemorate his roles, accomplishments, and their outcome. Names 30-50 ascend in scope from earth to heaven.)

"(30) GIL, who stores up grain in massive mounds,
"Who brings forth barley and flocks,
    grantor of the land's seed.

---

1. This passage may contain mythological material about a little-known deity, Sirsir, that is here worked into the Marduk story by association and syncretism. Sirsir, made into a name of Marduk, evidently figured in a tradition in which he slew the ocean in single combat.

"(31) GILIMMA, who established the bond of the gods,
    creator of enduring things, (80)
"The bridle(?) that curbed them,
    provider of good things.
"(32) AGILIMMA, the lofty one, uprooter of flood waves(?),
    who controls the sn[ow],
"Creator of the earth above the waters,
    establisher of things on high.
"(33) ZULUM, who assigned fields,
    measured off tracts(?) for the gods,
"Grantor of portions and food offerings,
    tender of sanctuaries. (85)
"(34) MUMMU, creator of heaven and netherworld,
    who administers (their) offices,
"Divine purifier of heaven and netherworld,
    is, secondly, (35) ZULUMMU,
"To whom no other among the gods was equal in strength.
"(35) GISHNUMUNAB, creator of all people,
    who made the world regions,
"Destroyer of the gods of Tiamat,
    who made mankind from parts of them. (90)
"(36) LUGALABDUBUR, the king who thwarted
    the maneuvers of Tiamat, uprooted [her] weapons,
"Whose support was firm in front and rear.
"(37) PAGALGUENNA, foremost of all lords,
    whose strength was supreme,
"Who was greatest of the gods his brethren, lord of them all.
"(38) LUGALDURMAH, king of the juncture of the gods,
    lord of the great bond, (95)
"Who was greatest in the abode of kingship,
    most exalted among the gods.
"(39) ARANUNNA, counsellor of Ea,
    fairest of the gods [his] fathers,
"Whose noble ways no god whatever could equal.
"(40) DUMUDUKU, whose pure dwelling
    is renewed in holy hill,

"Son of holy hill, without whom the lord of holy hill
    makes no decision. (100)
"(41) LUGALSHUANNA, king whose strength
    was outstanding among the gods,
"Lord, strength of Anu, who became supreme
    at(?) the nomination(?) of Anshar.
"(42) IRUGGA, who ravaged all of them amidst Tiamat,
"Who gathered all wisdom to himself, profound in perception.
"(43) IRQINGU, ravager of Qingu, ... of battle, (105)
"Who took charge of all commands, established lordship.
"(44) KINMA, leader of all the gods, grantor of counsel,
"At whose name the gods quake for fear like a whirlwind.
"(45) ESIZKUR shall dwell aloft in the house of prayer,
"The gods shall bring in their presents before him, (110)
"While they receive their due.[1]
"None besides him can create artful things,
"The four black-headed folk are his creatures,[2]
"No god but he knows how long they will live.
"(46) GIBIL, who maintained the ... of the weapon, (115)
"Who because of the battle with Tiamat
    can create artful things,
"Profound of wisdom, ingenious in perception,
"Whose heart is so deep
    that none of the gods can comprehend it.
"(47) ADDU shall be his name, the whole sky he shall cover,
"His beneficent roar shall thunder over the earth, (120)
"As he rumbles, he shall reduce the burden of the clouds,
    Below, for the people, he shall grant sustenance.
"(48) ASHARU, who, according to his name,
    mustered the gods of destinies,
"He has taken all peoples in his charge.
"(49) NEBIRU shall hold the passage of heaven and earth,
"So they shall not cross above and below
    without heeding him, (125)

---

1. The gods bring gifts and receive their income, with chiastic wordplay on "before him/receive" and "bring in/income ('due')."
2. That is, the people of the four points of the compass.

"Nebiru is his star which he made visible in the skies.
"It shall hold the point of turning around,
  they shall look upon him,
"Saying, 'He who crossed back and forth,
  without resting, in the midst of Tiamat,
'Nebiru ("Crossing") shall be his name,
  who holds the position in its midst'.
"He shall maintain the motions of the stars of heaven, (130)
"He shall herd all the gods like sheep.
"He shall keep Tiamat subdued, he shall keep her life cut short,
"In the future of mankind, with the passing of time,
"She shall always be far off, she shall be distant forever."
Because he created "places" and fashioned the netherworld, (135)
Father Enlil has pronounced his name (50) Lord of the World,
The Igigi-gods pronounced all the names.
When Ea heard (them), he was joyful of heart,
He said, "He whose name his fathers have glorified,
"His name, like mine, shall be 'Ea'.[1] (140)
"He shall provide the procedures for all my offices,
"He shall take charge of all my commands."
With the name "Fifty" the great gods
Pronounced his fifty names, they made his way supreme.[2]

(Composition and purpose of this text, its approval by Marduk.)

They must be grasped: the "first one" should reveal (them), (145)
The wise and knowledgeable should ponder (them) together,
The master should repeat, and make the pupil understand.
The "shepherd," the "herdsman" should pay attention,[3]
He must not neglect the Enlil of the gods, Marduk,
So his land may prosper and he himself be safe. (150)
His word is truth, what he says is not changed,
Not one god has annulled his utterance.

---

1. Marduk is now made god of wisdom and magic.
2. Marduk is here assigned the number fifty. In Mesopotamian scribal practice, the number 50 was used to write the name of Enlil, so herewith Marduk has replaced Enlil as supreme deity.
3. Kings and other rulers.

If he frowns, he will not relent,
If he is angry, no god can face his rage.
His heart is deep, his feelings all encompassing, (155)
He before whom crime and sin must appear for judgment.
The revelation (of the names) which the "first one"
    discoursed before him (Marduk),
He wrote down and preserved for the future to hear,
The [wo]rd of Marduk who created the Igigi-gods,
[His/Its   ] let them [   ], his name let them invoke. (160)
Let them sound abroad the song of Marduk,
How he defeated Tiamat and took kingship.

Story of the Flood

The Babylonian flood story, from a manuscript dating to the seventeenth century B.C., sets forth an interpretation of the creation of humanity, the flood, and the origins of human birth, marriage, procreation, and death, all of these themes brilliantly worked out in a cohesive plot. Humanity was created to provide servants for the gods; birth was instituted to allow them to reproduce. The flood was an attempt at population control when the human race had grown too numerous. When the flood proved too drastic a measure, population control was achieved by forbidding marriage and procreation to certain groups of people, and ordaining mortality for all.

The story exists in several versions that have been freely rearranged and combined here.

Tablet I

(Before mankind existed, the great gods imposed forced labor on the lesser gods.)

When gods were man,[1]	(1)
They did forced labor, they bore drudgery.	
Great indeed was the drudgery of the gods,	
The forced labor was heavy, the misery too much:	
The seven(?) great Anunna-gods were burdening	(5)
The Igigi-gods with forced labor.	
Anu their father was king,	
Their counsellor was the warrior Enlil,	
Their prefect was Ninurta,	
[And] their bailiff(?) [En]nugi.	(10)
They had taken the [ ] ... by the ...,	
They cast lots, the gods took their shares:	
Anu went up to heaven,	
[Enlil too]k the earth for his subjects(?),	

---

1. The line is a metaphor, meaning "when gods were (like) men" (in that they had to work). This does not mean that the gods were actually human beings; rather, they had to work as humans do. Use of singular "man" rather than "men" suggests that the poet sought to make his opening line artful by playing on the words "god" and "man."

[The bolt], the closure[1] of the sea, (15)
[They had gi]ven to Enki the leader.
[The Anunna-gods?] went up to heaven,
[The gods of the de]pths had descended.
[The Anunna-gods] in the he[ights] of heaven
[Burdened] the Igigi-gods [with forced labor]. (20)
[The gods] were digging watercourses,
[Canals they opened, the] life of the land.
[Those gods] were digging watercourses,
[Canals they opened, the] life of the land.
[The Igigi-gods dug the Ti]gris river, (25)
[And the Euphrates there]after.
[Springs they opened up from] the depths,
[Wells ...] they established.
[   ] the depth
[   ] of the land (30)
[   ] within it
[   ] they lifted up,
[They heaped up] all the mountains.
[years] of drudgery,
[   ] the vast marsh. (35)
They [cou]nted years of drudgery,
[and] forty years, too much!
[   ] forced labor they bore night and day.
[They were com]plaining, denouncing,
[Mut]tering down in the ditch, (40)
"Let us face up to our [foreman] the prefect,
"He must take off (this) our [he]avy burden upon us!
"[ ], counsellor of the gods, the warrior,
"Come, let us remove (him) from his dwelling;
"Enlil, counsellor of the gods, the warrior, (45)
"Come, let us remove (him) from his dwelling!"
[   ] made ready to speak,
[And said to the] gods his brethren,

---

1. Literally: "snare," precise sense not clear. The sea may be portrayed as a gigantic trap, holding all its fish within.

"[   ] the prefect of olden days(?)

(gap of about four lines, partly filled with a later fragment)

"[   ] let us kill [him]! (a)
"[   ] let us break the yoke!"
[   ] made ready to speak,
[Saying] to the gods his brethren,
"[   ] the prefect of olden days(?) ..." (e)
"The counsellor of the go[ds], the warrior,
"Come, let us remove (him) from his dwelling.
"Enlil, counsellor of the gods, the warrior,
"Come, let us remove (him) from his dwelling! (60)
"Now then, call for battle!
"Battle let us join, warfare!"
The gods heard his words,
They set fire to their tools,
They put fire to their spades, (65)
And flame to their workbaskets.
Off they went, one and all,
To the gate of the warrior Enlil's abode.
It was night, half-way through the watch,
The house was surrounded, but the god did not know. (70)
It was night, half-way through the watch,
Ekur was surrounded, but Enlil did not know!
Kalkal noticed it and ... [   ],
He touched the bolt and examined the [   ].
Kalkal woke [Nusku], (75)
And they listened to the clamor of [the Igigi-gods].
Nusku woke [his] lord,
He got [him] out of bed,
"My lord, [your] house is surrounded,
"Battle has run right up [to your gate]. (80)
"Enlil, your house is surrounded,
"Battle has [ru]n right up to your gate!"[1]
Enlil had [   ] ... to his dwelling.

---

1. Note the omission of a verb of speaking, indicating excitement and abruptness.

Enlil made ready to speak,
And said to the vizier Nusku, (85)
"Nusku, bar your gate,
"Get your weapons and stand before me."
Nusku barred his gate,
Got his weapons and stood before Enlil.
Nusku made ready to speak, (90)
And said to the warrior Enlil,
"My lord, your face is (gone pale as) tamarisk,
"Your own offspring! Why did you fear?
"My lord, your face is (gone pale as) tamarisk,
"Your own offspring! Why did you fear? (95)
"Send that they bring Anu down [here],
"And that they bring Enki be[fore yo]u."
He sent and they brought Anu down to him,
They brought Enki before him.
Anu, king of [hea]ven, was seated, (100)
The king of the depths, Enki, was [ ].
With the great Anunna-gods present,
Enlil arose, the debate [was underway].
Enlil made ready to speak,
And said to the great [gods], (105)
"Against me would they be [rebelling]?
"Shall I make battle [against my own offspring]?
"What did I see with my very own eyes?
"Battle ran up to my gate!"
Anu made ready to speak, (110)
And said to the warrior Enlil,
"The reason why the Igigi-gods
"Surrounded(?) your gate,
"Let Nusku go out [to discover it],
"[Let him take] to [your] so[ns] (115)
"[Your great] command."
Enlil made ready to speak,
And said to the [vizier Nusku],
"Nusku, open [your gate],
"Take your weapons, [stand before them]. (120)

"In the assembly of [all the gods]
"Bow down, stand up, [and expound to them] our [words]:

   'Anu, [your father],
   'Your counsellor, [the warrior] Enlil,
   'Your prefect, Ninurta, (125)
   'And your bailiff Ennugi have sent me (to say),

     "Who [is instigator of] battle?
     "Who [is instigator of] hostilities?
     "Who [declared] war,
     "[(That) battle has run up to the gate of Enlil]?" (130)

[Nusku opened] his gate,
[Took his weapons] and w[ent] ... Enlil.
[In the assembly of a]ll the gods,
[He knelt, s]tood up, expounded the c[omm]and,
"Anu, your father, (135)
"[Your counsellor, the] warrior Enlil,
"[Your prefect], Ninurta,
"And [your bailiff] Ennugi [have sent me (to say)]:

   'Who is [instigator of] battle?
   'Who is [instigator of] hostilities? (140)
   'Who [declared] war,
   '[(That) battle has run up to the gate of Enlil]?
   'In [   ]
   'He trans[gressed the command of] Enlil.'

"Every [one of us gods has declared] war; (145)
"We have set [   ] in the e[xcavation].
"[Excessive] drudgery [has killed us],
"[Our] forced labor was heavy, [the misery too much]!
"Now, every [one of us gods]
"Has resolved on [a reckoning?] with Enlil." (150)
Nusku took [his weapons   ],
He went, he [to his lord],
"My lord, [you sent] me to the [   ],
"I went [   ]
"I expounded [you]r great [command], (155)
"[trans]gressed it.

'[Every one of us] gods has declared war,
'We [have set   ] in the excavation.
'Excessive [drudgery] has killed us,
'Our forced labor [was heavy], the misery too much! (160)
'[Now, every] one of us gods
'Has resolved on a reckoning(?) with Enlil.'
When Enlil heard that speech,
His tears flowed.
Enlil ... [   ] his speech(?), (165)
And addressed the warrior Anu,
"I will go up with you, to heaven.
"Bear your authority, take your power,
"With the great gods in session before you,
"Summon one god, let them put a burial mound over him." (170)
Anu made ready to speak,
And addressed the gods his brethren,
"Why do we blame them?
"Their forced labor was heavy, their misery too much!
"[Every day   ], (175)
"[The outcry was] loud, [we could] hear the clamor.
[   ] to do,
[assigned] tasks ..."

(gap)

(The gap in the main edition is partly filled by the following fragment. This suggests that Enki echoes Anu's remonstrances, then goes on to propose creation of man to do the work of the laboring gods.)

Ea made ready to speak, (a)
And said to the gods [his brethren],
"What calumny do we lay to their charge?
"Their forced labor was heavy, [their misery too much]!
"Every day [   ] (e)
"The outcry [was loud, we could hear the clamor].
"There is [   ]
"[Belet-ili, the midwife], is present.
"Let her create, then, a hum[an, a man],

"Let him bear the yoke [   ], (j)
"Let him bear the yoke [   ]!
"[Let man assume the drud]gery of god ..."

(As the main manuscript resumes, Enki is speaking.)

"[Belet-ili, the midwife], is present,
"Let the midwife create a human being,
"Let man assume the drudgery of god."
They summoned and asked the goddess,
The midwife of the gods, wise Mami, (190)
"Will you be the birth goddess, creatress of mankind?
"Create a human being that he bear the yoke,
"Let him bear the yoke, the task of Enlil,
"Let man assume the drudgery of god."
Nintu made ready to speak, (195)
And said to the great gods,
"It is not for me to do it,
"The task is Enki's.
"He it is that cleanses all,
"Let him provide me the clay so I can do the making." (200)
Enki made ready to speak,
And said to the great gods,
"On the first, seventh, and fifteenth days of the month,
"Let me establish a purification, a bath.
"Let the one god be slaughtered, (205)
"Then let the gods be cleansed by immersion.
"Let Nintu mix clay with his flesh and blood.
"Let that same god and man be thoroughly mixed in the clay.
"Let us hear the drum for the rest of time,
"From the flesh of the god let a spirit remain, (210)
"Let it make the living know its sign,
"Lest he be allowed to be forgotten, let the spirit remain."[1]
The great Anunna-gods, who administer destinies,

---

1. I interpret this speech as follows: "Kill the one god (Aw-ilu) who had the "inspiration" (*ṭēmu*) for the rebellion, purify the executioners, but let a "spirit" (*eṭemmu*) remain from the slain god, this to be part of new-created man (*awēlu*). The pulsation of this spirit will be a perpetual reminder of the dead god."

Answered "Yes!" in the assembly.
On the first, seventh, and fifteenth days of the month, (215)
He established a purification, a bath.
They slaughtered Aw-ilu,[1] who had the inspiration,
    in their assembly.
Nintu mixed clay with his flesh and blood.
<That same god and man were thoroughly
    mixed in the clay.>
For the rest [of time they would hear the drum],[2] (220)
From the flesh of the god [the] spi[rit remained].
It would make the living know its sign,
Lest he be allowed to be forgotten, [the] spirit remained.
After she had mixed that clay,
She summoned the Anunna, the great gods. (225)
The Igigi, the great gods, spat upon the clay.
Mami made ready to speak,
And said to the great gods,
"You ordered me the task and I have completed (it)!
"You have slaughtered the god, along with his inspiration. (230)
"I have done away with your heavy forced labor,
"I have imposed your drudgery on man.
"You have bestowed(?) clamor upon mankind.[3]
"I have released the yoke, I have [made] restoration."[4]
They heard this speech of hers, (235)
They ran, restored, and kissed her feet, (saying),
"Formerly [we used to call] you 'Mami',
"Now let your n[am]e be
    'Mistress-of-All-the-Gods' (Belet-kala-ili)."

(Breaks off; the missing section, which describes the production of seven male and seven female foetuses, is supplied by the following, later fragment.)

  1. Aw-ilu may be a play on the Akkadian word for "man" (*awēlu*). Another version gives the name as Alla (Aw-ila?).
  2. Or heartbeat.
  3. That is, the only present given to mankind is something to complain of. Ironically, "clamor" will be the cause for the gods' sending the flood.
  4. That is, returned matters to their original state before the great gods had imposed labor on the lesser gods.

[   ] Ea said, (a)
Ea, [seated before her], was prompting her,
Belet-[ili] was reciting the incantation.
After she had recited her spell,
[She s]pat in her clay. (e)
She pinched off fourteen pieces of clay,
Seven she put on the right,
[Seven] on the left.
Between them the brick was placed.
She ... the headcovering(?)
        and ... the cutter of the umbilical cord, (j)
She summoned the wise and accomplished
Birth goddesses, seven and seven.
Seven produced males,
[Seven] produced females.
The midwife, creatress of destiny — (o)
They will crown(?) them in pairs,[1]
They will crown(?) them in pairs in her presence —
Mami laid down the designs for the human race:

"In the house of the pregnant woman about to give birth,
"Let the brick be in place for seven days, (t)
"That Belet-ili, the wise Mami, may be honored.
"Let the midwife rejoice in the house of the woman in labor.
"And when the pregnant woman gives birth,
"Let the mother of the baby deliver herself.
"A male (baby) to [   ] ..., (y)
"[A female (baby)] ..."

(gap)

[And the young girl ...] her breasts,[2]
[The youth ...] a beard,
[And hair ...] the cheek of the young man. (265)

1. That is, these foetuses will one day be married, male to female.
2. The first pair of human beings has grown from babyhood (somewhere after line y of the later fragment) to adolescence (Tablet I lines 263ff.) and has matured enough to reproduce (Tablet I line 267). In 268ff. the first mother-to-be is about to give birth.

[In the   ] ... and street
Wife and husband were [bliss]ful.
The birth goddesses were assembled,
And Nintu [sat rec]koning the months.
[At the] destined [time] they summoned the tenth month.   (270)
The tenth month[1] arrived;
... opened the womb.
Her face beaming and joyful,
She covered her head
And performed the midwifery.   (275)
She girded (the mother's) middle
As she pronounced a blessing.
She drew (a circle?) with meal and placed the brick,[2]
"I am the one who created, my hands have made it!
"Let the midwife rejoice in the sacrosanct woman's house.[3]   (280)
"Where the pregnant woman gives birth,
"And the mother of the baby is delivered,
"Let the brick be in place for nine days,
"Let Nintu, the birth goddess,[4] be honored.
"Always call Mami their [   ],   (285)
"[Always pra]ise the birth goddess, praise Kesh.[5]
"On [the tenth day?], when the bed is laid,
"(Then) let wife and her husband reach bliss together,
"At the time for being man and wife,
"They should heed Ishtar in the [   ] ... chamber.   (290)
"For the nine days let there be rejoicing,
"Let them [cal]l Ishtar Ishara.[6]
"[   ] at the destined time

(gap)

1. That is, nine months were completed.
2. The text implies that placing of a brick in the room where a woman was about to give birth was to be a common practice, but it is unknown outside of this composition.
3. This refers to a woman who has just given birth, so could not have intercourse for a taboo period. Line 287 refers to resumption of intercourse after delivery.
4. Variant: Belet-ili.
5. Sanctuary of the birth goddess.
6. Lines 289ff. refer to consummation of marriage. Ishara was another name for Ishtar.

(Mankind, now reproducing, is put to work to feed the gods.)

A man [   ]
Cleanse the dwelling (?) [   ]
The son to [his] father [   ]
... [   ]
They sat and [   ]   (320)
He it was who was carrying [   ]
He saw and [   ]
Enlil [   ]
They took up ... [   ]
They made n[e]w hoes and shovels,   (325)
They built the big canal banks.
For food for the peoples, for the sustenance of [the gods]

(large gap)

(Humanity reproduces continuously. Enlil is annoyed by their clamor and sends a plague to diminish it.)

[Twel]ve hundred years [had not gone by],
[The land had grown wide], the peoples had increased,
The [land] was bellowing [like a bull].   (345)
The god was disturbed with [their uproar],
[Enlil heard] their clamor.
[He said to] the great gods,
"The clamor of mankind [has become burdensome to me],
"I am losing sleep [to their uproar].   (350)
"[   ] let there be ague ..."

(three lines lost)

But he, [Atrahasis], his god was Enki,   (355)
[He was exceedingly wise].
He would speak [with his god],
And his god [would speak] with him!
Atrahasis [made] ready to speak,
And said to [his] lord,   (360)
"How long [   ]
"Will they impose the disease on us [forever]?"

(Another version reads)

"Ea,[1] lord, the peoples are groaning, (a)
"[The disease] from the gods is devouring the land.
"[Sin]ce you created us,
"[Will you] remove the disease, headpain, ague, and malady?"

Enki made ready to speak,
And said to his servant,
"The elders ... (365)
"... in ...
"[Command]:

   'Let heralds proclaim,
   'Let them raise a loud clamor in the land.

      "Do not reverence your (own) gods, (370)
      "Do not pray to your (own) goddesses,
      "Seek the door of Namtar,[2]
      "Bring a baked (loaf) before it.'"

"May the flour offering please him,
"May he be shamed by the gift and suspend his hand." (375)

(Another version reads)

[Ea made ready to] speak, and said to Atrahasis: (a)
"[Command:

   'Let her]alds [proclaim],
   'Let them silence the clamor in the land:

      "[Do not reverence your (own) gods],
      "Do not pray to your (own) goddesses, (e)
      "[   ] observe his rites,
      "[   ] the flour offering
      "[   ] before it
      "[   ] speak a blessing.'"

"[He will be shamed by the] gift [and set aside?] his hand." (j)

---

1. Ea is another name for Enki. Use of one or the other name in this translation depends upon which version of the text has been incorporated here.
2. God of plague.

(Atrahasis follows the instructions.)

Atrahasis received the command,
And assembled the elders to his gate.[1]
Atrahasis made ready to speak,
And said to the elders,
"Elders ... (395)
"[ ] ...
"[Command]:

   'Let heralds proclaim,
   'Let them raise a loud [clamor] in the land.

      "[Do not reverence] your (own) gods, (400)
      "[Do not] pray to your (own) [goddesses],
      "[Seek] the door of [Namtar],
      "[Bring a baked (loaf) before it.'"

"May the flour offering please him,
"May he be shamed by the gift and suspend his hand." (405)
The elders heeded [his] words,
They built a temple for Namtar in the city.
They commanded and the [heralds] proclaimed,
They made a loud clamor [in the land].
They did [not] reverence their (own) gods, (410)
They did [not] pray to [their (own) goddesses],
They sought [the door] of Namtar,
They [brought] a baked (loaf) before [it].
The flour offering pleased him,
[He was shamed] by the gift and suspended his hand. (415)
[The ague] left them,
They resumed [their clamor?],

    (two lines fragmentary)

    (Enlil next orders a famine.)

[Enlil] convened his assembly, and said to the gods his sons, (420)
"Do not lay contagion upon them (any longer)!
"[The peo]ples have not dwindled,
   but have become more numerous than before!

---

1. There seems to be no way to restore this and the next line from Enki's instructions in lines 365ff.

"I am disturbed [at] their clamor,
"[At] their uproar sleep cannot overcome me.
"Cut off provender for the peoples, (425)
"Let plants be scanty in their stomachs.
"Above, let Adad make scarce his rain,
"Below, let (rainfall) be blocked off and raise
      no flood from the depths.
"Let the fields reduce their yields,
"The grain goddess turn aside her bosom, (430)
"Let the black fields whiten,
"Let the broad plain produce salts,
"Let the earth's womb rebel,
"Let no plants come forth, no grains ripen.
"Let a malady be laid upon the peoples, (435)
"That the womb be constricted
      and give no safe birth to a child."
They cut off provender from the peoples,
Plants were scanty in their stomachs.
Above, Adad made scarce his rain,
Below, (the rainfall) was blocked off and raised
      no flood from the depths. (440)
The fields reduced their yields,
The grain goddess turned aside her bosom,
The black fields whitened,
The broad plain produced salts, earth's womb rebelled,
No plants came forth, no grains ripened. (445)
A malady was laid upon the peoples,
So that the womb was constricted
      and gave no safe birth to a child.
The bo[lt, the bar of the sea],
[Ea] watched over [together with his plants],
Above, [Adad made scarce his rain], (450)
Below, (rainfall) was blocked off
      [and raised no flood from the depths],
The fields reduced [their yields],
The grain goddess [turned aside her bosom],
[The black fields whitened],

[The broad plain] produced salts, [Earth's womb rebelled], (455)
[No plants] came forth, no grains [ripened].
[A malady was laid upon the peoples]
[That the womb was constricted
      and gave [no safe birth to a child].
[For one year they ate ...]
[   ] (460)
[When the second year came], they exhausted their stores,
[When the third year] came,
[The peoples' features] were distorted [by hunger].
[When the fourth year came], their [long] legs became short,
[Their broad shoulders] became narrow. (465)
[They walked about hunched] in the street.
[When the fifth year came], daughter saw mother [go in],
[But mother would not] open her door [to daughter].
[Daughter] watched [the scales (when) mother
      (was sold into slavery)],
Mother watched [the scales (when) daughter
      (was sold into slavery)]. (470)
[When the sixth year came],
      [they served up] daughter for a meal,
[They served up [son for sustenance]:
[They were filled on their own children?],
One [household] devoured another.
Their [faces] were encrusted [like dead malt]. (475)
[The peoples] were living [on the verge] of death.

[For th]e destiny of the man Atrahasis,
Ea, [his god], was heedful.
Did he not [speak] with his god?
His god Ea spoke with him. (480)
He left the gate of his god,
He placed his bed facing the river,
But the channels were quiet.

                (gap)

[When the second] year [came, they exhausted their stores],

[When] the third year [came], (485)
The peoples' [features] were distorted by [hunger].
When the fourth year [came], their [long] legs became short,
Their broad [shoulders] became narrow,
They walked about hunched in the street.
When the fifth year came, daughter saw mother go in, (490)
But mother would not open her door to daughter.
Daughter watched the scales (when) mother
    (was sold into slavery),
[Mother] watched the scales (when) daughter
    (was sold into slavery).
When the sixth year came,
    they served up [daughter] for a meal,
They served up son for sustenance: (495)
[They] were filled [on their own children?],
One household devoured another.
Their faces [were encrusted] like dead malt.
The peoples [were living] on the verge of [death].
The command which they received [ ] (500)
They entered and [ ]
The message of Atrahasis [ ]
"Lord, the land [ ]
"A sign [ ]

Tablet II

"[Command:

   'Let heralds proclaim],
   '[Let them make a loud] cl[amor] in the land.

      "Do not reverence your (own) gods,
      "Do not pray to your (own) [goddesses], (10)
      "Seek [the door of] Adad,
      "Bring a baked (loaf) [before it].'"

"[May the flour offering] please him,
"May he be shamed [by the] gift and suspend his hand.
"May he rain down mist in the morning, (15)

"May he stealthily rain down dew in the night,
"May the fields just as stealthily bear ninefold."
They built a temple for Adad in the city.
They commanded and the heralds proclaimed,
They made a loud clamor in the land.   (20)
They did not reverence their (own) gods,
They did [not] pray to their (own) goddesses,
They [sought] the door [of Adad],
[They brought] a baked (loaf) before it.
The flour offering pleased him,   (25)
He was shamed by the gift and suspended his hand.
He rained down mist in the morning,
He stealthily rained down dew in the night,
[The fields just as] stealthily bore ninefold.
[The famine?] left them,   (30)
They resumed their [clamor?]

(gap)

(Enlil is enraged and realizes that Enki has thwarted him. He proposes a flood to wipe out humanity and binds Enki by oath not to reveal his plans.)

He[1] was filled with anger [at Enki],
"[All we] great Anunna-gods
"Resolved together [on a rule].
"Anu and Adad watched over [the upper regions],   (35)
"I watched over the lower earth.
"Where Enki went,
"He released the yoke, he made restoration.[2]
"He let loose produce for the peoples,[3]
"He put [shade?] in the glare(?) of the sun."   (40)
Enlil [made] ready to speak,

---

1. Enlil.
2. That is, a return to conditions before the attempt to destroy the human race.
3. I take this speech to mean that Enki loosed a flood of fish upon the land and saved the people from starvation. The trick perhaps lay in the ambiguity of the word: Enki promised to send a flood of fish, which the gods understood to be a flood to overwhelm the land, but which turned out, intentionally no doubt, to be harvest for the starving human race. This incident is lost in a gap in the text.

He said to the vizier Nusku,
"Let them bring to me ... sons,[1]
"Let them [send] them into my presence."
They brought to him ... sons. (45)
The warrior [Enlil] said to them,
"[All we] great Anunna-gods
"Resolved together on a rule.
"Anu and Adad watched over the upper [regions],
"I watched over the lower earth. (50)
"Where you went
"[You released the yoke], you made restoration.
"[You let loose produce for the peoples],
"[You put shade?] in the glare(?) of the sun."

(gap)

(Enlil is explaining to the gods how Enki frustrated his murderous plans.)

"Adad [withheld?] his rain (55)
"[But   ] filled the fields
"[And] the clouds(?) covered [   ].
"[You (gods) must not] feed his peoples,
"[Nor] supply provisions on which the peoples thrive."
[The god] fretted for sitting idle, (60)
[In] the assembly of the gods, worry gnawed at him.
[Enlil] fretted for sitting idle,
[In] the assembly of the gods, worry gnawed at him.

(four lines fragmentary)

(Enlil is speaking.)

"[All we great Anunna-gods]
"[Resolved] together [on a rule],
"Anu and Adad watched over the upper regions, (70)
"I watched over the lower earth.
"Where you went
"[You] released the yoke, you made restoration.

---

1. Compare Tablet I lines 93, 95.

"[You] let loose produce for the peoples,
"[You put shade?] in the glare(?) of the sun." (75)

(gap)

"[She? imposed] your drudgery [on man],
"[You] have bestowed(?) clamo[r upon mankind].
"You slaughtered [the god], together with [his inspiration],
"[You] sat down and bath[ed yourselves].
"[   ] it will bring [   ] (80)
"You resolved on [a rule   ],
"Let (mankind) return to [its] la[ir?].
"Let us be sure to bind the leader Enki [ ] by an oath
         so that(?) he [   ].
Enki made ready to speak,
And said to the gods [his brethren], (85)
"Why would you bind me by oath [ ]?
"Am I to bring my hands against [my own peoples]?
"The flood that you are speaking of [to me],
"Who is that? I [do not know].
"Am I to produce [a flood]? (90)
"The task of that is [Enlil's].
"Let him [   ] choose,
"Let Shullat and [Hanish] go [in front],
"Let Errakal [tear out] the mooring poles,
"Let [Ninurta] go make [the dikes] overflow. (95)

(gap)

"Assemble ... [   ].
"Do not obey ... [   ]."
The gods commanded annihilation,
E[nlil] committed an evil deed against the peoples.

Tablet III

(gap)

(Atrahasis has had a dream from Enki, and wishes to know its meaning.)

Atrahasis made ready to speak,
And said to his lord,
"Make me know the meaning [of the dream],
"[ ] let me know, that I may look out for its consequence."
[Enki] made ready to speak, (15)
And said to his servant,
"You might say, 'Am I to be looking out while in the bedroom?'
"Do you pay attention to the message that I speak for you:

    'Wall, listen to me!
    'Reed wall, pay attention to all my words! (20)
    'Flee house, build boat,
    'Forsake possessions, and save life.
    'The boat which you build,
    '[ ] be equal [ ]

(gap)

    'Roof her over like the depths, (25)
    'So that the sun shall not see inside her,
    'Let her be roofed over fore and aft.
    'The gear should be very firm,
    'The pitch should be firm, make (her) strong.
    'I will shower down upon you later (30)
    'A windfall of birds, a spate(?) of fishes.'"

He opened the water clock and filled it,
He told it (the wall?) of the coming of the seven-day deluge.
Atrahasis received the command,
He assembled the elders at his gate. (35)
Atrahasis made ready to speak,
And said to the elders,
"My god [does not agree] with your god,
"Enki and [Enlil] are constantly angry with each other.
"They have expelled me from [the land?]. (40)

"Since I have always reverenced [Enki],
"[He told me] this.
"I can[not] live in [   ]
"Nor can I [set my feet on] the earth of Enlil.
"[I will dwell?] with <my> god in(?) the depths."   (45)
"[This] he told me [   ] ..."

(gap)

The elders [   ]
The carpenter [carried his axe],
The reed-worker [carried his stone].
[The rich man? carried] the pitch,   (50)
The poor man [brought the materials needed].

(gap)

Atrahasis [   ]

(gap)

Bringing [   ]
Whatever he [had   ]
Whatever he had [   ]   (55)
Pure (animals) he sl[aughtered, cattle] ...
Fat (animals) [he killed, sheep?] ...
He chose [and brought on] board.
The [birds] flying in the heavens,
The cattle(?) [and   of the cat]tle god,   (60)
The [creatures?   ] of the steppe,
[   ] he brought on board
[   ] ...
[   ] he invited his people
[   ] to a feast.   (65)
[   ] his family he brought on board.
While one was eating and another was drinking,
He went in and out; he could not sit, could not kneel,
For his heart was broken, he was retching gall.
The outlook of the weather changed,   (70)
Adad began to roar in the clouds.

The god they heard, his clamor.
He brought pitch to seal his door.
By the time he had bolted his door,
Adad was roaring in the clouds. (75)
As the furious wind rose,
He cut the mooring rope and released the boat.

(four lines lost)

[   ] the storm
[   ] were yoked
[Anzu rent] the sky with his talons,
[He   ] the land (85)
And broke its clamor [like a pot].
[   ] the flood [came forth],
Its power came upon the peoples [like a battle].
One person did [not] see another,
They could [not] recognize each other in the catastrophe. (90)
[The deluge] bellowed like a bull,
The wind [resound]ed like a screaming eagle.
The darkness [was dense], the sun was gone,
[   ] ... like flies
[the clamor?] of the deluge (95)

(two lines fragmentary)

[   ] the clamor of the de[luge]
It was trying [ ] of the gods.
[Enki] was beside himself, (100)
[That] his sons were carried off before him.
Nintu, the great lady,
Gnawed her lips in agony.
The Anunna, the great gods,
Were sitting in thirst and hunger. (105)
The goddess saw it, weeping,
The midwife of the gods, the wise Mami,
"Let the day grow dark,
"Let it turn back to gloom!
"In the assembly of the gods, (110)

"How did I agree with them on annihilation?
"Was Enlil so strong that he forced [me] to speak?
"Like that Tiruru, did he make [my] speech confused?[1]
"Of my own accord, from myself alone,
"To my own charge have I heard (my people's) clamor! (115)
"My offspring — with no help from me —
    have become like flies.
"And as for me, how to dwell in (this) abode of grief,
    my clamor fallen silent?
"Shall I go up to heaven,
"As if to live in a house of [plentiful store]s?
"Where has Anu gone to, the chief decision-maker, (120)
"Whose sons, the gods, heeded his command?
"He who, irrationally brought about the flood,
"And relegated the peoples to ca[tastrophe]?"

(gap)

Nintu was wailing [   ]
"... gave birth to(?) ... (125)
"As dragonflies a watercourse, they have filled the sea.
"Like rafts they lie against the e[dg]e,
"Like rafts capsized they lie against the bank.
"I saw and wept over them,
"I have exhausted my lamentation for them." (130)
She wept, giving vent to her feelings,
While Nintu wailed, her emotion was spent.
The gods wept with her for the land.
She had her fill of woe and thirsted for beer.
Where she sat, they too sat weeping, (135)
Like sheep, they filled a streambed.[2]
Their lips were agonized with thirst,
They were suffering pangs of hunger.
Seven days and seven ni[ghts]
There came the deluge, the storm, [the flood]. (140)
    Where it [   ]

1. The meaning of the reference to Tiruru is unknown.
2. The gods are hoping to find water to drink.

[   ] was thrown down

(gap of about sixty lines)

To the [four] winds [   ]
He cast [   ]
Providing food [   ] (205)
[   ]
[The gods sniffed] the savor,
They were gathered [like flies] around the offering.
[After] they had eaten the offering,
[Nin]tu arose to rail against all of them, (210)
"Where has Anu come to, the chief decision-maker?
"Has Enlil drawn nigh the incense?
"They who irrationally brought about the flood,
"And relegated the peoples to catastrophe?
"You resolved upon annihilation, (215)
"So now (the people's) clear countenances are turned grim."
Then she drew nigh the big ...s
Which Anu had and ... [   ]
"Mine is [their] woe! Proclaim my destiny!
"Let him get me out of my misery,
    let him show me the way(?). (220)
"Let me go out ... [   ]
"In [   ]
"Let [these] flies[1] be jewelry around my neck,
"That I may remember it [every?] day [and forever?]."
[The warrior Enlil] saw the vessel, (225)
And was filled with anger at the Igigi-gods.
"All we great Anunna-gods
"Resolved together on an oath.
"Where did life(?) escape?
"How did a man survive the catastrophe?" (230)
Anu made ready to speak,
And said to the warrior Enlil,
"Who could do this but Enki?

The episode is obscure and seems to contain a play on words.

"[   ] he revealed the command."
[Enki] made ready to speak, (235)
[And said to] the great gods,
"I did it [indeed] for your sakes!
"[I am responsible] for safeguarding li[fe].
"[   ] gods [   ]
"[   ] the flood (240)
"[   ] brought about
"[O Enlil,   ] your heart
"[   ] and relax.
"Impose your penalty [on a wrong-doer],
"[For] who is it that disregards your command?¹ (245)
"[   ] the assembly [   ]

(gap)

"[   ] it
"[   ] put,
"[   ] ... my heart."
[Enlil] made ready to speak, (250)
And said to Ea the leader,
"[Come], summon Nintu the birth goddess,
"[Do you] and she take counsel together in the assembly."
[Enki] made ready to speak,
And [said to] Nintu the birth goddess, (255)
"[You], birth goddess, creatress of destinies,
"[Establish death] for all peoples!
"[   ]
"[   ] let there be.

(one line missing?)

"Now then, let there be a third (woman) among the people,
"Among the people are the woman who has borne and the
    woman who has not borne.
"Let there be (also) among the people the (she)-demon,²

---

1. The thrust of the argument may be that he had sworn not to tell mankind of the flood, but did not swear to annihilate life.
2. "The-One-Who-Wipes-Out" (family names).

"Let her snatch the baby from the lap of her who bore it, (265)
"Establish high priestesses and priestesses,
"Let them be taboo, and so cut down childbirth.

(fragmentary lines, then large gap)

"How we brought about [the flood],
"But man survived the [catastrophe],
"You, counsellor of the [great] gods, (270)
"At [your] command have I brought a [   ] to be,
"This [my] song (is) for your praise.
"May the Igigi-gods hear, let them extol your great deed
    to each other.
"I have sung of the flood to all peoples:
"Listen!" (275)

When Ishtar Went to the Netherworld

In this poem, Ishtar decides to visit the netherworld and demands to be admitted. Her sister, Ereshkigal, queen of the netherworld, is suspicious and jealous, and instructs her gatekeepers to remove all of Ishtar's clothing as she enters. As she enters the netherworld naked, her sister sets upon her sixty disease demons and she dies. Sexual reproduction vanishes from the world; the gods need a way to bring Ishtar back to life. Ea, god of wisdom, sends a male prostitute to the netherworld, who so pleases Ereshkigal by adroit flattery that she grants him any wish. He asks for the body of Ishtar, as instructed by Ea. The enraged queen gives up the body, but dooms the prostitute to a squalid earthly existence. Ereshkigal orders the death god to bring someone else in Ishtar's stead and at the same time to get revenge on Ishtar. The death god finds Ishtar's lover, Tammuz, removes all signs of mourning for Ishtar's death from him, and gives him a ring and a flute to play on. The next part of the story is omitted in the Akkadian text, perhaps presumed as understood. When Ishtar returns from the netherworld to find her lover dallying with harlots and not in mourning, in a fit of jealous passion she offers him to the netherworld in her stead. In lines 132ff. the text switches abruptly to Tammuz's sister Belili, who, when she hears the wailing for her dead brother, institutes a ceremony for the dead.

This composition may have emerged from a Sumerian original. The present text is shorter than the Sumerian version of the same story, with large pieces omitted. The final episode of the text is so elliptical as to be incomprehensible to the modern reader. To him, the Akkadian text will seem poorly conceived in comparison to its Sumerian forerunner. In any event, the story is not without drama and narrative art.

> To the netherworld, land of n[o return], (1)
> Ishtar, daughter of Sin, [set] her mind.
> Indeed, the daughter of Sin did set [her] mind
> To the gloomy house, seat of the ne[therworld],
> To the house which none leaves who enters, (5)
> To the road whose journey has no return,
> To the house whose entrants are bereft of light,
> Where dust is their sustenance and clay their food.
> They see no light but dwell in darkness,

They are clothed like birds in wings for garments, (10)
And dust has gathered on the door and bolt.
When Ishtar reached the gate of the netherworld,
She said (these) words to the gatekeeper,
"Gatekeeper! Open your gate for me!
"Open your gate for me that I may enter! (15)
"If you will not open the gate that I may enter,
"I will break down the door, I will smash the bolt,
"I will break down the frame, I will topple the doors.
"I will raise up the dead to devour the living,
"The dead shall outnumber the living!" (20)
The gatekeeper made ready to speak,
Saying to the great one, Ishtar,
"Stay, my lady, do not cast it down.
"Let me go announce your name to the queen E[resh]kigal."
The gatekeeper went in and said to Ereshkigal, (25)
"Here is your sister Ishtar at [your gate],
"She who holds the great skip-rope,[1]
    who roils up the deep before Ea the [king?]."
When Ereshkigal heard this,
Her face went pallid as a cut-down tamarisk,
Her lips went dark as the lip of a vat. (30)
"What made her resolve on me?
    What has aroused bad feelings in her against me?
"Here now, shall I drink water
    with the (netherworld) Anunna-gods,
"Shall I eat clay for bread, shall I drink dirty water for beer?
"Shall I weep for the young men
    who have left [their] helpmeets?
"Shall I then weep for the young women
    who are wrenched from lovers' loins? (35)
"Shall I weep for the helpless infant
    who was taken before its time?[2]
"Go, gatekeeper, open [your] gate to her,

---

1. Symbol of the warlike Ishtar.
2. That is, if Ishtar succeeds in her plan, Ereshkigal will join the dead, instead of being their queen?

"Treat her according to the age-old rules."
Off went the gatekeeper and opened [the] gate to her,
"Enter, my lady, that Cutha[1] rejoice over you, (40)
"That the palace of the netherworld be glad at your presence."
He brought her in the first gate,
    he ... and removed the great tiara of her head.
"Why, gatekeeper, did you remove the great tiara of my head?"
"Enter, my lady.
    Thus the rules of the mistress of the netherworld."
He brought her in the second gate, he ...
    and removed the earrings of her ears. (45)
"Why, gatekeeper, did you remove the earrings of my ears?"
"Enter, my lady.
    Thus the rules of the mistress of the netherworld."
He brought her in the third gate,
    he ... and removed the beads of her neck.
"Why, gatekeeper, did you remove the beads of my neck?"
"Enter, my lady.
    Thus the rules of the mistress of the netherworld." (50)
He brought her in the fourth gate,
    he ... and removed the garment pin of her breast.
"Why, gatekeeper, did you remove the garment pin of my breast?"
"Enter, my lady.
    Thus the rules of the mistress of the netherworld."
He brought her in the fifth gate, he ... and removed
    the girdle of birth stones of her waist.
"Why, gatekeeper, did you remove the girdle of birth
    stones of my waist?" (55)
"Enter, my lady.
    Thus the rules of the mistress of the netherworld."
He brought her in the sixth gate,
    he ... and removed her bracelets and anklets.
"Why, gatekeeper, did you remove my bracelets and anklets?"
"Enter, my lady.
    Thus the rules of the mistress of the netherworld."

---

1. Cult center of Nergal, god of the netherworld.

He brought her in the seventh gate,
>he ... and removed the loincloth of her body. (60)
"Why, gatekeeper, did you remove the loincloth of my body?"
"Enter, my lady.
>Thus the rules of the mistress of the netherworld."
As soon as Ishtar had entered the netherworld,
Ereshkigal saw her and trembled with fury at her.
Ishtar, without thinking,
>sat(?) (in the place of honor) above her. (65)
Ereshkigal made ready to speak, and said
To Namtar her vizier these words,
"Go, Namtar, [take her from] my presence!
"Let loose against her sixty di[seases   ] Ishtar,
"Eye disease [against] her [eyes], (70)
"Side disease a[gainst] her [sides],
"Foot disease a[gainst] her [feet],
"Heart disease a[gainst her heart],
"Head disease [against her head],
"I [let them loose?] against all of her!" (75)
After the lady Ishtar [went down] to the netherworld,
The bull would not mount the cow,
>[the ass would not impregnate the jenny],
The [young man would not impregnate] the girl
>in the thoroughfare,
The young man slept in [his bedroom?],
The g[irl s]lept [by herself]. (80)
Papsukkal, vizier of the great gods,
>was downcast and his features [were gloomy].
He was dressed in mourning and [left] his hair unkempt.
Off went he in despair before Sin his father, weeping,
Before Ea the king [his] tears flowed down.
"Ishtar has gone down to the netherworld,
>she has not come up. (85)
"As soon as Ishtar went down to the netherworld,
"The bull will not mount the cow,
>the ass will not impregnate the jenny,

"The young man will not impregnate the girl
    in the thoroughfare,
"The young man has slept in his [bedroom?],
"The girl has slept by herself." (90)
Ea, in his wise heart, conceived (what was) called for,
He created Asushunamir, an impersonator.[1]
"Go, Asushunamir, make your way to the netherworld,
"Let the seven gates of the netherworld be opened before you.
"Let Ereshkigal see you and feel well-disposed towards you. (95)
"When she calms and her feelings are well disposed,
"Have her swear the oath of the great gods,
"Look up and set your mind on the waterskin,
"'Oh, my lady, let them give me the waterskin,
    that I may drink water from it.'"
When Ereshkigal heard this, (100)
She smote her thigh, she bit her finger.
"You asked of me the unaskable!
"Come, Asushunamir, I will curse you a great curse,
"Let me ordain you a fate never to be forgotten.
"May bread of public plowing be your food,[2] (105)
"May the public sewer pipe be your drinking place.
"The shadow of a wall be your station,
"The threshold be your dwelling.
"May drunk and sober slap your cheek!"
Ereshkigal made ready to speak, (110)
Saying these words to Namtar her vizier,
"Go, Namtar, knock at the Egalgina,[3]
"Decorate the thresholds with cowrie shells.
"Bring out and seat the (netherworld) Anunna-gods
    on thrones of gold,

---

1. Male prostitutes or transvestites were devotees of Ishtar. It is not clear how such a person could avoid being held by the netherworld. Perhaps a male in female costume "partook of both worlds" or could pass anywhere as an itinerant entertainer. The name means "He is resplendent as he comes forth."
2. Lines 105-106 may refer to homosexual activity.
3. Evidently a palace in the netherworld.

"Sprinkle Ishtar with water of life
    and take her from(?) my presence." (115)
Namtar went and knocked at the Egalgina,
He decorated the thresholds with cowrie shells,
He brought out and seated the (netherworld) Anunna-gods
    on thrones of gold,
He sprinkled Ishtar with water of life and brought her away.
He brought her out the first gate
    and returned to her the loin cloth of her body, (120)
He brought her out the second gate and returned to her
    her bracelets and anklets,
He brought her out the third gate and returned to her
    the girdle of birth stones of her waist,
He brought her out the fourth gate
    and returned to her the garment pin of her breast,
He brought her out the fifth gate
    and returned to her the beads of her neck,
He brought her out the sixth gate
    and returned to her the earrings of her ears, (125)
He brought her out the seventh gate
    and returned to her the great tiara of [her h]ead.
"If she does not pay you her ransom, bring [her] back here.
"Tammuz, her childhood lover,
"Bathe in a bath of pure water and a[noint with] fine oil,
"Dress him in a red garment,
    let him strike up a lapis flute [... a carnelian ring?], (130)
"Let prostitutes turn [his] mood." [1]
[The lady] Belili was put[ting right?] her jewelry,
[ ] eyestones with which she filled her l[ap?].
When she heard the wailing for her brother,
    Belili smote the jewelry of her body,
The eyestones which filled the Wild Cow's face(?). (135)
"Do not rob me of my only brother!

---

1. I assume here a gap in the narrative, including a narrative recapitulation of 128-131, Ishtar's catching sight of him, and Tammuz's removal to the netherworld by Namtar.

"On the day Tammuz (says) "Hurrah!"
   the lapis flute and carnelian ring (say) "Hurrah!"
"With him (say) "Hurrah!" the wailing men
   and wailing women,
"Let the dead come up and smell the incense."[1]

---

1. The meaning may be that when Tammuz emerges with a joyful shout from the netherworld, the dead will rise too. One has here, apparently, an aetiology for some cult festival. Other translations read "On the day Tammuz comes up to me, with him will come up ..."

How Nergal Became King of the Netherworld

The poem of Nergal and Ereshkigal relates how Nergal (also called Erra) became king of the netherworld. The story hinges on the isolation and sexual frustration of the queen of the netherworld, Ereshkigal. This aspect of the tale is related with warmth, even humor.

(The gods give a banquet. The chief god sends a message to Ereshkigal, queen of the netherworld.)

[Anu made ready to speak], (1)
[Saying to Gaga his messenger],
"[Let me send you, Gaga, to the Land of No Return],
"[To the house of Ereshkigal who dwells in the netherworld],
"[Saying], (5)

'[You are not able to come up],
'[Not (once) in a year can you come up before us].
'[We cannot go down],
'[Nor (once) in a month can we descend before you].
'[Let your messenger come here], (10)
'[Let him remove food from the table,
    let him receive your serving].
'[Whatever I give him, let him bring safely to] you.'"

[Gaga descended the long staircase] of heaven.
[When] he reac[hed the gate of Ereshkigal he said],
"[Gatekeeper], o[pen] the gate [to me]." (15)
"[Enter, Gaga], may the gate ble[ss you]."
He brought [the god G]aga in [the first gate],
He brought [the god] Gaga [in the second] gate,
He brought [the god] Gaga [in the third] gate,
He brought the god Gaga in the fourth gate, (20)
He brou[ght] the god Gaga in the fifth gate,
He br[ough]t the god Gaga in the sixth gate,
He br[ough]t the god Gaga in the seventh gate.
He entered her b[roa]d courtyard,
He knelt and k[issed] the ground before her. (25)
He straightened, stood, and said to her,

"Anu [your] father has sent [me],
"Saying,
   'You are not able to come up,
   'Not (once) in a year can you come up before us. (30)
   'We cannot go down,
   'Nor (once) in a month can we descend before you.
   'Let your messenger come here,
   'Let him remove food from the table,
      let him receive your serving,
   'Whatever I give him, let him bring safely to you.'" (35)
Ereshkigal made ready to speak,
   saying to G[aga] (these) words,
"Messenger of Anu our father, who has come to us,
"(I hope) all is well with Anu, Enlil, and Ea,
   the great gods?
"(I hope) all is well with Nammu and Nanshe,[1]
   the pure gods?
"(I hope) all is well with the husband
   of the Mistress of Heaven? (40)
"(I hope) all is well with Nin[urta, mightiest] in the land?"
Gaga made ready to speak, saying to Ereshkigal these words,
"All is well with Anu, Enlil, and Ea, the great gods,
"All is well with [Namm]u and Nanshe, the pure (gods),
"All is wel[l with the husband of the M]istress of Heaven, (45)
"All is we[ll] with Ni[nurt]a, the mightiest in the land."
[G]aga made ready to speak, saying to Ereshkigal these words,
"[   ] may all be well with you."
[Ereshkigal] made ready to speak, saying to Namtar,
   her messenger, these words,
"Nam[tar], my [messenger], let me send yo[u to] heaven
   to Anu our father. (50)
"Namtar, go up the long [staircase of heaven],
"Take food from the table, [receive my serving].
"Whatever Anu shall give [you, you must bring safely to me]."
[Namtar went up the long staircase of heaven]

---

1. Nammu and Nanshe were Sumerian goddesses.

(another version adds)

Up went N[amtar] to high heaven, (55)
He entered [the place] the gods were [se]ated(?).
They inter[rupted their talk?, stood, re]cei[ved] Namtar,
The messenger of their great sister.
They set out [food and drink],
    "Let him t[ake] her [food por]tion."

(Nergal refuses to stand. The messenger reports the offense to her mistress. She sends him back to bring her the offender. Namtar returns, but Nergal disguises himself.)

(gap)

Saying, "Where is the [one who] did not stand
    [in the presence of] my [mes]senger? (60)
"Bring him to m[e] that I may kill him."
Namtar came to speak to the gods,
They summoned him and the gods spoke with him, dea[th],
"Find the god who did not stand in your presence,
"Take him before your mistress." (65)
Namtar counted them; a god in the back was bald.
"The god who did not stand in my presence is not here."
Namtar went to [give] his report,
[Saying, "   I counted] them,
"[A god] in back [was bald], (70)
"[The god who did not stand in my presence] was not there."

(Ea remonstrates with Nergal.)

[Ea made ready to speak, saying to Nergal these words],
"[   ]
"[When he a]rrived a[t   ]
"[   ] the path [   ] (75)
"[The gods] all k[nelt before] him,
"[The great god]s, lords of destin[ies],
"[For he] bore the authority, the authority [of the gods],
"[The gods] who dwell in the netherworld.
"Why were you not [kneeling] before him? (80)
"[   ] I kept winking at you,
"But you were [affe]cting not to be aware.

"[You were not ...],
   y[our] e[yes] were looking at the ground."

(Nergal evidently replies that he is brave enough to face Ereshkigal's rage. Ea sees an opportunity, so gives Nergal detailed instructions how to enter the netherworld successfully. He is to build a chair of imitation substances on fine wood. In another version, Nergal weeps for fear, but Ea thinks of a way to save him.)

(gap)

[Nergal made ready to speak, saying to Ea these words],
"Let me proceed [   ]   (85)
"[   ] what you said.
"[   ] ... I will twine it double."
When Ea heard this, he said to himself,
"[Let me bring it] about that I entrust(?) ..."[1]
Ea made ready to speak, saying to Nergal these words: (90)
"Wayfarer, do you wish to go on your mission with a ...
   thorn(?) in your hand?
"Go down to the forest of sissoo-trees(?),
"Cut down sissoo(?), whitewood(?), cedar(?),
"Cut off f[rankincense?] and staffs."
[He went down to the forest of sissoo-trees?],   (95)
[He cut sissoo(?), whitewood(?), and c]edar(?)
He cut off frankincense(?) and fruit trees,
He made [a work], a throne of Ea, the leader.
[In imitation of] silver he colored with gypsum(?),
In imitation of lapis he colored with faience,   (100)
In imitation of gold he made multicolored
   with cobalt(?) and potash(?).
The work was complete, the throne done.
Then he (Ea) summoned him to give his instructions,
"Wayfarer, if you wish to go,
"[Take to] heart whatever instructions I [give you].   (105)
"When you arrive there,
"When they bring you a chair,

---

1. Uncertain. Ea evidently wishes to ensure that Nergal will survive the journey to the netherworld.

"Do not proceed to sit upon it.
"When the baker brings you bread, do not proceed to eat.
"When the butcher brings you meat, do not proceed to eat. (110)
"When the brewer brings you beer, do not proceed to drink.
"When someone brings water for your footbath,
    do not proceed to wash your [feet].
"When she goes in to bathe,
"And puts on her [ ] garment,
"She will let you see her body ... (115)
"You must not [become arous]ed as man and woman."
Nergal [   ]

          (gap)

[To the netherworld, Land of No Return],
[Nergal set his mind ...]
[To the gloomy house, seat of the netherworld], (120)
[To the house which none leaves who enters],
[To the road whose journey] has no return,
[To the house who entrants] are bereft of light,
[Where dust is their sustenance and] clay their food.
[They are clothed like bi]rds in wings for garments, (125)
[They see no light] but dwell in darkness,
[   ] moaning,
[they moan] like [do]ves.
[   ] ...
[The gatekeeper made ready to speak],
    saying to Nergal these words, (130)
"I shall take back report [concerning the wayfarer
    standing] at the gate."
[The gatekeeper went in to Ereshkiga]l to say (these) words,
"[Mistress, a certai]n [wayfarer] has com[e to us],
"[Wh]o will [identify?] him?"

          (gap)

    (Namtar is speaking.)

"[let me] identify him. (135)
"[I will look at] him outside the gate,

"I shall take back report [ ] to my mistress."
Namtar went and looked at Erra [through the ...] of the gate,
Namtar's face went pallid as a cut-down tamarisk,
His lips went dark as the lip of a vat. (140)
Namtar went to [his] mis[tress] to say (these) words,
"Mistress, that time you sent me [to] your father,
"When I entered the court of [Anu],
"[All the gods   ] knelt humbly,
"[The gods of the land] knelt humbly ... (145)
"The god who kept on st[anding] in my presence
"Is now come down to the Land of No Return."
[Ereshkigal made ready to speak, saying]
       to [Namtar, her messenger, (these) words],
"Namtar, you must not strive for divine supremacy,
       nor let your spirit imagine deeds of valor.
"Go up and take your seat on the throne, the royal dais, (150)
"Do you render the judgments of the vast netherworld.
"Let me go up to the heaven of Anu my father,
       that I may eat the food of Anu my father,
"And drink the beer of Anu my father.
"Go, Namtar, bring that god into my presence."
Namtar went and brought in the god Erra. (155)
When he entered the first gate, Pituh,
When he entered the second gate, Enkishar,
When he entered the third gate, Endashurimma,
When he entered the fourth gate, Nerulla,
When he entered the fifth gate, Nerubanda, (160)
When he entered the sixth gate, Endukuga,
When he entered the seventh gate, Ennugigi,
He entered her spacious court,
He knelt and kissed the ground before her,
He straightened, stood, and said to her, (165)
"Anu your father sent me to your presence,

    'Do you (be the one to) sit on this throne
    'And render the judgments of the great gods,
    'The great gods who dwell in the netherworld.'"

As soon as he came, they brought him a chair, (170)
He did not proceed to sit upon it.
The baker brought him bread,
    he did not proceed to eat his bread,
The butcher brought him meat,
    he did not proceed to eat his meat,
The cupbearer brought him beer, he did not
    proceed to drink his beer,
They brought him water for his footbath,
    but he did not proceed to wash his feet. (175)
Finally she went in to the bathing chamber,
She put on her [ ] garment,
She let him see [her body],
[He was not ar]oused as man for woman

        (gap)

Nergal ... [ ] (180)
She [went] in to the ba[th]ing chamber,
[She put on] garment,
[She let him see her body].
He [became aroused as man for woman],
They embraced [one another], (185)
Pa[ssionately they went] to bed.
One day, a second day they lay,
    [Queen Ereshkigal and Erra],
A third day, a fourth day [they lay,
    Queen Ereshkigal and Erra],
[A fifth day], a sixth day [they lay,
    Queen Ereshkigal and Erra].
[When the seventh] day [came], (190)
Nergal was [ ] for not being present [in heaven],
He ... after him [ ]
"Release me, sister, [ ]
"[Do not] make a fuss [at my going],
"I must go from(?) the Land of No Return." (195)
As for her, her [ ] turned dark.
[Nergal went strai]ght to [ ]

[To   ] the gatekeeper (he said these words),
"[Ereshkigal] your [mis]tress [has sent me, saying],
"'[I would send you to the heaven] of Anu [our father].'   (200)
"Let me out that [I may deliver] the message."
Nergal went [up the long staircase of heaven].
[When he reached] the gate of Anu, En[lil, and Ea],
Anu, Enlil, and [Ea saw him],
"The son of Ishtar [has come up to us]!   (205)
"[Ereshkigal] will look for [him to take him back].
"[Let] Ea his father [sprinkle him] with spring water
    that he be bald,
"Have a tic, be la[me, ... let him sit among all the gods]."
Ereshkigal [   ]
[Went into] the bath chamber [   ]   (210)
... [   ]
[   ] her body
... [   ]
She called out [   ]
"[Bring a] cha[ir   ]   (215)
"[Sprinkle the rooms with [   ] water,
"S[prinkle] the rooms with [   ] water,
"Sprin[kle] the rooms with [   ] water,
"[... the] two daughters of [   ] and Enmeshar,
"Sprinkle them with [water of] ...   (220)
"The messenger of Anu our father who came to us,
"Let him eat our bread, let him drink our beer."
Namtar made ready to speak,
Saying to Ereshkigal, his mistress, (these) words,
"[The messenger] of Anu your father, who came to us,   (225)
"Made off before daybreak."
[Eresh]kigal was crushed and let out a wail,
She fell [fr]om her chair to the ground,
[She got] up [from] the ground, her eyes raining tears,
Her tears ran down the sides of her nose,   (230)
"Erra, my voluptuous lover!
"I had not had my fill of his charms, but he left me!
"Erra, my voluptuous lover!

"I had not had my fill of his charms, but he left me!"
Namtar made ready to speak, saying to Ereshkigal, (235)
"Send me [to Anu] your [father], let me seize that god,
"[Let me fetch] him to you!"
[Ereshkigal made ready to speak],
    saying to Namtar (these) words,
"[to] Anu, Enlil, and Ea and say as follows,

    'Since I was a young girl, (240)
    'I have not known the play of maidens,
    'Nor have I known the frolic of little girls.
    '[That god whom] you sent, he has had intercourse
        with me, so let him lie with me.
    'Send me [that go]d that he be my husband
        and spend the night with me.
    'I am defiled, impure(?),
        I cannot render judgments for the great gods, (245)
    'The great gods who reside in the netherworld.
    'If [you do not] send t[hat] god,
    'Accor[ding to the authority of the netherworl]d
        and the great netherworld,
    'I shall raise up the dead to devour the living,
    'I shall make the dead outnumber the living!'" (250)

Up went Namtar the long staircase of heaven.
When he reached the gate of Anu, Enlil, and Ea,
[An]u, Enlil, and Ea saw him,
"[Wh]y are you come, Namtar?"
"Your [daught]er sent me, (255)
"Saying,

    'Since I was a young girl,
    'I have not known the play of maidens,
    'Nor have I known the frolic of little girls.
    'That god whom you sent,
        he has had intercourse with me,
        so let him lie with me. (260)
    'Send me that god that he be my husband
        and spend the night with me.

'I am defiled, impure(?),
    I cannot render judgments for the great gods,
'The great gods who reside in the netherworld.
'If you do [not] send that god,
<'According to the authority of the netherworld
    and the great netherworld,>   (265)
'I shall raise up the [dead to devour] the living,
'I shall make the dead [outnum]ber the living.'"

Ea made ready to speak, [saying to Namtar] (these) words,
"Na[mtar, come into] the cour[t of Anu],
"[   ]."   (270)
When he came into [the court of An]u,
All the gods kne[lt humbly   ],
[The god]s of the land k[nelt].
[He went straight to the] first one, but did not see that god,
He went straight [to a second, a thi]rd,
    but did not see that god.   (275)
Namtar went to speak to his mistress,
"My lady, [in the heaven of] Anu, your father,
    where you sent me,
"My lady, [there was a certain god, b]ald, with a tic, lame,
    [ ], sitting among all the gods."
"Go, seize that god, f[etch] (him) t[o m]e!
"Ea his father has spri[nkled him] with spring water,   (280)
"So he is bald, has a tic, is lame,
    [is sitting] among all the gods."
Up went Namtar the long staircase of heaven.
When he re[ached] the gate of Anu, Enlil, and Ea,
Anu, Enlil, and Ea saw him,
"Why are you come, Namtar?" "Your daughter sent [me],   (285)
"Saying, 'Seize that god, fetch him to m[e].'"
"Namtar, come into the court of Anu,
"Look for him ... and t[ake him]."
He went straight to the first, but did not see [that god],
He went straight to a [second, a thi]rd,
    [but did not see that god],   (290)

He went straight to [a fourth, a fifth,
   but did not see that god].
[   ] made ready to speak, saying to Ea [   ],
"[Na]mtar the messenger, who has come to [us],
"[Let him dr]ink water, bathe, anoi[nt his body] ..."

(gap)

"Let him not wrest away [   ].   (295)
"Erra, I shall make you go [   ] upon him [   ]
"I shall kill you ... [   ].
"Namtar, [   ] to [   ] your task.
"Erra [   ]
"All the authority of the great netherworld
   shall [I grant to you?].   (300)
"When you go from here,
"[You] shall c[arry the ...] of the throne¹
"[You shall car]ry [   ]
"[You shall carr]y [   ]
"You shall [carr]y [   ]   (305)
"You shall [carr]y [   ]
"You sh[all c]arry [   ]
"[   ]
"[   ] your chest."
[Nergal] took the word of [Ea] to heart,   (310)
He [   ] and readied his bow.
[Down went Ne]rgal the long stair[case of he]aven(?).
When he re[ache]d the gate of Eresh[kigal],
"Gatekeeper, op[en] the gate [to me]!"
The gatekeeper hung up his [   ] at the gate,   (315)
And would not allow him to take it,
The second one of the g[ate] hung up his [   ],
   and would not allow him to take it.
The third one [of the gate hung up his ...],
   and would not allow him to take it.

---

1. The implications of this episode remain obscure.

The fourth one [of the gate hung up his ...],
    and would not allow him to take it.
The fif[th one of the gate hung up his ...],
    and would not allow him to take it. (320)
[The sixth one of the gate hung up] his [...],
    [and would not allow him to take it].
[The seventh one of the gate hung up his ...],
    [and would not allow him to take it].
He en[ter]ed her broad court,
Approached her and burst out laughing.
He seized her by her coiffure, (325)
He [pulled] her from [the throne],
He seized her by her locks,
[   ] his arousal(?).
They embraced one another,
Passionately they went to bed. (330)
One day, a second day they lay,
    Queen Eresh[kigal and Er]ra,
A third day they lay, Queen Ereshkigal and Erra,
A fourth day they lay, Queen Ereshkigal and Erra,
A fifth day they lay, Queen Ereshkigal and Erra,
[A sixth day they lay, Queen Ereshkigal and Erra], (335)
[A seventh day they lay, Queen Ereshkigal and Erra].
 [Anu made ready to speak], saying
[To Gaga his messenger] these words,
"[Gaga, I sh]all send you [to the Land of No Return],
"[To the house of Ereshkiga]l,
    who dwells in the netherworld], (340)
"[Saying, 'That god] whom I sent to you,
"[Let him dwell with you] forever.
"[   ] upper regions,
"[   ] lower regions,

    (breaks off about twelve lines from the end)

How Adapa Lost Immortality

The story of Adapa reveals the goodwill and malice of the gods towards men. Adapa was the most perfect of mortals, a favorite of Ea's, whose cult he administered with wonderful assiduity. So great was his magical power that when a wayward breeze capsized his boat on an otherwise calm day, he cursed it and incapacitated it. When the absence of the wind was noticed in heaven, Adapa was summoned before Anu to give an account of himself. Ea admonished him to ingratiate himself with the vegetation deities standing at the door of the celestial palace. This he was to do by dressing himself in mourning for their seasonal absence from the land. These gods, amused, would put in a good word for him, and this is what occurred. Ea enjoined Adapa from accepting food or drink in heaven, though he might avail himself of the other offices of hospitality. Anu, after the intercession of the gods at the door, was so impressed that Ea would single out a man for his favor, that he offered him the hospitality fit for a visiting god. When Adapa declined the food and drink, which would have made him a god and released him from Ea's service, Anu was vastly amused by Ea's cleverness and his sage's stupidity, and so sent the swindled mortal back home.

The lessons of this simple text are numerous. Surely one is that if a man so perfect could not obtain immortality, despite his close relationship to a great god, who else could expect to? Even the apparent goodwill of the gods is limited; they will not gratefully manumit men from their service no matter how well performed.

Later Mesopotamian scholars incorporated the story into incantations as a means of identifying and localizing the magical powers of Adapa for medicinal ends. Some Assyriologists see in this text an aetiology for the origins of magic, though others will read here a somber Mesopotamian statement on the lot of mankind.

(about six lines lost)

Un[derstanding   ]   (1)
His utterance can command, like the utterance [of Anu],
He made him perfect in wisdom, revealing (to him)
    the designs of the land.
To him he granted wisdom, eternal life he did not grant him.
In those days, in those years, the sage, the citizen of Eridu,   (5)

Ea created him as ... among men,
The sage whose pronouncement no one gainsaid,
Able one, his perception of what pertains
    to the Anunna-gods was vast,
Pure, clean of hands, anointed one
    who was solicitous after divine rites,
He performed the baker's office with the baker,   (10)
He performed the baker's office with the bakers of Eridu,
Every day he (himself) made the food and drink
    for Eridu('s cult).[1]
He prepared the table with his own clean hands,
Nor without him was the table cleared.
He steered the boat,
    he made the daily fish catch for Eridu('s cult).   (15)
At that time Adapa, citizen of Eridu,
At the drawing of the [bo]lt of Ea to its socket(?),
Would each day set the bar himself.
[At] the sacred quay, the quay of "Heavenly Splendor,"
    he boarded the sailboat.
[Without? a st]eering oar his boat would drift downstream,   (20)
[Without? a ru]dder he could pilot his boat (upstream).
[Into the ... ocean, into the] wide sea

(fragmentary lines, gap)

He ma[de ready to speak, saying to the south wind],
"O south wind! [   ]
"I have done enough(?), let me [   ]   (25)
"O south wind, [gath]er against me your brothers,
    as m[any as there be],
"I will fracture your w[in]g!"
As soon as he said it,
The south wind's wing was fractured.
The s[outh wind] not having blown
    for seven days towards the land,   (30)
Anu called to his messenger Ilabrat,

---

1. That is, he was so concerned with correct ritual observance that he assumed personally even menial temple duties, such as the baking of sacrificial loaves.

"Why has the south wind not blown
    for seven days towards the land?"
His spokesman Ilabrat answered him,
"My Lord, Adapa, son of Ea,
    has fractured the south wind's wing."
When Anu heard this, (35)
He cried, "(Heaven) help (us)!" He rose from his chair,
"Se[nd word and let] them bring him here."
Ea, who knows the affairs of heaven, touched him,
[   ] made him wear his hair unkempt,[1]
[Had him put on] mourning weeds, (40)
Gave him instructions,
"[Adapa], you are to go [before Anu] the king,
"[You are to go up to heaven].
"When y[ou go up] to h[eav]en,
"[And draw near to Anu's door], (45)
"[Tammuz and Gizzi]da will be standing at Anu's door.
"When they see you, they will ask you,

    'Fel[low], for whom are you like this?
    'A[da]pa, why are you in mourning weeds?'
    'Two gods are disappeared from our land, (50)
    'That is why I am decked out so.'
    'Who are the two gods
        who have disappeared from the land?'
    'They are Tammuz and Gizzida.'

"They will look at each other and laugh and laugh,
"They will say a favorable word to Anu, (55)
"They will help you see Anu's benevolent side.
"When you come before Anu,
"They will proffer you food of death, do not eat!
"They will proffer you waters of death, do not drink!
"They will proffer you a garment, put it on. (60)
"They will proffer you oil, anoint yourself.
"Do not neglect the instructions I give you,
"Hold fast to the words which I have spoken."

---

1. A sign of mourning.

Anu's messenger reached him,

 'Adapa, who fractured the wing of the south wind, (65)
 'Send him to me!'"

He brought him along the [ro]ad to heaven,
He went up to heaven.
When he went up to heaven,
And drew near Anu's door, (70)
Tammuz and Gizzida were standing at Anu's door.
When they saw Adapa, they cried, "(Heaven) help (us)!
"Fellow, for whom are you like this?
"Adapa, why are you dressed in mourning?"
"Two gods have disappeared from the land, (75)
"So I am dressed in mourning."
"Who are the two gods who have disappeared from the land?"
"Tammuz and Gizzida."
They looked at each other and laughed and laughed.
When Adapa made his approach to Anu the king, (80)
Anu saw him and cried,
"Come now, Adapa, why did you fracture
 the wing of the south wind?"
Adapa answered Anu,
"My lord, I was fishing in the depths of the sea,
"For my master's temple. (85)
"The sea was like a mirror,
"Then the south wind blew upon me and capsized me.
"I spent the rest of the day in the home of the fish.
"In my fury, I cursed the [win]d."
There spoke up for [him Tammuz] and Gizzida, (90)
Saying a favorable word about him to Anu.
His heart grew calm, he became quiet.
"Why did Ea disclose what pertains to heaven and earth
"To an uncouth mortal,
"And give him a violent temper? (95)
"Since he has so treated him,
"What, for our part, shall we do for him?
"Bring him food of life, let him eat."

They brought him food of life, he did not eat.
They brought him waters of life, he did not drink. (100)
They brought him a garment, he put it on.
They brought him oil, he anointed himself.
Anu stared and burst out laughing at him,
"Come now, Adapa, why did you not eat or drink?
"Won't you live? Are not people to be im[mor]tal?" (105)
"Ea my lord told me,
    'You must not eat, you must not drink.'"
"Let them take him and [ret]urn him to his earth."

(another version of this episode)

[He ordered bread of life for him, he did not eat],
He ordered [water of life] for him, he did not drink. (100)
He ordered [oil] for him, he anointed himself,
He ordered a [gar]ment for him, he put it on.
Anu laughed uproariously at what Ea had done,
"Who else, of all the gods of heaven and netherworld,
    could d[o] something like this?
"Who else could make his command outweigh Anu's?"[1] (105)
Adapa [surveyed] from the horizon to the heights of heaven,
He saw the awesomeness of [   ].
[At that ti]me Anu imposed on Adapa an observance,
[Aft]erwards Ea released him.
[An]u ordained that he be distinguished
    for his leadership for all time.[2] (110)

(follows fragments of an incantation invoking Adapa's powers)

---

1. That is, by thwarting Anu's good intentions to give Adapa eternal life.
2. That is, he could not live forever, but would be famous forever.

Etana, the King without an Heir

The legend of Etana enjoyed particular popularity in Mesopotamian tradition. What now remains of the story may be outlined as follows. In Tablet I the gods are building a city for the human race, the lesser gods doing the work, the greater gods making the plans. When the city is completed and surrounded with defenses, a king is needed. Enlil looks over all the cult cities in the realm for a suitable candidate. This turns out to be Etana. Kingship is created and Etana is made the first king.

In Tablet II Etana the king has built some structures, including a temple for Adad, and a poplar tree grows there. A serpent takes up residence in the roots of the tree, an eagle in its crown. The two creatures swear an oath of friendship to each other. They produce their young and share the task of feeding them. As his children grow up, the eagle conspires to devour the serpent's children. One of his own children attempts vainly to dissuade him, a reversal of the usual wisdom motif whereby an elder advises a youngster. The eagle devours his friend's children.

When the serpent returns and discovers his children gone, he calls upon Shamash, lord of the oath, to witness the eagle's perfidy. Shamash hears his plaint and arranges for a wild ox to die. He enjoins the serpent to hide in the belly of the cadaver to seize the eagle when he comes to feed. He can then pluck his feathers and throw him into a pit to die of hunger and thirst. The ruse is successful, despite the warnings of the eagle's youngster, for the greedy eagle plunges into the carcass to feed and is captured by the vengeful serpent. The eagle's pleas for mercy are rejected, first by the serpent and second by Shamash. He is left to languish in a pit. Shamash is moved by his continued pleas, but, since the eagle violated an oath, the god cannot rescue him himself. He decides upon an agent, whom he advises the eagle to expect.

Meantime, Etana, the king, has been praying to Shamash for an heir. All of his efforts to produce one have proved unsuccessful, so his last hope is to find a certain plant of birth. Shamash tells Etana of the eagle's plight, and advises him to save the eagle in return for the bird's assistance in finding the plant of birth. Etana sets forth and approaches the pit.

Tablet III opens with a fragmentary episode, omitted here, in which the eagle is trying to persuade some birds to help him. Just then he catches sight of Etana and asks his help. The following exchanges are fragmentary, but it seems that the eagle temporizes and promises other gifts instead, to no avail. At last he consents to help Etana get the plant, if only he will save him from the pit. Etana throws something into the pit that allows the eagle to flutter his way out. The rest of the tablet is lost, but Etana and the eagle become comrades. There is a considerable gap at this point.

In Tablet IV the eagle is recounting to Etana a propitious dream he had which suggests to him that their perilous mission to secure the plant may be rewarded with success. Etana grasps the eagle's sides and wings, in a posture well known from Mesopotamian seal engravings, and the eagle carries him aloft. Higher and higher they go, until they reach the first stage of their journey in the sky. There, as foretold in the eagle's dream, they make obeisance to the great gods through whose celestial gates they are passing. After a gap in the text, it seems that the next stage of the journey is about to begin. Eagle and man set off, the man looking behind and recounting excitedly earth and ocean's rapid diminishment into the distance. But, the instant he loses sight of them altogether, Etana's courage fails him, and he begs to return to his city. The eagle plunges earthward and they land, without the plant.

At this point the tablet ends, so no one knows how the story ended. Perhaps, like Gilgamesh and Adapa, Etana had tried the impossible and lost the prize. Etana is known to have had a son in Mesopotamian tradition, at least in the Sumerian King List, so it is possible that a subsequent venture was successful, or that Etana achieved his goal in some other way.

Tablet I

They planned the city [   ], (1)
[The gods? laid its foundations],
[They planned the city? Kish?],
[The gods?] laid its foundations.
The Igigi-gods founded its brickwork [ ] (5)
"Let [ ] be their (the people's) shepherd,
"Let Etana be their architect, ..."
The great Anunna-gods, or[dainers of destinies],
[Sa]t taking their counsel [concerning the land],
The creators of the four world regions,
    [establishers of all physical form], (10)
By(?) command of all of them the Igigi-gods
    [ordained a festi]val f[or the people],

No [king] did they establish [over the teeming peoples].
At that time [no headdress had been assembled, nor crown],
Nor yet scepter [had been set] with lapis,
No throne daises(?) whatsoever [had been constructed]. (15)
The seven gods barred the [gates] against the multitude,
Against the inhabited world they barred [the gates ...],
The Igigi-gods surrounded the city [with ramparts?].
Ishtar [came down from heaven? to seek] a shepherd,
And sought for a king [everywhere]. (20)
Innina [came down from heaven? to seek] a shepherd,
And sought for a king e[verywhere].
Enlil examined the dais of(?) Etana,
The man whom Ishtar st[eadfastly   ]
"She has constantly sought ... (25)
"[Let] king[ship] be established in the land,
    let the heart of Kish [be joyful]."
Kingship, the radiant crown, throne, [   ]
He(?) brought and [   ]
The gods of the land[s   ]

(large gap)

Tablet II

[   ] which he called [   ] ...
    the "High Water," (1)
[   ] he had built a tower(?) [   ]
[   ] shrine for Adad, the god [   ]
In the shade of that shrine a po[plar] was growing [   ],
In its crown an eagle settled, (5)
A serpent ... at its root.
Daily they wa[tched the wild beasts].
[The eagl]e made ready to speak, [saying to the serpent],
"[Co]me, [let us make] friend[ship],
"Let us be comrades, [you] and I." (10)
[The serpent] made ready to speak, [saying to the eagle],

"[If indeed?] ... of friendship and [   ]
"[Then? let us swear a] mighty [oath of Shamash],
"An abomination of the gods [   ]
"Come then, let us set forth
    [and go up the high mountains (to hunt)], (15)
"Let us swear [an oath] by the netherworld."
Before Shamash the warrior they swo[re] the oath,
"Whoever [transgresses] the limits of Shamash [   ],
"May Shamash [deliver him] as an offender
    into the hands of the executioner,
"Whoever [transgresses] the limits of Shamash, (20)
"May the [mountains] remove [their pas]ses
    far away from him,
"May the oncoming weapon [make straight for him],
"May the trap and curse of Shamash overthrow him
    [and hunt him down]!"
After they had sworn the oath by the netherworld,
They set forth, going up the high mountains, (25)
Each day by turns watching for [the wild beasts].
The eagle would hunt down wild oxen and asses,
The serpent would eat, turn away,
    then his children would eat.
The serpent would hunt down buck and gazelle,
The eagle would eat, turn away,
    then [his] children would eat. (30)
The eagle would hunt down wild sheep and aurochs,
The serpent would eat, turn away,
    then his children would eat.
The serpent would hunt down b[easts of the field,
    crea]tures of the earth,
[The eagle would eat, turn aw]ay,
    then his children would eat.
... [   ] the food, (35)
The eagle's children grew big and flourished.
After the eagle's children were grown big
    and were flourishing,
The eagle's heart indeed plotted evil,

Evil his heart plotted indeed!
He set his thoughts upon eating his friend's young! (40)
The eagle made ready to speak, saying to [his children],
"I will eat the serpent's children, the serpent [ ],
"I will go up and d[well] in heaven,
"If I descend from the crown of the tree, ... the king."
The littlest fledgling, exceedingly wise,
    [said] these words to the eagle, his father, (45)
"Do not eat, my father!
    The net of Shamash will hu[nt you] down,
"The mesh and oath of Shamash will overthrow you
    and hunt you down.
"Whoever transgresses the limits of Shamash,
    Shamash [will deliver] him as an offender
    into the hands of the [executioner]!"
He did not heed them nor listen to [his sons' words],
He descended and ate up the serpent's [children]. (50)
In the evening of the same day(?),
The serpent ca[me], bearing his burden,
At the entrance to his nest [he cast down the meat].
[He loo]ked around, his nest was gone!
He looked down, [his children were] not [ ]! (55)
[The eagle had gouged] the ground with his talon,
The cloud of dust from the nest [darkened] the sky.
The serpent ..., weeping before Shamash,
[Before] Shamash [the warrior his tears ran down],
"I trusted in you, [O warrior Shamash], (60)
"I [was the one who gave provisions?] to the eagle,
"Now my nest [ ]!
"My nest is gone, [while his] ne[st is safe],
"My young are destroyed, [while his young are] sa[fe].
"He descended and ate up [my children]! (65)
"[You know], O Shamash, the evil he has done me,
"Truly, O Shamash, your net is the [wide] earth,
"Your trap is the [distant] heaven.
"[The eagle] must not es[cape] from your net,

"Th(at) malignant Anzu,
    who harbored evil [against his friend]!" (70)
[When he had heard] the serpent's lament,
Shamash made ready to speak, [and said] to [him],
"Go (your) way and cros[s the mountain],
"[I?] have captured for you a wi[ld ox].
"Open its insides, [rend its belly], (75)
"Set an ambush [in its belly],
"[Every kind of] bird of heaven [will come down
    to eat the meat].
"The eagle [will come down] with them [to eat the meat].
"[As] he will not know [the evil in store for him],
"He will sea[rch for] the juiciest meat [   ],
    he will walk about outside(?), (80)
"He will work his way into the covering of the intestines.
"When he comes inside, seize him by his wings,
"Cut off his wings, his pinions, and tailfeathers,
"Pluck him and cast him into a bottomless(?) pit,
"Let him die there of hunger and thirst." (85)
As Shamash the warrior commanded,
The serpent went and crossed the mountain.
Then did the serpent reach the wild ox,
He opened its insides, he rent its belly.
He set an ambush in its belly. (90)
Every kind of bird of heaven came down to eat the meat.
Did the [ea]gle know the evil in store for him?
He would not eat the meat [with] the other birds!
[The eagle] made ready to speak, saying to his children,
"[Co]me, let us go down and we too
    eat the meat of this wild ox." (95)
The little [fled]gling, exceedingly wise,
    said [these] words to the eagle [his father],
"Do not go down, father,
    no doubt the serpent is lurking inside the wild ox."
The eagle said to himself,
"Are the birds afraid? How is it they eat the meat in peace?"

He did not listen to them,
>   he did not listen to his sons' words, (100)

He descended and perched on the wild ox.
The eagle looked at the meat,
>   searching in front and behind it.

A second time he looked at the meat,
>   searching in front and behind it,

He walked around outside(?), he worked his way
>   into the covering of the intestines.

When he came inside, the serpent seized him by his wings, (105)
"You intruded ..., you intruded ... !
The eagle made ready to speak, saying to the serpent,
"Have mercy on me! I will make you such a gift
>   as a king's ransom!"

The serpent made ready to speak, saying to the eagle,
"If I release you, how shall I answer to Shamash on high? (110)
"Your punishment would turn upon me,
"Me, the one to lay punishment upon you!"
He cut off his wings, pinions, and tail feathers,
[He pluc]ked him and ca[st him into] a p[it],
That he should die [there] of hunger [and thirst]. (115)
[As for him, the eagle], ... [   ]
He kept on beseeching Shamash day after day,
"Am I to die in a pit?
"Who would know how your punishment
>   was imposed upon me?[1]

"Save my life, me, the eagle! (120)
"Let me cause your name to be heard for all time."
Shamash made ready to speak and said to the eagle,
"You are wicked and have done a revolting deed,
"You committed an abomination of the gods,
>   a forbidden act.

"Were you (not) under oath? I will not come near you. (125)
"There, there! A man I will send you will help you."
Etana kept on beseeching Shamash day after day,

---

1. That is, there is no exemplary value in his solitary death.

"O Shamash, you have dined from my fattest sheep!
"O Netherworld, you have drunk of the blood of my
 (sacrificed) lambs!
"I have honored the gods and revered the spirits, (130)
"Dream interpreters have used up my incense,
"Gods have used up my lambs in slaughter.
"O Lord, give the command!
"Grant me the plant of birth!
"Reveal to me the plant of birth! (135)
"Relieve me of my burden, grant me an heir!"
Shamash made ready to speak and sa[id] to Etana,
"Go (your) way, cross the mountain,
"Find a pit, [look insi]de,
"An eagle is cast within it. (140)
"He will reveal to you the plant [of birth]."
According to the command of the warrior Shamash,
Etana went (his) way.
He found the pit, he looked inside,
[The eagle was cast] with[in it]. (145)
There he was for him to bring up!

Tablet III

The eagle looked at him ...,
He said [   ] to Etana,
"You are Etana, king of the wild beasts,
"You are Etana, [   ] among(?) birds. (10)
"Bring [me] up from [thi]s [pi]t,
"Give me [   ] your hand,
"... [   ]
"I will si[ng] your [pra]ises for all time."

Etana [said] to the eagle (these) wor[ds], (15)
"(If) I save your life, [   ]
"(If) I br[ing you up fr]om the pit,
"[From th]at moment we [must be ...]"

(gap)

(the eagle finally accedes)

"[   ] to me ... [   ]
"From sunrise till [   ] (20)
"From his rising, where [   ]
"... [   ]
"I will grant you the [plant] of life."

When Etana h[eard] this,
He filled the front of the pit with [   ]. (25)
Next he threw in ... [   ].
He kept throwing in [   ] in front of(?) him,
The eagle ... from the pit.
As for him, he flapped [his wings].
[A first time and a second time ... the eagle ...] in(?) the pit, (30)
As for him, he flapped [his] w[ings   ]
[A third time] and a fourth time ... [the eagle ... in? the pi]t,
As for him, he flapped [his wings   ]
[A fifth and a sixth time   ] ...

(fragmentary lines, then gap)
(from another version)

He took him by the hand
    in his se[venth month (in the pit)], (35)
In the eighth month he brought him
    over (the edge) of his pit.[1]
The eagle took food like a ravening lion,
He gained strength.
The eagle made ready to speak and said to Etana,
"My friend! Let us be friends, you and I! (40)
"Ask of me whatever you desire and I shall give it to you."
Etana made ready to speak and said to the eagle,
"My eyes ..., open up what is hidden."

(gap)

---

1. Numerical parallelism, meaning that the eagle has been a long time in the pit, not that it took a month to get him out.

(Etana and the eagle are friends. Etana has dreams, which he relates to the eagle.)

"[   ] above
"[   ] at my feet." (45)
[The eagle made Etana] understand [the dream],
[   ] seated before him,
"[   ] your [dream] is propitious,
"[   ] burden¹ is brought,
"They will give [   ] (50)
"You have done [   ] of the people
"You will seize ... in your hand,
"The sacred bond² [   ] above
"[   ] at your feet."

Etana said to him, to the eagle, (55)
"My friend, [I saw] a second dream,
"[   ] reeds [   ] in the house,
"In all [   ], the whole land,
"They heaped up loads (of them) in piles.
"[   ] enemies, they were wicked serpents, (60)
"[   ] were coming before me,
"[   ] they were kneeling before me."

[The eagle made Etana] understand [the dream].
[   ] seated before him,
"[   ] your [dream] is propitious, (65)

(gap)

---

1. Here and in the next dream "weight" (*biltu*) and "tribute" (*biltu*) are used with a play on the words. Etana's ascent is no doubt referred to, his weight being borne by the eagle. In the second dream there is a wordplay on *biltu* "weight" and *elpetu* "reed," but the whole passage is too fragmentary to be understood.
2. A cosmic feature, being the linkage of heaven and earth.

Tablet IV

The eagle [made ready] to speak, [saying to Etana], (1)
"[My] fr[iend] ... that god [   ].
"[We] passed through the gates of Anu, Enlil, [and] Ea.[1]
"We did obeisance [together], yo[u] and I.
"We passed through the gates of Sin,
    Shamash, Adad, and Ishtar, (5)
"[We did obeisance together], yo[u] and I.
"I saw a house (with?) windows, [it had no] seal.
"I ... [   ] and went inside.
"A remarkable [young woman] was seated therein.
"She was imposing ..., beautiful of [fe]ature. (10)
"A throne was set out, the ground was trodden down,
"Under the throne [   ] lions were [c]rou[ching].
"As I went in, the lions [sprang at me?].
"I awoke with a start and shuddered [   ]."
The eagle [said] to him, to Etana, (15)
"My friend, the [   ] are obvious,
"Come, let me take you up to heaven.
"Put [your chest] against my chest,
"Put [your hands] against my wing feathers,
"Put [your arms] against my sides." (20)
He put [his chest] against his chest,
He put [his] hands against his wing feathers,
He put [his] hands against his sides,
Great indeed was the burden upon him.
When he bore [him] aloft one league, (25)
The eagle said to him, to Etana,
"Look, my friend, how the land is now!
"Examine the sea, lo[ok for] its boundaries."
"The land is hills ...[2]
The sea has become a stream(?)." (30)
When he had borne [him] aloft a second league,
The eagle said to him, to Etana,

---

1. That is, they are passing across the major portals of heaven.
2. Text ununderstandable, perhaps corrupt.

"Look, my friend, how the land is now!"
"The land is a hill."
When he had borne him aloft a third league, (35)
The eagle said to him, to Etana,
"Look, my friend, how the land i[s now]!"
"The sea has become a gardener's ditch."
After they had ascended to the heaven of A[nu],
They passed through the gates of Anu, Enlil, and Ea. (40)
The eagle and E[tana] did obei[sance to]gether.
At the gate of S[in   ]
[The eagle] and Etan[a did obeisance together].

(gap, fragmentary lines)

(another version of this episode)

"Through the power of Ishtar [   ]. (20)
"Put [your arms] against my sides,
"Put [your hands] against my wing feathers."
He put [his arms] against his sides,
He [put his hands] against his wing feathers.
[When he had borne him aloft] one league, (25)
"Look, my friend, how the land [is now]!"
"The land's [circumference?] is become
     one fifth of (its size).
"The vast sea is become like a paddock."
[When he had borne him aloft] a second league,
"Look, my friend, how the land [is now]!" (30)
"The land has become a garden plot [ ],
"And the vast sea has become a trough."
[When he had borne him aloft] a third [league],
"Look, my friend, how the land [is now]!"
"I looked, but could not see the land! (35)
"Nor were [my eyes] enough to (find) the vast sea!
"My friend, I won't go up to heaven!
"Set me down, let me go off to my city!"
One league he dropped him down(?),
Then the eagle plunged and caught him in his wings. (40)

A second league he dropped him down(?),
Then the eagle plunged and caught him in his wings.
A third league he dropped him down(?),
Then the eagle plunged and caught him in his wings.
Within three cubits of the earth [he dropped him down].   (45)
The eagle plunged, and ca[ught him in his wings].
The eagle [ ] and ..., while he, Etana, [   ].

(Two fragmentary lines, then breaks off. Nothing certain is known of the rest of the story.)

Anzu, the Bird Who Stole Destiny

This poem tells how the god Ninurta proved his valor and was acclaimed by the other gods as their deliverer. When the universe was still only partly organized, the Tigris and Euphrates rivers existed but no one worshipped the gods in separate sanctuaries yet, nor was there water for irrigation and rainfall. An eagle-like bird, Anzu, lived in a tree to the north of the land. His face was so horrible that even Enlil, chief of the gods, was taken aback when he saw it. Ea explains that he was a product of the flood waters, and suggests that his energies be harnessed by the chief god of Sumer. Enlil therefore puts the hideous bird in front of his own cella as a guardian.

The gods are given their responsibilities. The bird looks enviously upon Enlil's exercise of kingship and covets it for himself. While Enlil is in his bath, Anzu snatches and flies off with the tablet in which is the power to control all destinies, leaving Enlil and the other gods in disarray. The gods convene and seek a champion to recover the tablet and destroy the monster. Adad, god of rainstorms, is called but declines; Girra, god of fire, likewise. Shara, son of Ishtar, is no more eager than they. Throughout this portion of the story, as in the Epic of Creation, suspense and a feeling of helplessness are conveyed by the verbatim repetitions of speech and action, mostly the former. Thrice turned down, the gods are at a loss (Tablet I line 153).

Ea, god of wisdom, offers a plan that is gladly acceded to. Mami, the mother goddess, is named by a new name, Belet-ili "Mistress of the Gods," because her son, Ninurta, is to be champion of the gods. Mami, now Belet-ili, accepts this honor and orders her dutiful son to avenge his father's dishonor, thereby to allow the gods to reassert their authorities.

Ninurta marches off on his mission (Tablet II line 28) and confronts his opponent. Since Anzu has the tablet of destinies, he has efficacious incantations against any attack, so Ninurta's onslaught is stopped. Anzu orders the oncoming arrows to return to their original elements. Ninurta sends Sharur back to Ea to explain this impasse (Tablet II lines 87ff.). Ea sends him back with advice: cut off his wing feathers. When Anzu sees them fluttering about, he will order them to return to him. At that moment the arrow, which also has feathers on it, will find its mark. Again, lengthy repetitions are used to heighten suspense and delay resolution of the action.

In Tablet III Ea's suggestion is carried out. Ninurta succeeds in killing Anzu and regaining the tablet that controls destinies. The gods rejoice, but their festivity turns to consternation when the conquering hero does not return to yield the tablet back to Enlil. A messenger is sent to invite Ninurta's return. It appears, however, that Ninurta is not eager to return the tablet. At this point the text is damaged. When it resumes, Ninurta has returned and the gods are praising him as the most important among them. Various names of Ninurta are celebrated in a passage similar to Tablet VII of the Epic of Creation.

Tablet I

Son of the king of the inhabited world, splendid one,
    beloved of [Ma]mi, (1)
The mighty one will I ever sing, divine child of [En]lil,
Ninurta, the splendid one, beloved of Mami,
The mighty one will I ever praise, divine firstborn of Enlil.
Born (in) Ekur, leader of the Anu[nna-gods],
    Eninnu's[1] hope, (5)
Who [wa]ters(?) pen, garden, ..., land, and city,
Wave of battles, dancing one, sash of valor,
Tireless one whose onset raging fiends dread,
Hear the praise of the mighty one's power!
It is he who in his fierceness bound
    and fettered the stone creatures,[2] (10)
Overcoming soaring Anzu with his weapon,
Slaying the bull man in the midst of the sea.
Doughty, valorous, murderous with his weapon,
Mighty one, fleet of foot, always leader in fight and fray!
Before that, no dais had been built among the Igigi-gods, (15)
It was the Igigi-gods who knelt in their supremacy.
Tigris and [Euph]rates rivers had been fashioned,
But the [springs] were not bearing [their?] waters to the land.
The very seas [   ]
Clouds were absent from the horizon [   ] (20)
Then were the [Igigi-gods] convened from all parts,
To Enlil, their father, wa[rrior of the gods?],

---

1. Temple of Ningirsu at Lagash.
2. An allusion to a Sumerian poem called "Ninurta and the Stones."

Did his children bring [the news],
"Hee[d you well] the propitious word!
"On Hihi Mountain[1] a tree [   ]   (25)
"In its fork the Anu[nna-gods   ]
"It[2] bore Anzu [   ]
"[His] beak a saw [   ]
"[Go] out and [   ]

(four lines fragmentary)

At [his] clamor [   ]   (35)
The south wind [   ]
The massive [   ]
The voluminous [flooding crest   ]
The whirlwinds [   ]
They met and [   ]   (40)
The four winds [   ]
When the fat[her of the gods] saw him [ ]
He took what [they] said of him [to his heart],
He inspected Anzu closely [   ]
Debated with [himself   ]   (45)
"Who bore [   ]?
"Why this [   ]?"
[Ea] answered the query of his heart,
The Leader [said] to En[lil these words],
"No doubt the waters of the fl[ood   ]   (50)
"The pure waters of the gods of the deep [ ]
"The [   ] earth conceived him,
"He is the one [born] in the rocks of the mountain,
"It is Anzu you have seen [   ]
"Let him serve you ce[aselessly],   (55)
"Let him always block the way to the cella [seat]."

(gap)

---

1. Jebel Bishri(?), see How Erra Wrecked the World, Tablet IV lines 141, 143.
2. Perhaps the flood is meant; see line 50 below.

The god con[sented to the word] he spoke to him,
He took up holy places [   ]
And gave to all the [gods] their responsibilities.

He would reinstitute the decree (each morning?)
    and Anzu would hold [   ], (60)
Enlil entrusted him with the entrance to the cella,
    which he had wrought.
He was wont to bathe in pure waters before him.
His eyes looked upon the trappings of supremacy,
On his lordly crown, his divine apparel,
On the tablet of destinies in his hands
    Anzu was wont to gaze. (65)
He was wont to gaze, indeed, at the father of the gods,
    divine Duranki,
He resolved in his heart to make off with supremacy.
Anzu was wont to gaze on the father of the gods,
    divine Duranki,
He resolved in his heart to make off with supremacy!
"I myself will take the gods' tablet of destinies, (70)
"I will gather to myself the responsibilities of all the gods,
"I will have the throne for myself,
    and take power over authority,
"I will be commander of each and every Igigi-god."
His heart plotted the assault,
At the entrance to the cella, where he was wont to gaze,
    he bided (his) time. (75)
When Enlil was bathing in the pure waters,
Undressed(?), his crown set on the throne,
He took control of the tablet of destinies,
He took supremacy, [authority] was overthrown!
Anzu soared off and [made his way] to his mountain, (80)
Awful silence spread, deathly sti[llness] reigned.
Their father and counsellor Enlil was speechless.
The cella was stripped of its divine splendor.
[The gods] of the land converged,
    one after another, for a pl[an].

[A]nu made ready to speak, (85)
Saying to the gods his children,
"[Which] one would slay Anzu?
"He shall make for himself the greatest name
    in [eve]ry habitation."
They called the [irrigator], Anu's son,
Plan [ma]de(?), he said to him, (90)
They summoned Adad, the irrigator, Anu's son,
Plan [ma]de(?), he said to him,
"[O mighty] one, Adad, victorious Adad,
    let your battle not waver,
"[Blitz] Anzu with your weapon.
"[Let your name] be greatest among all the great gods, (95)
"You shall have no equal [among] the gods your brethren.
"Let there be daises to be built,
"Establish your holy places in the four [world regions],
"Let your [holy places] come into Ekur.
"[Show yourself] mighty before the gods,
    for your name shall be 'Mighty One'." (100)
[Adad] answered the command,
[To Anu] his father he said these words,
["My father], who would assault an inaccessible [moun]tain?
"[Which] of the gods your children can overcome Anzu?
"He took control of the [tablet of destinies], (105)
"He took away [supremacy], authority is overthrown.
"[Anzu] soared off and made his way to his mountain,
"His [utterance] is become like that of divine Duranki.
"[If he commands, the one he cur]ses will turn into clay."
The gods were despondent [at his utteranc]e. (110)
[He turned away, he refused to go].
[They called Girra, firstborn of Annunitum],
[Plan made?, he said to him],
"[O mighty one, Girra, victorious Girra,
    let your battle not waver].
"[Blitz Anzu with your weapon], (115)
"[Let your name be greatest among all the great gods],
"[You shall have no equal among the gods your brethren].

"[Let there be daises to be built],
"[Establish your holy places in the four world regions],
"[Show yourself mighty before the gods,
    for your name shall be 'Mighty One'." (120)
[Girra answered the command],
[To Anu his father he said these words],
"[My father, who would assault an inaccessible mountain]?
"[Which of the gods your children can overcome Anzu?
"[He took control of the tablet of destinies], (125)
"[He took away supremacy, authority is overthrown].
"[Anzu soared off and ma]de [his way to his mountain],
"[His utterance] is become like that of divine Duranki.
"[If he commands, the one he curses] will turn into clay."
The gods were despondent [at his utter]ance. (130)
[He turned away], he refused to go.
They [called] Shara, firstborn of Ishtar,
[Pl]an [made](?), he said to him,
"[O mi]ghty one, [Shara], victorious Shara,
    let your battle not waver.
"[Bli]tz Anzu with your weapon. (135)
"Let yo[ur name] be greatest among all the great gods,
"You shall have no equal among the gods your brethren.
"Let there be daises to be built,
"Establish your holy places in the four world regions,
"Let your holy places come into Ekur. (140)
"Show yourself mighty before the gods,
    for your name shall be 'Mighty One'."
Shara answered the command,
To Anu his father he said these words,
"My father, who would assault an inaccessible mountain?
"Which of the gods your children can overcome Anzu? (145)
"He took control of the tablet of destinies,
"He took away supremacy, authority is overthrown.
"Anzu flew off and [made his w]ay to his mountain.
"His utterance is become like that of divine Duranki.
"If he commands, the one he curses will turn into clay." (150)
The gods were despondent at his utterance.

He turned away, he refused to go.
The gods were spent and left off making proposals,
The Igigi-gods, (still) in session,
    were frowning(?) and in a turmoil.
The lord of wisdom, who dwells in the depths,
    the clever one, (155)
Was devising an idea in his cunning mind.
Ea devised wisdom(?) in his heart,
What he thought of in his mind he explained to Anu,
"Let me give a command and so find the god,
"For then I will appoint Anzu's conqueror in the assembly, (160)
"Let me be the one to find the god,
"For then I will appoint Anzu's conqueror in the assembly."
When the Igigi-gods [he]ard this speech of his,
The Igigi-gods, restored, did homage to him.
The Leader made ready to speak, (165)
[Saying t]o Anu and Dagan these words,
"Let them summon to me the mistress of the gods,
    the sister of the gods,
"The resourceful one,
    coun[sellor] of the gods [her] brethren.
"Let them proclaim her surpassing greatness
    in the as[sembly],
"Let all the gods honor [her] in their assembly. (170)
"[Then I will explain to her] the idea of my heart."
They summoned thither the mistress of the gods,
    the sister [of the gods],
The resourceful one, counsellor of the gods [her brethren].
They proclaimed her surpassing greatness [in the assembly],
The gods honored her in their assembly. (175)
Ea [explained the idea] from his cunning mind,
"Formerly w[e called you] 'Mami,'
"Now let 'Mistress of All the Gods' [be your name].
"Give (us) the mighty one, [your] superb [beloved],
"The broad-chested one who is ever leader in fight or fray. (180)
"Give (us) Ninurta, your superb beloved,
"The broad-chested one who is ever leader in fight or fray.

"[He shall be   ] lord in the assembly of the gods,
"He shall be proud in the [   ]
"In all [   ] (185)
"A holy place [   ]
"Lord [   ]
"A fes[tival   ]
"In [   ]."
[When she heard this speech of his], (190)
[She of surpassing greatness, the most exalted
    mistress of the gods, assented].
[When she spoke, the Igigi-gods rejoiced],
[Restored, they did homage to her].
[She summoned her son in the assembly of the gods].
Commissioning her heart's beloved, saying to him, (195)
"Be[fore Anu and Dagan   ]
"[They have discussed in the assembly]
    what has happened [to authority].
"[I bore] all the Igigi-gods,
"I made every [single one of them],
"I made all the A[nunna-gods]. (200)
"[To my brother I ...] supremacy,
"[I assigned] kingsh[ip of heaven] to Anu.
"Anzu has thrown into confusion
    [the kingship I appointed],
"The tablet of destinies, ... Anzu ... has taken control,
"He has snatched from Enlil, he has spurned your father. (205)
"He has snatched away authority,
    he has turned it over to himself.

Tablet II

"Blitz the way, choose (your) moment, (1)
"Make light come out for the gods I made.
"Launch your fullest attack,
"Let your ill winds go against him!
"Conquer soaring Anzu, (5)

"Flood the earth where he was made,
>bring chaos upon his dwelling.
"Let (your) armor clash against him,
"Let your fierce battle keep raging against him,
"May it have whirlwinds at their fullest to block him.
"Draw the bow, let the arrows bear poison, (10)
"Let your features turn into a fiend's,
"Send forth a mist so he cannot distinguish your face.
"Let your brilliant glow move against him,
"Let your radiance be glorious,
>you should have an awe-inspiring sheen,
"Let the sun not shine upon him, (15)
"Let the bright day turn to gloom for him.
"Kill him, conquer Anzu!
"Let the winds bear off his wing feathers as glad tidings,
"To the temple Ekur, to your father Enlil.
"Flood and bring mayhem to the mountain meadows, (20)
"Kill wicked Anzu!
"Let [king]ship (re-)enter Ekur,
"Let authority return [to the] fa[ther] who begot you.
"Let there be daises to be built,
"Establish your holy places [in the f]our [world regions], (25)
"[Let your shrine] come into Ekur.
"Show yourself mighty before the gods,
>for your name shall be 'Mighty One'."
The warrior heeded his mother's word,
Seething with fury, he made his way towards his mountain.
My Lord hitched up the seven battles, (30)
The warrior hitched up the seven ill winds,
The seven whirlwinds that make the dust dance.
He launched a terrifying assault, made war,
The winds were ready at his side for battle.
Anzu and Ninurta met on the mountainside. (35)
When Anzu saw him, he shook with fury at him,
He ground his teeth like a cyclone,
>he enveloped the mountain with his horrible glow.
He roared like a lion, seized with passion.

In his rage he cried to the w[arrior],
"I have carried off all possible authority, (40)
"So I control the responsibilities all the gods must do.
"Who are you who have to come fight with me?
    Account for yourself!"
He advanced upon him, saying to him,
The warrior Ninurta [answered] Anzu,
"I [am the son of] divine Duranki, (45)
"Upholder of the vast netherworld, of Ea, king of destinies!
"I am come to fight with you, your crusher!"
When Anzu heard what he said,
He let loose his piercing shriek within the mountain.
It grew dark, the face of the mountain was enveloped, (50)
The sun, light of the gods, became dark.
Adad roared in great (thunderclaps),
    the sign of Anzu was his clamor.
In the midst of the melee, the conflict,
    battle was joined, the deluge onset,
Armor was on the move, bathed in blood,
Clouds of death rained down, arrows flashed as lightning, (55)
Battle ran on, thundering between them.
The Mighty One, the splendid firstborn of Mami,
Hope of Anu and Dagan, beloved of the Leader,
Mounted the bow with a shaft,
From the handhold of the bow he sent against him an arrow. (60)
The shaft did not approach Anzu but returned!
Anzu cried out against it,
"Shaft which has come, go back to your thicket,
"Frame of the bow to your forests,
"Bowstring to the sheep's sinews,
    feather to the birds: go back!" (65)
Because he held the tablet of destinies of the gods in his hand,
The bowstring brought forth arrows,
    but they did not approach his body.
Battle die[d do]wn, attack was held back,
The fighting stopped,
    within the mountain they did not conquer Anzu.

He summoned Sharur¹ and commissioned him, (70)
"Tell Ea the Leader what you saw happen,
"Say this:

   'Lord, Ninurta had surrounded Anzu,
   'Ninurta was enveloped with the dust of battle.
   'He readied the bow, mounted the shaft, (75)
   'He readied the bow, shot the shaft towards him.
   'It did not approach Anzu but returned.
   'Anzu cried out against it,

      "Shaft which has come, go back to your thicket,
      "Frame of the bow to your forests, (80)
      "Bowstring to the sheep's sinews,
          feathers to the birds: go back!"

   'Because he was holding the tablet of destinies
      of the gods in his hand,
   'The bowstring brought forth arrows,
      but they did not approach his body.
   'Battle die[d d]own, attack was held back,
   'Within the mountain fighting was stopped, (85)
   'They did not conquer Anzu.'"

Sharur did obeisance, received the command,
Bore the battle message to Ea the Leader,
He repeated to Ea all the Lord told him,
"O lord, he says this, (90)

   'Ninurta had surrounded Anzu,
   'Ninurta was enveloped with the dust of battle.
   'He readied the bow, shot the shaft towards him,
   'The shaft did not approach Anzu but returned.
   'Anzu cried out against it, (95)

      "Shaft which has come, go back to your thicket,
      "Frame of the bow to your forests,
      "[Bowstr]ing to the sheep's [sinews],
          feathers to the birds: go back!"

---

1. Usually a deified weapon of Ninurta/Ningirsu, here a separate deity.

>   '[Because he was h]olding the [tablet of destini]es
>   of the gods in his ha[nd],
>   '[The bowstring brought forth arrows,
>   but they did not approach his body]. (100)
>   '[Battle died down, attack was held back],
>   '[Within the mountain fighting was stopped],
>   '[They did not conquer Anzu].'"

When [the Lea]der heard the words of his son,
He [called Sharur] and commissioned him, (105)
"[Repeat] to him, to your lord, what I say,
"Remember every[thing] I say for him.

>   'Do not tire in battle, strive for victory,
>   'Tire him out that he let his wings fall
>   to the brunt of the storm,
>   'Take, O lord, your darts towards the bottom, (110)
>   'Cut off his pinions and hurl them, right and left,
>   'Once he sees his feathers,
>   they will take away his (magic) words.
>   '"My wings!" to the wings he will cry; fear him still.
>   'Ready your bow, let the lightning shafts fly from it,
>   'Let pinions and wing feathers dance about like butterflies. (115)
>   'Kill him, conquer Anzu!
>   'Let the winds bear off his wing feathers as glad tidings,
>   'To the temple Ekur, to your father Enlil.
>   'Flood and bring mayhem to the mountain meadows,
>   'Kill wicked Anzu! (120)
>   'Let kingship (re-)enter Ekur,
>   'Let authority return [to the father] who begot you.
>   'Let there be daises to be built,
>   'Establish your holy places in the four world regions,
>   '[Let] your holy places come into Ekur. (125)
>   'Show yourself mighty be[fore the gods],
>   for your name shall be 'Mighty One'."

[Sharur did ob]eis[ance] and received the command,
Bo[re] off the battle message [to] his [lord],
Every[thing] Ea to[ld him he repea]ted to him,

'Do not ti[re] in battle, strive for victory, (130)
'Tire him out that he let his wings fall
    [to the brunt of] the storm.
'Take, O lord, your darts towards the bottom,
'Cut off his pinions and hurl them, right and left.
'Once he sees his feathers,
    they will take away his (magic) words.
'"My wings!" to the wings he will cry; [fear him] still. (135)
'Ready your bow, let the [lightning] shafts fly from it.
'Let pinions and wings dance about like butterflies.
'Kill him, conquer Anzu!
'Let the winds bear off his wing feathers as glad tidings
'To the temple Ekur, to your father Enlil. (140)
'Flood and bring [mayhem] to the mountain meadows,
'Kill wicked Anzu!
'Let kingship (re-)enter [Ekur],
'Let authority [return] to the father who begot you.
'Let there be [dais]es to be built, (145)
'[Estab]lish your holy places in the four world regions.
'[Let] your holy places [come into] Ekur.
'Show yourself mighty before [the gods],
    for your name shall be 'Mighty One'.'

The Lord heeded the words of Ea the Leader,
Seething with fury, he made his way towards his mountain. (150)
The Lord hitched up the seven battles,
[The warrior hitched up] the seven ill winds,
[The ...] whirlwinds [that make the dust swirl].
He launched a [terrifying] assault, made war,
[The winds were ready at his side] for his battle. (155)

Tablet III

(two lines fragmentary)

Armor ...
Constantly striking one another ... [ ]
The blazing of the fiery glare [   ] (5)
[ ] to the four winds, the storm [   ]
The weapons he struck and struck, in horrible protection,
Both were bathed in the sweat of battle.
Then Anzu grew tired,
    at the onslaught of the storm he dropped his wings,
The Lord took his darts towards the bottom, (10)
He cut off his pinions, hurled them right and left.
When Anzu saw his wings, they took away his (magic) words.
When he cried "My wings!" to the wings,
    the arrow flew against him,
The shaft passed through the ... of his heart,
He made his dart pass through pinion and wing, (15)
The shaft pierce through his heart and lungs.
He flooded, brought mayhem to the mountain meadows,
He flooded the vast earth in his fury,
He flooded the midst of the mountains,
He killed wicked Anzu! (20)
The warrior Ninurta took control of the tablet
    of the gods' destinies.
The wind bore Anzu's wingfeathers
As a sign of his glad tidings.
Dagan rejoiced when he saw his sign,
He summoned all the gods, saying to them in joy, (25)
"The Mighty One has outroared Anzu in his mountain,
"He has regained control of Anu and Dagan's weapons.
"Go to him, that he come to us,
"Let him rejoice, let him dance, let him celebrate,
"Let him stand with the gods his brethren,
    that he may hear the secret lore, (30)
    "[   ] the secret lore of the gods,

"Let [ ] grant him responsibilities ...
    with the gods his brethren."
[Ea?] made ready to speak,
Saying [to] Dagan (these) words,
"... he took the skin, (35)
"When he killed wicked Anzu in the mountains,
"The warrior Ninurta regained control of the tablet
    of the gods' destinies.
"Send to him, let him come to you,
"Let him place the tablet of destinies in your lap."
Enlil made ready to speak, (40)
Saying to Nusku his courier (these) words,
"Nusku, go outside,
"Bring Birdu[1] before me!"
He brought Birdu into Enlil's presence.
Enlil made ready to speak, (45)
Saying to Birdu (these) words,
"Birdu, I am sending you ...

(gap)

Ninurta [made] ready to speak,
[Saying these words] to Birdu,
"O Birdu, why did you come furiously to ...?" (50)
Birdu m[ade ready] to speak,
[Saying these words] to Ninurta his lord,
"My lord, [ ] to you,
"Your father Enlil sent me,
"Saying, (55)
  'The gods heard [   ]
  'That [you killed] wicked Anzu in the mountain.
  'They were joyful and glad, but [ ].
  'Before you [   ] ...
  'Go to him [   ] ... (60)
  'Let him rejoi[ce   ] ...

(three lines fragmentary)

---

1. A god.

Ninurta [made ready to speak, saying to Birdu], (65)
"Why [surrender] the trap[pings of kingship]?
"[My utterance has become] like that of the ki[ng of the gods].
"I will not re[turn] the tablet of destinies."

(fragmentary lines, then gap)

(A god is speaking to Ninurta.)

"Let [   ] not be built,
"[   ] Anzu in Ekur.
"[   ] the sign of the warrior, (115)
"Let him look upon wicked Anzu
    [in] the greatness of his might,
"O warrior, you could slay mountains in your might,
"You defeated Anzu, you could slay his might,
"You could slay the might of soaring Anzu!
"Because you were valiant and slew mountains, (120)
"You have made all enemies submit
    before your father, Enlil,
"O Ninurta, because you were valiant and slew mountains,
"You have made all enemies submit before your father, Enlil!
"You have gained lordship, each and every divine authority,
"For(?) whom besides you is the divine authority
    of the mountain? (125)
"Greatness has been given you at the daises of the gods
    of destinies,
"They called your lustrations 'Nisaba',
"They called your name in the furrow 'Ningirsu'.
"They assigned to you full shepherdship of the people,
"As king, they gave (you) your name
    'Guardian of the Throne'. (130)
"In Elam they gave (you) the name Hurabtil,
"In Susa they speak of you as Inshushinak.[1]

---

1. Elam and Susa are in southwestern Iran; the other cities and cult centers listed thereafter are Mesopotamian, so far as known.

"In Ibbi-Anu[1] they gave you the name
           'Master of Secret Lore',
"[   ] among the gods your brethren
"[   ] your father,   (135)
"They gave you your name '[Pabilsag]' in Egalmah,
"They [called] your name '[   ]' in Ur,
"[   ] you ... Duranki,
"[In Der] they speak of you as 'Ishtaran',
"[In   ] 'Zababa',   (140)
"[   ] they call as his name.
"Your valor [ ] Enlil over all the gods,
"[   ] to make surpassing your divinity,
"[   ] I praise you.
"In NI.SUR [they gave (you)] your name
           'Lugalbanda' in Egiskalamma,   (145)
"[In] Esikilla they gave (you) [your name]
           as 'Warrior Tishpak',
"In Bube in the Enimmankur [   ],
"In Kullab they called (you) by your name '[Pis]angunuk',
"[   ] Belet-ili your mother,
"[   ] lord of the boundary,   (150)
"[   ] Panigingarra,
"They called ... [   ]
"[   ] 'Papsukkal, the vanguard'.
"O ... lord, your names are surpassing great
           among the gods,
"Lord of understanding, capable and dreaded one,   (155)
"[   ] Ea the Leader, your father,
"[   ] battle and conflict,
"He [ ] you '[ ] of their lands'.

           (fragmentary lines, then breaks off)

---

1. Temple at Dilbat, a town in Babylonia.

How Erra Wrecked the World

How Erra Wrecked the World is one of the most original and challenging compositions in Akkadian. The text is a portrayal of violence: its onset, course, and consequences—how it needs to be recognized and feared as potentially the most powerful of forces. Violence can eliminate even the order ordained by the gods and sweep away in its frenzy all the hopes and accomplishments of civilization. The author, Kabti-ilani-Marduk, who may have lived in the eighth century B.C., must have seen and suffered the consequences of violence and civil strife. He gives witness to a society that had cast off restraints and so ceased to be in balance. If, the text tells, people understand the nature of violence, how it can rage out of control and overwhelm all, they can hope to avoid it. To the modern reader the most salient aspect of this text is its high level of feeling, the willingness of its author to experiment, and the complexity of its thought and structure.

Marduk, as chief Babylonian deity, plays a major role in this poem. He is portrayed as remote and all-wise; he knows Erra's plans even before Erra arrives at his temple. He speaks in sonorous, scholarly diction; there is never any doubt that he is king. Yet the poet is troubled that there could be disorder in his realm that could threaten even Marduk himself.

The form of the text is narrative poetry, most of it direct speech. Ishum, Erra's companion, is invoked near the beginning and plays a crucial role throughout the poem, though he is subordinate to Erra. The device, well known in Western literature, of telling the exploits of a hero from the standpoint of his closest companion, is attested here for the first time. While some narrative is in the third person, in one long passage (see Tablet II lines 115ff.), Erra narrates his own actions. This represents, in modern critical terms, an attempt to fuse narrative and the narrated, discourse and event. Such an experiment builds on a tradition of self-narrative by a deity in Mesopotamian poetry. Perhaps the same tradition is refurbished in a self-praise by Marduk of his own cult statue (Tablet I lines 150ff.), not to mention a description by Marduk himself of destruction done to Babylon (Tablet IV lines 40ff.). Some of Erra's actions are also narrated in the second person by Ishum (see Tablet III lines 98ff.).

The diction of this text seems strange, or at least idiosyncratic, to some modern readers. They are inclined to regard this as indicative of an author untutored in the finer points of Akkadian poetics. One might equally consider it a determined effort to refurbish a rich inventory of inherited expressions to lend them greater force, to do such violence, so to speak, to traditional usage as to command attention.

Tablet I

(Narrator invokes Marduk, chief deity of Babylon, and Ishum, vanguard and companion of Erra. Erra is restless and breaks into a soliloquy. He is anxious to fight and campaign, but hesitates through natural inertia. Speaking of himself in the third person, Erra says that what he needs to stir him to action is Ishum's encouragement [line 9].)

O king of all inhabited lands, creator of the wo[rld], (1)
O Hendursagga,[1] firstborn of Enlil [   ],
Holder of the "sublime scepter,"[2] herdsman
    of the black-headed folk, shepherd [of mankind],
O Ishum, "zealous slaughterer,"[3]
    whose hands are suited to brandish fierce weapons,
And to make his sharp spear flash, Erra, warrior of the gods,
    was restless in his dwelling, (5)
His heart urged him to do battle!
Says he to his weapons,
    "Smear yourselves with deadly venom!"
To the Seven, warriors unrivalled,
    "Let your weapons be girded!"
He even says to you, "I will take to the field!
"You are the torch, they will see your light,[4] (10)
"You are the vanguard, the gods will [   ],
"You are the stanchion, [zealous] slaughterer!
"(So) up, Erra, from laying waste the land
"How cheerful your mood will be and joyful your heart!

---

1. Another name for Ishum.
2. Translation of Hendursagga.
3. A learned Sumerian etymologizing of Ishum's name.
4. It is not clear who speaks lines 10-20. Erra may be describing himself, or the narrator may be speaking of Erra. As interpreted here, the narrative statement is that Erra is restless (5-9), while Erra's speech to Ishum, showing both inclination and disinclination to stir, includes the entire passage 10-20.

"Erra's limbs are slug[gish],
   like those of a mortal lacking sleep,   (15)
"He says to himself, 'Shall I get up or go to sleep?'
"He says to his weapons, 'Stay in the corners!'
"To the Seven, warriors unrivalled,
   'Go back to your dwellings!'
"Until you rouse him, he will sleep in his bedroom,
"He will dally with Mami his mate."   (20)

(With a second invocation, now of Ishum, the narrator introduces the terrible Seven, who stand ready to massacre the "black-headed folk," or Mesopotamians.)

O Engidudu "who patrols at night," "ever guiding the noble,"[1]
Who ever guides young men and women in safety,
   making light as day,
The Seven, warriors unrivalled, their divine nature is different,
Their origins are strange, they are terrifying,
Whoever sees them is numbed with fear.   (25)
Their breath of life is death,
People are too frightened to approach it!
Yet Ishum is the door, bolted before [them].
When Anu, king of the gods, sowed his seed in the earth,
She bore him seven gods, he called them the "Seven."   (30)
They stood before him, that he ordain their destinies.
He summoned the first to give his instructions,
"Wherever you go and spread terror, have no equal."
He said to the second, "Burn like fire, scorch like flame."
He c[ommanded] the third, "Look like a lion,
   let him who sees you be paralyzed with fear."   (35)
He said to the fourth, "Let a mountain collapse
   when you present your fierce arms."
To the fifth he said, "Blast like the wind,
   scan the circumference of the earth."

---

1. "Patrols at night" is a literal translation of the Sumerian epithet; "ever guiding" is a learned wordplay on the same epithet.

The sixth he enjoined, "Go out everywhere (like the deluge)
    and spare no one."
The seventh he charged with viperous venom,
    "Slay whatever lives."
After Anu had ordained destinies for all of the Seven, (40)
He gave those very ones to Erra, warrior of the gods,
    (saying), "Let them go beside you.
"When the clamor of human habitations
    becomes noisome to you,
"And you resolve to wreak destruction,
"To massacre the black-headed folk and fell the livestock,
"Let these be your fierce weaponry, let them go beside you." (45)

(The Seven offer the encouragement that Erra needs. In a rousing call to arms, they extol the heroic excitement of the campaign, the honor, prestige, and gratification it brings. The Seven claim vaguely that they are not respected enough, that others are growing more important than they. They bring up the old charge (see the Story of the Flood) that men make too much noise for the gods to sleep, although this was not the cause Erra had given for his own lack of sleep. The Seven claim further that there are too many wild animals on the loose. Their final claim, no doubt the most important one, is that they are bored and out of training.)

These are the ones who are in a fury,
    holding their weapons aloft,
They are saying to Erra, "Up, do your duty!
"Why have you been sitting in the city like a feeble old man,
"Why sitting at home like a helpless child?
"Shall we eat woman food, like non-combatants? (50)
"Have we turned timorous and trembling, as if we can't fight?
"Going to the field for the young and vigorous
    is like to a very feast,
"(But) the noble who stays in the city can never eat enough.
"His people will hold him in low esteem,
    he will command no respect,
"How could he threaten a campaigner? (55)
"However well developed is the strength of the city dweller,
"How could he possibly best a campaigner?

"However toothsome city bread,
   it holds nothing to the campfire loaf,
"However sweet fine beer,
   it holds nothing to water from a skin,
"The terraced palace holds nothing
   to the [wayside] sleeping spot! (60)
"Be off to the field, warrior Erra, make your weapons clatter,
"Make loud your battle cry that all around they quake,
"Let the Igigi-gods hear and extol your name,
"Let the Anunna-gods hear and flinch at the mention of you,
"Let (all) the gods hear and bend for your yoke, (65)
"Let sovereigns hear and fall prostrate before you,
"Let countries hear and bring you their tribute,
"Let the lowly hear and [per]ish of their own accord,
"Let the mighty hear and his strength diminish,
"Let lofty mountains hear and their peaks crumble, (70)
"Let the surging sea hear and convulse,
   wiping out (her) in[crease]!
"Let the stalk be yanked from the tough thicket,
"Let reeds of the impenetrable morass be shorn off,
"Let men turn cowards and their clamor subside,
"Let beasts tremble and return to clay, (75)
"Let the gods your ancestors see and praise your valor!
"Warrior Erra, why do you neglect the field for the city?
"The very beasts and creatures hold us in contempt!
"O warrior Erra, we will tell you,
   though what we say be offensive to you!
"Ere the whole land outgrows us, (80)
"You must surely hear our words!
"Do a kindly deed for the gods of hell,
   who delight in deathly stillness,
"The Anunna-gods cannot fall asleep
   for the clamor of mankind.
"Beasts are overrunning the meadows, life of the land,
"The farmer sobs bitterly for his [field]. (85)
"Lion and wolf are felling the livestock,

"The shepherd, who cannot sleep day or night
    for the sake of his flocks, is calling upon you.
"We too, who know the mountain passes,
    we have [forgotten] how to go,
"Cobwebs are spun over our field gear,
"Our fine bow resists and is too strong for us, (90)
"The tip of our sharp arrow is bent out of true,
"Our blade is corroded for want of a slaughter!"

(Erra brightens at this and asks Ishum why he does not proceed at once. Ishum remonstrates, saying that violence and destruction are evil. Erra, thoroughly aroused, launches into a self-praise. He is the bravest. If people do not respect the gods enough, and the others are too pusillanimous to do anything about it, he will remedy matters. Since the supposed lack of respect for him must be contrary to Marduk's wishes, Erra will cause Marduk to forsake his dwelling and thus bring about the punishment mankind deserves.)

The warrior Erra heard them,
What the Seven said pleased him like finest oil.
He made ready to speak and said to [Ish]um, (95)
"Why, having heard, did you sit by silent?
"Lead the way, let me begin the campaign!
"[ ] the Seven, warriors without rival,
"Make my fierce weapons¹ march at my side,
"But you be the vanguard and rear guard." (100)
When Ishum heard what he said,
He felt pity and said [to the war]rior Erra,
"O lord Erra, why have you pl[otted evil] against the gods?
"You have remorselessly plotted evil,
    to lay waste the lands and decimate [the people]."
Erra [made ready to sp]eak and said, (105)
To Ishum his vanguard he said [these words],
"Keep quiet, Ishum, listen to what I say.
"As concerns the people of the inhabited world,
    whom you would spare,

---

1. That is, the Seven.

"O vanguard of the gods, wise Ishum,
    whose counsel is always for the best,
"I am the wild bull in heaven, I am the lion on earth,   (110)
"I am king in the land, I am the fiercest among the gods,
"I am warrior among the Igigi-gods,
    mighty one among the Anunna-gods!
"I am the smiter of wild beasts,
    battering ram against the mountain,
"[I am] the blaze in the reed thicket,
    the broad blade against the rushes,
"I am banner for the march,   (115)
"I blast like the wind, I thunder like the storm,
"Like the sun, I scan the circumference of the world.
"I am the wild ram striding forth in the steppe,
"I invade the range and take up my dwelling in the fold.
"All the gods are afraid of a fight,   (120)
"So the black-headed folk are contemptuous!
"As for me, since they did not fear my name,
"And have disregarded Marduk's command,
    so he may act according to his wishes,[1]
"I will make Marduk angry, stir him from his dwelling,
    and lay waste the people!"

(*Erra repairs to Esagila and asks Marduk why his image is besmirched. Marduk, having, in his omniscience, seen Erra's intent, recounts what transpired last time he forsook his dwelling: the universe went topsy-turvy, living creatures were nearly wiped out by the ensuing catastrophe. When Marduk found that his cult statue had been sullied, he caused it to be rebuilt by sublime craftsmen who were later dismissed, never to return. Marduk waxes lyrical in praise of his own cult statue and the wonderful tree from which it was fashioned. The present image of Marduk, divinely created, could never be duplicated.*)

The warrior Erra set out for Shuanna,[2]
    city of the king of the gods,   (125)

---

1. Variant: "they act." As taken here, Erra will motivate Marduk to act as he really wanted to anyway, but had hesitated to for the reasons he gives in lines 134ff.
2. Babylon.

He entered Esagila, palace of heaven and earth,
> and stood before him.

He made ready to speak, saying to the king of the gods,

"Why has your precious image,[1] symbol of your lordship,
> which was full of splendor as the stars of heaven,
> lost its brilliance?

"Your lordly diadem, which made the inner sanctum shine
> like the outside tower,[2] (why is it) dimmed?"

The king of the gods made ready to speak, saying   (130)
To Erra, warrior of the gods, these words,

"O warrior Erra, concerning that deed
> you said you would do,[3]

"Once long ago indeed I grew angry,
> indeed I left my dwelling, and caused the deluge![4]

"When I left my dwelling,
> the regulation of heaven and earth disintegrated:

"The shaking of heaven meant:
> the positions of the heavenly bodies changed,
> nor did I restore them.   (135)

"The quaking of netherworld meant:
> the yield of the furrow diminished,
> being thereafter difficult to exploit.[5]

"The regulation of heaven and earth disintegrating meant:
> underground water diminished, high water receded.
> When I looked again, it was a struggle to get enough.

"Productivity of living offspring declined, nor did I renew it,

"Such that, were I a plowman,
> I (could) hold (all) seed in my hand.

---

1. The Akkadian word here translated as "precious image" can also be understood as "attire" or "fittings."

2. The meaning is that the inner shrine shone as brightly as if it were outside in open daylight.

3. That is, line 124.

4. "Deluge" may be used here metaphorically for "catastrophe," as the immediate consequence was low, not excessive, water (Tablet IV lines 46ff.), and no other Mesopotamian tradition associates Marduk with the deluge. However, a flood is implied in line 172.

5. Obscure. I take this to mean that the furrow could no longer be reliably "levied" for its "yield," that is, expected to give of its increase to the gatherer.

"I built (another) house and settled therein.[1] (140)
"As to my precious image,
    which had been struck by the deluge
    that its appearance was sullied,
"I commanded fire to make my features shine
    and cleanse my apparel.
"When it had shined my precious image
    and completed the task,
"I donned my lordly diadem and returned.
"Haughty were my features, terrifying my glare! (145)
"The survivors of the deluge saw what was done.
"Shall I raise my weapon and destroy the rest?
"I sent those craftsmen[2] down to the depths,
    I ordered them not to come up.
"I removed the wood and gemstone[3]
    and showed no one where.
"Now then, warrior Erra, as concerns that deed
    you said you would do, (150)
"Where is the wood, flesh of the gods,
    suitable for the lord of the uni[verse],
"The sacred tree, splendid stripling, perfect for lordship,
"Whose roots thrust down an hundred leagues through
    the waters of the vast ocean to the depths of hell,
"Whose crown brushed [Anu's] heaven on high?
"Where is the clear gemstone that I reserved for [ ]? (155)
"Where is Ninildum, great carpenter of my supreme divinity,
"Wielder of the glittering hatchet, who knows that tool,
"Who makes [it] shine like the day
    and puts it in subjection at my feet?

---

1. Perhaps a reference to (re)construction of Esagila after the catastrophe, or to a special building where his image was refurbished.
2. The divine craftsmen, or sages, who refurbished Marduk's image after it was damaged in the catastrophe.
3. The meaning is that the specific materials used to make the image are no longer to be had. The entire passage implies that the statue of Marduk dated to earliest time and could not be reproduced because it was not made by human hands.

"Where is Kusig-banda, fashioner of god and man,
    whose hands are sacred?
"Where is Ninagal, wielder of the upper and lower millstone, (160)
"Who grinds up hard copper like hide and who forges to[ols]?
"Where are the choice stones, created by the vast sea,
    to ornament my diadem?
"Where are the seven [sa]ges of the depths, those sacred fish,
    who, like Ea their lord, are perfect in sublime wisdom,
    the ones who cleansed my person?"

(Erra's reply is lost, but he may offer to produce suitable materials for refurbishing the statue. Marduk then asks who will ward off the forces of evil and chaos while he is being refurbished and is thereby non-combatant. Erra offers to reign in his stead. Marduk assents, forsakes his dwelling for repairs, and the universe is thrown into confusion.)

The warrior Erra [hea]rd him ... [ ],
He made ready to speak, saying to noble Marduk, (165)
"[craftsmen   ],
"[tree   ],
"Clear gemstone [from] its [pl]ace will I bring up."
When Marduk heard this,
He made ready to speak, saying to the [warrior] Erra, (170)
"(When) I rise [from] my dwelling,
    the regulation [of heaven and earth] will disintegrate,
"The [waters] will rise and sweep over the land,
"Bright [day will turn] to dar[k]ness,
"[Wh]irlwind will rise and the stars of heaven will be [ ],
"Ill winds will blow and the eyesight of living creatures
    [will be darkened?], (175)
"Demons will rise up and seize [ ],
"[They will ...] the unarmed one who confronts them!
"The gods of hell will rise up
    and smite down living creatures.
"Who will keep them at bay
    till I gird on my weaponry (once more)?"
When Erra heard this, (180)
He made ready to speak, saying to noble Marduk,

"O noble Marduk, while you enter that house,[1]
> fire cleanses your apparel and you return to your place,
"For that time I will govern and keep strong
> the regulation of heaven and earth,
"I will go up to heaven and issue instructions
> to the Igigi-gods,
"I will go down to the depths
> and keep the Anunna-gods in order. (185)
"I will despatch the wild demons to the netherworld,
"I will brandish my fierce weaponry against them.
"I will truss the wings of the ill wind like a bird's.
"At that house you shall enter, O noble Marduk,
"I will station Anu and Enlil to the right and left, like bulls."[2] (190)
Noble Marduk heard him,
The words which Erra spoke pleased him.

Tablet II

(Marduk leaves his palace, disaster ensues.)

He arose from his dwelling, an inaccessible place, (1)
He set out for the dwelling of the Anunna-gods.
He entered that house and sto[od before them].
Shamash looked upon him and let his protective radiance fall ...,
Sin looked elsewhere, and did not [leave?] the netherworld. (5)
Ill winds rose and the bright daylight was turned to gloom.
The clamor of the peoples throughout the land [was stilled].
The Igigi-gods were terrified and went up to h[eaven],
The Anunna-gods were [fright]ened
> and [went down] to the pit [of hell],
> [   ] the entire circumference [   ] (10)
> [   ] in the dust.
> [   ] let us see."

---

1. The special building where the cult image is refurbished.
2. The imagery seems to be of great winged bulls, such as stood at the entrances to certain Assyrian palaces.

[   ] its doors.
[   ] like the stars of heaven,

(gap)

(The gods convene to discuss the situation. Ea, intent upon restoring Marduk to his place, reasons that, even though the original sublime craftsmen cannot return, Marduk authorized reproductions of them to be made that are endowed with wondrous powers by Ea at Marduk's command. The repairs are proceeding well. Erra, while standing guard at the house where the work is being done lest harm approach, is taking the opportunity to usurp Marduk's power by keeping everyone away from him. So vainglorious is Erra's shouting that Ea resolves to see him humbled.)

"The diadem [   ]   (15)
"His heart [   ], let him make it happy.
"The governor's[1] [   ]
"The awe-inspiring radiance of [his] divine splendor [   ]
     his days [   ],
"[   ] like rain,
"[Let] Ea in the depths [   ] his springs,   (20)
"Let Shamash see ... [   ] and let the people [   ],
"Let Sin behold, and at his sign let him [   ] to the land.
"Concerning that work, Ea [   ] is expert(?)."
"The warrior Erra became very angry,
"Why, because of foam on the w[aters],[2] the ... of mankind,   (25)
"Which I myself created to bring offerings to the Anunna-gods,
"Did noble Marduk give up, not at the appointed time?
"He plotted to lay waste the lands and destroy their people!"
Ea the king considered and said these words,
"Even now that noble Marduk has arisen (from his dwelling),
     he did not command those craftsmen to c[ome up].   (30)
"How can images of them, which I made among mankind,
"Approach his sublime divinity, where no god has access?

---

1. Here possibly Erra, as temporary viceroy for Marduk, as opposed to the human governor who appears later in the poem.
2. In Tablet IV line 68, foam is used as a metaphor for the human race destroyed by the flood. Here it may refer to something transitory: why did Marduk sacrifice the human race for a passing whim (as it seemed to the speaker), and give the human beings over to Erra, when they were essential for feeding and maintaining the gods?

"He himself gave those same (human) craftsmen
    great discretion and authority,
"He gave them wisdom and perfect dexterity.
"They have made (his) precious image radiant,
    even finer than before.   (35)
"Warrior Erra has stationed himself before him,
    night and day without ceasing,
"Besetting the house for making radiant the precious image
    for the sovereignty of the king, and saying,
    'Don't come near the work!
    '[He who dr]aws near it —
        I will cut short his life and prolong his death agony.'
"[   ] let him hasten at the work,   (40)
"[   ] has no equal.
"[   ] Erra was speaking like a mortal,
"[   ] trying to rival the noble one,
"[   ] may he be humbled."
[The images of the craftsmen] made his precious image radiant, (45)
[   ] ...
[They set the ...] at his door(?)
[   ] king Shamash girds it on,
[   ] he reoccupied his dwelling,
[   ] brilliance was reestablished.   (50)
[All the gods   ] were gathered,
Erra [nob]le Marduk,
"Noble Marduk, [   ]
"Godlike, you [   ]
"Small to great, [   ]   (55)
[   ] Erra ... [   ]
[   ] ... his uproar was terrifying,
"[   ] ... the image,
"[   ] of your [lord]ship are raised up and establi[shed]."

(*The repairs successfully completed, Marduk has returned to his dwelling [line 49]. In a fragmentary passage, Marduk addresses the gods and orders them all to return to their dwellings. The gods are alarmed by astral omens that presage Erra's dominance.*)

The king of the gods [made ready] to speak and said, (60)
"[   ] and went up to heaven."
[   ] he commanded, "Return to your dwellings!"
[   ] ... his sign,
"[   ] upon your face,
"[   ] their peoples. (65)
"[   ] you did not turn back."
[He heard him], ... said [to the k]ing of the gods,
"The word of Marduk [   ] of the day."
He said to him [   ]
"Come now, [   ] (70)
"To destroy the lands [why did you plot?]."
Erra heard him [   ]
...
He entered [   ].
Anu heard in heaven [   ], (75)
He bowed his lofty head [   ].
Antu, mother of the gods, was aghast [   ],
She entered [her] cham[ber].
Enlil's [   ]

(gap)

[   ] father of the gods [   ] (80)
[   ] Enlil [   ]
Among the beasts, all of them [   ].
Erra among all the gods [   ].
Among the stars of heaven the Fox Star [ ]
Was shining bright and its radiance [   ] for him, (85)
The stars of all the gods were dazzling [ ],
Because they were angry with each other
    and noble Marduk [ ] put [   ],
"The star of Erra is shining bright and is radiant:
    ... of warfare.
"His awe-inspiring brilliance will ...
    and all people will perish(?).
"... the dazzling stars of heaven in his time are [dimmed?]. (90)
"... the ant, does it not rise [   ]?

"Among the beasts, the image of their star is the fox,
"Endowed with strength, a raging(?) lion [ ],
"Enlil is the father of [ ], he has [   ]."

(Even Ishtar, goddess of war, tries to calm Erra.)

Innina replied in the assembly of the gods [   ],   (95)
[ ] her words to Anu and Dagan [   ],
"Keep quiet, all of you, go into your chambers,
"Cover your lips, do not smell the in[cense],
"Do not debate noble Marduk's word, do not pl[ead   ]
"Until the days are drawn to a close,
       the [appointed time] passed,   (100)
"The word Marduk speaks is like a mountain where ...,
       he does not change (it) nor [ ]."

(gap)

Ishtar went, they entered the ...,
She pled with Erra, but he would not agree.
Ishum made ready to speak, saying (these) words to Ishtar,
"I have ... that of heaven over what is not of heaven,   (105)
"Erra is angry and will heed no one,
"Let him come to rest in the mountains, and I(?) ...
       the seed of the people which you spoke about to [ ],
"The sublime son of Enlil will not go on campaign without
       Ishum the vanguard before [him?]."

(Erra is furious. All he has done is to perform guard duty, and now has been sent home, his services no longer required, without a campaign. This is because he is the most valiant god — no evil rises to oppose him. This he fails to perceive, but, in his blind rage, he resolves to fight his war anyway, to show Marduk and Ea that he is not to be taken so lightly. Erra's self-praise turns into a self-narrative. This passage is unusual in Akkadian and has been subjected to varying interpretations. In favor of that offered here, note that first person narrative is nearly always past or future, hardly ever renderable as present and in progress. Since the passage cannot logically refer to the future, and since the past is difficult for grammatical reasons, we have here a present, first-person narrative, one of Kabti-ilani-Marduk's most interesting experiments.)

He was sitting in the E-meslam,[1] taking up his dwelling.
He thought to himself what had been done,[2] (110)
His heart being stung, it could give him no answer,
But he asked it what it would have him do.[3]
"Lead the way, let me begin the campaign!
"The days are drawn to a close,
    the appointed time has passed.
"I give the command and despoil the sun
    of his protective radiance, (115)
"By night I muffle the face of the moon.
"I say to the thunderstorm, 'Hold back [your] young bulls!
"'Brush aside the clouds, cut off sn[ow and rain]!'
"I will make Marduk and Ea mindful!
"[He] who waxed great in days of plenty,
    they bury him on a day of drought, (120)
"He who came by water,
    [they take him back] on a dusty road.
"I say to the king of the gods, 'Take your place in E[sagila],

    'They must do what you commanded,
        they must carry out your or[der].
    'The [black]-headed folk cry out to you,
        but do not accept their entreaties!'

"I obliterate [the land?] and reckon it for ruins, (125)
"I lay waste cities and turn them into open spaces,
"I wreck mountains and fel[l] their wildlife,
"I convulse the sea and destroy its increase,
"I bring the stillness of death upon swamp and thicket,
    burning like fire,
"I fell humankind, I leave no living creatures, (130)
"Not one do I retain, [nor any?] for seed to [ ] the land.
"I spare no livestock nor any living creatures,

---

1. Temple of Erra at Cutha.
2. That is, the successful completion of Marduk's repairs and his being packed off home again, needed no longer.
3. Obscure. As read here, Erra is furious at what he regards as high-handed treatment, and, consulting only his own wounded feelings, decides to go on a rampage. The lines imply that he debated with his "self," but took guidance from his heart (= emotions) alone.

"I dispatch the soldier from one city against another.
"Neither son nor father has a care for the other's well-being,
"Mother p[lots ev]il against daughter with a leer. (135)
"I let [yokels into] the abodes of gods,
    where harm must not approach,
"I settle the miscreant in the nobleman's dwelling.
"I let outlandish beasts into the shrines,
"I block access to any city where they appear,
"I send down beasts of the highlands, (140)
"Wherever they set foot,
    they bring the stillness of death to the thoroughfares,
"I cause beasts of the steppe not to stay in the steppe,
    but to traverse the city street.
"I make omens unfavorable,
    I turn holy places into foraging grounds,
"I let the demon "Upholder-of-Evil"
    into the dwellings of the gods,
    where no evil should go,
"I devastate the king's palace [ ] and turn it into a ruin, (145)
"I cu[t o]ff the clamor of [mankind] in [dwellings]
    and rob them of happiness,
"As [I] orchards like fire ...
"I let evil enter [ ]

Tablet III

(Erra's speech continues, as he glories in the horrors of war, anarchy, and privation. There follows a gap in the text.)

"[   ] heeds no one, (1)
"What he(?) reasoned [ ]
"Lions [   ]
"[   ]
"I make [ ] go towards [ ] (5)
"I confiscate [... their] households and cut short their lives,
"I as[sassinate] the righteous man who intercedes,
"I set the wicked cutthroat in the highest rank.

"I estrange people's hearts so father listens not to son,
"And daughter cavils spitefully to mother.   (10)
"I make their utterances evil, they forget their gods,
"They speak gross blasphemy to their goddesses.
"I stir up the [rob]ber and so cut off travel absolutely,
"People rifle one another's belongings in the heart of the city.
"Lion and wolf fell the livestock.   (15)
"I aggravate [ ] and she cuts off birth-giving,
"I deprive the nurse of the wail of toddler and infant.
"I banish the work song of harvest home from the fields,
"Shepherd and herdsman forget their field shelters.
"I cut the clothes from the bodies of men,
    the young man I parade naked through the city street,   (20)
"The young man without clothes I send down to hell.[1]
"The ordinary fellow has not so much as a sheep
    to offer up for his life,
"For the nobleman's divination lambs are few and precious.
"The patient yearns for a bit of roast to offer for his recovery,
"It does him no good, so he gets up and walks till he dies.   (25)
"I incapacitate the nobleman's mount like [ ],
"I cut [   ]

(fragmentary lines, then gap)

(The deed spoken and done, Ishum is remonstrating that Enlil has forsaken his city. Erra, in a frenzy, cries for more, and, having done enough himself, lets loose the Seven. Ishum, distressed at Erra's "over-kill," demands the reason for it.)

(Ishum is speaking, restored from IV 33-39)

"The stro[ng   ]
"Like the blo[od   ]
"[You homed their weaponry upon?] the people
    under special protection, [sacred to Anu and Dagan],[2]   (30)

---

1. Captives in war were sometimes paraded naked. Furthermore, the dead enter the netherworld naked; thus the people in the upper world are little better than dead.
2. Certain Mesopotamian cities were exempt from military service, taxes, or other obligations to the crown, and Erra has violated their charters.

"You [made] their blood course
       like [ditchwater in the city streets],
"You [opened their] arteries
       [and let the watercourses bear (their) blood away].
"Enlil [cried], "Woe!" [his heart was hardened],
"[He   ] from his dwelling,
"An irrever[sible curse rose to his lips], (35)
"He swore that [he would not drink from the watercourses],
"He was revol[ted by] their blood
       [and] would not enter [Ekur]."
Erra said these words to Ishum his vanguard,
"The Seven, warrior[s unrivalled   ]
"For all of them [   ] (40)
"Which no[ble   ]
"O [my] vanguard, [   ]
"Who can speak [   ]
"Who can [   ] like fire?
"Who can [   ] before [   ] (45)
"Who can [   ] like [   ]
"Who [   ]
"Who can [   ] Erra?
"The face of a r[avening] lion [   ]
"In the rage of [ ] heart [   ]? (50)
"Lead the way, [let me begin the campaign]!
"[Muster?] the Seven, warriors unrivalled,
"[Make] (them), fierce weaponry, [go at my side],
"And do [you] be [my] vanguard and [rear guard]."
When Ishum heard this [speech] of his, (55)
He felt pity and sa[id to himself?],
"Alas for my people, victims of Erra's fury [ ],
"Whom the warrior Nergal [overwhelmed]
       like the storm of battle [against] the demons,
"As if to kill that conquered god, his arms lose no tension,
"As if to snare wicked Anzu, [his net] is spread!"[1] (60)
Ishum made ready to speak,

---

1. That is, Erra is ready for even the most formidable encounter.

Saying to warrior Erra these words,
"Why have you plotted evil against god and man?
"And why have you remorselessly plotted evil
    against the black-headed folk?

(Erra replies exultantly that men are too stupid to understand the ways of the gods, so why take their part? Furthermore, Marduk did forsake his dwelling, so the world cannot be as it was before; that would be a denial of Marduk's centrality. Now Ishum narrates Erra's violent course in the second person, a literary experiment building upon the preceding. There follows a gap in the text.)

Erra made ready to speak, (65)
Saying to Ishum his vanguard these words,
"You (who) know the reasoning of the Igigi-gods,
    the counsel of the Anunna-gods,
"Would you give guidance to the black-headed folk
    and try to make them understand?[1]
"Why are you, indeed, talking like a know-nothing?
"You are advising me as if
    you knew not Marduk's command! (70)
"The king of the gods has risen from his dwelling!
"What of all lands has endured?
"He removed his lordly diadem:
"King and prince [ ] forget their duties.
"He has undone his girdle: (75)
"The bond of god and man is undone,
    impossible to tighten it again.
"Fierce fire made his precious image glow like the day
    and heightened his protective splendor,
"His right hand grasped the mace, his enormous weapon.
"Noble Marduk's glare is terrifying!
"As for me, what you said to me [ ], (80)
"O vanguard of the gods, wise [Ishum,
    whose counsels are sound],
"Why, just now, [did you   such a] speech?

1. That is, why would one privy to the minds of the gods bother with any attempt to make men understand them?

"Marduk's command is not [satisfactory to you]?"
Ishum made ready to speak, saying to [the warrior Erra],
"O warrior Erra ... [   ]　　　　　　　　　　(85)
"Mankind ... [   ]
"The livestock [   ]
"Swamps and reedbanks [   ]
"Now then, what you said, w[arrio]r Erra,
"One stood forth and you [   ] seven,　　　　　　　　(90)
"You killed seven and did not let go a single one,
"Take away the livestock [   ] ...
"O Erra, when you strike with your weapons,
"Mountains to[tter], the sea [con]vulses,
"Such a flash of [your] stan[chion], they look east,
　　　[as if to] see the sun [rise]!　　　　　　　　　　　　(95)
"The palace [   ]

　　　　　　　　　(gap of unknown length)

*(Ishum continues: Erra has taken over the universe, even Marduk's sanctuary.
　　　How can he now say that no one respects him?)*

Ishum made ready to speak, saying to the warrior Erra,
"O [war]rior Erra, you hold the leadrope of heaven,
"You are master of all the earth, lord in the land!
"You convulse the sea, obliterate mountains,　　　　　　　(100)
"You rule over man and herd beasts.
"The primeval sanctuaries are in your hands,
"You control Shuanna and command Esagila.
"You have gathered to yourself all authority,
　　　the gods revere you,
"The Igigi-gods stand in awe of you,
　　　the Anunna-gods are in dread of you.　　　　　　　(105)
"When you set forth counsel, even Anu heeds you,
"Even Enlil agrees with you.
　　　Aside from you, is there opposition?
"Except for you, is there battle?
"The armor of strife is yours alone!
"But you have said to yourself,
　　　'They hold me in contempt.'"　　　　　　　　　　　(110)

Tablet IV

(Ishum's speech continues, one of the longest in Akkadian literature. He narrates the horrors and destruction of civil war, refers to atrocities committed in Babylon by an invading army, and, in lines 36ff. quotes Marduk's moving lament for his city. In 45-49 Ishum goes on to quote Marduk's own description of the appalling conditions there. Ishum then describes events at Sippar, where the city walls are destroyed, and at Uruk, overrun by the barbarous Sutaeans. This fierce nomadic people even went so far as to interfere with the cult devotees of Ishtar, whose practices may have been abhorrent to the poet. In 63-64 Dur-Kurigalzu is referred to, and in 65ff. Ishtaran of Der curses his city. It is not clear where Ishum's speech ends, but the poem continues with a passionate portrayal of indiscriminate violence. In 115ff. Ishum points out that even with decimation of the populace Erra is not satisfied; he must ruin the guidance of the land, its government and sanctuaries, even that of Marduk himself.)

"O warrior Erra, you are the one
    who feared not noble Marduk's name![1]   (1)
"You have undone Dimkurkurra, "the bond of the world,"[2]
    the city of the king of the gods.
"You changed your divine nature
    and made yourself like a mortal,[3]
"You girded on your weaponry and entered Babylon.
"Inside Babylon you spoke like a rabble-rouser(?),
    as if to take over the city,   (5)
"The citizenry of Babylon, like reeds in a thicket,
    had no one in charge, so they rallied around you:
"He who knew nothing of weapons — his sword was drawn,
"He who knew nothing of archery — his bow was taut,
"He who knew nothing of fighting — set to the fray,
"He who knew nothing of wings — flew off like a bird.[4]   (10)
"The cripple could surpass the fleet of foot,
    the weakling could overpower the strong.

---

1. That is, granting that Erra is supreme, by virtue of Marduk's command, his continued fighting is tantamount to sin, since it would seem to admit of opposition, an apparent denial of Marduk's supremacy.
2. Babylon.
3. That is, by ravaging sanctuaries?
4. The reference seems to be to precipitous flight in the face of danger.

"They give voice to gross insolence against the governor
    who provides for their holy places,
"With their own hands they blockaded the gate of Babylon,
    their lifeline,
"They have torched the sanctuaries of Babylon
    like marauders of the land,
"You, the vanguard, took their lead! (15)
"You aimed your shaft at the innermost wall,
    "Woe! My heart!" it exclaims,
"You flung the seat of Muhra, its gatekeeper,
    into the blood of young men and girls,
"The inhabitants of Babylon themselves — they the bird,
    you the decoy —
"You snared in a net, caught and killed them, warrior Erra!
"You quit the city and have gone out to the outskirts, (20)
"You took on a lion's face and have entered the palace.
"When the troops saw you, they girded on their weapons,
"The heart of the governor, avenger of Babylon, turned to fury.
"He issued orders to his army to plunder,
    as if plundering enemies,
"He incited the commander to atrocities, (25)

   'You, my man, for that city I am sending you to,
   'Fear no god, respect no man!
   'Do young and old alike to death!
   'Spare no one, not even the baby sucking milk!
   'You shall plunder the accumulated wealth of Babylon!' (30)

"The royal troops drew up and have invaded the city,
"With flashing shafts and outstretched blades,
"You homed their weapons upon those under special protection,
    sacred to Anu and Dagan.
"You made their blood course like ditchwater in the city streets,
"You opened their arteries
    and let the watercourses bear their blood away. (35)
"When the great lord Marduk saw that, he cried 'Woe!'
    and his heart was hardened,
"An irreversible curse rose to his lips.

"He swore that he would not drink from the watercourses,
"He was revolted by their blood and would not enter Esagila,

   'Alas for Babylon,
      whose crown I fashioned luxuriant as a palm's,
      but which the wind has scorched!   (40)
   'Alas for Babylon,
      that I had laden with seed, like an evergreen,
      but of whose delights I could not have
      what I hoped for!
   'Alas for Babylon,
      that I tended like a thriving orchard,
      but whose fruit I could not taste!
   'Alas for Babylon,
      that I suspended like a gemstone seal
      on the neck of the sky!
   'Alas for Babylon,
      that I clasped in my hand like the tablet of destinies,
      not handing it over to anyone else!'

"[And this too has] noble Marduk said,   (45)
   '[   ] from former days [ ]
   'Let one quit the wharf: he shall cross
      at two cubit's depth of water on foot,[1]
   'Let one go down sixty fathoms in a well,
      not one man shall keep himself alive (on the water),
   'Let them (still have to) punt the fishing boat
      a hundred leagues out in the open sea!'

"As for Sippar, the primeval city,
      through which the lord of the world did not allow
      the deluge to pass, because it was precious to him,   (50)
"You destroyed her ramparts against the will of Shamash,
      and threw down her fortifications.

---

1. The sense may be that there will be so little water at the city docks that one can walk across the riverbed, starting at the pier, and the water will scarcely reach to one's waist. Cutting off of water could also be a military maneuver.

"As for Uruk, the dwelling of Anu and Ishtar, the city
    of courtesans, harlots, and prostitutes (for the cult),
"Whom Ishtar deprived of husbands
    and reckoned as her own(?),
"There Sutaean nomads, men and women,
    bandy war whoops![1]
"They turned out the actors and singers (of) Eanna,   (55)
"Whose manhood Ishtar changed to womanhood
    to strike awe into the people,
"The wielders of daggers and razors,
    vintner's shears and flint knives,
"Who take part in abominable acts
    for the entertainment of Ishtar,[2]
"A haughty, remorseless governor you placed over them,
"He harassed them and interfered with their rites.   (60)
"Ishtar was angered, she flew into a rage against Uruk,
"She stirred up the enemy and swept clean the country,
    like granules on the water's face.
"The dweller in Parsa had no respite
    from lamenting the destroyed Eugal-sanctuary.[3]
"The enemy you roused has no desire to stop.
"Ishtaran responded thus,   (65)

'You turned the city Der[4] into a wasteland,
'You fractured her populace like reeds,
'You extinguished their clamor
    like the (dying hiss of) foam on the water's face!
'And as for me, you did not spare me
    but gave me over to the Sutaean nomads!
'For the sake of my city Der,   (70)
'I will judge no disputed truth,
    nor make any ruling for the land,

---

1. The Sutaeans, from the point of view of the Mesopotamian city dweller, were marauding nomadic people.
2. The cult of Ishtar was associated with prostitution, both male and female (lines 52, 56), and, perhaps, self-mutilation (57).
3. Parsa is to be identified with Dur-Kurigalzu, a large city northwest of Babylon.
4. Important Mesopotamian city near present-day Badra, near the Iranian frontier.

'I will give no guidance nor aid in understanding.
'Men forsook truth and took up violence,
'They abandoned justice and were plotting wickedness.
'Against (but) one country I raised up seven winds. (75)
'He who did not die in battle will die in the epidemic,
'He who did not die in the epidemic,
    the enemy will plunder him,
'He whom the enemy has not pl[undered],
    the bandit will murder him,
'He whom the bandit did not murder,
    the king's weapon will vanquish him,
'He whom the king's weapon did not vanquish,
    the prince will slay him, (80)
'He whom the prince did not slay,
    a thunderstorm will wash him away,
'He whom the thunderstorm did not wash away,
    the sun will parch him,
'He who has gone out in the world,
    the wind will sweep him away,
'He who has gone into his home,
    a demon will strike him,
'He who has gone up to a high place
    will perish of thirst, (85)
'He who has gone down to a low place
    will perish in the waters!
'You have obliterated high and low place alike.
'The man in charge of the city says to his mother,[1]
    "If only I had stuck in your womb
        the day you bore me,
    "If only our lives had come to an end, (90)
    "If only we had died together,
    "For you gave me a city whose walls are destroyed!
    "Its people are the beasts,
        their god is he who hunts them down.

---

1. As the text stands, it is difficult to decide who speaks what lines; the reading offered here is only a suggestion.

> "He it is whose net is tight-meshed: those engaged
> cannot slip through but die a violent death."

'He who begot a son, saying, (95)

> "This is my son,
> "When I have reared him he will requite my pains,"

'I will put that son to death, his father must bury him,
'Afterwards I will put that father to death,
but he will have none to bury him.
'He who built a house, saying (100)

> "This is my home,
> "I built it for myself, I shall spend my leisure in it,
> "On the day fate claims me, I shall fall asleep inside,"

'I will put him to death and wreck his home,
'Afterwards, though it be wreckage(?),
I will give it to another.' (105)

"O warrior Erra, you have put the righteous man to death,
"You have put the unrighteous man to death,
"He who sinned against you, you put him to death,
"He who did not sin against you, you put him to death,
"The high priest, assiduous with divine offerings,
you put to death, (110)
"The functionary who served the king you put to death,
"The old man on the doorstep you put to death,
"The young girls in their bedrooms you put to death,
"Even then you found no appeasement whatsoever!
"Even then you told yourself, 'They hold me in contempt!' (115)
"Even then you said to yourself, O warrior Erra,

> 'I will strike down the mighty, I will terrorize the weak,
> 'I will kill the commander, I will scatter the troops,
> 'I will wreck the temple's sacred chamber, the rampart's
> battlement, the pride of the city I will destroy!
> 'I will tear out the mooring pole so the ship drifts away, (120)
> 'I will smash the rudder so she cannot reach the shore,
> 'I will pluck out the mast, I will rip out the rigging.
> 'I will make breasts go dry so babies cannot thrive,

'I will block up springs so that even little channels
   can bring no life-sustaining water.
'I will make hell shake and heaven tremble, (125)
'I will make the planets shed their splendor,
   I will wrench out the stars from the sky,
'I will hack the tree's roots
   so its branches cannot burgeon,
'I will wreck the wall's foundation so its top tumbles,
'I will approach the dwelling of the king of the gods,
   that no direction be forthcoming!'"

(Erra is gratified that the extent of his power is recognized; he has at last won his respect. He decrees that the rabble of the world should fight on; at length Babylon shall rule what is left. Erra then allows Ishum to campaign against a mountain that is apparently the homeland of the Sutaeans, the human arch-villains of the narrative. Erra has destroyed most of the world, but Ishum now puts violence to useful purpose.)

The warrior Erra heard him, (130)
The speech that Ishum made pleased him like finest oil.
Thus spoke the warrior Erra,
"The Sealand the Sealand,[1] Subartu Subartu,
   Assyrian Assyrian,
"Elamite Elamite, Kassite Kassite,
"Sutaean Sutaean, Gutian Gutian, (135)
"Lullubaean Lullubaean, land land, city city,
"House house, man man, brother brother must not spare
   (one another), let them kill each other!
"Then, afterwards, let the Akkadian arise to slay them all,
   to rule them, every one."
The warrior Erra said these words to Ishum his vanguard,
"Go, Ishum, the matter you spoke of,[2] do as you wish." (140)

---

1. This and the following list the countries surrounding Babylonia to the south, north, east, and west, partly in contemporaneous, partly in archaizing terms. "Akkadian" in 138 refers to an unnamed Babylonian king whose victories are here "prophesied."
2. If there was a referent for this speech, it is now missing in one of the gaps in the poem.

Ishum set out for the mountain Hehe,[1]
The Seven, warriors unrivalled, fell in behind him.
When the warriors reached the mountain Hehe,
He raised his hand, he destroyed the mountain,
He reckoned the mountain Hehe as level ground.   (145)
He cut away the trunks of the cedar forest,
The thicket looked as if the deluge had passed over,
He laid waste cities and turned them into open spaces,
He obliterated mountains and slew their wild life,
He convulsed the sea and destroyed its increase,   (150)
He brought the stillness of death upon swamp and thicket,
 burning like fire,
He cursed the wildlife and returned it to clay.

Tablet V

(Erra, in a last boast, addresses the gods. He praises Ishum and points out, not without pride, that in his rage and valor he, Erra, had made the blunder of attacking the leadership of the universe as well as its subjects. Were it not for Ishum's timely intervention, who knows where Erra's terrible strength might have led him? Ishum rejoins that this is all very well, but would Erra please calm himself now that his point has been made?)

After Erra was calmed and took up his own abode,   (1)
All the gods were gazing at his face,
All the Igigi-gods and Anunna-gods stood in awe.
Erra made ready to speak, saying to all the gods,
"Quiet, all of you, learn what I have to say.   (5)
"No doubt I intended evil in the bygone lapse,
"I was angry and wanted to lay waste the people.
"Like a hireling, I took the lead ram from the flock,
"Like one who did not plant an orchard,
 I was quick to cut it down,
"Like a scorcher of the earth,
 I slew indiscriminately good and evil.   (10)

---

1. Homeland of the Sutaeans.

"One would not snatch a carcass
    from the jaws of a ravening lion,
"So too no one can reason where one is in a frenzy.
"Were it not for Ishum my vanguard,
    what might have happened?
"Where would your provider be, where your high priest?
"Where your food offering? You would smell no incense." (15)
Ishum made ready to speak,
    saying to the warrior Erra these words,
"Quiet, warrior, hear what I have to say,
"No doubt this is true, now, calm down, let us serve you!
"At a time you are angry, where is he who can face you?"

(Erra returns to his home and pronounces a blessing upon Babylon, that she will at last prevail over her enemies and wax rich on the tribute of her foes throughout the world.)

When Erra heard this, his face beamed, (20)
Like radiant daylight his features glowed.
He entered E-meslam and took up his abode,
He called Ishum to tell him the sign,
To give him instructions concerning
    the scattered peoples of Akkad,
"Let the people of the country, who had dwindled,
    become numerous again, (25)
"Let short and tall alike traverse its paths,
"Let weak Akkadian fell mighty Sutaean,
"Let one drive off seven like sheep.
"You shall make his cities into ruins
    and his highlands into open ground,
"You shall take massive booty from them
    (and put it) in Shuanna, (30)
"You shall reconcile the angry gods with their own abodes,
"You shall make gods of livestock
    and grain descend (once more) to the land,
"You shall make mountain deliver its yield, sea its produce,
"You shall make the ruined fields deliver produce.

"Let the governors of all cities haul their massive tribute
    into Shuanna, (35)
"Let the [ru]ined temples lift their heads like rays of the sun,
"Let Tigris and Euphrates bring abundant water,
"Let the governors of all cities make the provider for Esagila
    and Babylon their lord."

(Erra's speech melds into that of the narrator. The poet introduces himself by name, and explains that the text, or "sign" of the god, was approved by Erra himself after it was revealed to the author in a half-waking state. Having become a sign, the text acquires prophylactic powers.)

Praise to the great lord Nergal and warrior Ishum
    for years without number!
How it came to pass that Erra grew angry and set out
    to lay waste the lands and destroy their peoples, (40)
But Ishum his counsellor calmed him and left a remnant,
The composer of its text was Kabti-ilani-Marduk,
    of the family Dabibi.
He revealed it at night, and, just as he (the god?)
    had discoursed it while he (K.) was coming awake,
    he (K.) omitted nothing at all,
Nor one line did he add.
When Erra heard it he approved, (45)
What pertained to Ishum his vanguard satisfied him.
All the gods praised his sign.[1]
Then the warrior Erra spoke thus,
"In the sanctuary of the god who honors this poem,
    may abundance accumulate,
"But let the one who neglects it never smell incense. (50)
"Let the king who extols my name rule the world,
"Let the prince who discourses the praise of my valor
    have no rival,
"Let the singer who chants (it) not die from pestilence,
"But his performance be pleasing to king and prince.

---

1. This poem.

"The scribe who masters it shall be spared in
 the enemy country and honored in his own land, (55)
"In the sanctum of the learned, where they shall constantly
 invoke my name, I shall grant them understanding.
"The house in which this tablet is placed,
 though Erra be angry and the Seven be murderous,
"The sword of pestilence shall not approach it,
 safety abides upon it.
"Let this poem stand forever, let it endure till eternity,
"Let all lands hear it and praise my valor, (60)
"Let all inhabitants witness and extol my name."

II
KINGS AND THEIR DEEDS

Legends of Sargon of Akkad

BIRTH LEGEND OF SARGON

Sargon of Akkad (ca. 2334–2279 B.C.) was remembered in Mesopotamian tradition as a successful warrior king who founded the first empire in history. Various poems about his exploits were composed for centuries after his death.

  This fragment of a pseudonymous text of uncertain character purports to tell the story of his birth and early life. Language and content point to a first millennium date for this composition. The point of this narrative may not be that Sargon was of humble origins but rather, as offspring of a high priestess, he was noble by birth, as confirmed by his subsequent success.

> I am Sargon the great king, king of Agade. (1)
> My mother was a high priestess, I did not know my father.
> My father's brothers dwell in the uplands.
> My city is Azupiranu, which lies on Euphrates bank.
> My mother, the high priestess, conceived me,
>   she bore me in secret. (5)
> She placed me in a reed basket, she sealed my hatch with pitch.
> She left me to the river, whence I could not come up.
> The river carried me off, it brought me to Aqqi, drawer of water.
> Aqqi, drawer of water, brought me up as he dipped his bucket.
> Aqqi, drawer of water, raised me as his adopted son. (10)
> Aqqi, drawer of water, set (me) to his orchard work.
> During my orchard work, Ishtar loved me.
> Fifty-five years I ruled as king,
> I became lord over and ruled the black-headed folk.
> I ... [   ] hard mountains with picks of copper, (15)
> I was wont to ascend high mountains,
> I was wont to cross over low mountains.
> The [la]nd of the sea I besieged three times, I conquered Dilmun.
> I went up to great Der, I [   ],
> I destroyed [Ka]zallu and [   ]. (20)

Whatsoever king who shall arise after me,
[Let him rule as king fifty-five years],
Let him become lo[rd over and rule] the black-headed folk.
Let him [ ] hard mountains with picks [of copper],
Let him be wont to ascend high mountains, (25)
[Let him be wont to cross over low mountains].
Let him besiege the [la]nd of the sea three times,
[Let him conquer Dilmun].
Let him go up [to] great Der and [ ].
... from my city Agade

(breaks off)

SARGON, KING OF BATTLE

This epic poem opens with Sargon fretful for battle. He convenes his warriors to tell them that he plans a campaign to a distant place, the name of which is lost, and speaks of a rebellion against his suzerainty there. In lines 8ff. a soldier attempts to dissuade him, arguing that the journey is arduous and life is comfortable where they are in his city, Agade.

In the meantime Nur-daggal, king of Burushhanda, a city in Anatolia, taunts Mesopotamian merchants resident in his kingdom because, as he believes, Sargon could never come to help them. The merchants, upset, send a delegation to Sargon, offering him rich booty in return for his campaign. Sargon's soldiers are disinclined to accept, but this is the opportunity that Sargon has been yearning for, so he launches a campaign.

The army traverses a wondrous forest. Nur-daggal, unaware of the advance, is confident that the Euphrates(?), not to mention the forest, will prove an impassable barrier, and his troops echo his confidence. No sooner has Nur-daggal spoken than Sargon bursts into the city, smites down his finest warriors, and demands his submission.

Nur-daggal's fabulous court is the scene of his humiliation. Sargon takes his seat and jeeringly parrots Nur-daggal's boasts. Nur-daggal, incredulous, confesses that some divine agency must have brought Sargon, then asks to be restored to his kingdom as a vassal. Sargon accepts and Nur-daggal offers tribute of exotic fruits never before seen in Mesopotamia. After three years in Burushhanda, Sargon departs.

[The king of battle, emiss]ary(?) of Ishtar, [who made firm?]
    the foundations(?) of the city Agade [   ], (1)
[Might]y one in battle, king of the campaign(?) [ ],
[Sargon   ] speaks of war!
Sargon, [mighty in battle], [   ] his fierce weapons.
The palace of Sargon [assembles], he says this wo[rd to them], (5)
"O my warriors! The land of [   ]
"[   ] thinks of war, (though) I made it submit [   ]."

[   ] brought [   ], Sargon was held in contempt [by   ].
"[O lord of a]ll daises, the road that ... [you wish] to travel
    [is a most difficult path], grievous to go.
"The Burushhanda road [that you wish to travel],
    is a road I worry about, (10)
"Did we ever [undertake such a] mission?
"(Here) we sit on chairs and have plenty of rest,
"Of a sudden [we set forth and] our arms have given out,
    and our knees become exhausted from traversing the road."

[Nur-daggal made] ready to speak,
    saying to the messenger of the merchants,
"[So where is Zababa], the campaigner who makes straight
    the way and spies out the regions of the earth? (15)
"[So where is the lord of a]ll daises,
    who [ ] from sunrise to sunset?"
[   ] the merchants vomited up (what was in)
    their stomachs, mixed with bile,
"In a storm [   ] ... and pluck the Kishite from Agade!
"We have invoked [Sargo]n, king of the universe:
    'Come down to us that we may receive strength,
        for we are no warriors. (20)
    'Let us be responsible equally for the [ ] ...
        of the king's journey,
    'Let the king be responsible for those who stand
        in battle with him,
    'Let the king [ ] impose (tribute) of gold, let Sargon's
        warriors give him a silver mine.'"

"[O] our [lord], we must go, outrages are being committed
     in the ... of your god, Zababa."
[After the] merchants assembled, they entered the palace.   (25)
After they entered [the palace], the warriors would not
     accept the [   ] of the merchants.
Sargon made ready to speak and said,
"[I am the] king of battle! The city Burushhanda which arose,
     let us(?) see its troops in campaign!
"[What is] its direction? Which is its mountain?
     What is the road?
     Which one is it that goes (there)?"
"[The road th]at you wish to travel is a most difficult path,
     grievous to go,   (30)
"[The road to Burushha]nda that you want to go,
     the road that I worry about, is a mission of seven(?) leagues."

[Sargon entered] the massive mountains,
     in which are chunks of lapis and gold,
[a]pricot tree, fig tree, boxwood, sycamore,
     evergreen(?) trees with seven cones,
[   ] let them strike *urtu*-plants — search
     for its crown seven leagues! — bramble,
[   ] all the [fruits?] which for seven leagues
     the trees cast down,   (35)
The border of the [   ] of the trees, sixty cubits, in all,
     seven leagues,
[   ] elevation, sixty cubits.

          (fragmentary lines, then gap)

"[   ] troops [   ]."

[these were] the words that they said.
Nur-da[ggal] made ready to speak
     and spoke to [his] war[riors], saying,   (40)
"[Sargo]n will not come as far as we are.
"Riverbank and high water will surely prevent him,

"The massive mountain will surely make a reed thicket,
   forest, grove(?), and woods hung about with tangles."
His warriors answered him, to Nur-daggal they said,
"Which are the kings, past or future, which king is he
   who has come here and will have seen our lands?" (45)
Nur-daggal had not spoken when Sargon surrounded his city
   and widened the gate two acres!
He cut through ... his ramparts and smote
   the most outstanding of the general's men!

[Sar]gon set up his throne in front of the city gate,
Sargon made ready to speak,
   [sa]ying to his warriors these words,
"Now then! Nur-daggal, favored of Enlil, (50)
"[Let them br]ing him in, let me see him submit!"

[With] the gem-studded [crown?] on his head,
   and lapis footstool at his feet,
With fifty-five attendants [he] sat before him.
Since he was seated on a throne of gold,
   the king was enthroned like a god.¹
[Wh]o is ... like the king? (55)
Nur-daggal was made to sit before Sargon.

Sargon made ready to speak, saying to Nur-daggal,
"Come, Nur-daggal, favored of Enlil, you said,
   'Sargon will not come as far as we are!
   'Riverbank and high water will surely prevent him. (60)
   'The massive mountain will surely make a reed thicket,
      forest, it will surely produce a grove(?),
      and a woods of tangles!'"
Nur-daggal made ready to speak, saying to Sargon,
"My lord, no doubt your gods lifted up(?)
   and brought your soldiers across.
"[   ] to cross the river.

---

1. Grammatically it is not clear whether Sargon or Nur-daggal is being described here.

"What lands could rival Agade? What king could rival you? (65)
"You have no adversary, you are their mighty opponent.
"Your opponents' hearts are seared,
"They are terrified, and left paralyzed with fear.
"Restore (to) them [city], field, and lea,
    the lord (to be your) ally in charge of it."

"[We have ...] to his place and come around to it, (70)
"Its fruit let him render: apricot, fig, medlar, grape,
"[ ], pistachio, olive, as never before.
"Never need we come around to it again,
    let him render [its fruit].
"May the city be at peace, may I fetch fine things."
In going [the path] and staying, who (ever) followed Sargon? (75)
He withdraws from the city,
Three years [in the city] he has stayed.

(The End)

Legend of Naram-Sin

Naram-Sin (ca. 2254-2218 B.C.), grandson of Sargon, was the subject of a richly embroidered literary tradition. Although a successful warrior king, he was portrayed in later times as a luckless sovereign nearly overwhelmed by uncanny disasters.

This text takes the form of a fictitious stela, beginning with a self-introduction of the king, turning to the autobiographical narrative, and concluding with blessings on the reader who heeds its words. It relates how a supernatural host devastated Naram-Sin's armies and land. While the story is based on a series of battles Naram-Sin fought against coalitions of foreign and Mesopotamian enemies, the events are here fictionalized and presented as a divine judgment against an arrogant and impetuous king who fails to heed unfavorable omens.

The principal message of this text is that kings who carry out projects in the face of unfavorable omens are doomed to catastrophe. This renders more specific the general caution of Mesopotamian proverbs, prophecies, and oracles that deal with self-preservation of the king, and stresses the importance of divination, especially extispicy, for important decisions. This text combines the cautious, even pessimistic approach of wisdom literature with a theme more common in poetry: affirmation that man's highest duty is to transmit knowledge and experience to the future.

[Open the foundation box] and read well the stela (1)
[That I, Naram-Sin], son of Sargon,
[Have written for] all time.
[Enmerkar? ruled the land], then passed away,
[My father ruled the land], then passed away, (5)
[I became r]uler of the land.
[When the years] passed,
[When the   ] came,
[Ishtar chan]ged her mind,
[Against ... she ...-ed] and rode. (10)
[I inquired of the] great [gods]:
[Ishtar, Ilaba?], Zababa, Annunitum,
[Shullat, Hanish, Shamash] the warrior.
[I summoned] and charged [the diviners].
[Seven upon seven extispicies I] made, (15)
[I set up ho]ly reed altars.

[The diviners spoke to me thus]:
"[ ] the 'thread' [   ]¹
"[ ] the 'mark' [   ]
"[   ] (20)
"[ ] you [ ] ... yourself,
"Until [the host?] of the great gods."
Enmerkar [the king?]² the judgment ... which Shamash
    [gave him] —
The judgment for him, the decision (binding on) his ghost,
    the ghosts of [his children],
The ghosts of his family, the ghosts of his descendants —
    (the judgment of) Shamash [the warrior] — (25)
The Lord of Above and Below, the lord of the Anunna-gods,
    lord of the ghosts (of the dead),
Who drink muddy water and drink no clear water —
(Enmerkar) whose wisdom and weaponry captured,
    defeated, and killed that host,
Did not write (that judgment) upon a stela, nor leave (it) for me,
Nor did he publish his name, so I did not bless him. (30)
Troops with bodies of "cave birds," humans with raven faces
Did the great gods create.
In the earth which the gods made was its ...,
Tiamat suckled them,³
Belet-ili their mother made (them) fair. (35)
Inside the mountain(s) they grew up, became adults,
    got their stature.
Seven kings they were, allies, glorious in form,
360,000 were their troops.
Anu-banini⁴ their father was king; their mother was named Melili,
Their eldest brother, their vanguard, was named Memandah, (40)

---

1. Technical terms of divination.
2. Enmerkar, a Sumerian ruler of the first dynasty of Uruk (early third millennium B.C.), was the subject of several Sumerian epic poems. Why Naram-Sin cites Enmerkar is unclear, nor is any story now known wherein he triumphs over an enemy host.
3. Compare Tiamat's role as creatress of monsters in the Epic of Creation.
4. This is the name of a historical personage who may have lived about the time of Naram-Sin of Agade. The other names are unknown and presumably imaginary.

Their second brother was named Midudu,
Their third brother was named [ ]pish,
Their fourth brother was named Tartadada,
Their fifth brother was named Baldahdah,
Their sixth brother was named Ahubandih, (45)
Their seventh brother was named Harzishakidu.
They rode against the shining mountains,
A soldier seized them, they smote their thighs (in frustration).
At the beginning of their incursion,
    when they invaded Burushandar,[1]
The entire region of Burushandar was destroyed, (50)
Pulu was destroyed,
Puramu was destroyed.
"Should I go out beyond Nashhuhuhhu [ ]?[2]
"Should I strike out(?) into the midst of that host
    whose camp is Shubat-Enlil?"[3]
Then they s[ettled down] inside Subartu,[4] (55)
They destroyed the (upper?) Sealands[5] and invaded Gutium,[6]
They destroyed Gutium and invaded Elam,[7]
They destroyed Elam and arrived at the seacoast,
They killed the people of the (sea) crossing,[8]
    they were thrown to [ ],
Dilmun, Magan, Meluhha,
    whatever is in the midst of the sea they killed.[9] (60)
Seventeen kings with 90,000 troops
Came with them to support them!

1. An echo of Burushhanda, a wealthy commercial city in south central Anatolia.
2. All unknown, and presumably fabulous or corrupted toponyms.
3. Shubat-Enlil, modern Tell Leilan in the Habur region, was an important city at the end of the third millennium B.C.
4. Subartu, as used here, was a traditional name for northern Mesopotamia.
5. I take this to refer to the "Upper Sea," a vague term that at different times may refer to the Mediterranean, the Black Sea, and perhaps Lake Van.
6. As used here, a traditional term for the mountainous regions east and northeast of Mesopotamia.
7. Southwest Iran.
8. May refer to peoples whose abodes could only be reached by a sea voyage, that is, the lands mentioned in line 60.
9. In the third millennium, Bahrain, Oman/Makran, and the Indus Valley respectively.

I summoned a soldier and charged him,
"I [give you a lance] and a pin,
"Touch them with the lance, [prick them] with the pin. (65)
"If [blood] comes out, they are human like us.
"If no blood comes out, then they are spirits, ill fate,
"Phantoms, evil demons, handiwork of Enlil."
The soldier brought back his report [to me],
"I touched them with [the lance], (70)
"I pricked them with [the pin], and blood came out."
I summoned the diviners and charged them,
[Seven] upon seven extispicies I performed,
[I set up] holy reed altars,
I inquired of the great gods (75)
Ishtar, Ilaba(?), Zababa, Annunitum,
Sh[ullat, Hanish], Shamash the warrior.
The breath of the great gods, the spirit did not allow me to go.
Speaking to myself, thus I said,
"What lion observed divination? (80)
"What wolf consulted a dream interpreter?
"I will go, as I like, like a brigand,
"And the (very) lance of Ninurta I will grasp!"[1]
When the following year had come,
I sent out 120,000 troops against them, not one returned alive. (85)
When the second year arrived, I sent out 90,000 troops
    against them, not one returned alive.
When the third year arrived, I sent out 60,700 troops against
    them, not one returned alive.
I was confounded, bewildered, at a loss, anxious, in despair.
Speaking to myself, thus I said,
"What have I left for a reign? (90)
"I am a king who brings no well-being to his land,
"A shepherd who brings no well-being to his flock.
"How shall I place myself that I may proceed effectively?

---

1. The significance of the "lance of Ninurta" is unclear; perhaps a term for "taking the bull by the horns."

'Fear of lions, death, plague, convulsions,
'Panic, ague, economic collapse, starvation, (95)
'Want, anxiety of every kind came down upon them.
'Above, in [the earth?], there was a deluge,
'Below, in [the netherworld?],
    there was [an earthquake?].'"
Ea, lord of the city [of that host?],
Spoke to the [gods his brethren] and said, (100)
"O great gods [   ],
"You told me [to make this host],
"And the dirt [of my finger nails?] you [spat on?]."[1]
When New Year of the fourth year arrived,
At the prayer to Ea, [sage] of the great gods, (105)
[When I offered] the holy offerings of New Year,
I [received] the holy instructions.
I summoned the diviners and [charged them],
Seven upon seven extispicies I performed.
I set up holy reed altars, (110)
I inquired of the great gods
Ishtar, Ilaba(?), Zababa, Annunitum,
[Shullat and Hanish, Shamash the warrior].
The [diviners spoke to m]e [thus],
  "[ ] will bear [   ] (115)
  "[ ] will be [   ]
  "[ ] you have [   ]
  "[ ] sent down ... [   ]
  "[ ] blood [   ]."
From their midst twelve troops flew off from me, (120)
I went after them in haste and hurry [ ],
I overcame those troops,
I brought those troops back [   ].
Speaking to myself, [thus I said],
"Without divination (of liver), flesh, and entr[ails],
    [I will not] lay [hand on them to kill?]." (125)

1. The enemy host was formed from the dirt of his fingernails, then, perhaps, given life by divine spittle.

[I performed] an extispicy concerning them:
The breath of the great gods [ordered] mercy for them.
The shining Morning Star spoke from heaven thus,
"To Naram-Sin, son of Sargon:
"Cease, you shall not destroy the perditious seed! (130)
"In future days Enlil will raise them up for evil.
"It (the host) awaits the angry heart of Enlil,
"O city! Those troops will be killed,
"They will burn and besiege dwelling places!
"O city! They will pour out their blood! (135)
"The earth will diminish its harvests,
    the date palms their yield.
"O city! Those troops will die!
"City against city, house against house will turn.
"Father to father, brother to brother,
"Man to man, companion to friend, (140)
"None will tell the truth to each other.
"People will teach untruth, strange things [will they learn].
"This hostile city they will kill,
"That hostile city (another) hostile city will capture.
"Ten quarts of barley will cost a mina of silver, (145)
"No strong king ... will have been in the land."
To the great gods I brought (the captives) as tribute,
I did not lay hand on them to kill.
Whoever you may be, governor, prince, or anyone else,
Whom the gods shall name to exercise kingship, (150)
I have made a foundation box for you,
    I have written you a stela,
In Cutha in the Emeslam,
In the cella of Nergal have I left it for you.
Behold this stele,
Listen to the wording of this stela: (155)
You should not be confounded,
    you should not be bewildered,
You should not be afraid, you should not tremble,
Your stance should be firm.
You should do your task in your wife's embrace.

Make your walls trustworthy, (160)
Fill your moats with water.
Your coffers, your grain, your silver,
    your goods and chattels
[ ] bring into your fortified city.
Gird on your weapons, (but) stay out of sight,
Restrain your valor, take care of your person. (165)
Though he raids your land, go not out against him,
Though he carries off(?) your livestock, go not nigh him,
Though he eats the flesh of your soldiery(?),
Though he murders [   ],
Be moderate, control yourself, (170)
Answer them, "Yes, my lord!"
To their wickedness, repay kindness,
To kindness (add) gifts and gratifications.
You should not trespass against them.
Let expert scholars tell you my stela. (175)
You who have read the stela and placed yourself that you
    can proceed effectively,
You (who?) have blessed me, so may a future one bless you.

Tukulti-Ninurta Epic

Tukulti-Ninurta I, a tragic and fascinating Assyrian king of the thirteenth century B.C., began his reign with significant conquests, including parts of northern Syria, Anatolia, and Babylonia. In Babylon he ruled as king for seven years. Royal agents included scholarly and literary manuscripts among the booty brought back from Babylonia. These may have stimulated literary activity in Assyria and provided writers with new themes and language.

The epic of Tukulti-Ninurta is the product of a mature and learned master steeped both in Babylonian and Assyrian tradition. The text presents a distinctive, turgid splendor of language, with rare words and convoluted syntax. The idioms of treaties and diplomacy, penitential psalms and laments, heroic tales, hymnography, and commemorative inscriptions are freely used. Close to the troubled monarch was a brilliant scholar and poet whose work appealed to his taste.

As part of his booty, Tukulti-Ninurta brought the statue of Marduk from his temple in Babylon to Assur. The image remained in Assur for a century, to the Babylonians a maddening symbol of their political and military impotence. Furthermore, large numbers of Babylonians and Kassites were resettled in Assyria. The extent to which the king and his scholar attempted to cultivate Babylonian ways and religion at Assur is unknown. Marduk's image was treated with respect. Discontent with the influx of Babylonian ideas into Assyria may have contributed to Tukulti-Ninurta's downfall.

Having reached the natural limits of his conquests early in his reign, Tukulti-Ninurta turned his formidable energies to a massive, even frenetic building campaign. After living in the "Old Palace" at Assur, he reconstructed a palace built by his father, Shalmaneser I. Soon thereafter he cleared a large residential area and built yet another palace with walls to connect it to the fortified sector of the city. Hardly was this done when he began to build a whole new city, Kar-Tukulti-Ninurta, across the Tigris and thus isolated from the traditional capital of the land. There he seems to have shut himself up in suspicion of all around him.

The king's outrageous demands on his subjects for building enterprises opened the way for a successful conspiracy against him led by his own son. Tukulti-Ninurta was seized and murdered in his new palace.

(Praises of the god Assur and of the king, Tukulti-Ninurta)

Listen to his praise, the praises of the king of [ ] lords, (1)
I ex[tol] the [ ] of lord of the world, the Assyrian Enlil,
Let his mighty power, his [ ] be spoken of,
[Hear] how great his weapons were over his enemies!
I extol and praise Assur, king of [the gods], (5)
The great kings also [ ]
Whom [he ...] in the campaign against Kadm[uhi],
And (whom) by command of the w[arrior] Shamash [he ...],
Aside from the forty kings of [Nairi]
Whom, in his reign [ ] (10)
The triumph of his lordship [ ]

(gap)

(Introduction of the protagonist: the valiant Tukulti-Ninurta [in the broken section] and his antagonist, the treacherous Kashtiliash [as the text becomes intelligible]. The Babylonian gods become angry with Kashtiliash and forsake his sanctuaries, a sign of impending doom. After a gap in the text, there is a fragmentary hymn to Tukulti-Ninurta, with allusions to his birth and upbringing. In line 25 Kashtiliash is referred to again. He disdains his sworn treaty [of friendship and non-aggression?] and plots war.)

[ ] against enemies [ ]
[ ] [ ]
[ ] no(?) surviving [ ]
[ ] which cannot be faced [ ] (15)
[ ] the wicked [ ]
[ ] and the disobedient [ ]
[ ] ... [ ]
[the dis]obedient [ ]
[ ] command [ ] (20)

(gap)

[ ] and [ ]
[ ] to transgress [ ]
[ ] ... [ ]
[ ] ... light [ ]
[ ] the end of the reign of [ ] (25)

[w]arrior of heaven and netherworld.
[   ] which he took by force [   ]
[   ] the land which he ruled [   ]
[   ] ... [   ]
[   ] Ishtar, the high point of the land of Akkad [   ]   (30)
[fr]om(?) lordship the king of the Kassites
[guilt] which cannot be expunged.
[The gods became angry at] the king of the Kassite's betrayal
    of the emblem [of Shamash],
Against the transgressor of an oath, Kashtiliash, the gods
    of heaven and netherworld [   ].
They were [angry] at the king, the land, and the people [ ],   (35)
They [were furious and with] the willful one,
    their shepherd.
His lordship, the lord of the world,[1]
    became disturbed, so he [forsook] Nippur,
He would not approach [ ] (his) seat at Dur-Kurigalzu.
Marduk abandoned his sublime sanctuary, the city [Babylon],
He cursed his favorite city Kar-[   ].   (40)
Sin left Ur, [his] holy place [   ],
Sh[amash became angry] with Sippar and Larsa,
Ea [ ] Eridu, the house of wisdom [   ],
Ishtaran became furious w[ith Der   ],
Annunitum would not approach Agade [   ],   (45)
The lady of Uruk cast [off her   ]:
(All) the gods were enraged [   ]
[ ] on account of the verdict [   ]

                (gap)

[   ] his ..., Assur.
[   ] the gods, lord of judgment,   (50)
[   ] he has none to calm him,
[   ] bears him
[   ] he made light of the oath of the gods!
[   ] ... defeat,

---

1. Enlil.

[Who obeys] the gods' intents on the battlefield, (55)
[   ] he made the weapons glorious.
Glorious is his heroism,
    it [ ] the dis[respectful] front and rear,
Incendiary is his onrush,
    it burns the disobedient right and left.
His radiance is terrifying; it overwhelms all foes,
Every pious king of the four world regions
    stands in awe of him. (60)
When he bellows like thunder, mountains totter,
And when he brandishes his weapon like Ninurta,[1]
    all regions of the earth everywhere hover in panic.
Through the destiny of Nudimmud, he is reckoned as flesh
    godly in his limbs,[2]
By fiat of the lord of the world, he was cast sublimely
    from the womb of the gods.
It is he who is the eternal image of Enlil, attentive to the
    people's voice, the counsel of the land, (65)
Because the lord of the world appointed him to
    lead the troops, he praised him with his very lips,
Enlil exalted him as if he (Enlil) were his (Tukulti-Ninurta's)
    own father, right after his firstborn son![3]
Precious is he in (Enlil's) family, for where there is
    competition, he has of him protection.
No one of all kings was ever rival to him,
No sovereign stood forth as his battlefield opponent. (70)
[   ] falsehood, crime, repression, wrong-doing,
[   ] the weighty ... the divine oath and went
    back on what he swore.
[   ] the gods were watching his furtive deed,
[   ] though he was their follower.
[   ] the king of the Kassites made light of what he swore, (75)
He committed a crime, an act of malice.

---

1. An oblique reference to the king's name.
2. Nudimmud was a name for Ea as creator.
3. That is, the god Ninurta.

[Although the one] ... kept changing [   ],
    (the other's) word is sure,
[Although the one ...], (the other) is one who pleas
    for divine mercy always.
[   ] and shall not be expunged.
[   ] ... offenses were numerous. (80)
[   ] he turned back on a command
[   ] he spoke hostility
[   ] put his trust in ...
[   ] he longed for battle
[   ] stratagem (85)

(gap)

(The Assyrians capture Babylonian merchants, who were evidently spying in Assyria, and bring them before the king. He spares them out of respect for international custom. In a prayer to Shamash, god of justice, the king states that he has been faithful to the treaty, explains how it was made, reminds the god that he oversees sworn treaties, and calls on him for a favorable outcome in his contest with the evildoer. In lines 109ff. Tukulti-Ninurta sends a message to Kashtiliash, reminding him of the long history of relations between their two lands, and charging him with violation of the treaty. The letter may have ended on a conciliatory note, offering the opportunity for reaffirmation of the oath despite the Kassite's willful violation of it.)

Within the confines of the land of [Assyria   ] he imposed an
    ordinance, lest any secret [of the land?] go out.
They came [   ] very much ...
Those who bore the in[signia?] of the king of the Kassites,
    merchants were captured at night(?),
They brought [them] before Tukulti-Ninurta,
    lord of all peoples, bound together.
The king gathered(?) [them] in the place of Shamash,
    he perpetrated no infamy, (90)
(But) he sustained them,
    he did a good deed for the lord of Babylon:
He released the merchants ..., bearers of money bags,

He had them stand before Shamash and anointed
 their heads with oil.¹
The tablets(?) of the king of the Kassites, the seal
 impression which he had made official,²
He reconfirmed(?), before Shamash he [ ], his utterance
 he presented in measured words to the god, (95)
"O Shamash, [ ] lord, I respected(?) your oath,
 I feared your greatness.
"He who does not [ ] transgressed before your [ ],
 but I observed your ordinance.
"When our fathers made a pact before your divinity,
"They swore an oath between them
 and invoked your greatness.
"You are the hero, the valiant one, who from of old
 was unalterable judge of our fathers, (100)
"And you are the god who sets aright,
 who sees now our loyalty.
"Why has the king of the Kassites from of old invalidated
 your plan and your ordinance?
"He had no fear of your oath, he transgressed your
 command, he schemed an act of malice.
"He has made his crimes enormous before you,
 judge me, O Shamash!
"But he who committed no crime [against] the king
 of the Kassites, [act favorably towards him], (105)
"By your great [ ] bestow the victory ...
 on the observer of oaths,
"[He who does not] your command,
 obliterate his people in the rout of battle!"
[The wi]se [shepherd], who knows what should be done,
 waxed wroth, [his frigh]tening brilliance
 became enraged.

---

1. A ceremony of release.
2. Probably refers to official letters given by the king to the merchants as bonafide commercial agents. If the men acted as spies, this was presumably a violation of "commercial immunity," but Tukulti-Ninurta is careful to protect them as merchants, despite their questionable status.

He sent a message [to Kashtili]ash the wicked,
    the obstinate, the heedless,
"[Whereas] formerly you [forswore] what belonged
    to the time of our forefathers' hostilities,   (110)
"[Now] you face Shamash with false testimony about us.
"[Enlil-nera]ri, my forefather, king of all peoples, ... [ ]
"[Against? Kur]igalzu, (he) pursued
    the oath of the gods, [   ]
"[Adad-n]erari, my grandfather, [   ]
"[ ] Nazimaruttash [ ] in battle [   ]   (115)
"[ ] Shalmaneser, perceiver of his princeship, [   ]
"[ ] the lives of their [   ] ...
"[   ] ...
"[ ] ... [   ]
"[ ] among all lands he is the unalterable judge,   (120)

              (gap)

(The Babylonian king replies insolently to Tukulti-Ninurta's letter, while preventing the Assyrian messenger from returning, a diplomatic snub of the time. After a gap of uncertain size, in lines 129-134 Kashtiliash is threatening Tukulti-Ninurta, and, beginning in line 135, Tukulti-Ninurta replies in righteous wrath.)

[   ] the land
[e]nemies
[   ] he sent a [mes]sage
[   ] he had decided upon a good deed,
[   ] he affirmed the compact.   (125)
[Kashtiliash said, "...] your good deed!
    Detain the messenger (here)!
"[   ] don't let the [merchan]ts cross!
"[   ] take away!

              (gap)

"[Against] your camp ... like a thunderstorm [   ]
"[ ] like a flood that spares no [   ]   (130)
"[ ] your valiant warriors like [   ]
"[ ] the mighty onslaught of the Kas[site] army

"[   ] every stratagem in the onslaught of battle [   ],
"[   ] your warriors on an [ill-fated] day [   ]!"
[The king], the wise shepherd,
    [who knows] what should be done, [   ],   (135)
[To Kashtilia]sh, the wicked, the obstinate,
    king of the Kassites [   ],
"[The ...], Kashtiliash, of your forefathers you [   ],
"[   ] in the unp[lundered?] sanctuaries,
"[   ] my [   ], to set straight [   ]
"[   ] your warriors who [   ] combat   (140)
"[   ] of my land which you plundered [   ],
"[   ] the troops that you made off with [   ],

(Tukulti-Ninurta exchanges letters with Kashtiliash and indicts him for his misdeeds. Tukulti-Ninurta calls upon Shamash to resolve their differences and to vindicate his adherence to the treaty by making him victorious in trial by battle. Kashtiliash is paralyzed with fear at the prospect and offers a soliloquy on his impending doom. After a gap in the text, Tukulti-Ninurta invades Babylonia and the doomed and desperate Kassite goes berserk.)

"And the borders of your territories [   ],
"Why did you retreat and [   ] the road from which there
    is no escape?
"And why are you turning afraid,
    and ... without engagement [   ]?   (145)
"You have plundered my whole land, [   ] pillage,
"You have made away with the armies of Assur,
    before hostilities even, you have [   ].
"The [   ] have steadily cast down in untimely death,
"Their [wives] are become widows in undue season.
"I raise aloft, therefore, the tablet of oath between us, and
    call upon the Lord of Heaven [   ]!   (150)
"You have showed forth a crime that [   ] us both to
    the battlefield,
"Saying: 'I released your father(?), I took no revenge.'

"That you have plundered my unarmed people
    is an offense to us[1] forever!
"When we face one another in battle, let the judgment
    between us be ... [ ].
"We shall meet that day just as a righteous man plunders
    the [ ] of a thief.   (155)
"Reconciliation cannot be made without conflict [ ],
"Nor can there be good relations without a battle,
    so long as you do not [ ].
"(And) until I expose your hair fluttering behind you[2] and
    you have [disappeared] to an untimely death,
"Until my eyes, in the battle with you, shall see ...,
    slaughter, and ...,
"So come to me in the battle of servants (of the gods?),
    let us get to the bottom of the matter together!   (160)
"From this festival of battle may the transgressor of oath not
    away, may they cast away(?) his corpse!"
Tukulti-Ninurta, having put his trust in his observance
    of the oath, was planning for battle,
While Kashtiliash, insofar as he had trespassed the command
    of the gods, was altered within himself,
He was appalled on account of the appeal to Shamash
    and became fearful and anxious
    about what was laid before the gods.
The mighty king's utterance constricted his body
    like a demonic presence.   (165)
So Kashtiliash deliberated with himself, "I did not listen to
    what the Assyrian (said),
    I made light of the messenger.
"I did not conciliate him, I did not accept his favorable
    intention before.
"Now I understand how grievous the crimes of my land are
    become, how numerous its sins.

---

1. "Us" may refer to Tukulti-Ninurta and the Assyrian people.
2. That is, in flight.

"Mortal punishments have smitten me down,
    death has me in its grip!
"The oath of Shamash sets upon(?) me,
    it catches me by the hem, (170)
"You have entered in evidence against me an unalterable
    tablet with the seal impression of m[y forefather]s,
"They too have intro[duced evidence] before me,
    a [ ] whose wording cannot be changed!
"My forefathers' treaty, which was not violated, [ ]
"Thus did the just judge, the unalterable, the valiant one,
    [Shamash] establish the case against me!
"As for the plundering which my forefathers did,
    I [have made it worse]! (175)
"For it is I, indeed, who have put my people into a pitiless
    hand, a grasp [from which there is no escape].
"Into a narrow strait with no way out
    I have gathered [my land].
"Many are my wrong-doings before Shamash,
    [great are] my misdeeds,
"Who is the god that will spare my people
    from [catastrophe]?
"The Assyrian is ever heedful of all the gods [ ] (180)
"He ... the lords of our oath,
    ... of heaven and netherworld,
"I shall not examine in the extispicy
    (the signs for) "fa[ll of the regime],"
"The omens for well-being of my army
    are [gone] from my land,
"The signs within the [ ] are ...
"The security of my house's foundation [ ] was never firm. (185)
"Whatever my dream(s), they are terrifying [ ]
"Omnipotent Assur glowers at me [ ]!"
This too: "Quickly, let me cast: [ ]
"To what shall I [ ] my omen?"
This too: "Let me know: For ba[ttle] (190)
"How long [ ]?
"... [ ]

"Let me learn the secret [   ]
"Will he overcome me and [   ]?
"Like an inferno or a cyclone [   ]?   (195)
"He has closed in on me and [   ],
"So death [   ]!"
He was exhausted [   ]

(gap)

[   ] he entered, and the city Akka[d   ]
And like a thunderstorm against the creatures of [... he ...]   (200)
[As for] Kashtiliash, king of the Kassites,
    who had yearned [for battle],
And whose fondest hopes were ecstatic at comb[at   ],
He jumped from his chair and [   ] his table.
He twitched, he flung away the meat, he [   ],
He discarded his royal adornment in [   ].   (205)
He could not swallow a bite [   ].
The dining tray was not ... where he arose [   ],
The seats of his palace, which used to be firm(?) [   ].
He mounted his chariot and harangued the hor[de?   ],
He said to his army, "I fought with [   ]!"   (210)
The king of the Kassites rushed hither and yon like a [   ],
He sought all over the groves [for a place to hide   ],
He went away then turned back, with [   ].
He fled as if he were quarry, like a [   ].
No fervor raised he, with the [   ],   (215)
Nor could he [   ] his victory(?) against Annunitu.
He did not look behind him, [nor] over his soldiers [did he ...]
[Nor] over his own offspring, the creation of [   ]
Kashtiliash, like one in [   ]
The dust of death [   ]   (220)

(Despite his doom, the obstinate Kashtiliash refuses to yield, and seeks to evade Tukulti-Ninurta's advance. Kashtiliash prefers guerilla tactics to a direct confrontation. Tukulti-Ninurta challenges him to a fight, but Kashtiliash stalls, hoping for a change of fortune. An indecisive battle is fought, apparently when Kashtiliash tries to surprise the Assyrians.)

[ ] with the point of his ar[row   ]
Which he sent off [   ]
The king of the Kassites did not trust ... [   ]
He summoned against him [   ]
He rained down upon him [   ]   (225)
Kashtiliash went out [   ]
"Surely our lord's treaty ... [   ]
"He will not leave the innermost [   ]
"Until he catches him alive [   ]."
They carried off the king [   ]   (230)
And the hero of his warriors [   ]
He would not submit(?) to Tukulti-Ninurta [   ]
Nor before his warriors did he [   ]
Where the weapon of Assur joins [battle   ]
The river banks were trampled, the cities [   ]   (235)
The king overcame the city [   ]
He turned to Annunitu [   ]
He became lord of the distant city
     which [   ] had never [   ]
He reckoned the land for devas[tation   ]
The king set to [   ]   (240)
He established for many a distant league [   ]
He dammed up the conflu[ence   ]
He repaired the paths [   ]
He overcame the city(?) [   ]

(gap)

Another time he ... [   ]   (245)
But he did not submit before Tukulti-Ninurta [   ]
Nor would he face him [in battle   ]
Another time he ... [   ]
He was drawn up in [   ]
He decided(?) [   ]   (250)
Tukulti-Ninurta ordered [   ]
A messenger to Kashtiliash to [   ]
"How much longer is [your army] to flee?
"You keep changing your army around by command [   ]."

Saying, "For what day are you keeping
   the [weapons] of combat [ ]?   (255)
"And which of your weapons stands by for which day?"
Saying, "I am stationed in your land, [I] cult center,
"I plundered all the cities you had and [ ] your people!"
Saying, "When will your usual insolence
   [provoke you] to battle?
"The fury and slaughter you wanted so much
   we will soon show!   (260)
"Surely now you have courage, for the month of the spring
   flood, the water will be your ally.
"And you have pitched your camp in remote places,
   trusting in G[irra],[1]
"But in the dry season, when the peak flood ends,
   and the god ... with fire,
"In what remote place will you trust to save your people?
"My army is camped not many leagues from you,   (265)
"And as for you, all your chariotry is in readiness and
   your army is massed.
"Attack me, then, like a brave man,
   fight the battle that you strive so hard to attain!
"Show your weapon, find release in the battle
   that your fondest hopes burned for!"
Kashtiliash gave the command for battle,
   but was anxious and agitated,
Saying, "Tukulti-Ninurta, your army should stand fast
   until the appointed time of Shamash arrives.   (270)
"Do not begin your fighting until the right season to fight me!"
Saying, "This is the day your people's blood will soak the
   the pastures and meadows,
"And, like a thunderstorm, I will make the levelling flood
   pass over your camp."
He dragged out the message-sending as a ruse
   until he could draw up his warriors,

---

1. The heat?

And until he had made ready his battle plan,
    the chariotry was held back. (275)
Then he despatched his army,
    but Girra held it back like a serious mutiny.
He brought his army across secret hideouts,
    blocking the crossing.
The valiant warriors of [Assur] espied the Kassite king's
    preparations,
They did not have their armor on, but sprang forward like lions,
Assur's unrivalled weapon met the onslaught of [his] ar[my?] (280)
And Tukulti-Ninurta, the raging, pitiless storm,
    made [their blood] flow.
The warriors of Assur [struck] the king of the Kassites
    like a serpent,
A mighty attack, an irresistible onslaught [ ] upon them.
Kashtiliash turned his [face] to save himself.
The weapon of Enlil, lord of the world,
    which hems in enemies, shattered [his troops], (285)
The ... of battle, his allies were slaughtered like cattle,
    [his] nobles [ ]
Governors perished, warriors [ ]
    [ ] the forefinger of the lord of the world.

(gap)

(After Kashtiliash's flight, the Assyrian troops urge their king to a decisive encounter, no matter what the cost to them. In lines 311ff. the major battle is fought at last. Kashtiliash is defeated, but any account of his fate is lost in a gap in the text. According to an inscription of Tukulti-Ninurta, Kashtiliash was captured and brought to Assur: "(I) trod with my feet upon his lordly neck.")

The k[in]g ... [ ]
His warriors ... [ ] (290)
"My lord, since the beginning of your reign [ ],
"Battle and hardship have been our holiday and plea[sure].
"You urge us to prepare for the melee [ ],
"With the propitious sign of your lordship
    let us proceed like men!

"In your royal reign no king has stood equal to you, (295)
"Your exalted power has been set over the whole world,
    the seas, and the mountains.
"With the wrath of your scepter you have made to submit
    all regions, in all quarters,
"You spread the might of your land to territories
    beyond count, you established (their) boundaries.
"Kings know your valor and live in fear of battle with you.
"They bear your frightfulness like slander and falsehood
    homing in on the source.[1] (300)
"Now plan against the king of the Kassites,
    destroy his forces before the season!
"Rout the ranks he has set up, burn(?) his chariotry!
"For how much longer in the future
    is he to plot this evil against us?
"Plotting basely against us, he plans murder by wont.
"Daily he hopes to destroy the land of Assur, his threatening
    finger is stretched out towards it. (305)
"He strives constantly to take control of
    the Assyrians' kingship.
"Let us join battle, let him live to draw breath who advances,
    let him die who turns back! (You say),
"'While I was at peace he ended our friendly relations(?),'
    so proceed with the battle!
"[ ], when they encouraged you before on the battlefield.
"And you will gain, our Lord, by command of Shamash,
    a victorious name over the king of the Kassites!" (310)
The lines of battle were drawn up,
    combat was joined on the battlefield.
There was a great commotion,
    the troops were quivering among them.
Assur went first, the conflagration of defeat burst out
    upon the enemy,
Enlil was whirling(?) in the midst of the foe, fanning the blaze,

---

1. I take this line to mean that just as lies come home to roost on the liar, so too the king's frightfulness cannot be avoided by those lesser kings; in fact, it sticks to them like some evil that they richly deserve.

Anu set a pitiless mace to the opponent, (315)
Sin, the luminary, laid upon them the tension of battle.
Adad, the hero, made wind and flood pour down
    over their fighting,
Shamash, lord of judgment, blinded the eyesight of the army
    of Sumer and Akkad,
Valiant Ninurta, vanguard of the gods,
    smashed their weapons,
Ishtar flailed her jump rope, driving their warriors berserk! (320)
Behind the gods, his allies, the king at the head of the army
    sets to battle,
He let fly an arrow, the fierce, overwhelming,
    crushing weapon of Assur, he felled one slain.
The warriors of Assur cried, "To battle!"
    as they went to face death,
They gave the battle cry, "O Ishtar, spare (me)!"
    and praise the mistress in the fray,
They are furious, raging, taking forms strange as Anzu. (325)
They charge forward furiously to the fray
    without any armor,
They had stripped off their breastplates,
    discarded their clothing,
They tied up their hair and polished(?) their ... weapons,
The fierce, heroic men danced with sharpened weapons.
They blasted at one another like struggling lions,
    with eyes aflash(?), (330)
While the fray, particles drawn in a whirlwind,
    swirled around in combat.
Death, as if on a day of thirsting,
    slakes itself at the sight of the warrior.
    [   ] furiously he attacked and turned north,

(gap)

(The victorious Assyrians plunder Babylonia, including prisoners and treasures. Tukulti-Ninurta plunders collections of cuneiform tablets and brings them back to Assyria. He lavishly adorns temples there and in his royal city, Kar-Tukulti-Ninurta. In the concluding lines the poet praises the king.)

[   ] the population of the cities.
[   ] his [off]spring, the offspring of [   ] (335)
[   ] the throne, the boundary stone [   ]
[   ] daughters of princes, dwelling in [   ]
[   ] their infants, sons and daughters.
[   ] the enclosure of which ... for leagues,
[   ] the treasure of [ ] he plundered.[1] (340)
[   ] innumerable subjects
[he di]d seven times in excess
[   ] he took special care for their lives
[   ] who could pile up their [   ]?
[   ] a trustworthy house. (345)
[so]ldiers, number of chariots,
[   ] the treasure of(?) the king of the Kassites,
[fr]om report of(?) the battle
[   ] scepter
[   ] of the land (350)
[   ] war vehicles

(gap)

Treasure [   ],
Tablets of [   ],
Scribal lore [   ],
Exorcistic texts [   ], (355)
Prayers to appease the gods [   ],
Divination texts ... the ominous marks(?)
    of heaven and earth,
Medical texts, procedure for bandaging [   ],
The muster lists of his ancestors [   ],
Records of(?) ... slaves(?), overseers(?), and soldiers [   ]: (360)
Not one was left in the land of Sumer and Akkad!
The rich haul of the Kassite king's treasure [   ]
He filled boats with the yields for Assur [   ]
And the glory of his power was seen [   ]
[To] his victorious power the gods, lords [of   ] (365)

---

1. A late Babylonian chronicle states that Tukulti-Ninurta took booty from Esagila, carried off the cult statue of Marduk, installed a governor, and ruled as king in Babylon for seven years.

[To] the great gods he bestowed fine [   ]
Gold and silver were [not] precious in his sight,
He dedicated [ ] to the gods of his land.
He decorated [Ehur]sag-kurkurra[1] with [   ],
[He Ekurm]esharra,[2] dwelling of Enlil of the Assyrians,   (370)
[   ] of the city Baltil[3] with pure red gold,
[He the san]ctuary of the Igigi-gods,
[   ] jewelry of fine [gold].
[   ] he praises his god As[sur   ],
Assur, who established him
    [for king]ship of his land [   ].   (375)
Adad [   ] the [   ] of his weapons,
[   ] which he rendered him [   ] greatly,
[   ] the weapons which he ... [   ]
[the oa]th which Tukulti-Ninurta [sw]ore
    after Shamash [   ].
Let me [   ] the designs of the gods,   (380)
[   ] let me set the [   ] of the gods in the mouth
    of the people!
[   ] to the lyre bearer let me [   ]
[   ] ... of the gods, the people who [   ]
Let me proclaim his companion [   ]
[ ] established like heaven and earth till [remotest] days.   (385)
[The gods?] of Sumer and Akkad whose ... he praised,
[   ] whom he praised, he became lord [   ].
[   ] the oath of the gods [   ]
[   ] the snare[4] of Shamash his reign [   ]
[   ] of the oath of the gods, observer of [   ]   (390)
He established [the   of the lands of Sumer] and Akkad.
[ ] of Nabu, sage, wise, of vast u[nderstanding],
[who in the land of Sumer] and Akkad has no rival,
    who ...

---

1. The cella of the Assur temple in Assur.
2. The Assur temple in Kar-Tukulti-Ninurta, Tukulti-Ninurta's newly built royal city south of Assur.
3. Another name for Assur, apparently, the oldest part of the city.
4. The punishment reserved for violators of oaths.

[   ] the depth of his understanding [   ]
[   ] the ultimate praise, his inscription [   ]   (395)
[Tu]kulti-Ninurta, the ...
    which he took [   ] he [   ]
[   ] you who have no riva[l   ]

(small gap)

Nebuchadnezzar and Marduk

Nebuchadnezzar I (1124-1103 B.C.) was a successful and energetic monarch whose name became a byword in later Babylonian historical and literary tradition. He ascended the throne of Babylon (or Isin?) when Babylonian fortunes were at an ebb. The Kassite dynasty had been deposed after nearly half a millennium. Assyrians and Elamites had successively invaded. The Elamite king had deported one of Nebuchadnezzar's predecessors and removed the statue of Marduk from his temple at Babylon.

Nebuchadnezzar marched against the Elamites in a series of campaigns. At first turned back by an outbreak of plague among his soldiery, he later mounted a surprise attack during the summer hot season, routed his foe, and recovered the statue of Marduk. The return of the statue occasioned a burst of patriotic literary activity.

THE SEED OF KINGSHIP

This composition alludes to the remote descent of Nebuchadnezzar I, king of Babylon, from Enmeduranki, an antediluvian cultural figure, sage, and king of Sippar. This extraordinary claim may be interpreted in various ways. During this period, Babylonian scholars interested themselves in the remote ancestry of individuals, texts, and institutions for antiquarian, political, social, heuristic, and perhaps even patriotic reasons. In particular, Nebuchadnezzar I asserts that his claim to the throne antedated that of the Kassites and that of the Amorite kings of Babylon (most of the second millennium) and could be anchored in remotest known Babylonian tradition at Sippar (the only city still important at his time that was believed to have antedated the flood). Perhaps some connection was posited between this personage and the king's lineage in order to assert a revival of native Babylonian tradition. In any case, the text was composed in both Sumerian and Akkadian, an unusual undertaking at such a late date.

Praise is [for him w]hose mig[ht is]
    over the universe for eternity, (1)
Whose anger [is grievous but whose re]lenting is sweet,
    glorious to praise![1]
In his power are casting down and setting up, he reveals
    to future peoples how to watch for his sign.
Nebu[chadnezzar], king of [Babylon], who sets in order all
    cult centers, who maintains regular offerings,
He (Marduk) exalted his [wisdom] and made him foremost, (5)
He (Marduk) made great [his might],
    he exalted his great destiny.[2]
[Nebuchadnezzar], king of Babylon, who sets [in order a]ll
    cult centers, who maintains regular offerings,
Scion of royalty remote (in time), seed which has been
    watched for[3] since before the deluge,
Descendant of Enmedura[nki], king of Sippar, who instituted
    the sacred diviner's bowl, who held the cedar,[4]
(And) who took his place before Shamash and Adad,
    the divine judges,[5] (10)
Foremost son of [Ninurta-nadin]-shumi, just king, faithful
    shepherd who makes firm the foundations of the land,
Superb offspring(?) of Adad and Gula, the great gods,
    of Nippurian descent and lineage eternal,
Foremost attendant of Shuzianna,[6] twin sister of Anshar,
Nominated by Anu and Dagan,
    chosen by the steadfast hearts of the great gods am I!
It came to pass that in the reign of a previous king
    the signs changed: (15)
Good vanished and evil was prevailing,

1. Compare Poem of the Righteous Sufferer Tablet I lines 1ff. and the Epic of Creation Tablet VII lines 153ff.
2. That is, Marduk chose Nebuchadnezzar to be the agent of his return to Babylon.
3. Compare line 3 above, where "watching for" is also alluded to. The poet may have had a specific omen in mind.
4. Enmeduranki, an antediluvian king of Sippar, is here credited with being an early practitioner of oil divination.
5. A reference to divination, particularly hepatoscopy.
6. A healing deity known as "The Lady of Babylon."

The Lord became angry and waxed furious.
He commanded that the gods of the land forsake it, its people
    went out of their minds, they were incited to falsehood.
The guardian of well-being became furious and went up to
    heaven, the protective genius of justice stood aside,
[ ], the guardian of living creatures, over[threw] the people,
    and they all became as if they had no god! (20)
Malignant demons filled the land,
    remorseless plague penetrated the cult centers,
The land was diminished, its counsel changed.
The vile Elamite, who did not hold precious [the gods],
    whose battle was swift,
    whose onslaught was quick to come,
Laid waste the habitations, ravaged the gods,
    turned the sanctuaries into ruins!
Marduk, king of the gods, who ordains the destinies
    of the lands, observed all — (25)
When the Lord is angry,
    the Igigi-gods in [heaven] can[not] bear his fury,
His frightfulness is terrifying,
    no man can withstand his glowering —
The hardest ground sustained not his tread,
    oceans trembled [at] his rage,
No rock withstood his footstep,
    the gods of the universe knelt before him!
All existence(?) is entrusted to his power,
    when he grew angry, who could appease him? (30)
[ ] who learned [ ] him and sees his artfulness,
[ ] himself [ ] the capable Enlil of the gods,
[ ] the I[gigi-gods], solicitous prince,
[ ] who in [ ] adorned with splendor,
    enthroned in terrifying radiance,
The powerful one [ ], whose leadership excels (35)
    (gap)

(Marduk allows Nebuchadnezzar to defeat the Elamites and bring his statue home.)

[ ] the arms of whomsoever the weapon touched turned
    stiff of their own accord, as if dying of cold,
    and their corpses were spread far and wide,
He (Marduk) made (it) pass over above and below,
    right and left, front and rear, like the deluge;
    what was inside the city, outside the city,
    in the steppe, in the open country,
    he filled with deathly stillness and turned into a desert.
[?] the servant who revered him,
    who was assiduous in prayer,
    obedient, and constantly awaiting his revelation,
    ceased not from praying until he (Marduk) would
    fulfill his heart's desire,
[?] "until I behold his lofty figure, dejection of heart will
    never depart from my person, even for a day,
    nor can I have full term of sleep in night's sweet lap!"
[On account of] my most distressing lamentations,
    my ardent prayers, my entreaties,
    and the prostration that I performed in lamentation
    before him daily, his profound(?) heart(?) took pity,
    and he relented, [Marduk it was?] who resolved
    to go to the "New City." (40)
He, having set forth from the evils of Elam,
    having taken the road of jubilation,
    the path of gladness, and the way (that signified his)
    hearing and acceptance of their prayers,
The people of the land looked upon his lofty, suitable,
    noble form, as they acclaimed his brilliance,
    all of them paying heed to him.
The Lord entered and took up his comfortable abode,
Ka-sushi(?),[1] his lordly cella, beamed for joy.
The heavens bore him their abundance, earth its yield,
    sea its catch, and mountains their tribute: (45)
Their gifts beyond compare, or that tongue could tell,
Their massive tribute to the lord of lords!

---

1. A temple in Babylon.

Many sheep were slaughtered, grown bulls were provided
    in abundance, food offerings were magnificent,
    incense was heaped up,
Aromatics gave off sweet fragrance,
[ ] offerings were [   ], full of gladness. (50)
[   ], there was rejoicing,
[Gods of hea]ven and netherworld exult
    as they [lo]ok upon valiant Marduk,
[   ] a song of praise of his valor,
[   ] who makes the kettle and snare drums glow(?).

(end of text)

NEBUCHADNEZZAR'S PLEA

This epic-style poem recounts in summary fashion the events dealt with in more detail in the next composition.

When Nebuchadnezzar [the king] dwelt in Babylon,	(1)
He would roar like a lion, would rum[ble] like thunder,	
His illustrious great men would roar like lions.	
[His] prayers went up to Marduk, lord of Babylon,	
"Have mercy on me, in despair and pros[trate],	(5)
"Have mercy on my land, which weeps and mourns,	
"Have mercy on my people, who wail and weep!	
"How long, O lord of Babylon,	
will you dwell in the land of the enemy?	
"May beautiful Babylon pass through your heart,	
"Turn your face towards Esagila which you love!"	(10)
[The lord of Babylon] heeded Nebuchadnezzar['s prayer],	
[ ] befell him from heaven,	
"I command you with my own lips,	
"[A word of] good fortune do I send you:	
"[With] my [help?] you will attack the Westland.	(15)
"Heed your instructions, [ ]	
"Take me [from El]am to Babylon.	
"I, [lord of Bab]ylon, will surely give you Elam,	
"[I will exalt] your [kingship] everywhere."	
[ ] the land of [ ] and seized [ ] of? his gods	(20)

(breaks off)

NEBUCHADNEZZAR IN ELAM

A carved stone monument commemorating a grant of land and exemptions by Nebuchadnezzar I to one of his officers in the Elamite campaign, Sitti-Marduk, opens with a literary description of the campaign, the work of the scribe Enlil-tabni-bullit.

(1) When Nebuchadnezzar, pious and preeminent prince, of Babylonian birth, aristocrat of kings, valiant governor and viceroy of Babylon, sun god of his land, who makes his people flourish, guardian of boundaries, establisher of measuring lines(?), righteous king who renders a just verdict, valiant male whose strength is concentrated on warfare, who wields a terrible bow, who fears no battle, who felled the mighty Lullubi[1] with weaponry, conqueror of the Amorites,[2] plunderer of the Kassites,[3] preeminent among kings, prince beloved of Marduk, was sent forth by Marduk, king of the gods, he raised his weapon to avenge Akkad.

(14) From Der, sanctuary of Anu, he made an incursion for a distance of thirty leagues. He undertook the campaign in July. With the heat glare scorching like fire, the very roadways were burning like open flames! There was no water in the bottoms, and drinking places were cut off. The finest of the great horses gave out, the legs of the strong man faltered. On goes the preeminent king with the gods for his support, Nebuchadnezzar presses on, nor has he a rival. He does not fear the difficult terrain, he stretches the daily march!

(25) Sitti-Marduk, head of the house of Bit-Karziabku,[4] whose chariot did not lag behind the king his lord's right flank, held his chariot back.

---

1. Literary term for "mountain people."
2. Literary term for "(uncivilized, nomadic) West Semites," perhaps here a reference to inhabitants of the Trans-Tigridian region.
3. Perhaps used here as a literary term for Zagros-mountain peoples.
4. A Kassite eponymous tribal domain. Sitti-Marduk was thereby a member of the Kassite nobility.

(28) So hastened the mighty king, and reached the bank of the Ula river.[1] Both kings met there and made battle. Between them a conflagration burst out, the face of the sun was darkened by their dust, whirlwinds were blowing, raging was the storm! In the storm of their battle the warrior in the chariot cannot see the other at his side.

(35) Sitti-Marduk, head of the house of Bit-Karziabku, whose chariot did not lag behind the king's right flank, and who held his chariot back, he feared no battle (but) went down to the enemy and went furthest in against the enemy of his lord. By the command of Ishtar and Adad, gods who are the lords of battle, Hulteludish, king of Elam, retreated and disappeared. Thus king Nebuchadnezzar triumphed, seized Elam, and plundered its possessions.

(Text continues with record of the exemptions made to Sitti-Marduk's ancestral lands.)

---

1. Karun river.

NEBUCHADNEZZAR TO THE BABYLONIANS

A fragmentary manuscript preserves a letter, evidently addressed by Nebuchadnezzar to the Babylonians, telling them of his victory in Elam and recovery of Marduk's statue.

[To the citizenry of Babylon], of protected status, leaders learned and wise, [   ], men of business and commerce, great and small, [thus says Nebuchadnezzar, v]iceroy of Enlil, native of Babylon, the king, your lord, [   ] on a stele: [   ] you should know [that the great lord Marduk, who] was angry at all the holy places for a long time, took [pity] on Babylon. He gave me in his majesty the [sublime] command, [in?] the awe-inspiring sanctuary [Esagila] he ordered me to take the road of march to [the land of] Elam.

I gave reverent heed [to the command of the great lord] Marduk, assembled the army of Enlil, Shamash, and Marduk, and set forth towards [the land of] Elam. On I went, traversing distant [ways], waterless roads, night and d[ay.   At the] Ulaya River, the enemy, the vile Elamite, [blocked] the watering place in the gr[oves   ] the troops [ ] traversed. I could give no water, nor could I relieve their fatigue.

He advanced, hurtling his arrows, weapons [brandished] in battle. Through the might of Enlil, [Shamash, and Marduk, which] has no [equ]al, I overwhelmed(?) the king of Elam, defeating him ... His army scattered, his forces dispersed, [   ] deathly still, he(?) ravaged his (own) land, abandoned his strongholds, and disappeared.

I hastened on [ ] I beheld the [great lord] Marduk, lofty warrior of the gods, and the gods of the land [of Babylonia whom?] he commanded to convene with him. I raised [   ] ... and set up a wailing, I brought the great lord [Marduk] in procession and set out on the road to his homeland.

(Rest fragmentary. The king commands the restoration of Marduk and his treasures to Esagila.)

Tiglath-Pileser and the Beasts

A student's tablet from Assur preserves a short, epic-style poem about a campaign of the Assyrian king Tiglath-Pileser I (1115-1077 B.C.) against mountain peoples, cast in a metaphor of a hunter stalking wild game.

> [Who curbs] foes, trampler of his enemies, (1)
> [Who hunts] mountain donkeys,
>   flushes the creatures of the steppe,
> [The Hunter]: Assur is his ally, Adad is his help,
> Ninurta, vanguard of the gods, [go]es before him.
> The Hunter plans battle against the donkeys, (5)
> He sharpens(?) his dagger to cut short their lives.
> The donkeys listened, they gamboled alert,
> The Hunter's terror had not come down upon them.
> They were bewildered, "Who is it that stalks us?
> "Who is it, not having seen who we are, who
>   tries to frighten us all? (10)
> "Our ... will cut off the high mountains,
> "Our dwelling place lies in the ... of the mountain.
> "Let the wind send flying the hunter's snare!
> "May the shootings(?) of his bow
>   not rise high enough to reach(?) (us) assembled!"
> The Hunter heard the chatter of the mountain beasts — (15)
> Their speech was anxious, their words troubled,
> "Mouth or muscles, men are what they're born!"[1]—
> To the warriors who will make the breaches(?)
>   over the mountain he says,
> "Let us go and bring massacre upon the mountain beasts,
> "With our sharpened(?) weapons we will shed their blood." (20)
> He performed an extispicy for his appointed time,
> He raged like a thunderstorm,
>   (like the) sun he was hitching up his chariotry.
> A journey of three days he marched [in one].

---

1. Obscure, translation doubtful. Perhaps this is a proverbial expression, "a man's a man for a' that." Lines 15-18 may be out of sequence.

Even without sunshine a fiery heat was among them,
He slashed the wombs of the pregnant, blinded the babies, (25)
He cut the throats of the strong ones among them,
Their troops saw(?) the smoke of the (burning) land.
Whatever land is disloyal to Assur will turn into a ruin.
Let me sing of the victory of Assur, the mighty,
    who goes out to c[ombat],
Who triumphs over the cohorts of the earth! (30)
Let the first one hear and te[ll it] to the later ones!

The King of Justice

This text recounts certain signs and wonders of the reign of a Neo-Babylonian king (seventh or sixth century B.C.) that illustrate his concern for justice and the gods' favor for him. Of particular interest is the fullest description of a water ordeal to come down from antiquity. Important parts of the text are missing, notably the beginning and end, that latter of which contained, among other things, a description of the king's domain (unfortunately too fragmentary to translate).

i

(At the beginning remains of about twenty-seven lines of text are preserved. These suggest that the composition opened with a third person peroration with numerous dependent clauses ["He who ..."], with reference to the "Lord of Lords," climaxing in the mention of Babylon and the king's name [lines 10-11]. Thereupon the text may move into an account of his divinely directed birth and upbringing, and how he was chosen for dominion over the land.)

ii

... (2) nor would he make a decision concerning them (the cripple or widow). They would eat each other like dogs. The strong would oppress the weak, while they had insufficient means to go to court for redress. The rich would take the belongings of the lowly. Neither governor nor prince would appear before the judge on behalf of the cripple or widow, they would come before the judges but they would not proceed with their case; a judge would accept a bribe or present and would not consider it (the case).[1] They (the oppressors) would not receive an injunction (such as this):

(9) "The silver which you loaned at interest you have increased five-fold! You have forced households to be broken up, you have had fields and meadowland seized, families were living in front and back yards. You have taken in pledge servants, slaves, livestock, possessions, and property. Although you have silver and interest in

---

1. Not clear. The line may mean that judges were bribed not to hear cases, not that the poor were unable to muster the fee to give to a judge to have a case heard.

full, these (mortgaged properties) remain to yourselves."[1]

(14) A man who had nothing came before him, but he, the judge who had made the decision, drawn up a tablet, and sealed it, threw the tablet away and would not give (it) to him. Were the man to pursue him (the judge), he risked his life. Having no recourse, he would let out a cry and set up a sh[ou]t, invoking the lord of lords, "Award (me) my silver and interest, against (these) people!" [He (the judge) would not aw]ard it (to him), nor would he comfort them (widow and cripple), come to their help (the oppressed), nor consider (the case of the impoverished).

(22) For the sake of due process he (the king) did not neglect truth and justice, nor did he rest day or night! He was always drawing up, with reasoned deliberation, cases and decisions pleasing to the great lord Marduk (and) framed for the benefit of all the people and the stability of Babylonia. He drew up improved regulations for the city, he rebuilt the law court. He drew up regulations ... his kingship is forever. *(one line gone).*

iii

(2) The innocent man would take the ... [   ]. A man who returned to that law court (to reopen a case), such that, a tablet [having been written] and sealed, he was returning a second time for false and dishonest purposes, the king commanded the troops to cut off his head and paraded it through the land. The head ... cut off, he made a likeness of that man's head, and he had (the following) written upon that man's head and fastened forever after to the outer gate of that law court for all the people to see, "(This was) a man whose case was judged, whose tablet of verdict was written and sealed, but who afterwards changed and came back for judgment. His head was cut off on this wise." Base and wicked men would see it, abscond, and never be heard of again.

(14) He put a stop to bribes and presents among the people, he gave the people satisfaction, he caused the land to dwell in tranquility, allowing none to do them any alarm. He pleased his

---

1. Translation doubtful. It seems that the rapacious creditor, though paid, has not let the debtor take his pledged property back.

lords Sin, Shamash and Ishtar — they being Lord and Lady — (and) Nabu who dwells in Esagila and Ezida, <and who loves his kingship>. They (the gods) were reconciled in his reign on account of the regular offerings.

(21) A man charged a man with murder but did not prove it. They were brought before him (the king) and he ordered them (to be taken) above Sippar, to the bank of the Euphrates, before Ea, king of the depths, for trial. The troops of the guard, keeping both under close surveillance all night, lit a fire. At daybreak the prince, governor, and troops assembled as the king commanded, and took their places around them. Both went down (and) ... the river. Ea, king of the depths, in order to [ ] his royal beloved (and) in order to see justice [done, did] what always had [ ] ... [The first] ... he had jump in, he (the river god) brought him safely t[o the bank]. The one who had charged him with murder sank in the water. From morning until noon no one saw him nor was aught heard of [him]. As for the troops of the guard, who had stood around them at the riverbank from evening until daybre[ak], their hearts sank and they set out to search [ ], "What shall we report? How shall we answer the king?" When the king heard, he was furious at the troops. A courier was coming and going, "Did you not watch over the man? Has he gotten across the river and lain down in the open country?" Since none saw him at any time, they could not answer. Anxious boat(?) riders went along the river, bank to bank, checking the edge. When high noon came his corpse rose up from the river. He had been struck on the head, blood was running from the ears and nostrils. The top of his head was burned, as if with fire, his body was covered with sores. The people saw, and spoke (? of it) in reverence; all the world was borne down with awe. The enemy, the wicked one, and the hostile betook themselves into hiding.

(iv 24) On another occasion, another man den[ounced] another man. He swore an oath by Shamash (that he had not), and had no fear of the magic circle[1] [of Shamash], the great lord who is Marduk, residing in Esagila *(one line lost).*

---

1. Oaths to Shamash could be sworn standing inside a magic circle.

V

(1) [ ] he built anew. He hitched up strong horses to wagons. It being his desire, the foremost of them were laden with an offering to the gods, they lost no time hurrying along with (it).

(4) Before him (Marduk), every day, without ceasing, for food he gave him to eat abundant mighty oxen, fine fatted rams, [ ], geese, ducks, [wild fowl, pigeons], dormice, s[trings] of f[ish], cultivated [fr]uit in enormous [quantities], the [prid]e of orchards, [apples], figs, pomegranates, grapes, dates, imported dates, [dried figs?], [rai]sins, abundant vegetables, the [delight] of the garden, fine mixed beer, honey, ghee, refined oil, best quality milk, sweet emmer beer, fine wine. The finest of grain and vine of all mountains and lands, the best of what was his, the fair products of mountains and seas he offered in abundance before the great gods. What no one had ever done to such an extent, they received, in perpetuity, from his pure hands, and blessed his kingship. [In] conquering from Egypt to Hume, Piriddu, Lydia, [Mar]hashi, king of [remote] regions [ ] *(breaks off)*

III
Divine Speech

Prophecies

A group of letters from Mari, a city on the Middle Euphrates, reports prophecies spoken by people in a trance-like state. Most of these have to do with current events or are general warnings to the reigning king, Zimri-Lim (19th century B.C.), to protect himself.

FROM THE GODDESS ANNUNITUM

They will put you to the test with a revolt. Watch over yourself! Set in position around yourself trustworthy(?) servants whom you love, so they can watch over you. You must not go anywhere by yourself! But those men who would put you to the test, I will deliver those men into your power.

FROM THE GODDESS ANNUNITUM

O Zimri-Lim! Even though you have no regard for me, I will smite(?) on your behalf. I will deliver your enemies into your power ...

FROM THE GOD DAGAN

The peace initiatives of the king of the city of Eshnunna are treachery, water flows under the straw. But I will capture him for the very net he meshes; I will destroy his city; and I will make plunder of his ancient possessions.

FROM THE GOD DAGAN

O Babylon, what are you trying to do? I will assemble you for net and sword. I will deliver homes and possessions of the seven allies into the power of Zimri-Lim!

Letters from Gods

Some messages from the gods were conveyed in written form. Two examples from Mari, addressed to King Zimri-Lim, are given below.

FROM ISHTAR OF NINEVEH

Thus says Ishtar of Nineveh: I will station you at my side with my powerful weapons. Build me at Mari a house for a sleeping place. I order you as follows: when there is two hours march to your enemies, quickly kindle a fire. Then let Hadbu-Malik the courier extinguish it.

FROM SHAMASH

Thus says Shamash: I am lord of the land. Let them dispatch at once to Sippar, city of life, a great throne for my sumptuous dwelling and your daughter whom I required of you. Now the kings who affronted [you] and who have raided you time and again have been [given] into your power. Even now funeral pyres are given [to you] in the land!

Marduk Prophecy

This text purports to be a speech of the god Marduk in which he relates his history prior to the time of Nebuchadnezzar I. He explains that he is wont to traverse the universe; implicitly one is not to be surprised then at his peregrinations. He dwelt for a while among the Hittites (the image was captured by a Hittite king in 1594), and then returned to Babylonia. Marduk then speaks of a stay in Assyria (Baltil, image captured by Tukulti-Ninurta I). He blessed Assyria during his residence there. No such blessing is in store for Elam, whose attack on Babylon in the time of Kudur-nahhunte resulted in the transport of the statue of Marduk to Elam. In fact, a terrible fate is foretold for Elam. Marduk speaks warmly of a prince who is to arise and restore the land, who will bring him home again, and through whose good offices he will be reconciled to Babylon once more. Babylon will then flourish as never before.

The Marduk Prophecy may have been composed to glorify Nebuchadnezzar I and perhaps suggest to him specific benefactions (last column). The "future" there revealed included detailed recommendations about some otherwise unknown cult centers.

(1) O Haharnum, Hayyashum,[1] Anu, Enlil, Nudimmud, Ea, ..., Nabium, great gods who are learned in my mysteries! Now that I am ready for a journey, I will tell you my name.

(2) I am Marduk, great lord, the most lofty one, he who inspects, who goes back and forth through the mountains, the lofty one, inspector, who smites(?) lands, he who goes constantly back and forth in the lands from sunrise to sunset, am I!

(3) I gave the command that I go to Hatti, I put Hatti to the test, there I set up the throne of my supreme godhead. For twenty-four years I dwelt there. I made it possible for Babylonians to send (commercial) expeditions there, and they marketed(?) its [ ] goods and property [in] Sippar, Nippur, [and Babylo]n.

(4) A king of Babylon arose [and] led [me in procession to] ... Babylon, ..., fair was the processional way of Babylon! The crown of my [supreme godhead] and the image of [ ] workmanship [ ]. Water and [propitious] winds [ ]. Three days [ ] the crown of

---

1. Two little-known primeval deities, presumably cited here so as not to give primacy to the better-known and younger deities in the list.

my supreme godhead [ ], and the image of [ ] workmanship to my body did I [ ]. I returned, [and for Babylon I said], "Bring [your tribute, ye] lands [to Babylon!]." *(gap)*

(5) [The king? of] Baltil was pleasing [to me], the temple of Baltil was [.... to me]. His [temple]s [shone] like gems, I bestowed [ ] and abundance [upon him] ... [Month, day, and y]ear [I blessed him]. Having drawn up with him troops of Enlil, I set upon him wings like a bird and I delivered all [lands] (into his power), I blessed the land of Assur. I gave him the [tablet?] of destinies, I granted him stability. [ ] ... [I retur]ned, and for Babylon I said, "Bring your tribute, ye lands! ..."

(6) I am Marduk, great lord, lord of destinies and decision am I! Who (but me) made this journey? I have returned from whence I have gone, it was I who ordered it. I went to the land of Elam, and that all the gods went, it was I who ordered it. I cut off the offerings to the temples, I caused gods of cattle and grain to go away to heaven. The goddess of fermentation sickened the land, the people's corpses choked the gates. Brother consumed brother, comrade slew his comrade with a weapon, free citizens spread out their hands (to beg of) the poor! Authority was restricted, injustice afflicted the land, rebellious kings diminished the land, lions cut off travel, dogs [went mad] and bit people. As many as they bit did not live but perished! I fulfilled my days, I fulfilled my years. I resolved to return to my city Babylon and to Ekur-sagila. I spoke to all the ... It was I who ordered it, "Bring your tribute, ye lands, to Babylon! ..."

(7) A king of Babylon will arise, he will renew the marvelous temple, the Ekur-sagila. He will create the plans of heaven and earth in Ekur-sagila, he will double(?) its height. He will establish exemptions for my city Babylon. He will lead me in procession to my city Babylon and bring me into eternal Ekur-sagila. He will restore my (processional) boat, he will inlay its rudder with precious metal, he will [cover] its [com]ing with gold leaf. The boatmen who serve [it] he will bring aboard. They will be divided to [right] and left. The king will [ ] from(?) the dock(?) of Esagila *(gap, then some following fragmentary lines which deal with the restoration of another processional ship.)*

(8) ... [this prince] will see the benevolence of the god. [The years of] his reign will be long.

(9) He will make [Ekur]-Ekishnugal shine [like] a gem, the sanctuary of Ningal, the sanctuary of Sin, to[gether] with their treasures, possessions, and properties ... *(fragmentary lines, gap)*

(10) ... He will provide for the city and gather in the scattered ones. Ekur-Egalmah and the other sanctuaries he will make shine like gems. (The goddesses) Ningal, Gula, and Kurnunitum ... he will bring back to their favorite temples. This prince will cause his land to browse on the splendor of his pastures, and his days will be long ... [ ] He will make the sanctuaries shine like gems. He will bring back all their gods. He will gather in the scattered land and make firm its foundations.

(11) The gate of heaven will be open,[1] [ ] ... will get [ ] forever. (The god) Ningirsu will prevail: The watercourses will bring fish. Field and acreage will be full of yield. The winter crop will last till the summer harvest, the summer crop till the winter. The harvest of the land will be bountiful, market prices will be favorable. Wickedness will be rectified. Obscurities will be brought to light. Clouds will always be visible.[2] Brother will have consideration for brother, son will revere father like a god. Mother will [ ] daughter, bride will be mar[ried] and r[evere her husband]. There will always be consideration among the people. The young man will [always bear] his burden(?). This prince will [ru]le [all] lands.

(12) Finally, I and all the gods will be reconciled with him. He will smash Elam, he will smash its cities, he will dismantle its fortresses. He will lift the great king of Der from his unsuitable position, change his desolation, [ ] his bad situation, take him by the hand, and bring him into Der and (its temple) Ekur-Dimgal-kalamma forever.

(13) 40 quarts of [ ], 40 quarts of [ ], 10 quarts of flour, 1 quart of [ ], 1 quart of honey, 1 quart of butterfat, 1 quart of figs(?), 1 quart of raisins, 1 quart of alabastron [oil], 1 quart of finest [ ] without alkali(?), 1 regular sheep, a fatted calf will be burned for this spirit. Month, day, and year I will bless him!

---

1. A reference to rainfall?
2. Favorable prognosis.

Oracles to Assyrian Kings

ESARHADDON AND ISHTAR

Esarhaddon (680-669 B.C.) ruled the Assyrian empire in one of its most powerful and prosperous periods. This king is sometimes reputed to have been unusually superstitious and much under the influence of exorcists and diviners. These devised elaborate rituals for him to avoid evils, real or imagined.

Tablets from Nineveh preserve prayers of Esarhaddon and his son, Assurbanipal, together with divine responses, or oracles. About fifty such oracles are known.

> I am Ishtar of [Arbela]. O Esarhaddon, king of the land of As[syria], I give long days and eternal years to Esarhaddon, my king in the City,[1] in Nine[veh], Calah, and Arbela. I am your great midwife, I your good wetnurse. I have made firm your throne for long days and eternal years under the great heavens. I watch over you in a golden abode in the midst of heaven.
>
> Fear not, O king! I have taken you in trust, I did not disappoint you. I made [your] trust, I did not let [you] come to shame. I brought you over the river in good order(?). O Esarhaddon, legitimate heir of Ninlil, ..., I will finish off your enemies with my own hands. Esarhaddon, king of the land of Assyria, is a cupful of lye, an axe weighing (only) two shekels.[2]
>
> In the City I give you long days and eternal years, O Esarhaddon, in Arbela, I am your good shield.

---

1. Assur.
2. This may mean that Esarhaddon is ineffective as a warrior without Ishtar's assistance.

ASSURBANIPAL AND NABU

[I sin]g your praise, O Nabu, among the great gods. [Among?] my [ill-wisher]s, may my life not be continually sought. I keep turning to you, O most valorous of the gods his brethren, [in the temple of the lady of] Nineveh. [You are the tru]st of Assurbanipal henceforth, for all time. [Since childhood I] have cast myself at the feet of Nabu, [watch over me], O Nabu, among my ill-wishers!

Listen(?), O Assurbanipal, I am Nabu! Until the end of time, your feet shall not falter, your hands shall not tremble, nor shall these your lips weary of continual prayer to me, nor shall your tongue stumble at your lips, for I shall ever grant you fair speech. I shall raise your head and make you proud in Emashmash.[1]

(Nabu continues) That, your eloquent mouth, which always implores the lady of Uruk, and your own person, which I created, keep imploring me to remain(?) in Emashmash, your destiny, which I created, keeps imploring me as follows, "Bring good order(?) to Egashankalamma." Your spirit keeps imploring me as follows, "Prolong the life of Assurbanipal."

Assurbanipal, on bended knee, keeps praying to Nabu his lord, "Listen(?), O Nabu, do not forsake me! My life is inscribed before you, my spirit is entrusted to the lap of Ninlil. Listen(?), do not forsake me among my ill-wishers!"

A dream-god answered him from the presence of Nabu his lord, "Fear not, Assurbanipal, I will give you long life, I will entrust fair breezes with your spirit. This, my eloquent mouth, will ever bless you among the great gods."

Assurbanipal, spreading his hands, kept praying to Nabu his lord, "May he who seized the feet of the Queen of Nineveh not be

---

1. Temple of Ishtar at Nineveh.

disgraced among the great gods! May he who grasps the hem of the Lady of Uruk not be disgraced among his ill-wishers. Do not forsake me, O Nabu, do not forsake my life among my adversaries!"

"You were young, O Assurbanipal, when I left you to the Queen of Nineveh, you were a baby, O Assurbanipal, when you sat on the knee of the Queen of Nineveh. Her four teats were set in your mouth, with two you were suckled and with two you drew milk for yourself. Your ill-wishers, O Assurbanipal, will fly off like insects from the water's surface, they will be squashed at your feet like bugs in springtime. You will stand, O Assurbanipal, opposite the great gods, that you may praise Nabu."

IV
Hymns and Prayers
Individual Prayers

To Adad

This is a grateful paean to the beneficent rain storm.

> O Adad, [thun]derer, splendid, mighty god, (1)
> [ter]ror, doughty warrior,
> [Who forms?] clouds, who curtains daylight,
> ... everything,
> Who wields lightning, master of the deluge, (5)
> Who administers heaven, mountains, seas,
> Your [na]mes are [good], your invocation is heard abroad.
> At [your] clamor the mountains rejoice,
> The meadows are joyous, the fields are happy,
> [The people] are exuberant,
>   they sound praises of your valor! (10)
> You relieve dr[yn]ess by night and day,
> You make abundant greenery, you reconcile the angry.
> Maintain your kindnesses [to] me, your servant,
> Ordain mercy for me, let me sound your praises,
> Let me extol your good [names] to the numerous peoples! (15)

To Dumuzi

Tammuz/Dumuzi is celebrated in various Sumerian religious poems as the shepherd boy who wooed and married the youthful Inanna/Ishtar and subsequently met a violent death. He was also known as a netherworld deity, and is here referred to as a son of Ea (Nudimmud, line 2). The following incantation prayer appeals to Dumuzi in his aspects as shepherd and lover of Ishtar.

> O lord Dumuzi, awe-inspiring shepherd of Anu, (1)
> Lover of Ishtar the queen, eldest son of Nudimmud,
> O mighty one, leader without rival,
> Who eats pure loaves baked in embers,
> Who is clad in a cloak and carries a staff, (5)
> Who drinks water from a ... waterskin,
> Creator of everything, lord of the [sheep]fold,
> You are the lofty prince, the noble one!
> Drive away from me the "evil gazer," the worker of evil,
> [Who] has fixated upon me
>   and is trying to cut short my life. (10)
> Herewith I bring you my life!
> I hand him over to an evil spirit, a merciless demon,
> Let him be cut off from me, grant me life!
> Tear out the "evil gazer" who is present in my body,
> Let me sound your praises
>   until the end point of these (my) days. (15)

To Ea

As god of wisdom, knowledge, and skill, Ea was a particular favorite among diviners and exorcists; indeed, magic was one of his special concerns. Excerpted from an exorcistic work, this bilingual prayer expresses the exorcist's hope for success and professional high repute.

>   O Ea, king of the depths, finder of [good counsel], (1)
>   I am the exorcist your servant.
>   Come to my right hand, hasten to my left,
>   Set your sacral spell for mine,
>   Set your sacral utterance for mine, (5)
>   Make my sacral word effective,
>   Make what I say successful.
>   Command that my procedures be pure,
>   Let me succeed wherever I shall go.
>   Let the person I treat become well. (10)
>   Let favorable comments precede me,
>   Let favorable gestures follow me.
>   Be my protective genius,
>   Be my good fortune!
>   May Marduk, the god who brings (me) success, (15)
>   [Bring] success wherever my going.
>   Let the patient's (personal) god speak of your greatness,
>   Let this man sound your praises,
>   I too, the exorcist, let me sound your praises!

To Ea, Shamash, and Marduk

Ea, god of wisdom, Shamash, god of justice, and Marduk, son of Ea, were a group frequently invoked in magical prayers and rituals. Marduk is sometimes referred to with a by-name, Asalluhi, as in the second prayer. Their functions in such contexts are not normally differentiated, save that, in a general way, Ea provides the spell, Marduk the effective execution of it, and Shamash the powers of purification. In this respect the last line of the second prayer is unusual.

AGAINST CONGENITAL GUILT

O Ea, Shamash, and Marduk, what is my guilt? (1)
An abomination has confronted me,
    evil has me in its power.
My father begot me, my mother bore me,
They laid their plans and like a snake I [   ],[1]
From the dark within I came forth and saw you, O Shamash! (5)
An ill wind has brought down my branches,
A mighty tempest has bent low my crown.
My pinions were shorn like a bird's,
I moulted my plumage, I could not fly.
Paralysis has seized my arms, (10)
Debility has befallen my knees.
I moan like a dove night and day.
I am feverish and weep bitterly,
Tears are coursing from my eyes.
O Shamash, abatement is within your reach: (15)
Dispel, drive off the guilt of my mother and father.[2]
Go away, curse (upon me)!
Drive it away, O Ea, king of the depths,

---

1. This line may express parents' hopes and ambitions for their child. The "snake" is an image for the child wriggling through the birth canal from the womb (the "dark within" of line 5). The sense of the whole passage seems to be that the first thing this sufferer did was to behold the sun, so his life began auspiciously. Furthermore, the sun should know all about him, since he was born as he is now. This speaker is evidently wrestling with the problem of personal guilt.

2. The text seems to impute the sufferer's trouble to his parents, who made him the mere human that he is.

[and A]salluhi, lord of exorcism!
May my guilt be 3600 leagues far distant,
May the river accept (it) from me
    and take (it) down within. (20)
O Ea, Shamash, and Marduk, come to my help!
Let me be clean in your presence,
    let me be pure before you.

AGAINST ANY EVIL

This prayer could be used against the consequence of any unfavorable omen.

O Ea, Shamash, and Asalluhi, great gods, (1)
You are the ones who judge cases for the land.
Ordainers of destinies, the ones who draw up designs,
Apportioners of lots for heaven and earth,
In your power is decreeing of destinies
    and drawing-up of designs, (5)
The destiny of life is yours to ordain,
The design of life is yours to draw up,
The ruling for life is yours to render.
Your spell is life, your utterance well-being,
    your speech is life.
You are the ones to pass judgment on the land, (10)
Who tread the vast netherworld, who tread
    the distant heavens, as far as the heavens extend.
O opponents of evil, upholders of good,
Who obliterate evil signs and portents,
    terrifying, evil, foul dreams,
Who cut the wicked skein,
    who make defensive magic effective,
Wherever there are signs and portents,
    as many as there are, (15)
I, so-and-so, son of so-and-so,
Whose (personal) god is so-and-so,

Whose (personal) goddess is so-and-so,
Against whom evil signs keep occurring,
I am afraid, frightened, and terrified! (20)
Let me escape the evil (portended by)
    an eclipse of the moon,
The evil (portended by) an eclipse of the sun,
The evil (portended by) the stars (and) the stars of Ea,
    Anu, and Enlil,
The evil (portended by) the planets
    that approach the path of the stars,

(gap and fragmentary lines)

The signs and evil portents, (1')
[Lest I perish, be injured], or be turned ov[er to] a demon,
[Let a good] wind [blow] and this evil not,
[Let] the [south] wind [blow] but this evil not,
[Let] the [no]rth wind [blow] but this evil not, (5')
[Let] the east wind [blow] but this evil not,
Let the west wind blow but this evil not!
At your sublime command, which cannot be altered,
And your firm assent, which cannot be changed,
Let me live in well-being! (10')
O Ea, Shamash, and Asalluhi, let me sound
    at this very time praises of your great divinity,
O Shamash, make great the exorcism which Marduk,
    sage of the gods, performs.

To Family Ghosts

While Mesopotamians believed in the finality of death and a dreary eternity in a dusty, cheerless netherworld, they accepted as well the possibilities of traffic with spirits of the dead. Survivors of the deceased were responsible for providing food and water for the spirit in the netherworld. Spirits of the dead not properly interred or cared for might exercise a baneful influence. There is evidence at various periods for a household ancestral cult as well.

O ghosts of my family, progenitors of the grave(?), (1)
My father, my grandfather, my mother, my grandmother,
    my brother, my sister,
My family, kith, and kin,
    as many as are asleep in the netherworld,
I have made my funerary offering,
I have libated water to you, I have cherished you, (5)
I have glorified you, I have ho[no]red you.
Stand this day before Shamash and Gilgamesh,[1]
Judge my case, render my verdict!
Hand over to Namtar, messenger of the netherworld,
The evil(s) present in my body, flesh, and sinews! (10)
May Ningizzida, prefect of the vast netherworld,
    guard them well,
May Pituh, great gatekeeper of the netherworld,
    [cover?] their faces.
Seize (them) and send (them) down
    to the Land of No Return!
May I, your servant, live in well-being,
Let me be purified [in] your name from witchcraft, (15)
Let me libate cool water in your drinking pipe,[2]
Revive me, let me sound your praises!

---

1. Here a netherworld deity.
2. Conduit for water to the netherworld where the dead could receive fresh water, if offered to them by the living.

To Girra

Girra was the god of fire. He was invoked in magical procedures where figurines or symbols of an enemy were melted or burned as a way of returning harm for harm.

MELTER

O stately Girra, firstborn of Anu, (1)
Pure offspring of sublime Shalash,[1]
Stately, ever-renewing,
    eternal requirement(?) of the gods,
Giver of food portions to the Igigi-gods,
Who imparts brilliance to the Anunna, the great gods, (5)
Raging Girra, who burns up canebrakes,
Brave Girra, who destroys trees and rocks,
Who burns up evil ones, the tribe of sorcerer and sorceress,
Who destroys malefactors,
    the tribe of sorcerer and sorceress,
Stand by me this day in my case, (10)
Overcome the seditious, corrupter(?), the evil one!
Just as these figurines dissolve, melt, drip away,
Let my sorcerer and sorceress dissolve, melt, drip away.

JUDGE

O Girra, mighty one, terrifying storm, (1)
You govern gods and sovereigns,
You judge the case of the oppressed man and woman.
Stand by me in my case, and, like the warrior Shamash,
Judge my case, render my verdict! (5)
Burn up my sorcerer and my sorceress,
Consume my enemies,
    devour those who are wicked to me,
Let your furious storm overcome them!

---

1. Normally the wife of Adad or Dagan, but here assigned to Anu.

To Gula

This hymn extols in alternating stanzas Gula, goddess of healing, and her spouse, using different names. The text is unusual because of the author's "signature" in the concluding lines. It is a work of great learning; rare and dialectal words abound. The hymn makes numerous allusions to mythology and may quote directly other compositions. It was popular in learned circles and was quoted in an ancient commentary. It is also attested in an ancient list of famous authors of the past and their putative literary works.

The frame of the composition is a third-person prayer by Bullutsa-rabi. He introduces the goddess in the first stanza and concludes the whole composition with a prayer that she intercede for him. The goddess speaks her own praises, a well-attested mode in Akkadian. She discourses upon her astral character, her elevation to a position of authority, her interest in agriculture, her unalterable word, her healing abilities, her control of destinies, her sexual attractiveness, her upbringing and education, marriage, and scholarship.

The poet thereby proceeds from her general attributes of divinity, her role, function, and physical attributes to her major "rites of passage" and concludes with praise of her medical learning. Perhaps this aspect of her persona was of particular appeal to the poet, who says he is sick and in need of her ministrations. By contrast, her spouse is consistently portrayed as a fierce and terrible warrior, without developing a theme. Gula's personality is more complex; she has more names than her husband. Despite the dual structure of the hymn, the goddess is clearly the author's primary interest.

i

The goddess is the most capable of all deities who sit on daises, (1)
"I am noble, I am lordly, I am splendid and sublime.
"My station is on high, I am a woman of dignity.
"I excel among goddesses,
"Great is my star in heaven, my name in the netherworld. (5)
"Fair it is to hold me in mind, (it is) good health and life.
"People discourse of me (in) sickness (and in) health,
"My great name is Nintinugga.[1]

---

1. Sumerian healing deity, "Lady Who Revives the Dead."

ii

"My spouse is the warrior, son of Enlil, the mighty,
"Valorous one, trampler of the foe, (10)
"Who crushes the enemy, (but) who makes the righteous stand,
"Who fulfilled Enlil's wishes, whose strength is sublime,
"The strong lord who slew Anzu,
"[   ] the responsibility of (Enlil's) supremacy.[1]
"[   ] to whom Ninlil listens, (15)
"Ninurta, the merciful offspring of heaven,
"Pure progeny, heir of Esharra.[2]

iii

"I was sought out, for E[nli]l chose me among goddesses,
"He looked up [ ], he fell in love with me.
"He wed me [for the ...] his supremacy, (20)
"He allotted the management of Esharra [ ] into my hands.
"He added [   ] procedures,
"He [   ] me,
"He made fair my name [   ] among goddesses.
"He called [me   ] Nin-[ ], I have no rival. (25)

iv

"[(My spouse is)] the great master of portions,
"Pure light of heaven, the one who calls for the work song,
"Resettler of devastated agricultural lands,
"Pursuer, wild bull with head held high,
"Who seized ..., who split stones[3] and begot grains, (30)
"Heaper up of grain piles,
    who performed the great festival for Enlil,
"Who makes teeming mankind live in abundance,
    who resettles abandoned mounds,
"Stately, tall of form, pure shining son of Anu,
"Mightiest of the gods, great Ningirsu.

---

1. Allusion to Anzu, the Bird Who Stole Destiny (above, Part I).
2. A temple of Enlil in Nippur, hence the author is saying "son of Enlil."
3. Allusion to a Sumerian poem in which Ninurta kills stone monsters.

v

"Opener of the furrow, director of daybreak, (35)
"Who drives out the (plow) ox, mistress of (its) track,
"Beloved of the stars which are the signs for plowing,
"Who silos fodder for the oxen,
"Who grants good work to the plowman,
"Mistress of basket, seed grain, plow, plowfield, share,
    and field hand(?), (40)
"Who stretches out the measuring cord, cubits,
    and measuring rod,
"Who carries a stylus as she works, doing the accounts,
"Mother Nanshe,[1] mistress of the field boundary am I.

vi

"My towering husband is an honored noble of heaven,
"Clad in awesomeness and divine splendor, (45)
"Who makes heaven and netherworld quake,
    lofty one among the Igigi-gods,
"Who charges through canebrakes, who dances in battle,
"Who examines the heights of heaven,
    who investigates the bottom of the netherworld,
"Who implements wise counsel, master of decisions,
"Who gathers to himself wisdom, of profound intelligence, (50)
"Reared by the depths, splendid one, offspring of Mami,
"Rider of all the winds, lord of battle and warfare,
"Great storm, brilliant of feature, lord of lords, Ninazu.[2]

vii

"I am sublime in heaven, I am queen in the netherworld,
"Among the gods I have no peer, (55)
"Among goddesses I have no equal.
"I am mistress of the depths, Ea's place,
"Lofty and great are my responsibilities.

---

1. A goddess at home in the Lagash region, not usually equated with Gula, but perhaps through Ningirsu (Lagashite god) = Ninurta; see also line 34.
2. "Lord Physician," a Sumerian deity (usually a brother of Ninurta).

"The limits I (set) cannot be changed,
"(My) command cannot be altered. (60)
"My name is great, I am sublime,
"I tower in my stance, I am enormous in form.
"I grant portions to all the gods.
"I am daughter, I am bride, I am spouse,
    I, indeed, manage the household, (65)
"Wife of the foremost one, Pabilsag,[1]
"Ninkarrak,[2] mistress of counsel, am I.

viii

"The lofty one, favorite of the gods, Anu's son,
"He is the foremost one, surpassing all lords.
"The Igigi-gods consult with him,
    the shining breastplate(?) of heaven. (70)
"Great is fear of him among the gods,
    every one of them is in awe of his name,
"They await his command.
"He is the foremost one, towering hero, noble,
    virile one, bastion,
"He is firm of foot in heaven, powerful in the depths,
"Great in the netherworld, sublime in Ekur, (75)
"Cherished son of Enlil,
"Pure offspring of Nin<lil>,
"Double of Anu, the warrior Ninurta.

ix

"I am the physician, I can save life,
"I carry every herb, I banish illness. (80)
"I gird on the sack with life-giving incantations,
"I carry the texts which make (one) well.
"I give health to mankind.
"(My) clean dressing salves the wound,
"(My) soft bandage relieves the pain. (85)

---

1. Sumerian deity, husband of Nininsina, a healing goddess.
2. Healing goddess.

"At my examination, the moribund revives,
"At a word from me, the feeble one arises.
"I am merciful, [I am] kindly [ ]
"The mighty man [   ]
"I am she who gives [   ] (90)
"Ninigiziba[ra   am I].

x

"My beloved is the young man ... [ ]
"The mighty one, endowed with strength [ ]
"Overpowering lord whose vigor cannot be equalled;
"Towering, with stately physique,
    standing ready to charge mountains, (95)
"Lovely, adorned with allure, and gorgeous all over,
"Who dances in the pride of young manhood, adorned with joy,
"First fruits of the harvest song, whose look is abundance,
"Fierce, irresistible, overcoming foes,
"Crusher of stones, Zababa.[1] (100)

xi

"I am a warrior, skilled through experience,
"I am the spouse of the mighty one, light of the gods.
"I make decisions, I give commands,
"In Esharra (my) way is sublime,
"In Ekur, dwelling of the gods, (my) dwelling is on high. (105)
"I have mercy on the weak, I enrich the destitute,
"I bestow life on the one who reveres me.
"I make straight the path of the one who seeks after my ways,
"I am the great one, daughter of Anu, mother Ba'u,[2]
    life of the people.

xii

"My beloved is the warrior, foremost one, king of kings, (110)
"Furious one, slayer who tangles (in) battle,

---

1. A warrior god sometimes equated with Ninurta.
2. Sumerian goddess, wife of Ningirsu.

"Launcher of the deluge,
"Who loves [   ] and bride.
"Being merciful, he heeds prayers,
"He turns the wicked and enemies into clay. (115)
"He burns the roots of all disobedient like reeds,
"Ninurta, foremost of the vanguard, mighty son of Enlil.

xiii

"I am fairest voiced among goddesses,
"I am the most beautiful among queens,
"I am the most attractive among young women, (120)
"I am the most seemly among fine ladies.
"I have been given to his divinity,
"I am led to the foremost one, lord of the gods.
"My face is attractive,
"I am seductive to the mighty one, son of the lord of the gods. (125)
"I have come into his pure place,
"Into awe-inspiring Eshumesha,[1]
"Into (its) Ekashbar, house of destinies, place of commands,
"I am Ungalnibru,[2] the pure princess.

xiv

"Lofty one, lord who is the very greatest in heaven, (130)
"Terror of whom makes all lands quake(?),
"Fear of whom envelops the mountain[s],
"He wears the heavens on his head, like a tiara,
"He is shod with the netherworld, as with [san]dals.
"He holds in his grasp commands that no [god kn]ows of, (135)
"At his glance ... [   ]
"Swift [   ], multiplying prosperity,
"[   ], trampler, lofty Uta'ulu.[3]

---

1. Temple of Ninurta and spouse at Nippur.
2. Sumerian epithet, "Queen of Nippur."
3. Another name for Ninurta.

xv

"Antu bore me, cherished me steadfastly,
"She taught me fair counsel, adorned me with charm, (140)
"She gave me to the fullest the joys of young girls.
"Anu my father named me according to his own name,
"He made me excel among my brothers.
"Ea in the depths gave me in full of his wisdom,
"He gave me the tablet stylus from his own hand, (145)
"He entrusted to me the physician's craft,
    a secret of the gods,
"Enlil chose me as bride for the mighty one, his son.
"I am Gula, mistress of heaven and netherworld.

xvi

"Foremost one, slayer, mountain, overwhelmer of the sea,
"Irresistible storm, battle deluge, (150)
"Instigator of discord, declarer of war,
"Who brings opponents to submission, mastering the foe,
"Mighty one who relies on his own strength,
"Savage, pitiless, who musters the ill wind, who grants victory,
"Esharra's trust, sublime son, who takes his own high rank, (155)
"Avenger of the father who begot him,
"Pure god, deserving of kingship,
"My fair spouse, Lugalbanda."[1]

---

1. Legendary Sumerian king of Uruk, who, like Ninurta, contested with Anzu.

xvii

"...
"My allure is compelling ... [ ] (160)
"I am adorned with ... [   ]
"My [ ] are ...
"My [ ] are piping,
"I wear(?) a ...
"When I go in procession, charm falls like the dew, (165)
"When I come in there is splendor,
"In my bed ...
"There is no one like me,
"I am Ninsun,[1] the merciful goddess.

xviii

"My beloved is the favorite among goddesses, (170)
"He wears on his head a tiara with superb horns,
"He wields sharp weapons,
"He leads about fierce storm demons,
"Conqueror of all mountains,
"Who overthrew hard stones, as many as there were, (175)
"He forced to submit those
    who were insubmissive to Enlil,
"Strongest of the strong, slayer of slayers, Lugalbanda.

xix

"I am merciful, I hear (prayer) from afar off,
"I fetch up the dead from the netherworld,
"I am girded with the leather bag,
    I ... the scalpel and knife. (180)
"I examine the weary, I watch over the sick,
    I open(?) the sore,
"I am mistress of life.
"I am physician, I am diviner, I am exorcist,

---

1. "Wild Cow," mother of Gilgamesh.

"I, who am expert in calculations,
    no one has explained (to me) a single wedge,[1]
"I ... every one of them.   (185)
"There is life in my [   ],
"I am Ninlil, the merciful [goddess]."

xx

[ ] bo[th] gods [   ],
Have mercy on the servant who fears your divinity [ ]!
Heed what he says, stand by him when he prays,   (190)
Accept his entreaty, listen to his words,
Take your seats (of judgment) and administer his case,
Set right his confusion, illumine his darkness.
Let him strip his mourning weeds,
    let him put on (normal) clothes.
That servant, meek and lowly,   (195)
May his life be prolonged at the unalterable command
    of your great divinity.
O Gula, great lady, whose help is Ninurta,
Intercede for him with the mighty one,
    your splendid spouse,
That he bring forth recovery for Bullutsa-rabi,
That he may kneel before you daily.   (200)

---

1. This may refer to calculation of propitious times or the time suffering could be expected to last; compare Poem of the Righteous Sufferer (see Part V) Tablet II line 1.

To Ishtar

Ishtar, one of the most complex figures in Mesopotamian religion, is early attested as a goddess of warfare and as the morning and evening star. Partly through syncretism with the Sumerian goddess Inanna, she became as well a goddess of fertility, reproduction, and love. She is often portrayed as harsh, capricious, and vindictive; fearless and joyful in the battle fray; urgent, ardent, and alluring as a lover. She was also associated with prostitution, sexual impersonation, self-mutilation, and homosexuality. Penitential and devotional literature tends to stress her valor and queenly tenderness.

SING OF THE GODDESS

After the opening invocation, this poem treats first the attractions of Ishtar's body, then focuses upon her features, suffused with pleasure, and her head, which is bedizened with love charms. Mention of her eyes leads to consideration of the well-being her regard can bestow, especially, in the fifth strophe, on a woman who hopes for harmonious love. The poet thinks then of Ishtar's might and splendor — who could withstand such power? This leads to her role as queen of heaven, the morning and evening star; she reigns supreme with her spouse, the sky, and the lesser lights stand before her, partaking of her brilliance. As the gods await her command, the poet introduces the Babylonian king, Ammiditana (ca. 1683-1647 B.C.), who bears rich offerings, whose domains she ensures — may his long life be her command.

i

> Sing of the goddess, most awe-inspiring goddess,
> Let her be praised, mistress of people,
> > greatest of the Igigi-gods.
>
> Sing of Ishtar, most awe-inspiring goddess; let her be praised,
> Mistress of women, greatest of the Igigi-gods.

ii

> She is the joyous one, clad in loveliness,
> She is adorned with allure, appeal, charm.

Ishtar is the joyous one, clad in loveliness,
She is adorned with allure, appeal, charm.

iii

In her lips she is sweetness, vitality her mouth,
While on her features laughter bursts to bloom.
She is proud of the love charms set on her head,[1]
Fair her hues, full-ranging, and lustrous her eyes.

iv

This goddess, right counsel is hers,
She grasps in her hand the destinies of all that exists.
At her regard, well-being is born,
Vigor, dignity, good fortune, divine protection.

v

Whispers, surrender, sweet shared captivation,
Harmony too she reigns over as mistress.
The girl who invokes(?) finds (in her?) a mother,
Among women(?) one mentions her, invokes her name.

vi

Who is it that could rival her grandeur?
Her attributes are mighty, splendid, superb.
Ishtar this is, who could rival her grandeur?
Her attributes are mighty, splendid, superb.

vii

She it is who stands foremost among the gods,
Her word is the weightiest and prevails over theirs.
Ishtar stands foremost among the gods,
Her word is the weightiest and prevails over theirs.

---

1. The love charm, sometimes a personification, may here be something worn, like a necklace or headband.

viii

She is their queen, they relay her commands,
All of them bow down before her:
They go to her (in) her radiance,
Women and men fear her too.

ix

In their assembly her utterance is noble, surpassing,
She is seated among them as an equal to Anu their king,
She is wise in understanding and perception.
Together they make their decisions, she and her lord.[1]

x

There they sit together on the dais
In the temple chamber, abode of delights,
The gods stand in attendance before them,
Their ears awaiting what those mouths will command.

xi

Their favorite king, whom their hearts love most,
Ever offers in splendor his pure offerings,
Ammiditana offers before them
His personal, pure libation of cattle and fatted lambs.

xii

She has asked of Anu her spouse long life hereafter for him,
Many years of life for Ammiditana
Has Ishtar rendered to him as her gift.

xiii

By her command she gave him in submission
The four world regions at his feet,
She harnessed the whole of the inhabited world to his yoke.

---

1. Anu is meant. "Lord" may be a term of endearment here.

xiv

What she desires, this song for her pleasure
Is indeed well suited to his mouth,
    he performed for her Ea's own word(s).[1]
When he heard this song of her praise, he was well pleased with him,
Saying, "Let him live long, may his (own) king always love him."[2]

O Ishtar, grant long life enduring to Ammiditana,
    the king who loves you, (long) may he live!

        (its antiphon)[3]

GREAT PRAYER

I implore you, lady of ladies, goddess of goddesses,   (1)
Ishtar, queen of all the inhabited world,
    who governs the peoples,
Irnini, you are noble, the greatest of the Igigi-gods,
You are powerful, you are queen, exalted is your name.[4]
You are the luminary of heaven and earth,
    the valiant daughter of Sin,   (5)
Who brandishes weapons, who prepares for battle,
Who gathers to herself all rites, who dons the lordly tiara.
O Mistress, splendid is your greatness, exalted over all the gods.
Planet for the warcry, who can make harmonious
    brothers set at one another,
Who can always grant a comrade,   (10)
Strong(?) one, mistress of the tilt, who gores mountains,
Gushea, whose mail is combat, clothed in chilling fear.

---

1. This refers to the artfulness of the text, which pleases Ea, god of wisdom.
2. "King" may mean the god of Ammiditana's city, Babylon.
3. This refers to the lines in the ruled-off section. The poem may have been performed or sung antiphonally.
4. Or: "are your names."

You render final judgment and decision,
> the command for heaven and netherworld,
Chapels, sanctuaries, altars, and daises are attentive to you.
Where is not your name, where are not your rites? (15)
Where are your designs not put into effect,
> where are your daises not set up?
Where are you not great, where are you not exalted?
Anu, Enlil, and Ea have lifted you high, they have made
> your authority greatest among the gods,
They have given you the highest rank among all the Igigi-gods,
> they have made your (heavenly) station highest of all.
At the thought of your name, heaven and netherworld quake, (20)
The gods totter, the Anunna-gods tremble.
Mankind extols your awe-inspiring name,
You are the great one, the exalted one.
All the black-headed[1] folk, living creatures, mankind,
> praise your valor.
You are the one who renders verdicts
> for subject peoples in truth and justice, (25)
You look upon the oppressed and abused
> and always set them right.
Have mercy, mistress of heaven and earth,
> shepherdess of the human race!
Have mercy, mistress of holy Eanna,[2] the pure treasury!
Have mercy, mistress whose feet weary not,
> whose legs are strong to run!
Have mercy, mistress of combat and of every melee! (30)

O splendid lioness of the Igigi-gods,
> who renders furious gods submissive,
Most capable of all sovereigns,
> who grasps the leadrope of kings,
Who opens the veils of all young women,

---

1. The Mesopotamians.
2. Sanctuary of Anu and Ishtar at Uruk.

You rise up, bring yourself down,
>   great is your valor, O valiant Ishtar,
Shining torch of heaven and earth,
>   brilliance of all inhabited lands. (35)
Furious in irresistible onslaught, hero to the fight,
Fiery glow that blazes against the enemy,
>   who wreaks destruction on the fierce,
Dancing one, Ishtar, who masses the multitude,
Goddess of men, Ishtar of women,
>   whose intentions no one can learn,
Wherever you look the dead come to life, the sick arise, (40)
The unjustly treated prosper at the sight of you.
I myself call upon you, your exhausted, desperate,
>   most stricken servant,
Look upon me, mistress, accept my entreaty!
Look steadfastly upon me, hear my prayer!
Speak a word of mercy for me, let your feelings be eased. (45)
Have mercy on my wretched person,
>   which is full of confusion and perturbation!
Have mercy on my most stricken heart,
>   which is full of tears and sighing!
Have mercy on my wretched omens,
>   confused and perturbed!
Have mercy on my anguished household,
>   which moans for grief!
Have mercy on my feelings,
>   which abide in tears and sighing! (50)
Irninitum, raging lion, may your heart be calmed.
Furious wild bull, may your feelings be eased.
May your benevolent eyes rest upon me,
Look upon me with your beaming features!
Drive off the evil witchcraft from my person,
>   let me see your shining light! (55)
How long, my mistress, will my opponents glower at me,
And with lies and falsehood plot evil against me?
My harassers and ill-wishers are raging against me,

How long, my mistress,
>   will imbeciles and weaklings surpass me?
The feeble has gone on ahead, I have lagged behind, (60)
The weak have grown strong, I have grown weak.
I churn like a wave which an adverse wind masses,
My heart soars and flutters like a bird of heaven.
I moan like a dove, night and day,
I am ..., I cry bitterly. (65)
My feelings are most stricken from crying "Woe!" and "Alas!"
I, O my god, O my goddess, what have I done?
I am dealt with as if I did not revere my god and my goddess.
Disease, headpains, decline, and ruin beset me,
Constraints, averted faces, and anger beset me, (70)
Wrath, rage and fury of gods and men.
I have experienced, O my mistress, days of darkness,
>   months of gloom, years of grief,
I have experienced, O my mistress,
>   a judgment of upset and turmoil.
Death and misery have a hold on me,
My chapel is deathly still, my sanctuary is deathly still, (75)
A ghastly stillness has fallen upon my household,
>   my courtyard, and my fields,
My god's face is turned some other place,
My relations are scattered, my fold dispersed.
I am attending you, my mistress, waiting for you,
I implore you, absolve my debt! (80)
Absolve my crime, misdeed, sin, and wrong-doing!
Forget my sin, accept my plea,
Loose my fetters, set me free!
Make straight my path, let me pass through the street,
>   proud and radiant among the living.
Speak, that from your speaking the angry god be reconciled, (85)
That the goddess who became furious relent!
May my dark and smoky hearth burn clear,
May my snuffed-out torch burst to flames,
May my scattered relations regroup themselves,
May my paddock enlarge and my fold expand, (90)

Accept my supplication, hear my prayer!
Look steadfastly upon me, ...
How long, my mistress,
 will you be angry and your face averted?
How long, my mistress,
 will you be enraged and your feelings in a fury?
Turn towards me your cast-down head,
 resolve on a favorable word! (95)
Like water, the standing pool(?) of a canal,
 may your feelings come to ease.
Let me trample down like dirt those who rage against me!
Make submissive those furious against me
 and flatten them under my feet!
May my prayers and entreaties sit well with you,
May your magnificent forbearance be with me, (100)
That those who see me in the street
 may magnify your name,
And that I too may proclaim your divinity and
 valor to the black-headed folk,
"Ishtar is pre-eminent, Ishtar is queen,
"The lady is pre-eminent, the lady is queen,
"Irnini, the valiant daughter of Sin, has no rival." (105)

AGAINST SORCERY

O pure Ishtar, lofty one of the Igigi-gods, (1)
Who makes battle, who brings about combat,
Most stately and perfect of goddesses,
At your command, O Ishtar, humankind is governed.
The sick man who sees your face revives, (5)
His bondage is released, he gets up instantly.
At your command, O Ishtar, the blind man sees the light,
The unhealthy one who sees your face becomes healthy.
I, who am very sick, I kneel, I stand before you,
I turn to you to judge my case, O torch of the gods, (10)
I have seen your face, may my bonds be released.

Do not delay, I am confused and anxious.
I live like one bastinadoed.
I did what you said to do, O Ishtar!
A sorcerer or a sorceress, (15)
Whom you know, but I do not know,
With magic rites of malice and assassination,
Which they have worked in your presence,
Have laid figurines of me in a grave,
Have come to assassinate me! (20)
They have worked in secret against me,
    I work against them openly!
By your sublime command, which cannot be altered,
    And your firm "yes," which cannot be changed,
May whatever I say come true.
Let life come forth to me from your pure utterance,
(May) you (be the one to say) "What a pity about him!"
    O you who are the (supreme) goddess among the gods. (25)

To Marduk

Marduk, god of Babylon, emerged as pre-eminent in the Babylonian pantheon during the second half of the second millennium B.C. Although his original role as a vegetation deity and warden of spring waters is alluded to in devotional literature, he is often appealed to as father, warrior, and ruler.

In this prayer, an agnostic theme, taken up at length in the Poem of the Righteous Sufferer and penitential psalms, is balanced with expressions of goodwill (lines 12f.) and resignation (lines 14f.). The unanswered cries of the penitent provide a dramatic opening address, at once a reminder of the penitent's past observance and a description of his physical and emotional distress. His becoming an old man through Marduk's punishment (line 6) suggests that youth is a metaphor for his happy condition prior to Marduk's punishment, rather than his actual youth. This figure is carried through by the conclusion, whereby the suppliant becomes, if forgiven, a child of his god again. Although there is scarcely a line in this poem that does not have parallels elsewhere, the harmony and effectiveness of the whole are striking and set this composition apart as a masterpiece.

> O warrior Marduk, whose anger is the deluge, (1)
> Whose relenting is that of a merciful father,
> I am left anxious by speech unheeded,
> My hopes are deceived by outcry unanswered,
> Such as has sapped my courage, (5)
> And hunched me over like an aged man.
> O great lord Marduk, merciful lord!
> Men, by whatever name,
> What can they understand of their own sin?
> Who has not been negligent,
>   which one has committed no sin? (10)
> Who can understand a god's behavior?
> I would fain be obedient and incur no sin,
> Yes, I would frequent the haunts of health!
> Men are commanded by the gods to act under curse,
> Divine affliction is for mankind to bear. (15)
> I am surely responsible for some neglect of you,
> I have surely trespassed the limits set by the god.

Forget what I did in my youth, whatever it was,
Let your heart not well up against me!
Absolve my guilt, remit my punishment, (20)
Clear me of confusion, free me of uncertainty,
Let no guilt of my father, my grandfather, my mother,
    my grandmother, my brother, my sister,
      my family, kith, or kin
Approach my own self, but let it be gone!
If my god has commanded (it) for me,
    purify me as with medicaments.
Commend me into the hands of my (personal) god
    and my (personal) goddess for well-being and life, (25)
Let me stand before you always in prayer, supplication,
    and entreaty,
Let the fruitful peoples of a well-ordered land praise you.
Absolve my guilt, remit my guilt!
O warrior Marduk, absolve my guilt, remit my guilt!
O great lady Erua-Sarpanitu, absolve my guilt, (30)
O Nabu of the good name, absolve my guilt,
O great lady, Tashmetu, absolve my guilt,
O warrior Nergal, absolve my guilt,
O gods who dwell \<in\> Anu's \<heaven\>,
    absolve my guilt!
The monstrous guilt that I have built up from my youth, (35)
Scatter it hence, absolve it sevenfold.
Like my real father and my real mother,
Let your heart be reconciled to me.
O warrior Marduk, let me sound your praises!

To Nabu

Nabu, son of Marduk and Sarpanitum, was god of the scribal arts. This sad prayer reflects on the joy of premature happiness and the bitterness of premature sorrow. All has gone by too quickly, and the suppliant begs that his life be made worth living.

(gap)

 O Nabu, lest I sin, O son of the Lord, [lest] I offend, (1)
 [On account of the heed]less deeds of my ancestors and
  kinfolk, who heedlessly neglected
  [the rites of Tashmetu],[1]
 I have longed [for] Ezida,[2] the high ground,
  the house in which we put our trust,
 I have longed for Ezida, the threshold of delight, ...
 [Even as] an infant(?), I have longed for the collegium,
  to take my place in (its) house of learning, (5)
 My strength was the precious offerings
  of the temple of Nabu,
 I was ever mindful of its beauties,
  it was the fire of Ezida that stoked my heart.
 I gained wealth,
  I attained what I wanted ahead of my time.
 (Now) old age has me bedridden prematurely,
 I am wasted by suffering,
  as if I were not fearing your divinity. (10)
 I weep, for I have not seen the beauty of my life.
 I have become the smallest of the small,
  I am become the lowest of the low,
 My (begging) hands are outstretched
  (even) to the poverty-stricken who frequent my door,
 I have entreated slaves and slavegirls,
  whom I used to buy in commerce,

---

1. Wife of Nabu.
2. Sanctuary of Nabu at Borsippa, south of Babylon.

When I moved against an enemy,
>   a sorceress splashed water on my back. (15)

I am cut off from my community,
>   enemies of (my) family glower at me,

Anguish, sickness are upon me,
>   I am stricken with weakness.

I keep crying out to estranged gods,
>   raising my hands (in prayer) in heed of my goddess.

I have gone everywhere for a mother,
>   she has shrunk from me and is clawing at me.

Death has tantalized me like a precious stone. (20)

I constantly go up to the roof to jump off,
>   but my life is too precious, it turns me back.

I try to encourage myself,
>   what is there for me to encourage?

I try to keep control of my thoughts,
>   but what is there for me to control?

O Nabu, where is your forgiveness,
>   O son of the [Lo]rd, where are your oracles?

Where is your favorable breeze
>   which wafts over your weakling (subjects)? (25)

O lord, how long will there be darkness
>   in my time of trouble?

The sun lights up for the land, (but) for me [   ].

Prosperity rains down on the people,
>   (but) for me rains down [ ] and gall.

My life is spent, O account-keeper of the u[niverse],
>   where shall I go?

I have reached death's door, O Nabu,
>   why have you forsaken me? (30)

Do not forsake me, my lord,
>   for the [com]pany of my numerous ill-wishers,

To the hands ... of my sorceress do not forsake me,
>   O god called by the good name!

I am a weakling who fears you,
>   do not shame me in public!

I am a guardian of truth,
> do not destroy the truth [I have] guarded!

May the lonely one not die,
> who has called up to you, O lord! (35)

O Nabu, take the hand of the fallen one
> who attends your divinity,

Spare the life of the weakling,
> whom ill-wishers hemmed in,

Whom baleful witches have splashed with conjured water.
Let the dead man revive [by your] breeze,
Let his squandered life become gain! (40)

To Nusku

Nusku, courier of the gods, was invoked as a protective, beneficent deity.

FORFENDER OF NIGHTMARES

O Nusku, you are companion to the sun, (1)
You are the judge, judge (my) case!
This dream which was brought to me in the evening,
    midnight, or morning watch,
Which you understand but I do not,
If it is propitious,
    may the good (it portends) not pass me by, (5)
If it is evil, may the evil (it portends) not overtake me,
It is not for me!
Just as this pulled-up reed cannot return to its place,
And (as) this hem cut from my garment,
Being cut from it, cannot return to my garment, (10)
So may the evil (portended by) this dream,
Which was brought to me in the evening, midnight,
    or morning watch,
Not overtake me, it is not for me!

PROTECTOR AGAINST SORCERY

O Nusku, most great one, offspring of Anu, (1)
Likeness of (your) father, firstborn of Enlil,
Raised in the depths, creation of Enanki,[1]
I have raised a torch, I have made you glow.
A sorcerer has bewitched me, bewitched me
    with the sorcery he worked against me, (5)
A sorceress has bewitched me, bewitched me
    with the sorcery she has worked against me,

---

1. "Lord of heaven and netherworld," a name for Ea.

A male witch has bewitched me, bewitched me
    with the witchcraft he has worked against me,
A female witch has bewitched me, bewitched me
    with the witchcraft she has worked against me,
A worker of spells has bewitched me, bewitched me
    with the spells she has worked against me!
Those who have made figurines that are figurines of me,
    who have made a likeness of my features, (10)
Who have taken of my spittle,
    who have plucked out (a lock) of my hair,
Who have cut off a piece of my clothing,
    have collected dust where my feet have passed,
May Girra, the warrior, dissipate their spells!

To Shamash

GREAT HYMN

This hymn to the sun god, Shamash, begins with Shamash as the all-seeing sun (1-20), whose energies and responsibilities lead him over the entire world every day (21-52). His importance in divination is alluded to (53f.), as well as his role in oaths, treaties, and contracts (55f.). His ability to illumine the darkest places leads to a celebration of his role in investigation, trial, and verdict (56-64). Mention of his concern for travelers and the homeless (65-74) is followed by a fragmentary passage dealing with his interceding mercy (75-82?) and his inexorable retribution against the wicked (83?-102). An interesting passage (103-121), perhaps another independent composition inserted here, delves into his role as supervisor of honest business transactions. Shamash can see through the cleverest fast-talk and the most stringent false denial (122-128). He is the principal divine communicant with the perplexed, the lost, meek, venturesome, and the most wretched human beings beyond the pales of civilization (129-148). This leads to a reflection upon his relationship to the human race as a whole; he grants knowledge, and receives joyous cultic observances in return, including beer at wharfside in honor of his interest in commerce and shipping (149-162). In a climactic paean, the hymnist marvels at the sun's universal dominion, extending to the unseen corners and depths of the cosmos (163-175). He considers the alternately harsh and tender qualities of the god (176-185?). The text is fragmentary at the end, but may conclude with reference to a ceremony and a plea for the god's goodwill.

Illuminator of all, the whole of heaven, (1)
Who makes light the d[arkness for mankind] above and below,
Shamash, illuminator of all, the whole of heaven,
Who makes light the dark[ness for mankind a]bove and below,
Your radiance [spre]ads out like a net [over the world], (5)
You brighten the g[loo]m of the distant mountains.
Gods and netherworld gods rejoiced when you appeared,
All the Igigi-gods rejoice in you.
Your beams are ever mastering secrets,
At the brightness of your light,

>   humankind's footprints become vis[ible].   (10)
> Your dazzle is always seeking out [   ],
> The four world regions [you set alight] like fire.
> You open wide the gate of all [sanctuaries],
> You [   ] the food offerings of the Igigi-gods.
> O Shamash, mankind kneels to your rising,   (15)
> All countries [   ].
> Illuminator of darkness, opener of heaven's bosom,
> Hastener[1] of the morning breeze (for?) the grain field,
>   life of the land,
> Your splendor envelops the distant mountains,
> Your glare has filled all the lands.   (20)
> Leaning over the mountains, you inspect the earth,
> You balance the disk of the world in the midst of heaven
>   (for) the circle of the lands.
> You make the people of all lands your charge,
> All those king Ea, the counsellor,
>   has created are entrusted to you.
> You shepherd all living creatures together,   (25)
> You are their herdsman, above and below.
> You cross regularly through the heavens,
> Every day you traverse the vast earth.
> High seas, mountains, earth, and sky,
> You traverse them regularly, every day, like a ...[2]   (30)
> In the lower regions you take charge of the netherworld gods,
>   the demons, the (netherworld) Anunna-gods,
> In the upper regions you administer all the inhabited world.
> Shepherd of the lower regions, herdsman of the upper regions,
> You, Shamash, are regulator of the light for all.
> You cross time and again the vast expanse of the seas,   (35)
> [Whose] depths not even the Igigi-gods know.
> [O Sham]ash, your radiance has gone down to the deep,
> [The hairy hero-m]an of the ocean can see your light.

1. Or, "who heats," in which case the meaning would be that the rising sun heats the breezes of morn from their night coolness.
2. Word broken, perhaps "cultivated field" or the like, in which case the sun is like a conscientious farmer going over his domain.

[O Shamash], you tighten like a noose, you shroud like a mist,
Your [bro]ad protection is cast over the lands. (40)
Though you darken each day, your face is not eclipsed,
For by night you traverse [the below?].[1]
To far-off regions unknown and for uncoun[ted] leagues
You have persevered, O Shamash,
    what you went by day you returned by night.
Among all the Igigi-gods there is none who does such
    wearisome toil but you, (45)
Nor among the sum total of the gods one
    who does so much as you!
At your rising the gods of the land assembled,
Your fierce glare covered the land.
Of all the lands of different tongues,
[You] know their intentions, you see their footprints. (50)
All humankind kneels before you,
[O Sha]mash, everyone longs for your light,
[From] the diviner's bowl to the knots of cedar,[2]
[You are] the most reflective of dream interpreters,
    explicators of night visions.
[The parties to] contracts[3] kneel before you, (55)
[Be]fore you both wicked and just kneel down.
[No one] goes down to the depths without you.[4]
You clear up the case of the wicked and criminal,
[   ]
He pours out sleep [   ] (60)
You send back (to court?) the rogue surrounded
    by [false witnesses],
You rescue from the brink of hell
    the [innocent] one tied up in a lawsuit,[5]

---

  1. The meaning may be that even though the sun sets, his brightness remains undimmed as he passes the other side of heaven, so he is not to be considered in unfavorable eclipse.
  2. Cedar was used in the diviner's ritual. Perhaps totality is implied, "from alpha to omega."
  3. Sworn documents, such as treaties and contracts, were Shamash's area of concern.
  4. This may refer to a water ordeal.
  5. Lines 61-62 may refer to the comfortable(?), scot-free evildoer being packed off for legal action, while the just man is rescued from the machinations of the law.

What you pronounced in just verdict, O Shamash, [ ],
Your utterances are manifest, they cannot be changed,
    [you show] no favoritism.
You give support to the traveler whose j[ourney] is trying, (65)
To the seafarer in dread of the waves you lend [aid],
You are wont to g[uide] the roamer(?) on unexplored routes,
You always guide [on the ro]ad
    any who turn towards [Shamash].
You rescued from the flashflood
    the [mer]chant bearing his purse,[1]
You bring up the one gone down to the deep,
    you set wings upon him. (70)
You reveal havens in sea and [wastelan]ds,
You show the exile roads he did not know.
[You set free] the one in hid[den dungeon],
You save the displaced cast in prison.
[You reconcile promptly] the god
    [who is angry] with someone, (75)
Upon seeing ... [ ]
You stand by(?) the si[ck man]
You investigate the cause [ ]
You bear [ ]
From the Land of No Return you [ ] (80)
The angry(?) goddesses [ ]
You are exalted [ ]
O Shamash, with [your] battle net [you]
From your meshes no [can escape].
He who, in taking an oath [ ], (85)
For the one who does not fear [ ],
Your wi[de] net is spread [ ].
The man who co[vets] his neighbor's wife,
He will make to [ ] before his appointed day.
A snare is set for him, the wicked man will [ ], (90)
Your weapon makes straight for him,
    there [will be no]ne to save him.

---

1. The bag used by commercial agents to carry their means, and, by extension, "capital."

[His] own father will not be present at his trial,
Nor will his own brothers reply to the judge's queries.
He is caught unawares in a metal trap!
You blunt the horns of a scheming villain, (95)
The perpetrator of a cunning deal is undermined.
You show the roguish judge the (inside of) a jail,
He who takes the fee but does not carry through,
    you make him bear the punishment.
The one who receives no fee
    but takes up the case of the weak,
Is pleasing to Shamash, he will make long his life. (100)
The careful judge who gives just verdicts,
Controls the government, lives like a prince.
What return is there for the investor in dishonest dealings?
His profits are illusory, and he loses his capital.
He who invests in long-range enterprises(?),
    who returns (even?) one shekel to the ... [ ], (105)
Is pleasing to Shamash, he will make long his life.
He who [commits] fra[ud] as he holds the ba[l]ances,
Who switches weights,[1] who lowers the [ ],
(His) profits are illusory, and he lo[ses the capital].
The one who is honest in holding the balance,
    [ ] plenty of [ ], (110)
Whatever (he weighs) will be given to him in plenty [ ].
He who commits fra[ud] as he holds the dry measure,
Who pays loans by the smaller standard,
    demands repayment by the extra standard,
Before his time, the people's curse will take effect on him,
Before his due, he will be called to account,
    he will bear the consequence(?). (115)
No heir will (there be) to take over his property,
Nor will (there be) kin to succeed to his estate.
The honest merchant who pays loans by the [ex]tra(?)
    standard, thereby to make extra virtue,

---

1. That is, buys with a heavy standard and pays back with a light one, taking advantage of varying local standards of weight.

Is pleasing to Shamash, he will grant him extra life,
He will make (his) family numerous,
    he will acquire wealth, (120)
[His] seed will be perpetual as the waters
    of a perpetual spring.
For the man who does virtuous deeds,
    who knows not fraud,
The man who always says what he really means,
    there will be [ ],
The seed of evildoers wi[ll not be perpetual].
The nay-sayers' speeches are before you, (125)
You quickly analyze what they say.
You hear and examine them,
    you see through the trumped-up lawsuit.
Each and every one is entrusted to your hands,
You make their omens the right ones for them,
    you resolve what perplexes.
You heed, O Shamash, prayer, supplication, and blessing, (130)
Obeisance, kneeling, whispered prayer, and prostration.
The feeble one calls you as much as his speech allows him,
The meek, the weak, the oppressed, the submissive,
Daily, ever, and always come before you.
He whose family is far off, whose city is distant, (135)
The shepherd [in] the afflictions of the wilderness,
The herdsman in trouble, the keeper of sheep among
    the enemy, come before you.
O Shamash, there comes before you the caravan,
    in anxious progress,
The travelling merchant, the agent carrying capital.
O Shamash, there comes before you
    the fisherman with his net, (140)
The hunter, the archer, the driver of the game,
The fowler among his snares comes before you,
The skulking thief who hates the daylight,
The bandit on the wilderness paths comes before you,
The wandering dead, the vagrant spirit come before you, (145)
O Shamash, you have listened to them all.

You did not hold back(?) those who came before you,
> you heeded them,
For my sake, O Shamash, do not despise them!
You grant wisdom, O Shamash, to humankind,
You grant those seeking you your raging, fierce light. (150)
[You make] their omens [the rig]ht ones for them,
> you preside over sacrifices.
You probe their future in every way.
You grant wisdom to the limits of the inhabited world.
The heavens are too puny to be the glass of your gazing,
The world is too puny to be (your) seer's bowl. (155)
On the twentieth of the month
> you rejoice with mirth and joy,[1]
You dine, you drink fine brew,
> the tavernkeep's beer at wharfside.[2]
They pour barkeep's beer for you, you accept it.
You are the one who saved them,
> surrounded by mighty waves,
You accept from them in return their fine, clear libations. (160)
You drink their sweet beer and brew,
You are the one who makes them achieve
> the goals they strive for.
You release the ranks[3] of those who kneel to you,
You accept prayers from those who are wont to pray to you.
They revere you, they extol your name, (165)
They(?) praise your greatness(?) forever.
Imposters, those whose tongues urge sedition,
Who, like clouds, have neither face nor ap[pro]ach(?),
Those that go all over the wide earth,
Those that tread the lofty mountains, (170)
The hairy hero-men [of the oce]an, filled with fearsomeness,
The yield of the ocean, which goes all over the deep,
The catch of the rivers, (are?) what pass,
> O Shamash, before you.

1. In Mesopotamian menology, the twentieth of the month was Shamash's day.
2. Refers to Shamash's protection of travelers and commercial venturers (see lines 65ff.).
3. This could mean that the submissive are spared the discipline reserved for the others.

Which are the mountains that are not arrayed in your beams?
Which are the corners of the earth that are not warmed
    by the brightness of your rising? (175)
Brightener of gloom, illuminator of shadow,
Penetrator of darkness, illuminator of the wide world,
Who makes daylight shine,
    who sends down the heatglare of midday to the earth,
Who makes the wild world glow like flame,
Who can shorten the days and lengthen the nights, (180)
[Who can cau]se cold, frost, ice, (and) snow,
[Who shuts ... the ga]te, the bolt of heaven,
    opens wide the doors of the inhabited world,
[Who is master of] strike-point and pin, latch,
    and handlebar,[1]
[Who ...] is relentless, (but) bestows life,
[Who ...] the captive in a fight to the death. (185)
[rea]son, counsel, deliberation, advice,
[   ] ... of morning(?) to the wi[despread] people
[   ] throne, rule, [   ]
[   ] strength, [   ]

(gap of three lines)

[   ] shining, your splendid abode,
[   ] a banquet for(?) the four world regions.
[gover]nor, high priest, and prince, (195)
[   ] may they bring you their tribute.
[   ] in a libation the yield of the lands,
[   ] may your throne dais be renewed,
[   ] whose utterance cannot be changed,
[May Aya, your sp]ouse, say to you in the bed chamber,
    ["Be appeased!"] (200)

---

1. A contrast is implied between the parts that lock the door and those that open it, suggesting a chiasm with the preceding line.

PROTECTOR OF THE KING

This prayer was used in the ritual series "House of the Ritual Bath." This was a royal lustration procedure that took place in various bathing chambers of a bath house, during which an officiant pronounced some prayers and the king others. While many of the officiant's were in Sumerian, the king was expected to speak only Akkadian prayers. Each stage was accompanied by elaborate rituals. The basic procedure involved washing off evil from the king and transferring it magically to those believed to be the source of it. In this instance a figurine is splashed with the dirty wash water. One cycle of this series was devoted to Shamash, from which this prayer has been excerpted.

(said by the king)

O Shamash, king of heaven and earth, lord of truth and justice, (1)
You are purifier of god and man.
O Shamash, I take my place before you
    in the reed booth of the house of the ritual b[ath],
O Shamash, I do not know who has a hold over me,
    assuming a woman, here is a figurine (to represent) her.
O Shamash! Since it is made of pure barley,[1]
    which creates mankind, (5)
The figurine is like a (human) shape,
    the head is like a (human) head,
The shape of the body is like the shape of a (human) body.
O Shamash! This is the figurine of the witch
    (who is doing the) sorcery, who has harassed me,
    who is making the attempt against me,
Who has said to a sorceress, "Bewitch!"
    who has said to a harasser "Harass!"
    who has incited another, (10)
Who has made me eat (bewitched) bread,
    who has made me drink (bewitched) beer,
Who has made me wash in (bewitched) water,
    who has made me anoint with (bewitched) oil,

---

1. The figurine is made of a grain paste.

Who has made me eat (bewitched) food:
Because of whatever she made me eat,
    because of whatever she made me drink,
Because of whatever she made me wash with,
    because of whatever she made me anoint with,
    or dispatched against me, (15)
Because she pronounced my name with evil intent,
    interred symbols of me,
Made figurines of me and took my measurements,
Collected dust grains from my footprints, took up my spittle,
Plucked out a lock of hair, cut off a piece of my clothing,
    snooped for something bad about me,
Because she has made accusations against me,
    hampered me, seized me, polluted me, (20)
Has made me full of stiffness and debility,
Has seized my heart,
    has turned the heart <of my god> against me,
Has twisted my muscles, weakened my strength,
Has overthrown my arms, hobbled my feet,
Has set upon me discord, ill temper,
    misery, anxiety, panic, (25)
Terror, cursing, fear, worry, loss of sleep,
    speechlessness, depression,
Misery, dissatisfaction, illness,
Has cast "dog tongue"[1] between us,
O Shamash, this is she, here is her figurine!
Even though she is not here, her figurine is here! (30)
I wash the water off upon her,
    whatever is known to me of her or not known,
I pollute her with it, let her receive it from me.
She has worked against me furtively,
    but I wash myself off on her openly before you.
Through the greatness of Ea and the procedures of Asalluhi, (35)
Through the command of Marduk and Sarpanitum,
Through the command of Nabu and Tashmetum,

---

1. Meaning unknown, perhaps expression for "bad blood."

I wash myself off upon her, I bathe myself off upon her.
Just as the water is cleared from my body
    and goes upon her and her form,
So do I cast off upon her wrong and bondage!
May all evil in my person, flesh, and sinews (40)
Be cleared like the water from my body
    and go against her and against her form!
O Shamash, her own wicked intents and actions
    turn against her and her form.
On account of the evil of signs and [bad, unfavorable] portents
    which are [present] in my palace [and in my land],
O Shamash, may my sorceress fall but I rise,
May she be hamstrung but I proceed, (45)
May she be polluted but I become pure,
May she die but I live!
O Shamash, let me proceed straight on my way,
    according to your judgment.
O Shamash, since I did not work against her
    — it was she who worked against me —
O Shamash, since I did not harass her
    — it was she who harassed me — (50)
I have washed myself off upon her,
    I have bathed myself in water upon her,
I have polluted her, may she receive it from me!
Just as the water is cleared from my body
    and goes to this (figurine),
May all evil in my person, my flesh, my sinews
Be cleared from my body and leave my body. (55)

AGAINST THE CONSEQUENCES OF A NIGHTMARE

You have burst into light, Shamash, (1)
    from the Mountain of Cedars,
The gods rejoice on account of you,
    mankind is glad on account of you.
The diviner brings you cedar, the widow a flour offering,
The poor woman oil, the rich man a lamb from his wealth.
I bring you a lump of earth, product of the depths. (5)
You, lump, product of the depths,
Part of me is pinched off in you,
Part of you is pinched off in me.
My clay is mixed with your clay,
Your clay is mixed with my clay.
Just as you, lump, dissolve and disappear
    when I throw you into water to dissipate you, (10)
So may the evil [portended by the dream] I had last night,
Which I had of a god, which I had of a king,
    which I had of a noble, which I had of a prince,
    which I had of a dead man, which I had of a living man,
Which I went around ... right ... left,
May it, like you, fall into water to dissipate,
Dissolve, and disappear!
Sheep of the storm, slaughtered with a knife of the wind, (15)
The dead eat it and drink it, it is nothing but wind!
Just as the instep of the foot does not come near the heel,
May the evil (portended) by the dream I had during the night
    not approach me nor come near me!

HOMECOMING

This prayer, designated to be used at sunset, portrays the sun coming home to his abode, Ebabbar, at the end of the day. His gates hail him, his steward escorts him inside, his wife meets him happily, and he has his evening meal.

    O Shamash, when you enter innermost heaven, (1)
    May the pure bolt of heaven greet you,
    May the door of heaven salute you.
    May Justice, your beloved vizier, bring you straight in.[1]
    Show your splendor to the Ebabbar, your lordly dwelling. (5)
    May Aya, your beloved wife, meet you happily,
    May she make you relax,
    May your godly meal be set before you.
    O youthful warrior Shamash, let them ever praise you.
    O lord of Ebabbar, go straight on your path, (10)
    Make straight your way, go the true course to your dwelling.
    O Shamash, you are judge of the land, administrator of its verdicts.

---

1. Wordplay in the original, justice and straightness having the same root.

To a Personal God

Belief in personal gods, supposed to act as protectors and intercessors for the individual, is widely expressed in Assyro-Babylonian literature. Pleas to them express a range of feelings such as guilt, frustration, sorrow, even anger and reproof.

GOD OF MY FAMILY

O my god, my lord, who created my name, (1)
Guardian of my life, producer of my progeny,
O angry god, may your heart be calmed,
O angry goddess, be reconciled with me.
Who knows where you dwell, O my god? (5)
Never have I seen your pure standing place (or sleeping) chamber.
I am constantly in great distress: O my god, where are you?
You who have been angry with me, turn towards me,
Turn your face to the pure godly meal of fat and oil,
That your lips receive goodness. Command that I thrive, (10)
Command (long) life with your pure utterance.
Bring me away from evil that, through you, I be saved.
Ordain for me a destiny of (long) life,
Prolong my days, grant me (long) life!

FURIOUS GOD

My god, I did not know (how) [har]sh
    [your] punishment would be! (1)
I have sworn lightly a solemn oath by your name,
I have disregarded your rites, I went too far,
I have skirted(?) your duty in difficulty,
I have trespassed far beyond your limits. (5)
I certainly did not know, much [ ].
My crimes being (so) numerous, I do not know all I did.
O my god, clear, forego, dispel your ire,

Disregard my iniquities, accept my entreaties,
Transmute my sins into good deeds. (10)
Your hand is harsh, I have seen your punishment.
Let him who does not revere his god and goddess
  learn from my example.
O my god, be reconciled, O my goddess, relent!
Turn hither your faces to the entreaty of my prayer.
May your angry hearts be calmed, (15)
May your feelings be soothed, permit me reconciliation,
Let me ever sing your praises, not to be forgotten,
  to the numerous peoples.

To Any God

According to its subscription, this address, consisting of a prayer, confession, lament, and concluding supplication, could be used for any deity.

> May (my) lord's angry heart be reconciled, (1)
> May the god I do not know be reconciled,
> May the goddess I do not know be reconciled,
> May the god, whoever he is, be reconciled,
> May the goddess, whoever she is, be reconciled, (5)
> May my (personal) god's heart be reconciled,
> May my (personal) goddess's heart be reconciled,
> May (my) god and (my) goddess be reconciled (with me)!
> May the god who [has turned away] from me
>   [in anger be re]conciled,
> May the goddess [who has turned away from me
>   in anger be reconciled], (10)
> [I do not know] what wrong [I have done],
> [   ] the wrong [   ].
> [My god did not call my name] with favor,
> [My goddess did not call my name] with favor,
> [My god did not] pronounce my name [with favor], (15)
> [My goddess did not pronounce my name with favor].
> I could not eat for myself the bread I found,[1]
> I could not drink for myself the water I found.
> I have perpetrated un[wittingly] an abomination to my god,
> I have unwittingly violated a taboo of my goddess. (20)
> O (my) lord, many are my wrongs, great my sins,
> O my god, many are my wrongs, great my sins,
> O my goddess, many are my wrongs, great my sins,
> O god, whoever you are, many are my wrongs,
>   great my sins,
> O goddess, whoever you are, many are my wrongs,
>   great my sins! (25)
> I do not know what wrong I have done,

---

1. That is, he offered it all to his gods in vain.

I do not know what sin I have committed,
I do not know what abomination I have perpetrated,
I do not know what taboo I have violated!
A lord has glowered at me in the anger of his heart, (30)
A god has made me face the fury of his heart,
A goddess has become enraged at me
    and turned me into a sick man,
A god, whoever he is, has excoriated me,
A goddess, whoever she is, has laid misery upon me!
I keep on searching, but nobody will help me, (35)
When I wept, they would not draw near,
When I would make a complaint, no one would listen,
I am miserable, blindfolded, I cannot see!
Turn towards me, merciful god, as I implore you.
I do homage to you, my goddess,
    as I keep groveling before you, (40)
O god, whoever you are, [turn towards me,
    I implore you],
O goddess, [whoever you are, turn towards me,
    I implore you],
O lord, tur[n towards me,
    I implore you],
O goddess, lo[ok upon me,
    I implore you],
O god, [whoever you are, turn towards me,
    I implore you], (45)
O goddess, whoever [you are, turn towards me,
    I implore you]!
How long, O my god,
    [until your furious heart is calmed]?
How long, O my goddess,
    [until your estranged heart is reconciled]?
How long, O god whosoever you are,
    until y[our angry heart is calmed]?
How long, O goddess, whosoever you are,
    until your estranged heart is reconciled? (50)
Men are slow-witted and know nothing,

No matter how many names they go by,
> what do they know?
They do not know at all if they are doing good or evil!
O (my) lord, do not cast off your servant,
He is mired in a morass, help him! (55)
Turn the sin which I perpetrated into virtue,
Let the wind bear away the wrong I committed!
Many are my crimes, strip them off like a garment,
O my god, though my wrongs be seven times seven,
> absolve my wrongs,
O my goddess, though my wrongs be seven times seven,
> absolve my wrongs, (60)
O god, whosoever you are, though my wrongs be
> seven times seven, absolve my wrongs,
O goddess, whosoever you are, though my wrongs be
> seven times seven, absolve my wrongs,
Absolve my wrongs, let me sound your praises!
As if you were my real mother, let your heart be reconciled,
As if you were my real mother, my real father,
> let your heart be reconciled!

Royal Prayers

Coronation Prayer for Assyrian Kings

Three tablets dating sometime after the reign of Tukulti-Ninurta I preserve a new year's coronation ritual of the kings of Assyria dating to the latter half of the second millennium B.C. When the text begins, the king is being hailed and carried into the Assur temple. He distributes gifts of silver and gold which are received by the priests. The king makes an offering to Assur and various other gods. The royal diadem is then set before the altar. After a procedure with a garment that is not clear, the ritual continues with the placing of a gold ring. The priest crowns the king with a turban-like headdress, here rendered "diadem," and speaks the prayer translated below. This sums up Assyrian imperial doctrine, with its religious and territorial emphasis.

> May Assur and Ninlil, owners of your diadem, (1)
> Let you wear the diadem on your head for a century.
> May your foot go fair in Ekur and so too your hands in prayer
>   to Assur your god.
> May your priesthood and the priesthood of your sons go fair
>   before Assur your god.
> With your just scepter, enlarge your country. (5)
> May Assur grant you authority, hearing, and obedience,
>   truth and peace.

Prayer at the Gods' Repast

This prayer was said in honor of the Assyrian king when the gods were served a cultic repast. One manuscript names a late Assyrian king, Assur-etil-ilani (ca. 626-623 B.C.), but the prayer dates earlier than his time.

> He who made this repast, who provided food and drink to the gods, grant that he administer far and wide forever more. May he exercise the high priesthood (of Assur), kingship, and universal dominion. May he attain a ripe old age. To him who heeds these words be barley, silver, oil, wool; salt of Bariku[1] for their food, and oil for their lamps. Live, prosper, and enjoy good fortune! May the rites of the repast for the Mighty Ones in the land of Assyria be eternal. May Assur bless the one who provided this repast, Assur-etil-ilani.

---

1. An esteemed variety of imported salt.

Assurnasirpal I, on Occasion of Illness

The Assyrian king Assurnasirpal I (1050-1032 B.C.) speaks here of his rise to power. He credits Ishtar of Nineveh with the divine favor that led to his success, and reminds her of various compensatory achievements, including restoration of images and construction of a magnificent bed for her. In view of their past relationship, the king asks the goddess for remission of his illness. The mood and message of this text recall the righteous sufferer tradition in Mesopotamian literature.

i

I will tell of [ ] that befell me:	(1)
To the creatress of wis[dom], the praiseworthy ... [goddess],	
To her, who dwells in Emashmash,[1]	
[ ] I shall tell of myself,	
To the queen of the gods, into whose hands [all]	
responsibilities are bestowed,	
To the lady of Nineveh, the lofty [of the gods],	(5)
To the daughter of Sin, twin sister of Shamash	
— she exercises all kingship —	
To her, who renders verdicts, the goddess of all there is,	
To the mistress of heaven and netherworld,	
who accedes to entreaties,	
To her, who hears prayers, who accepts lamentations,	
To the merciful goddess, who loves justice,	(10)
Ishtar, whose portion it is to keep alive(?):	
I set forth before you all the anxieties that I undergo,	
May your ear turn to my weary utterance,	
May your feelings take pity on my ailing speech!	
Look upon me, Mistress, may your heart be pained	
as I turn to you.	(15)

ii

I am Assurnasirpal, your ailing servant,
    Humble, revering your divinity, responsible, your beloved,

---

1. Temple of Ishtar at Nineveh.

Who ensures your divine sustenance,
>who unfailingly supplies your food offerings,

Who looks forward to your festivals,
>who provides for your shrine,

Who provides generously the beer that you want and enjoy, (20)
Son of Shamshi-Adad, a king who revered the great gods.
I was formed in mountains unknown to you, lady.
I was not mindful of your dominion,
>my prayers were not continual,

The people of Assyria did not know me nor did they
>confront your divine presence.

Yet it was you, Ishtar, terrifying dragon of the gods, (25)
That appointed me by your desire
>and wished that I should rule.

You took me from the mountains and named me to be
>shepherd of the peoples,[1]

You established for me a just scepter
>until the world grows old.

It was you, Ishtar, who made glorious my name!
It was you who granted me the power to save and requite
>those who were loyal. (30)

From your mouth came (the command) to repair the divine
>(images) that were stored away,

It was I who repaired the ruined sanctuaries,
I rebuilt the damaged divine images
>and restored them to their places,

I ensured their divine allotments and sustenance forever.
It was I who had made a couch of boxwood,
>a well-appointed bed for your divine repose, (35)

The interior of which I overlaid
>with the finest gold cunningly wrought,

Which I adorned with the choicest precious stones from
>the mountain(s) like a [ ].[2]

---

1. According to some scholars, this is an oblique reference to an irregularity in the royal succession.
2. The old tablet from which the existing manuscript was copied was evidently damaged here, as well as in lines 41 and 59–70.

I consecrated it, I filled it with splendor to behold,
I made it shine like the sun's brilliance, a seemly sight.
I provided it a place in the Emashmash,
    your favorite abode that you love, (40)
In what way have I neglected you
    that I should draw upon myself [such hardship]?
You have blanketed me with disease,
    why am I at my last gasp?
[ ] ... my sinews, in form a wreck.
[Panic], phobia, [ ] choked off(?) my life

(fragmentary lines)

iii

Constantly [ ] I pray to your ladyship,
I sob before your divinity [ ] ...
[ ] who does not fear your divinity,
    who commits abominations, (60)
How have I incurred no sins or misdeeds (before) that I
    should draw upon myself [punishment (now)]?[1]
I am constantly in a state of anxiety, [I abide] in darkness,
I am cut off and shall not see [offspring],
I forsook(?) my royal throne and [   ]
I do not go near the meal I am to eat, [ ] (65)
Beer, the support of life, [is become] disgusting [to me],
I loathe the sennet and sounding of strings, [kingship's] due,
Thus am I deprived of the joys of living! [ ]
My eyes (once) sharp-hued can perceive nothing,
I do not hold [my head] high, [but gaze at]
    the surface of the ground. (70)
For how long, Mistress, have you afflicted me with this
    interminable illness?

---

1. That is, perhaps, he was never blameless; what unusual behavior justifies the goddess's anger?

iv

I am Assurnasirpal, in despair, who reveres you,
Who grasps your divine hem, who beseeches your ladyship:
Look upon me, let me pray to your divine ladyship(?),
You who were angry, take pity on me,
    may your feelings be eased! (75)
May your ever benevolent heart grow pained on my account,
Drive out my illness, remove my debility!
From your mouth, Mistress, may the command
    for mitigation fall!
Have pity on your (once) favored viceroy[1] who never changes,
Banish his despair! (80)
Take his part with your beloved Assur, the [warr]ior,
    father of the gods!
I will praise your divinity forever,
I will magnify the [nob]le one among the gods of heaven
    and netherworld!

---

1. A title of the Assyrian kings expressing their subservience to Assur, the national god and deified city.

Sargon II, for His New City

Sargon II (721-705 B.C.) came to the throne under mysterious circumstances. He may not have been of royal lineage nor in direct line for succession. He proved to be a valorous warrior and undertook an extensive series of campaigns, on one of which he died in battle.

Sargon II constructed a new capital city for himself at Dur-Sharrukin, modern Khorsabad, not far from Nineveh. This city was destined to be occupied for less than fifty years and lies today as an impressive memorial to the will of a single man. Its grandiose plan included numerous temples and a royal palace. The prayers translated here were composed for the new temples at Dur-Sharrukin. Each appeals to a specific aspect of the deity's powers: rainfall (Adad), protection (Assur, Nabu), wisdom and spring water (Ea), progeny (Ningal), strength and prowess (Ninurta), and truth (Sin).

TO ADAD

This prayer was inscribed on the threshold of the entrance to the Adad-temple at Dur-Sharrukin.

> O Adad, irrigator of heaven and earth, who brightens daises, for Sargon, king of the world, king of Assyria, governor of Babylon, king of the land of Sumer and Akkad, builder of your cella, bring the rains from heaven and the floods from underground in good season. Garner grain and oil in his leas, make his subjects lie down in safe pastures amidst plenty and abundance. Make firm the foundations of his throne, let his reign endure.

TO ASSUR

This prayer concluded an inscription on the pavement of a palace gate at Dur-Sharrukin.

> May Assur, father of the gods, look steadfastly with the radiance of his holy features upon this palace. May its renewal always be ordered, until distant days. Let it be established from his holy utterance that protective spirit and safeguarding god be on the watch day and night within it and never leave its sides.
>
> At his command may the sovereign who built it live to a ripe old age. From his holy lips may (these words) fall, "May he who made it grow old, far into the future." May he who dwells therein rejoice within, in good health, happiness, and blithe spirits. May he enjoy well-being in full measure.

TO EA

This prayer was inscribed on the entrance to the Ea-temple at Dur-Sharrukin. It addresses Ea using his byname Ninshiku, which may mean "leader" or the like.

> O Ninshiku, lord of wisdom, creator of all and everything, for Sargon, king of the universe, king of Assyria, governor of Babylon, king of the lands of Sumer and Akkad, builder of your cella, make your underground depth open up, send him its spring waters, provide his leas with plentiful, abundant water. Ordain for his destiny great wisdom and profound understanding, make his project(s) succeed, may he enjoy well-being in full measure.

TO NABU

This prayer was inscribed on the threshold and around the steps in the sanctuary area of the Nabu-temple at Dur-Sharrukin.

> O Nabu, universal scribe, who checks on all, look steadfastly, in the fidelity of your heart, upon Sargon, king of the universe, king of Assyria, governor of Babylon, king of the lands of Sumer and Akkad, builder of your cella, and direct your just countenance upon him. Grant him days of good health till furthest time, ordain for his destiny years of happiness. Make his reign last as long as heaven and earth, let him continue to exercise shepherdship of all lands. May his support endure as (this) structure and its platform.

TO NINGAL

This prayer was inscribed on the threshold of the entrance to the Ningal-temple at Dur-Sharrukin.

> O preeminent lady, exalted Ningal, [inter]cede for Sargon, king of the universe, king of Assyria, governor of Babylon, king of the land of Sumer and Akkad, builder of your cella, with Sin, your beloved spouse, speak a word favorable of him that his reign be [sta]ble. Let him ordain his destiny to live a life long of days. May his offspring hold dominion over all inhabited regions till the end of time.

TO NINURTA

This prayer was inscribed on the threshold of the entrance to the Ninurta-temple at Dur-Sharrukin.

> O Ninurta, athlete of surpassing strength, bestow old age upon Sargon, king of the universe, king of Assyria, governor of Babylon, king of the land of Sumer and Akkad, builder of your cella. May he enjoy well-being in full measure. Make firm his reign in Esagila and Esharra. Guide straight his steeds, safeguard his teams, grant him [un]rivalled strength and manly might, make his weapon at the ready that he kill his foes.

TO SIN

This prayer was inscribed on the threshold of the entrance to the Sin-temple at Dur-Sharrukin.

> O Sin, pure god who renders verdicts and discloses decisions,[1] look steadfastly in the fidelity of your heart upon Sargon, king of the universe, king of Assyria, governor of Babylon, king of Sumer and Akkad, builder of your cella, and direct your just countenance upon him. Grant him days of good health till furthest time, ordain for his destiny years of happiness, make his reign last as long as heaven and earth, make firm his throne over the four world regions.

---

1. Reference to divination.

Assurbanipal, Pious Scholar

The last great Assyrian king, Assurbanipal, succeeded to the throne of the empire in 669 B.C. Among his many military achievements was the destruction of Elam, the traditional enemy of Babylonia.

At Assurbanipal's order was assembled a library at Nineveh, the largest known collection of Akkadian literary and scholarly texts. Among the colophons scribes appended to the manuscripts they copied for Assurbanipal's library are prayers for the king and his muse.

> I, Assurbanipal, king of the universe, king of Assyria, on whom Nabu and Tashmetu have bestowed vast intelligence, who acquired penetrating acumen for the most recondite details of scholarly erudition, no predecessors of whom among kings having any comprehension of such matters, I wrote down on tablets Nabu's wisdom, the impressing of each and every cuneiform sign, and I checked and collated them. I placed them for the future in the library of the temple of my lord Nabu, the great lord, at Nineveh, for my life and for the well-being of my soul, to avoid disease, and to sustain the foundations of my royal throne. O Nabu, look joyfully and bless my kingship forever! Help me whenever I call upon you! As I traverse your house, keep constant watch over my footsteps. When this work is deposited in your house and placed in your presence, look upon it and remember me with favor!

Nebuchadnezzar II, for His Public Works

The Neo-Babylonian kings were heirs to the great conquests of Assyria after its destruction by the Medes and their allies towards the end of the seventh century B.C. Numerous prayers in the names of the Neo-Babylonian kings are preserved in building inscriptions. Their language bespeaks great piety and reverence. The long reign of Nebuchadnezzar II (604-562 B.C.) saw Babylon the greatest city of its time. New temples and a royal palace were built, the remains of which are still visible today. The prayers which follow come from texts commemorating building projects of this energetic and successful king.

TO MARDUK

This prayer concludes an inscription commemorating reconstruction of the old palace and construction of a new one at Babylon.

> What is there besides you, my lord? You have promoted the reputation and vouchsafed an honorable career to the king you love, whose name you pronounce, who is pleasing to you. I am the prince whom you preferred, your handiwork. It was you who created me and vouchsafed me kingship over all peoples. According to your favor, O lord, which you are always ready to bestow upon all of them, make your sublime lordship merciful upon me, instill in my heart reverence for your divinity, grant me what you please that you sustain my life.

TO NABU

This prayer concludes an inscription commemorating construction of a temple for Nabu at Borsippa.

> O Nabu, true heir, sublime courier, victorious one, beloved of Marduk, look joyfully upon my works for (my) favor. Grant me the gift of eternal life, venerable old age, a firm throne, an enduring reign, slaying of foes, conquest of the enemies' land. Proclaim from your steadfast tablet, which fixes the limits of heaven and netherworld, long days and a prolonged old age. Make my works acceptable to Marduk, king of heaven and netherworld, the father who begot you. Speak favorably of me, may this ever be on your lips, "Nebuchadnezzar is surely a provident king."

TO NABU AND MARDUK

This prayer, written out on a brick, concludes an inscription commemorating construction of a processional street in Babylon.

> O Nabu and Marduk, as you go joyfully in procession through these streets, may words favorable of me be upon your lips. As I proceed before you within the(se streets), may I live a life enduring till distant days, in good health and [satisfac]tion forever.

TO NINMAH

This prayer concludes an inscription commemorating reconstruction of the temple of the birth goddess in Babylon.

> O Ninmah, merciful mother, look joyfully! May words in my favor be upon your lips. Multiply my descent, make numerous my posterity, administer in safety childbirth among my descendants.

Nabonidus, for His Public Works

Nabonidus (555-539 B.C.) came to the throne under obscure circumstances, ending a period of political instability. His reign was marked by religious controversy, for he promoted the cult of the moon god to an extent some Babylonians found offensive. He spent part of his reign at Teima, in northern Arabia, for reasons that are as yet unexplained, but which may have to do with the growing power of the Medes across the northern flanks of Mesopotamia. After his return to Babylon his policies seem to have met increased resistance, though his theological innovations are not yet fully understood. The invading armies of Cyrus the Persian entered Babylon without hindrance, and this ended native rule in Babylonia. Some of the prayers translated below give elusive hints as to the personality and religious convictions of this complex and interesting man.

TO MARDUK

This prayer forms part of an inscription commemorating reconstruction of the Shamash temple in Larsa.

> O lord, foremost of the gods, prince Marduk, without you no dwelling is founded nor is its design laid out. Were it not for you, who could do what? O lord, at your sublime command, let me do what is pleasing to you.

TO MARDUK

This prayer forms part of an inscription commemorating reconstruction of the Ehulhul, temple of the moon god in Harran.

> Let me be king after your own heart, I who, in my ignorance, had no thought of kingship, whom you, lord of lords, have given more responsibility than others you have named and who held dominion from of old. Prolong my days, let my years endure, that I may be the provider [for your sanctuary].

TO SHAMASH

This prayer forms part of an inscription commemorating reconstruction of the Ebabbar, temple of Shamash in Sippar.

O Shamash, sublime lord, as you enter Ebabbar, seat of your repose, may the gates, entrances, chapels, and courtyards rejoice before you like flowers(?).[1] As you take up your residence in your lordly cella, your judiciary seat, may the gods of your city and of your household put your feelings in repose, may the great gods please you. May Aya the great bride, who dwells in the bedchamber, keep your features ever aglow and speak favorably of me every day.

With your radiant features and joyful face look joyfully upon my precious handiwork, my good deeds, my inscription and my royal statue. May words in my favor be upon your lips, pronounce my name for all time. Let the house I built endure, may your dwelling be perpetual within it. May the god of the house, the design of the house, the crossbeams, lintel, doorframe, sill, bolt, threshold, anteroom, and door leaves guard my step and make straight your going, in your presence extol my deeds, and night and day may they invoke favor for me.

At your sublime command, which cannot be altered, at the word of your great divinity, which cannot be transgressed, may truth, justice, and the divine judge of the gods who sits before you, set for my feet a way of well-being and wealth, a path of truth and justice. May your sublime courier who stands before you, Bunene, whose counsel is good, who rides (your) chariot, who sits on the driver's seat, whose onslaught cannot be withstood, who hitches up the valorous steeds whose legs tire not going or returning, who parades before you in street and way, make favorable report of me and advise you that my kingship be lengthy of days, may he come to your aid in your precious mission. Send beside me the divine splendor of your lightning bolt, symbol of dominion and the

---

1. Meaning uncertain, the simile may be that of a field full of spring flowers that seems to rejoice as the sunlight approaches.

awesomeness of kingship, to plunder the land of my enemy. May I overwhelm my foe's land, may I kill my adversaries, may I partake of the booty of my enemy, may I garner to my land the possessions of all lands.

May I be a provident king who renews holy places, who completes sanctuaries for all time. At the invocation of my eminent name may all my enemies become timorous and weak, may they bow down before me. May they bear my yoke till distant days and bring their massive tribute before me in my city Babylon. May my dwelling be eternal within Babylon, may I enjoy the thoroughfare of its byways in full measure, may my service endure in Esagila and Ezida, which I love. Before lord Nabu and Nergal, my gods and the gods of the entire new year's festival house of the Enlil of the gods, Marduk, may I always, for all time, proceed to offer flour sacrifices, to care for Edadihegal,[1] and to entreat the lord of lords.

TO SHAMASH

This prayer forms part of an inscription commemorating reconstruction of the Ebabbar, temple of Shamash in Sippar.

O Shamash, great lord of heaven and earth, light of the gods his ancestors, offspring of Sin and Ningal, as you enter the Ebabbar, your beloved house, as you take your place upon your eternal dais, look joyfully upon my good works, mine, Nabonidus, king of Babylon, the prince who provides for you, who pleases you, builder of your sublime cella. Each day as you rise and set, make my signs favorable in sky and terrain. Receive my entreaties and accept my prayers. May I hold dominion forever with the legitimate scepter and staff which you let me hold in my hand.

---

1. Unclear, perhaps the name of a structure.

Diviners' Prayers

Extispicy, or divination by examination of the entrails of a lamb (exta), required a series of prayers and rituals, culminating in sacrifice and examination of the animal. The prayer and rituals are replete with legal imagery: the procedure is a "case"; inducements are offered for a favorable decision; the outcome is a "verdict"; the principal gods concerned are Shamash, god of justice, and Adad, god of thunder. The prayers were intended to attract the god's attention, to enlist his help for proper procedure, and to elicit, if possible, a favorable verdict for the client. Often the specific favorable features of the exta are itemized together with the more general requests of the prayer. Where the client's name was to be given, the manuscripts refer to "so-and-so, son of so-and-so."

The Cedar

O Shamash, I place in my mouth sacred cedar, (1)
For you I knot it in a lock of my hair,
For you I place in my lap bushy cedar.

I have washed my mouth and hands, (5)
I have wiped my mouth with bushy cedar,
I have tied sacred cedar in a lock of my hair,
For you I have heaped up bushy cedar.
Cleansed now, to the assembly of the gods
    draw I near for judgment. (10)
O Shamash, lord of judgment, O Adad, lord of prayers
    and acts of divination.
In the ritual I perform, in the extispicy I perform,
    place the truth!

O Shamash, I place incense in my mouth,
... sacred cedar, let the incense linger! (15)
Let it summon to me the great gods.
In the ritual I perform, in the extispicy I perform,
    place the truth!

O Shamash, I hold up to you water of Tigris and Euphrates,
Which has carried to you cedar and juniper
    from the highlands. (20)
Wash yourself, O valiant Shamash,
Let the great gods wash with you.
And you too, Bunene, faithful messenger,
Wash yourself in the presence of Shamash the judge.

O Shamash, to you I hold up something choice, (25)
... sacred water for the flour.
O Shamash, lord of judgment,
    O Adad, lord of prayers and divination,
Seated on thrones of gold, dining from a tray of lapis,
Come down to me that you may dine, that you may sit
    on the throne and render judgment!
In the ritual I perform, in the extispicy
    I perform, place the truth!

O Shamash, I hold up to you a lordly tribute,
Which in the courtyard of the gods to you [ ]. (35)
O Shamash, lord of judgment, O Adad l[ord of acts of]
Divination, seated on thrones of gold,
Dining from a tray of lapis, come down to me
That you may sit on the throne and render judgment!
In the ritual I perform, in the extispicy I perform,
    place the truth! (40)

O Shamash, I hold up to you seven and seven sweet loaves,
The rows of which are ranged before you.
O Shamash, lord of judgment, O Adad, lord of divination,
Seated on thrones of [gold], dining from a tray of lapis, (45)
Come [down to me] that you may eat,
That you may sit on the throne and render judgment.
In the ritual I perform, in the extispicy I perform,
    place the truth!

O Shamash, I hold up to you the plentiful yield of the gods,
>   the radiance of the grain goddess. (50)
O Shamash, lord of judgment, O Adad, lord of divination,
In the ritual I perform, in the extispicy I perform,
>   place the truth!

O Shamash, I have laid out for you the plentiful yield of
>   the gods, the radiance of the grain goddess,
O Shamash, lord of judgment, O Adad,
>   lord of prayer and divination, (55)
In the ritual I perform, in the extispicy I perform,
>   place the truth!

Take your seat, O valiant Shamash,
Let there be seated with you the great gods,
Let Anu, father of heaven, Sin, king of the tiara, (60)
Nergal, lord of weaponry, Ishtar, lady of battle
Be seated with you.
In the ritual I perform, in the extispicy I perform,
>   place the truth!

The Sacrificial Gazelle

This prayer is notable for its lyrical portrayal of the growth of a young gazelle in the wilderness. It forms part of a group of diviner's prayers arranged for the offering of specific animals.

O Shamash, lord of judgment, O Adad, lord of divination, I bring and ask your blessing upon a pure fawn, offspring of a gazelle, whose eyes are bright-hued, whose features are radiant(?), a pure, tawny sacrificial animal, offspring of a gazelle, whose mother bore him in the steppe, and the steppe set its kind protection over him. The steppe raised him like a father, and the pasture like a mother. When the warrior Adad saw him, he would rain abundance(?) upon him in the earth's close: grass grew up, he would rejoice in (its) fullness, the ... of the livestock would sprout luxuriantly. He would eat grass in the steppe; never would he want for water to drink at pure pools. He would feed on the ...-plants and then return (to his haunts). He who never knew a herdsman [ ] in the steppe, from whom the lamb was kept away, I ask your blessing (upon him as my offering). O Shamash and Adad, stand by me! In what I say and pray, [in whatsoever I d]o, in the inquiry I ask your blessing on, let there b[e] truth!

The Sacrificial Lamb

[O Shamash, lord of judgment, O Ada]d, lord of divination, I bring and ask your blessing upon (this) yearling [lamb] which no ram has mounted, into which [no] beast's seed has fallen. It ate grass on the plains, it always drank water from pure pools, the male lamb was kept away from it. I ask your blessing upon (this) lamb, I set in this lamb's mouth pure cedar in bunches, sprigs, and sweet sap. O Shamash and Adad, stand by me in this lamb (offering). In what I say and pray, in whatsoever I do, in the inquiry I ask your blessing on, let there be truth!

Will Ur-Utu Be Alive and Well?

This prayer is a general oracular inquiry about the well-being of Ur-Utu, a priest or professional man attached to the local temple in a village near Sippar in the Old Babylonian period. He was presumably one of the leading citizens of the community.

> O God, my lord Ninsianna, accept this offering, stand by me when this offering is made, place there an oracle of well-being and life for Ur-Utu, your servant! Concerning Ur-Utu, your servant, who is now standing by this offering, from April 20 until April 20 of the coming year, six times sixty days, six times sixty nights, by command of a god, by command of a goddess, by command of a king, by command of a noble, by command of a commoner, by command of fate or regulation, by any command whatsoever, will Ur-Utu be alive and well? From April 20 until April 20, six times sixty days, six times sixty nights, until next year, will Ur-Utu be alive and well? In his household: his wife, his sons, his daughters, his brother, his sister, his near and distant kin, his neighbor, anyone on (his) street who likes him? In the ritual I perform ... Will Ur-Utu be alive and well? Place an oracle of well-being and life for Ur-Utu!

Letter Prayers

Kussulu to the Moon-God

This bitter harangue, written on a pierced cylinder, is addressed to the moon-god by a certain Kussulu. He loaned money to a certain Elali without a written document, but was instead content with the debtor's four-fold oath in the precinct of the moon-god's temple at Ur, and, apparently, a symbolic gesture. Perhaps Kussulu had wanted to avoid the costs of a scribe and witnesses. The debtor failed to repay. He married and raised a family, although a consequence of breaking an oath was supposed to be infertility. Kussulu had no recourse save a direct appeal to the gods concerned by the broken oath to exercise their power and thereby prove their greatness.

O Nanna, you are king of heaven and earth, I put my trust in you. Elali, son of Girnisa, has wronged me, judge my case!

Having no money, he approached me. He paid his debts with my money. He married, he had a son and daughter. He did not satisfy me, he did not repay my money in full, he has wronged me, his creditor(?). But I put my trust in Nanna!

In the orchards facing Ekishnugal[1] he swore: "May I be damned if I wrong you!" He swore at the Main Gate, under the weapon which you love, he swore inside the Main Court facing Ekishnugal, facing Ningal of the Egadi, before Ninshubur ... of the Main Court, before Alamush, before Nanna-Vanguard and Nanna-Reinforcement he swore: "May I be damned if I wrong you or your sons!" He said, "These gods be my witness."

Moreover, in the orchards facing Ekishnugal, before Nanna, before Shamash, he swore this: "May I, Elali, be damned if I wrong Kussulu! May Elali have no heir before Nanna and Shamash (if he wrongs)!"

(One says): "The false swearer (by) Nanna and Shamash shall be a leper, he shall be destitute and not have a male heir." Elali swore by Nanna and Shamash and has wronged me! May Ninshubur,

---

1. Temple of the moon-god at Ur.

master of property rights, stand (as witness), may Nanna and Shamash judge my case! Let me see the greatness of Nanna and Shamash!

Ur-Nanshe to Ninsianna

This prayer, addressed to the goddess Ninsianna in the form of a letter, complains that she has not been looking after her protégé, Ur-Nanshe.

Say to Ninsianna, thus says Ur-Nanshe: What have I done to you that [ ]? I cannot hold up my head for misery! For ..., I do not have enough food to eat, nor do I have decent clothes for myself, nor can I limber up my bones with oil. Misery has crept into my heart like a weed(?). I really must complain [ ]

(gap and four fragmentary lines)

Apil-Adad to "God My Father"

In this letter, addressed to his personal god, Apil-Adad complains of being neglected, and asks him to send a letter to Marduk, god of Babylon.

Say to God my father, thus says Apil-Adad your servant. Why have you been so neglectful of me? Who might there be to give you a substitute for me? Write to Marduk who loves you, ... my debt. Let me see your face, let me kiss your feet![1] Consider my family, old and young! For their sakes take pity on me, let your assistance reach me!

---

1. "Let me see your face," that is, "show yourself capable of doing something." "Let me kiss your feet," that is, "do something that I may have cause to be grateful to you."

V
Sorrow and Suffering

Dialogue between a Man and His God

This text deals with the problem of guilt and a man's relationship to his god.

> A young man was imploring his god as a friend, (1)
> He was constantly supplicating, he was [praying to?] him.
> His heart was seared, he was sickened with his burden,
> His feelings were somber from misery.
> He weakened, fell to the ground, prostrated himself. (5)
> His burden had grown too heavy for him,
>   he drew near to weep.[1]
> He was moaning like a donkey foal separated
>   (from its mother),
> He cried out before his god, his master.
> His mouth a wild bull, his clamor two mourners,
> [His] lips bear a lament to his lord. (10)
> He recounts the burdens he suffered to his lord,
> The young man expounds the misery he is suffering:
> "My Lord, I have debated with myself, and in my feelings
> "[ ] of heart: the wrong I did I do not know!
> "Have I [ ] a vile forbidden act?
> "Brother does not de[sp]ise his brother, (15)
> "Friend is not calumniator of his friend![2]
> "The [ ] does not [ ]

        (large gap)

> "[From] when I was a child until I grew up,
>   (the days?) have been long, when ... [ ]?
> "How much you have been kind to me, how much
>   I have blasphemed you, I have not forgotten.

---

1. That is, in order to weep near a statue or cult symbol.
2. If the god is a friend, he will not treat the sufferer unjustly.

"In[stead?] of good you revealed evil, O my lord, (20)
    you made [ ] glow ...
"My bad repute is grown excessive, it ... to (my) feet.
"It [rains] blows on my skull(?).
"Its [ ] turned my mouth ... to gall.

(large gap)

[ ] he brought him to earth,
[ ] he has anointed him with medicinal oil, (25)
[ ] food, and covered his blotch,
He attended him and gladdened his heart,
He ordered the restoration of his good health to him:
"Your disease is under control,
    let your heart not be despondent!
"The years and days you were filled with misery are over. (30)
"Were you not ordained to live,
"How could you have lasted the whole
    of this grievous illness?
"You have seen distress, ... is (now) held back.
"You have borne its massive load to the end.
"I flung wide your access(?), the way is open to you, (35)
"The path is straight for you, mercy is granted you.
"You must never, till the end of time, forget [your] god
"Your creator, now that you are favored.
"I am your god, your creator, your trust,
"My guardians are strong and alert on your behalf. (40)
"The field will open [to you] its refuge.
"I will see to it that you have long life.
"So, without qualms, do you anoint the parched,
"Feed the hungry, water the thirsty,
"But he who sits there with burning e[yes], (45)
"Let him look upon your food, melt, flow down,
    and dis[solve].[1]

---

1. Perhaps a reference to an ill-wisher who will see the sufferer's good fortune and melt away magically.

"The gate of life and well-being is open to you!
"Going away(?), drawing near, coming in, going out:
    may you be well!"

Make straight his way, open his path:
    May your servant's supplication reach your heart!

Poem of the Righteous Sufferer

The Poem of the Righteous Sufferer is a poetic monologue, opening and concluding with hymns, that tells how a certain noble gentleman, once important and prosperous, for no apparent reason was driven to disgrace and disease by the god Marduk. His story is set forth as exemplary of the two sides to divine character, anger and forgiveness, and as exemplary of the unfathomable will of the gods.

The poem opens with a hymn setting forth contrasts of Marduk's nature and then proceeds to the narrative (Tablet I line 41). The speaker loses his luck and his personal defenses are lowered, exposing him to misfortune. He consults experts (line 52), to no avail. He loses favor at court (line 55) and paints a vivid picture of seven base conspirators excitedly clamoring over the advantages they plan to take of his downfall (lines 59-64). Physical disintegration sets in (lines 70ff.), followed by social ostracism. He is reviled everywhere and suffers financial setbacks (lines 99ff.). He loses his post and a long period of depression and foreboding ensues (lines 103ff.). He still hopes for deliverance (lines 119-120).

As Tablet II opens, a year has elapsed, longer than such suffering is usually visited upon a man. Prayer and consultation are to no avail. One would think he was godless (Tablet II lines 12-22), but he was always scrupulous in his observances of god and sovereign. Does that matter (lines 33ff.)? Can anyone hope to understand the will of the gods? People's fortunes rise and fall — what is the lesson in that?

The speaker has no further opportunity for reflection as he comes down with a textbook of illnesses (Tablet II lines 50ff.). Pains, agony, malfunction, disability crush him. He can neither eat nor drink (Tablet II lines 86ff.). He falls bedridden (Tablet II lines 95ff.) and writhes helplessly in filth and torment. Continued consultations with experts yield nothing. He is given up for lost, his tomb is made ready, grave goods set out, his wretched obituary written (Tablet II lines 114ff.; compare also Tablet I line 13). Gloom settles over his loved ones.

As he lapses into the coma of death, the sufferer, whose name is now revealed to be Shubshi-meshre-Shakkan, sees a dream visitant: a young man in fine clothes (perhaps a personification of the speaker's own self in better days?). The apparition promises him relief and dries up his sores. The ministrant speaks on behalf of a lady, who may be Sarpanitum, Marduk's wife (see Tablet IV fragment C, lines 55-56). She may have interceded with her husband on behalf of the sufferer, a common motif in Mesopotamian literature. In Tablet III lines 16-18 the sufferer tries vainly to convince his skeptical family of the truth of what he saw. In a second vision, a man washes him off with water and massages him. In a third, a female figure intercedes for him in oblique terms; thereupon a scholar appears with a written text that contains the wording for his release (Tablet III line 41). Signs are sent so the people will believe; Marduk forgives him his misdeeds. The sufferer's illnesses are thereupon cured, he begins to eat and drink, gets out of bed, and testifies to his health.

Tablet IV opens with Shubshi-meshre-Shakkan's testimony that it was Marduk who saved him. He goes through a river ordeal to prove himself guiltless, then goes to the temple of Marduk. His progress through the city echoes the note of encouragement for the human race sounded by the name of each gate and quarter and fulfills the implications of the names. In Tablet IV lines 35ff. he makes lavish thank offerings; finally, in Tablet IV lines 49-50, he gives a banquet for the citizenry at the site of his intended entombment. In a closing hymn, the Babylonians proclaim the wondrous healing power of Marduk to rescue mankind. So great is this healing power that it can heal even the most terrible of afflictions — those sent by Marduk himself.

The text sets forth a Mesopotamian notion of guilt and divine power. The modern term "righteous sufferer" is a misnomer when applied to this and comparable texts; at least, Shubshi-meshre-Shakkan was not so confident of his righteousness as Job. The author of Job makes clear that Job's suffering had nothing to do with his righteousness, but was a test of faith. Here the speaker says that, so far as he knows, he has been righteous, and whatever his fault may have been (who can know?), he is sorry for it and begs forgiveness. There is none of the defiance and bitterness of Job. In short, this text sees suffering and redemption as signs of divine power, while Job sees them as tests of human strength. Despite these differences, the two documents belong to a common Near Eastern literary tradition. Each works out its version of the problem of divinely inflicted human suffering in an original manner.

The reader is left to conclude that Marduk can redeem anyone, no matter how lost to the human race. This sounds a note of optimism that for the author outweighs his despair and agnosticism. In expatiating this theme, the poet drew freely on a vast store of knowledge to lend his text richness and broad scholarly appeal. The product is one of the finest literary monuments of Mesopotamian antiquity.

Tablet I

I will praise the lord of wisdom, solicitous god, (1)
Furious in the night, growing calm in the day:
Marduk! Lord of wisdom, solicitous god,
Furious in the night, growing calm in the day:
Whose anger is like a raging tempest, a desolation, (5)
But whose breeze is sweet as the breath of morn.
In his fury not to be withstood, his rage the deluge,
Merciful in his feelings, his emotions relenting.
The skies cannot sustain the weight of his hand,
His gentle palm rescues the moribund. (10)
Marduk! The skies cannot sustain the weight of his hand,
His gentle palm rescues the moribund.
He it is, in the brunt of whose anger, graves are dug,
At the same moment, raised the fallen from disaster.
He glowers, protective spirits take flight, (15)
He regards, the one whose god forsook him returns.
His severe punishment is harsh and speedy,
He stops short and quickly returns to his natural state.
He is bull-headed when cherishing his beloved(?),[1]
Like a cow with a calf,
      he keeps turning around watchfully.[2] (20)
His scourge is barbed and punctures the body,
His bandages are soothing, they heal the doomed.
He speaks and makes one incur many sins,
On the day of his justice liability and guilt are dispelled.
He is the one who afflicts with demons of shaking-disease, (25)
Through his sacral spell chills and shivering are driven away.
Who ... the flood of Adad, the blow of Erra,
Who reconciles the wrathful god and [god]dess,
The lord divines the gods' inmost thoughts,
  (But) no [god] understands his behavior! (30)

---

1. A wordplay on "beloved"(?) and "wild bull" may be intended, resumed by "cow" in the following line. Variant: "love for me"(?).

2. The image, well known in Near Eastern art, appears to be that of the maternal cow turning to lick the newborn calf.

Marduk divines the gods' inmost thoughts,
Which [god] understands his mind?
As heavy his hand, so compassionate his heart,
As brutal his weapons, so life-sustaining his feelings.
Without his consent, who could cure his blow? (35)
Against his will, which one could stay his hand?
I, who touched bottom like a fish,
    will proclaim his anger,
He quickly granted me favor, as if reviving the dead.
I will teach the people that his kindness is nigh,
May his favorable thought take away their [guilt?]. (40)
From the day the Lord punished me,
And the warrior Marduk became furious with me,
My own god threw me over and disappeared,
My goddess broke rank and vanished.
He cut off the benevolent angel who (walked) beside me, (45)
My protecting spirit was frightened off,
    to seek out someone else.
My vigor was taken away,
    my manly appearance became gloomy,
My dignity escaped and lit on the roof.
Terrifying signs beset me:
I was forced from my house, I wandered outside. (50)
My omens were confused,
    they were contradictory every day,
(Even) with diviner and dream interpreter
    my course was undecided.
What was said in the street portended ill for me,
When I lay down at night, my dream was terrifying.
The king, incarnation of the gods, sun of his peoples, (55)
His heart hardened against me,
    turning tolerance to ill-will.
Courtiers were plotting hostile action against me,
They mustered themselves to instigate base deeds:
If the first "I will make him end his life"
Says the second "I ousted (him) from his command!" (60)
So likewise the third "I will get my hands on his post!"

"I'll come into property!" vows the fourth
As the fifth subverts the mind of fifty,
Sixth and seventh follow on his heels![1]
The clique of seven have massed their forces, (65)
Merciless as fiends, the likeness of demons.
So one is their body, (but seven) their mouths.
Their hearts fulminate against me, ablaze like fire.
Slander and lies they try to lend credence against me.
My eloquent mouth they checked, as with reins, (70)
My lips, which used to discourse,
    became those of a deaf man.
My resounding call struck dumb,
My proud head bent earthward,
My stout heart turned feeble for terror,
My broad breast brushed aside by a stripling, (75)
My far-reaching arms were pinned by my clothing.
I, who walked proudly, learned slinking,
I, so grand, became servile.
To my vast family I became a loner,
As I went through the streets, I was pointed at, (80)
I would enter the palace, eyes would squint at me,
My city was glowering at me like an enemy,
Belligerent and hostile would seem my land!
My brother became my foe,
My friend became a malignant demon, (85)
My comrade would denounce me savagely,
My colleague kept the taint to(?) his weapons for bloodshed,
My best friend made my life an aspersion.
My slave cursed me openly in the assembly (of gentlefolk),
My slave girl defamed me before the rabble. (90)
An acquaintance would see me and make himself scarce,
My family set me down as an outsider.
A pit awaited anyone speaking well of me,
While he who was uttering defamation of me forged ahead.

---

1. . Literally: "like his protective spirit."

One who relayed base things about me
    had a god for his help, (95)
For the one who said "What a pity about him!"
    death came early,
The one of no help, his life became charmed,
I had no one to go at my side, nor saw I a champion.
They parceled my possessions among the riffraff,
The sources of my watercourses they blocked with muck, (100)
They chased the harvest song from my fields,
They left my community deathly still,
    like that of a (ravaged) foe.
They let another assume my duties,
And appointed an outsider to my prerogatives.
By day sighing, by night lamentation, (105)
Monthly, depression, despair the year.
I moaned like a dove all my days,
Like a singer, I moan out my dirge.
My eyes endure(?) constant crying,
My cheeks scald from tears, as if eroded(?). (110)
My face is darkened from the apprehensions of my heart,
Terror and panic have jaundiced my face.
The wellsprings of my heart quaked in unremitting anxiety,
I was changeable(?) as a flickering fire,
Prayer was disorder, like an exploding flame, (115)
My entreaty was like the fracas of a brawl.
My sweet-lipped discourse was murky, obscure,
When I turned a biting comment, my gambit was stifled.
"Surely in daylight good will come upon me!
"The new moon will appear, my sun will shine!" (120)

Tablet II

One whole year to the next! The (normal) time passed.	(1)
As I turned around, it was more and more terrible.	
My ill luck was on the increase, I could find no good fortune.	
I called to my god, he did not show his face,	
I prayed to my goddess, she did not raise her head.	(5)

The diviner with his inspection
    did not get to the bottom of it,
Nor did the dream interpreter with his incense
    clear up my case.
I beseeched a dream spirit, but it did not enlighten me,
The exorcist with his ritual did not appease divine wrath.
What bizarre actions everywhere! (10)
I looked behind: persecution, harassment!
Like one who had not made libations to his god,
Nor invoked his goddess with a food offering,
Who was not wont to prostrate, nor seen to bow down,
From whose mouth supplication and prayer were wanting, (15)
Who skipped holy days, despised festivals,
Who was neglectful, omitted the gods' rites,
Who had not taught his people reverence and worship,
Who did not invoke his god, but ate his food offering,
Who snubbed his goddess, brought (her) no flour offering, (20)
Like one possessed(?), who forgot his lord,
Who casually swore a solemn oath by his god:
    I, indeed, seemed (such a one)!
I, for my part, was mindful of supplication and prayer,
Prayer to me was the natural recourse, sacrifice my rule.
The day for reverencing the gods was a source
    of satisfaction to me, (25)
The goddess's procession day was my profit and return.
Praying for the king, that was my joy,
His sennet was as if for (my own) good omen.
I instructed my land to observe the god's rites,
The goddess's name did I drill my people to esteem. (30)
I made my praises of the king like a god's,
And taught the populace reverence for the palace.

I wish I knew that these things were pleasing to a god!
What seems good to one's self could be an offense to a god,
What in one's own heart seems abominable
    could be good to one's god! (35)
Who could learn the reasoning of the gods in heaven?
Who could grasp the intentions of the gods of the depths?
Where might human beings have learned the way of a god?
He who lived by (his) brawn died in confinement.
Suddenly one is downcast, in a trice full of cheer, (40)
One moment he sings in exaltation,
In a trice he groans like a professional mourner.
People's motivations change in a twinkling!
Starving, they become like corpses,
Full, they would rival their gods. (45)
In good times, they speak of scaling heaven,
When it goes badly, they complain of going down to hell.
I have ponde[red] these things;
    I have made no sense of them.
But as for me, in despair, a whirlwind is driving(?) me!
Debilitating disease is let loose upon me: (50)
An evil vapor has blown against me [from the] ends
    of the earth,
Head pain has surged up upon me from the breast of hell,
A malignant spectre has come forth from its hidden depth,
A relentless [ghost] came out of its dwelling place.
[A she-demon came] down from the mountain, (55)
Ague set forth [with the] flood [and sea?],
Debility broke through the ground with the plants.
[They assembled] their host, together they came upon me:
[They struck my he]ad, they closed around my pate,
[My features] were gloomy, my eyes ran a flood, (60)
They wrenched my muscles, made my neck limp,
They thwacked [my chest], pounded(?) my breast,
They affected my flesh, threw (me) into convulsions,
They kindled a fire in my epigastrium,
They churned up my bowels, they tw[isted] my entrails(?), (65)
Coughing and hacking infected my lungs,

They infected(?) my limbs, made my flesh pasty,
My lofty stature they toppled like a wall,
My robust figure they flattened like a bulrush,
I was dropped like a dried fig, I was tossed on my face. (70)
A demon has clothed himself in my body for a garment,
Drowsiness smothers me like a net,
My eyes stare, they cannot see,
My ears prick up, they cannot hear.
Numbness has spread over my whole body, (75)
Paralysis has fallen upon my flesh.
Stiffness has seized my arms,
Debility has fallen upon my loins,
My feet forgot how to move.
[A stroke] has overcome me, I choke like one fallen, (80)
Signs of death have shrouded my face!
[If someone th]inks of me, I can't respond to the inquirer,
"[Ala]s!" they weep, I have lost consciousness.
A snare is laid on my mouth,
And a bolt bars my lips. (85)
My way in is barred, my point of slaking blocked,
My hunger is chronic, my gullet constricted.
If it be of grain, I choke it down like stinkweed,
Beer, the sustenance of mankind, is sickening to me.
Indeed, the malady drags on! (90)
For lack of food my features are unrecognizable,
My flesh is waste, my blood has run dry,
My bones are loose, covered (only) with skin,
My tissues are inflamed, afflicted with gangrene(?).
I took to bed, confined, going out was exhaustion, (95)
My house turned into my prison.
My flesh was a shackle, my arms being useless,
My person was a fetter, my feet having given way.
My afflictions were grievous, the blow was severe!
A scourge full of barbs thrashed me, (100)
A crop lacerated me, cruel with thorns.
All day long tormentor would torment [me],
Nor at night would he let me breathe freely a moment.

From writhing, my joints were separated,
My limbs were splayed and thrust apart. (105)
I spent the night in my dung like an ox,
I wallowed in my excrement like a sheep.
The exorcist recoiled from my symptoms,
While my omens have perplexed the diviner.
The exorcist did not clarify the nature of my complaint, (110)
While the diviner put no time limit on my illness.
No god came to the rescue, nor lent me a hand,
No goddess took pity on me, nor went at my side.
My grave was open, my funerary goods ready,
Before I had died, lamentation for me was done. (115)
All my country said, "How wretched he was!"
When my ill-wisher heard, his face lit up,
When the tidings reached her, my ill-wisher,
    her mood became radiant.
The day grew dim for my whole family,
For those who knew me, their sun grew dark. (120)

Tablet III

Heavy was his hand upon me, I could not bear it! (1)
Dread of him was oppressive, it [me].
His fierce [pun]ishment [ ], the deluge,
His stride was ..., it ... [ ]
[Ha]rsh, severe illness does not ... [ ] my person, (5)
I lost sight of [aler]tness, [ ] make my mind stray.
I gro[an] day and night alike,
Dreaming and waking [I am] equally wretched.
A remarkable young man of extraordinary physique,
Magnificent in body, clothed in new garments, (10)
Because I was only half awake, his features lacked form.
He was clad in splendor, robed in dread —
He came in upon me, he stood over me.
[When I saw him, my] flesh grew numb.
[ ] "The Lady(?) has sent [me], (15)
"[ ]."

>   [ ] I tried to tell [my people],[1]
>   "[ ] sent [for me]."
>   They were silent and did not [speak],
>   They heard me [in silence and did not answer].   (20)
>   A second time [I saw a dream].
>   In the dream I saw [at night],
>   A remarkable purifier [   ],
>   Holding in his hand a tamarisk rod of purification,
>   "Laluralimma,[2] resident of Nippur,   (25)
>   "Has sent me to cleanse you."
>   He was carrying water, he po[ured it] over me,
>   He pronounced the resuscitating incantation,
>   he massaged [my] bo[dy].
>   A third time I saw a dream.
>   In my dream I saw at night: (30)
>   A remarkable young woman of shining countenance,
>   Clothed like a person(?), being li[ke] a god,
>   A queen among peoples [   ],
>   She entered upon me and [sat down] ... [   ]
>   She ordered my deliverance [   ]
>   "Fear not!" she said, "I [will   ]   (35)
>   "Whatever one sees(?) of a dream [   ]."
>   She ordered my deliverance, "Most wre[tched] indeed is he,
>   "Whoever he might be,
>   the one who saw the vision at night."[3]
>   In the dream (was) Ur-Nintinugga, a Babylonian(?) ...
>   A bearded young man wearing a tiara,   (40)
>   He was an exorcist, carrying a tablet,
>   "Marduk has sent me!

---

1. These three lines may mean that when the sufferer told of his dream to his family, no one believed him. For the restoration, see line 47 below, where they need a sign to be convinced.

2. An academic Sumerian name, typical of Babylonia of the second half of the second millennium B.C.

3. These are oblique references to the sufferer, perhaps meaning something like "whoever has seen this vision should have pity taken upon him."

"To Shubshi-meshre-Sakkan[1] I have brought a sw[athe],
"From his pure hands I have brought a sw[athe]."
He has entru[sted] me into the hands of my ministrant. (45)
[In] waking hours he sent a message,
He reve[aled] his favorable sign to my people.
I was awake in my sickness, a (healing) serpent slithered by.[2]
My illness was quickly over, [my fetters] were broken.
After my lord's heart had quiet[ed], (50)
(And) the feelings of merciful Marduk were ap[peased],
[And he had] accepted my prayers [   ],
His sweet [relen]ting [   ],
[He ordered] my deliverance!: "He is g[reatly trie]d!"
[   ] to extol [   ] (55)
[   ] to worship and [   ]
[   ] my guilt [   ]
[   ] my iniquity [   ]
[   ] my transgression [   ]
He made the wind bear away my offenses. (60)

(The exact placement of the following lines is unknown.)

[He applied] to me his spell
    which binds [debilitating disease],[3]
[He drove] back the evil vapor to the ends of the earth,
He bore off [the head pain] to the breast of hell, (5')
[He sent] down the malignant spectre to its hidden depth,
The relentless ghost he returned [to] its dwelling,
He overthrew the she-demon, sending if off to a mountain,
He replaced the ague in flood and sea.
He eradicated debility like a plant, (10')
Uneasy sleep, excessive drowsiness,
He dissipated like smoke filling the sky.

---

1. The name of the sufferer. This time the object of mercy is more specific than the preceding. Note that Marduk is named here for the first time since the opening of the poem.
2. The serpent, like the serpents of Aesculapius, was sometimes associated with the goddess of healing.
3. See Tablet II lines 50ff.

The turning towards people(?) with "Woe!" and "Alas!"
> he drove away like a cloud, earth ... [   ].

The tenacious disease in the head,
> which was [heavy] as a [mill]stone,

He raised like dew of night, he removed it from me. (15′)

My beclouded eyes,
> which were wrapped in the shroud of death,

He drove (the cloud) a thousand leagues away,
> he brightened [my] vision.

My ears, which were stopped
> and clogged like a deaf man's,

He removed their blockage, he opened my hearing.

My nose, whose bre[athing] was choked
> by symptoms of fever, (20′)

He soothed its affliction so I could breathe [freely].

My babbling lips, which had taken on a h[ard crust?],
> He wiped away their distress(?)
> and und[id] their deformation.

My mouth, which was muffled,
> so that proper speech was diffi[cult],

He scoured like copper and r[emoved] its filth. (25′)

My teeth, which were clenched
> and locked together firmly,

[He op]ened their fastening, fre[ed?] the jaws(?).

My tongue, which was tied and [could] not converse,
[He] wiped off its coating
> and [its] speech became fluent(?).

My windpipe, which was tight and choking,
> as though on a gobbet, (30′)

He made well and let it si[ng] its songs like a flute.

My [gul]let, which was swollen so it could not take [food],
Its swelling went down and he opened its blockage.

My [   ], which [   ]
[   ] above [   ] (35′)
[which] was darkened like [   ]

(three damaged lines, then gap)

Tablet IV[1]

(Fragment A)

The Lord [   ] me, (1)
The Lord took hold of me,
The Lord set me on my feet,
The Lord revived me,
He rescued me [from the p]it, (5)
He summoned me [from destruc]tion,
[   ] he pulled me from the river of death.
[   ] he took my hand.
[He who] smote me,
Marduk, he restored me! (10)
He smote the hand of my smiter,
It was Marduk who made him drop his weapon.
[He   ] the attack of my foe,
It was Marduk who [   ]

(Two fragmentary lines, then gap. Insert here, perhaps, two lines known only from an ancient commentary.)

At the place of the river ordeal, where people's fates are decided,
I was struck on the forehead, my slavemark removed.

(Fragment B)

[   ] which in my prayers [   ]
[With] prostration and supplication [ ] to Esagila [ ]
[I who went] down to the grave
    have returned to the "Gate of [Sunrise]."[2]
[In the] "Gate of Prosperity" prosperity was [given me]. (20)
[In the] "Gateway of the Guardian Spirit" a guardian spirit
    [drew nigh to me].
[In the] "Gate of Well-being" I beheld well-being.
In the "Gate of Life" I was granted life.

1. The assignment of fragments to this tablet and their arrangement are uncertain.
2. This and the following are gates in Babylon.

In the "Gate of Sunrise" I was reckoned among the living.
In the "Gate of Splendid Wonderment"
    my signs were plain to see. (25)
In the "Gate of Release from Guilt"
    I was released from my bond.
In the "Gate of Petition"(?) my mouth made inquiry.
In the "Gate of Release from Sighing" my sighs were released.
In the "Gate of Pure Water"
    I was sprinkled with purifying water.
In the "Gate of Conciliation" I appeared with Marduk, (30)
In the "Gate of Joy" I kissed the foot of Sarpanitum.
I was assiduous in supplication and prayer before them,
I placed fragrant incense before them,
An offering, a gift, sundry donations I presented,
Many fatted oxen I slaughtered, butchered many ..., (35)
Honey-sweet beer and pure wine I repeatedly libated.
The protecting genius, the guardian spirit,
    divine attendants of the fabric of Esagila,
I made their feelings glow with libation,
I made them exultant [with] lavish [meals].
[To the threshold, the bolt] socket, the bolt, the doors (40)
[I offered] oil, butterfat, and choicest grain.
[   ] the rites of the temple.

(large gap)

(insert here four lines quoted in an ancient commentary?)

I proceeded along Kunush-kadru Street in a state of redemption.
He who has done wrong by Esagila, let him learn from me.
It was Marduk who put a muzzle on the mouth of the lion
that was devouring me. (45)
Marduk took away the sling of my pursuer
and deflected his slingstone.

(Fragment C)

[ ] golden grain [   ]
[He?] anointed himself with sweet cedar perfume,
    upon him [ ]
A feast for the Babylonian(s?) [   ]
His tomb he(?) had made [was set up] for a feast! (50)
The Babylonians saw how [Marduk] can restore to life,
And all mouths proclaimed [his] greatness,
"Who (would have) said he would see his sun?
"Who (would have) imagined
    that he would pass through his street?
"Who but Marduk revived him as he was dying? (55)
"Besides Sarpanitum, which goddess
    bestowed his breath of life?
"Marduk can restore to life from the grave,
"Sarpanitum knows how to rescue from annihilation.
"Wherever earth is founded, heavens are stretched wide,
"Wherever sun shines, fire blazes, (60)
"Wherever water runs, wind blows,
"Those whose bits of clay Aruru pinched off (to form them),
"Those endowed with life, who walk upright,
"[Tee]ming mankind, as many as they be,
    give praise to Marduk!
"[   ] those who can speak, (65)
"[   ] may he rule all the peoples
"[   ] shepherd of all habi[tations]
"[   ] floods from the deep
"[   ] the gods [   ]
"[   ] the extent of heaven and netherworld, (70)
"[   ]
"[   ] was getting darker and darker for him."

A Sufferer's Salvation

This composition is known from a fourteenth(?)-century manuscript from Ugarit in Syria. As preserved, the text does not deal with the causes of the sufferer's punishment, but portrays his privations and afflictions before glorifying Marduk, his redeemer.

(gap of about fifteen lines)

Evil [portents?] were continually set again[st me]	(1)
My omens were obscure, they became like [ ]	
The diviner could not reach a ruling concerning me,	
The "Judge"[1] would give no sign.	
The omens were confused, the oracles mixed up.	(5)
Dream interpreters used up incense, diviners lambs,	
Learned men debated the tablets (? about my case),	
They could not say when my affliction would run its course.	
My family gathered round to bend over me before my time,	
My next of kin stood by ready for the wake.	(10)
My brothers were bathed in blood like men possessed,	
My sisters sprinkled me with fine(?) oil from the press.	
Until the Lord raised my head,	
And brought me back to life from the dead,	
Until Marduk raised my head,	(15)
And brought me back to life from the dead,	
I could eat scant bread,	
[I took for my] drink bilge(?) and salt pools.	
[When I lay down], sleep would not overcome me,	
[I would lie aw]ake my whole night through.	(20)
My heart [ ] me, my(!) mind ...,	
I was wasting away(?) from the sickness I suffered.	
[I] was made most anxious [ ]	
My [te]ars [had to serve] as my sustenance.	
[Lest] Marduk be forgotten,	(25)
That Marduk be praised:	

1. Shamash?

Were it not for Marduk, breath had gone from me,
[The mou]rner would not have cried out 'Alas for him!'
I praise, I praise, what the lord Marduk has done I praise!
[I praise, I praise], what the angry (personal) god [has done]
    I praise! (30)
[I praise, I praise], what the (personal) goddess [has done]
    I praise!
Praise, praise, do not be bashful, but praise!
[He it] is, Marduk, I entreat(?) him, I entreat(?) him,
[He it] was who smote me, then was merciful to me,
He scuttled(?) me, then moored me, (35)
He dashed me down, then grabbed me (as I fell),
He scattered me wide, then garnered me,
He thrust me away, then gathered me in,
He threw me down, then lifted me high.
He snatched me from the maw of death, (40)
He raised me up from hell.
He smashed my smiter's weapon,
He wrested the shovel from the digger of my grave.
He opened my shrouded eyes,
He made my [sp]eech intelligible, (45)
He [   ] my ears.

        (breaks off)

The Babylonian Theodicy

The Theodicy takes the form of a debate between two friends on divine justice. The sufferer, a younger son without means, sees everywhere around him strength and wealth being equated with right and justice, while poverty is considered a crime. The gods take no notice of strict obedience to their rites and concede nothing to the serious seeker after understanding. Even injustice is of divine origin. As the debate proceeds, always with great courtesy and eloquence, the sufferer craves his friend's indulgence by acknowledging that his doubts about divine justice were merely fruits of his personal circumstances, and were themselves faults of the kind he has normally tried to avoid. He concludes by voicing, in effect, a challenge to his gods to take better care of him in the future — at least, mercy and a greater sense of divine responsibility are his only hope. The reader is left to judge whether or not he concludes with a vote of no confidence.

The poem is a technical *tour de force*. Within a constrictive rhythmic scheme of four units to the line, the author begins each ten-line stanza with the same syllable. The beginnings of each stanza, read vertically, form an acrostic, which reads, "I, Saggilkinamubbib, am adorant of god and king."

I. Sufferer

O sage, [   ], come, [let] me speak to you, (1)
[   ], let me recount to you,
[   ] ...
[I ...], who have suffered greatly, let me always praise you,
Where is one whose reflective capacity is as great as yours? (5)
Who is he whose knowledge could rival yours?
Wh[ere] is the counsellor to whom I can tell of woe?
I am without recourse, heartache has come upon me.
I was the youngest child when fate claimed (my) father,
My mother who bore me departed to the land of no return, (10)
My father and mother left me, and with no one my guardian!

II. Friend

Considerate friend, what you tell is a sorrowful tale,
My dear friend, you have let your mind harbor ill.
You make your estimable discretion feeble-minded,
You alter your bright expression to a scowl. (15)
Of course our fathers pay passage to go death's way,
I too will cross the river of the dead,[1]
    as is commanded from of old.
When you survey teeming mankind all together,
The poor man's son advanced, someone helped him get rich,
Who did favors for the sleek and wealthy? (20)
He who looks to his god has a protector,
The humble man who reveres his goddess will garner wealth.

III. Sufferer

My friend, your mind is a wellspring of depth unplumbed,
The upsurging swell of the ocean that brooks no inadequacy.
To you, then, let me pose a question, learn [what I would say]. (25)
Hearken to me but for a moment, hear my declaration.
My body is shrouded, craving wears me do[wn],
My assets have vanished, my res[ources?] dwindled.
My energies have turned feeble, my prosperity is at a standstill,
Moaning and woe have clouded [my] features. (30)
The grain of my mead is nowhere near satisfying [me],
Beer, the sustenance of mankind, is far from being enough.
Can a happy life be a certainty?
    I wish I knew how that might come about!

IV. Friend

My well-thought-out speech is the ulti[mate] in good advice,
But you [make?] your well-ordered insight [sound] like babble. (35)
You force [your ...] to be [sca]tter-brained, irrational,
You render your choicest offerings without conviction.

---

1. Hubur, here the Mesopotamian equivalent of the Styx or the "River Jordan." The line may also refer to the forefathers rather than the speaker, "They say from of old 'I must cross the river of death.'"

As to your [ever]lasting, unremitting desire [ ],
The [fore]most protection [lies] in prayer:
The reconciled goddess returns to [   ], (40)
The re[conciled gods] will take pity on the fool(?),
    the wrong-doer.
Seek constantly after the [rites?] of justice.
Your mighty [   ] will surely show kindness,
[   ] ... will surely grant mercy.

V. Sufferer

I bow down before you, my [comrade],
    I apprehend your w[isdom], (45)
[   ] what you say.
Come, let me [tell you],
The on[ager], the wild ass, that had its fill of [wild grass?],
Did it carefully ca[rry out?] a god's intentions?
The savage lion that devoured the choicest meat, (50)
Did it bring its offerings to appease a goddess' anger?
The parvenu who multiplies his wealth,
Did he weigh out precious gold to the mother goddess
    for a family?
[Have I] withheld my offerings? I prayed to my god,
[I] said the blessing over the regular sacrifice
    to my goddess, my speech [ ]. (55)

VI. Friend

O date palm, wealth-giving tree, my precious brother,
Perfect in all wisdom, O gem of wis[dom],
You are a mere child,
    the purpose of the gods is remote as the netherworld.
Consider that magnificent wild ass on the [plain],
An arrow will gash that headstrong trampler of the leas! (60)
Come, look at that lion you called to mind,
    the enemy of livestock,
For the atrocity that lion committed, a pit yawns for him.
The well-heeled parvenu who treasured up possessions,

A king will put him to the flames before his time.
Would you wish to go the way these have gone? (65)
Seek after the lasting reward of (your) god.

VII. Sufferer

Your reasoning is a cool breeze,
    a breath of fresh air for mankind,
Most particular friend, your advice is e[xcellent].
Let me [put] but one matter before you:
Those who seek not after a god can go the road of favor, (70)
Those who pray to a goddess have grown poor and destitute.
Indeed, in my youth I tried to find out the will of (my) god,
With prayer and supplication I besought my goddess.
I bore a yoke of profitless servitude:
(My) god decreed (for me) poverty instead of wealth. (75)
A cripple rises above me, a fool is ahead of me,
Rogues are in the ascendant, I am demoted.

VIII. Friend

O just, knowledgeable one, your logic is perverse,
You have cast off justice, you have scorned divine design.
In your emotional state you have an urge
    to disregard divine ordinances, (80)
[   ] the sound rules of your goddess.
The strategy of a god is [as remote as] innermost heaven,
The command of a goddess cannot be dr[awn out].
Teeming humanity well understands trouble,

(fragmentary lines, then large gap)

XIII. Sufferer

I will forsake home [   ]
I will crave no property [   ]
I will ignore (my) god's regulations, [I will] trample on his rites. (135)
I will slaughter a calf, I will [ ] the food,
I will go on the road, I will learn my way around distant places.
I will open a well, I will let loose a fl[ood?],

I will roam about the far outdoors like a bandit.
I will stave off hunger by forcing entry
    into one house after another, (140)
I will prowl the streets, casting about, ravenous.
Like a beggar I will [   ] inside [ ],
Good fortune lies afar off [   ].

XIV. Friend

My friend, [you have] resolved [upon]
The transactions of mankind,
    which you had no urge to [   ], (145)
[   ] are in your mind,
Your discretion has forsaken [you   ]

(fragmentary lines)

XV. Sufferer

(four lines lost)

Daughter says [unjust words] to her mother.
The fowler who casts [his net] is fallen (into it), (160)
All in all, which one [will find] profit?
Many are the wild creatures that [   ],
Which among them has gotten [   ]?
Shall I seek son and daughter [   ]?
Shall I not leave behind what I find [ ]? (165)

XVI. Friend

O modest, submissive one, who [ ] all [   ],
Your mind is always receptive, most precious one [ ],

(fragmentary lines, then gap)

XVII. Sufferer

The son of a king is clad [in rags?],
The son of the destitute and naked is dressed in [fine raiment?].
The maltster [can pay in] finest gold,

While he who counted red gold shoulders a [debt?].
He who made do with vegetables [sates himself]
    at a princely banquet, (185)
While the son of the eminent and wealthy
    (has only) carob to eat.
The man of substance is fallen, [his income] is removed.

(fragmentary lines, gap)

XX. Friend

You have let your subtle mind wander,
[   ] you have overthrown wisdom.
You have spurned propriety, you have besmirched (every) code.
Far will be the workman's basket from him who ... (215)
[   ] is established as a person of importance,
[   ] he is called a scholar,
He is well served, he gets what he wants.
Follow in the way of a god, observe his rites,
[   ] be ready for good fortune! (220)

(gap)

XXII. Friend

As for the rascal whose good will you wanted, (235)
The ... of his feet will soon disappear.
The godless swindler who acquires wealth,
A deadly weapon is in pursuit of him.
Unless you serve the will of a god, what will be your profit?
He who bears a god's yoke shall never want for food,
    though it may be meager. (240)
Seek after the favorable breeze of the gods,
What you lost for a year you will recoup in a moment.

XXIII. Sufferer

I have looked around in society, indications are the contrary:
God does not block the progress of a demon.
A father hauls a boat up a channel, (245)

While his firstborn sprawls in bed.
The eldest son makes his way like a lion,
The second son is content to drive a donkey.
The heir struts the street like a peddler,
The younger son makes provision for the destitute.[1] (250)
What has it profited me that I knelt before my god?
It is I who must (now) bow before my inferior!
The riffraff despise me as much as the rich and proud.

XXIV. Friend

Adept scholar, master of erudition,
You blaspheme in the anguish of your thoughts. (255)
Divine purpose is as remote as innermost heaven,
It is too difficult to understand, people cannot understand it.
Among all creatures the birth goddess formed,
Why should offspring be completely unmatched(?)?
The cow's first calf is inferior, (260)
Her subsequent offspring is twice as big.
The first child is born a weakling,
The second is called a capable warrior.
Even if one (tries to) apprehend divine intention,
    people cannot understand it.

XXV. Sufferer

Pay attention, my friend, learn my (next) parry, (265)
Consider the well-chosen diction of my speech.
They extol the words of an important man
    who is accomplished in murder,
They denigrate the powerless who has committed no crime.
They esteem truthful the wicked to whom tr[uth] is abhorrent,
They reject the truthful man who he[eds] the will of god. (270)
They fill the oppressor's st[rongroom] with refined gold,
They empty the beggar's larder of [his] provisions.
They shore up the tyrant whose all is crime,

---

1. The meaning may be that the elder expects the world to provide him a living, while the younger provides for others as well as himself.

They ruin the weak, they oppress the powerless.
And as for me, without means, a parvenu harasses me. (275)

XXVI. Friend[1]

Enlil, king of the gods, who created teeming mankind,
Majestic Ea, who pinched off their clay,
The queen who fashioned them, mistress Mami,
Gave twisted words to the human race,
They endowed them in perpetuity with lies and falsehood. (280)
Solemnly they speak well of a rich man,
"He's the king," they say, "he has much wealth."
They malign a poor man as a thief,
They lavish mischief upon him, they conspire to kill him.
They make him suffer every evil
    because he has no wherewithal(?). (285)
They bring him to a horrible end,
    they snuff him out like an ember.

XXVII. Sufferer

You are sympathetic, my friend, be considerate of (my) misfortune.
Help me, see (my) distress, you should be cognizant of it.[2]
Though I am humble, learned, supplicant,
I have not seen help or succor for an instant. (290)
I would pass unobtrusively through the streets of my city,
My voice was not raised, I kept my speaking low.
I did not hold my head high, I would look at the ground.
I was not given to servile praise among my associates.
May the god who has cast me off grant help, (295)
May the goddess who has [forsaken me] take pity,
The shepherd Shamash will past[ure] people as a god should.[3]

---

1. One would expect this speech from the sufferer rather than the friend. Is the text in disorder, or is he swayed by the sufferer?
2. That is, in judging his interlocutor's state of mind, the friend should weigh his dire circumstances and not condemn him too harshly.
3. That is, a just god takes proper care of his subjects.

Lament for a City

This lament, known from a tablet of the Hellenistic period, is cast in an antique Sumerian style, in the manner of a lament for Tammuz, lover of Ishtar, patron deity of Uruk. The text deals primarily with the devastation of war and the cries of women deprived of their husbands.

> "O grieving (women) of Uruk, O grieving (women) of Akkad,
>   I am prostrate!" (1)
> The goddess of Uruk wept, whose attendant was gone,
> The goddess of Uruk wept, whose loincloth was snatched away.
> The daughter of Uruk wept,
>   the daughter of Akkad was crying aloud.
> The face of the daughter of Larak was shrouded
>   with the fringe of her garment. (5)
> The goddess of Hursagkalamma wept,
>   who was deprived of her husband.
> The goddess of ... wept, whose seven brothers were killed,
>   whose eight brothers-in-law were prostrate.
> The goddess of Akkad wept, whose sandals were mangled,
>   whose lord, in whom she delighted, was killed.
> The goddess of Kesh wept, sitting in the alleyway,
>   the lord of her house slain by a lynx(?).
> The goddess of Dunnu wept,
>   "For whom the couch, for whom the coverlet?
>   For whom do I treasure the coverlet,
>   (now) deathly still?" (10)
> The daughter of Nippur wept,
>   "Finishing the task was for Gutians!"[1]
> Her cheeks were sore (from weeping),
>   she was deprived of her husband, in whom she delighted.
> The goddess of Der <wept>,
>   "Finishing the task was for Gutians!"

---

1. "Gutians" was a term for hateful barbarian invaders.

\<Her\> cheeks were sore (from weeping),
> she was deprived of her husband, in whom she delighted.

She whose city was wrecked, whose ancestral home
> was broken into and desecrated, (cried) (15)

"(O women), weep for Uruk, (my) headband caught in thorns,
"As for me, I do not know where I stepped in the tempest.
"(O women), weep for Larak, [ ], I am deprived of my cloak,
"My eyes cannot look upon ..., slashing of mother's wombs,
"(O women), weep for Nippur, silence dwells upon me. (20)
"The heavens have shrouded me,
"My chair that supported me has been overturned upon me.
"The lord has deprived me of my spouse,
> the husband in whom I delighted!"

Who Has Not Sinned?

Be it [offen]se, crime, iniquity, sin, (1)
[I] have offended against my god,
    I have sinned against my goddess.
I have (indeed) perpetrated [all] my crimes,
    all my sins, all my iniquities.
[I] gave my word, then changed (it),
    I was trusted but did not deliver.
I did [un]seemly deeds, I said something harmful. (5)
I repeated [what should not be spoken of],
    harmful (speech) was on my lips.
[I was ig]norant, I went too far!
Absolve, my god ... [   ]
Let my [iniquities] be dissolved,
    [transmute] my sins into good deeds.
You decide [   ] (10)
Save safe and sound the one who sinned [   ]!
Who is there who is guilty of no sin against his god?
Which is he who kept a commandment forever?
All human beings there are harbor sin.
I, your servant, have committed every sin, (15)
I stood before you, (but) I ... falsehood,
I uttered lies, I indulged crimes,
I spoke harmful words, you know what they are.
I committed an abomination against the god who created me,
I acted sacrilegiously, I kept on doing evil. (20)
I envied your vast possessions,
I yearned for your precious silver,
I lifted my own hand to touch what should not be touched.
I entered the temple without being pure,
I committed one terrible outrage after another against you, (25)
I went beyond your limits of what was offensive to you,
I cursed your divinity in the rage of my heart.
I have persisted in every sort of crime,
I kept on going as I liked and incurred iniquity.
It is enough, O my god, let your heart be calmed! (30)

May the goddess who grew angry be pacified completely.
Dissolve the ire you harbored in your heart,
May your inmost self, which I swore by,
    be reconciled with me.
Though my crimes be numerous, clear my debt,
Though my iniquities be seven(-fold),
    let your heart be calmed.   (35)
Though my [si]ns be numerous,
    show great mercy and cleanse [me].
[O my god], I am exhausted, grasp my hand,
[from the gr]ound and hold up [my] head,
[   ] save my life!

    (thirteen lines fragmentary)

Let the day be joyful [for] the shepherd of the people,   (40)
[Let me si]ng of you, let me p[r]aise your divinity,
Let me sound your praises [to] the numerous [peoples]!

The Piteous Suffer

This lament portrays the suffering of a man who believes himself forsaken by his god.

(gap)

[In agony of] heart, in terrible weeping, (1)
He abides in grief.
With bitter plaint, agony of heart,
Terrible weeping, terrible grief,
He moans like a dove, in crushing distress, night and day. (5)
He lows like a cow to his merciful god,
He keeps setting forth his bitter grief,
He abases himself before his god in supplication.
He weeps and knows no restraint in sobbing:
"Shall I speak of what I did?
    What I did is unspeakable! (10)
"Shall I repeat what I said?
    What I said should not be repeated!
"O my god, shall I speak of what I did?
    What I did is unspeakable!
"O my lord, shall I speak to someone (of it)?
    It is unspeakable!
"Shall I repeat what I said?
    What I said should not be repeated!
"I am deaf, I am blindfolded, I cannot see. (15)
"You have gone beyond what you intended,[1]
"Let your sweet breeze wa[ft upon me].
"I am caught up like reeds in the wind.
"My god, [absolve] my sin,
"My god, look steadfastly upon me from your abode, (20)
"Take pity on me, may your angry heart be calmed,
"[May your heart, like a real mother's, like a real father's],
    be [restored],
[Like a real mother's, like a real father's, may it be restored]."

---

1. I take this to mean that the punishment has exceeded the limits imagined by the sufferer to have been imposed upon it by the god.

Elegy for a Woman Dead in Childbirth

This poem tells the story of a woman's death in childbirth as if she were narrating it herself. Her pleas and those of her husband fail to move Belet-ili, goddess of birth.

> Why are you cast adrift, like a boat in midstream, (1)
> Your planking stoven, your mooring rope cut?
> With shrouded face, you cross the river of the City.[1]
>
> How could I not be cast adrift,
>   how could my mooring rope not be cut?
> The day I carried the fruit, how happy I was, (5)
> Happy was I, happy my husband.
> The day I went into labor, my face grew overcast,
> The day I gave birth, my eyes grew cloudy.
>
> I prayed to Belet-ili with my hands opened out,
> 'You are mother of those who give birth, save my life!' (10)
> Hearing this, Belet-ili shrouded her face,
> 'You [   ], why do you keep praying to me?'
>
> [My husband, who lov]ed me, uttered a cry,
> '[   ] me, the wife I adore!'
>
> (gap)
>
> [All ...] those days I was with my husband, (15)
> While I lived with him who was my lover,
> Death was creeping stealthily into my bedroom,
> It forced me from my house,
> It cut me off from my lover,
> It set my foot toward the land from which I shall not return. (20)

---

1. Assur is meant.

VI
LOVE AND SEX

Love Charms

SEATED ON HER THIGHS

The purpose of this very early love charm is to enable a man to win a woman's favor by magical procedure. (a) The speaker invokes the god of wisdom and incantations, saying that the love charm sits in the lap of the goddess of love, surrounded by aromatic "sap." (b) The speaker sends off two demonic maidens to fetch some of this sap. The speaker asserts control over the woman he desires, apostrophizing her (c). In (d), through vegetation metaphors, the speaker describes his approach towards her and summons her to search for him. Part (e) may be the imagined internal whisperings of erotic desire awakened in the woman by the love charm, while in (f) the spell has taken hold. In the final line, Ea conjures the helpless girl that she find no release from desire till her union with her would-be lover.

(a)

Ea loves the love charm, (1)
The love charm, son of Ishtar,
[Sea]ted on her thighs, in the sapflow of the incense-tree.

(b)

... you two beautiful maidens,
You are come into bloom, you went down to the garden, (5)
To the garden you went down.
You cut the sapflow of the incense-tree.

(c)

I have seized your mouth for saliva!
I have seized your lustrous eyes!
I have seized your vulva for urine! (10)

(d)

I climbed into the garden of the moon[1]
I cut through poplar to her ...
Seek for me among the boxwood,
As the shepherd seeks for the sheep,
The goat her kid,   (15)
The ewe (her) lamb,
The jenny her foal.

(e)

"His arms are two garlands of fruit,
"His lips are oil and ...-(plant?).
"A cruse of oil (is) in his hand,   (20)
"A cruse of cedar oil (is) on his shoulder,"
(So) the love charms have bespoken her,
Then driven her to ecstasy!

(f)

I have seized your mouth for love-making!
By Ishtar and Ishara[2] I conjure you: (25)
May you find no release from me
Till your neck and his neck lie close beside!

---

1. Obscure. "Garden" presumably means his beloved's sexual parts.
2. Goddess of love.

HORNS OF GOLD

This charm opens with a description of the love charm (a). The speaker hopes that the woman of his choice will remain available (b), and that he can acquire power over her (c). He concludes by apostrophizing her (d).

(a)

Love charm, love charm! (1)
Its horns are of gold,
Its(!) tail of pure lapis,
It is placed in Ishtar's heart.

(b)

I called to her, but she did not come back to me, (5)
I whistled at her,[1] but she did not look at me.
If she is "consecrated," may her lover fall,
If she has been taken, may her accuser fall.[2]

(c)

(May the) marriageable girl, the free-born young lady,
Fall at my clamor, at my shout. (10)
May the dough fall from her hands,[3]
May the little boy(?) at her side ... to her.

(d)

You set up your household for your household utensils,
Look upon me as if (I were) a leash!
Follow me around like a calf! (15)
Why did you bind your head with my love, like a headband?

(six lines fragmentary)

---

1. This may refer to the prolonged hiss that serves throughout the Near East today as a "wolf whistle."
2. If she is pure, may any would-be lover not deflower her; if she has been deflowered, may her accuser not prove his case.
3. This and the next line may refer to domestic tasks, one involving food preparation and the other child care (her younger brother?), that the beloved will be unable to perform while the charm affects her heart.

LOOK AT ME!

These spells are intended for men and women in love who wish to attract or to arouse sex partners.

(a)

(She)

"With dog slaver, thirst(?), hunger(?), (1)
"Slap in the face, deflection of eye,
"I have hit you on the head, I have driven you out of your mind!
"Set your thinking to my thinking,
"Set your reason to my reason! (5)
"I hold you in restraint, as Ishtar held Dumuzi,
"(As) liquor binds him who drinks of her,[1]
"I have bound you with my mouth for breaths,
"With my vulva for urination,
"With my mouth for spitting, (10)
"With my vulva for urination.
"May no rival come to you!
"Dog is crouching, pig is crouching,
"You too keep crouching on my thighs!"

(Ritual follows.)

(b)

(She)

"Look at me, feel tension like (a taut harp) string, (1)
"May your heart glow as with liquor,
"Keep bursting forth like the sun upon me,
"Keep renewing yourself for me like the moon,
"... may your love ever be new." (5)

(Ritual follows.)

---

1. Or, "I have bound you (as) liquor ..."

(c)

(She)

"Get your legs underway, Erra-bani,[1] (1)
"Get your middle in motion,
"Let your sinews follow after."

(He)

"Let your heart rejoice,
"Let your spirits be happy, (5)
"I will swell large as a dog!
"Your ... are like a hobble-rope,
"Don't let them go limp(?) on me!"

(Love incantation)

(d)

(He)

"Stay awake at night, (1)
"Don't go to sleep in the day,
"You shall not sit down nights!"

(Love incantation)

(e)

(She)

"Beloved, beloved, (1)
"You, whom Ea and Enlil installed,
"As Ishtar sits on dais,
"As Nanay sits in chamber,
"I close you in! (5)
"High priestesses love burning(?),
"Wives despise their husbands!
"Cut off her stuck-up nose,
"Set her nose under my foot!
"Just as her love was too strong for me, (10)
"So may my love be too strong for her love."

(Love incantation)

Personal name, whether real or proverbial is unknown.

(f)

(He)
"Why are you as hard as a thorn in a thicket, (1)

(She)
"Why is your desire as perverse as a child's?

(He)
"Why is your face so hostile?
"Why am I invisible, do not exist?

(She)
"In your heart lies a dog, lurks a pig, (5)
"You lie down with me and I'll pluck out your bristle,
"Take what you have in your hand and put it into my hand."

(Incantation ...)

(g)

(She)
"Where is your heart going? (1)
"Where are your eyes lo[oking]?
"Let [your heart come] to me!
"Let [your eyes look at] me!
"Look at me l[ike   ] (5)
"Gaze at me [   ]
"You will [hunger for] me like bread,
"You will [thirst for] me like beer.
"...

(Love incantation)

(h)

(She)

"[Arousal], arousal! (1)
"It ke[eps its place] in his heart.
"Let me give you cool water to drink,
"Let me give you ice and coolants.
"Your heart is vigor, like a wolf, (5)
"Like a lion, may splendor possess you.
"Spring, O arousal of Nanay!"

(i)

(She)

"Arousal, arousal! (1)
"He [comes upon me] like a wild bull,
"He [keeps springing at me] like a hound,
"L[ike a lion he is furious] in his onset,
"Li[ke a wolf] he goes where he lists. (5)
"...
"I [broke the ...] of his heart,
"I will cross him like a bri[dge],
"The Tigris river is under [him].
"Spring, [O arousal] of Nanay!" (10)

(j)

(She)

"Arousal, arousal! (1)
"I will step over you like a threshold,
"I will traverse you like open gro[und],
"Spring, O [ar]ousal of Nanay!"

(Incantation, using? a lump of salt)

(k)

(She)

"Big mouth, floppy ears, Iddin-Damu, (1)
"Open your mouth like a ...-fish.
"Your heart is a ...-plant.
"I lapped at your heel,
"I took the ... (5)
"I caught your leg.
"Cuddle me like a puppy,
"M[ount] me like a dog!"

(Incantation, using soap-plant)

(l)

(She)

"I have hit you on the head, (1)
"You will squirm around me on the ground like a [   ],
"You will ... the ground like a pig,
"Until I'll have my way, like a child!"

(m)

"Both onion and ox stick up a blade, (1)
"As river moistened its banks,
"I make myself moist,
"I make my body moist.
"I have opened my seven doors for you, Erra-bani, (5)
"...
"Bring the constant gnawing of your heart to an end on me!"

THE HARPSTRING

Wind blow, orchard shake, (1)
Clouds gather, droplets fall!
Let my potency be (steady as) running river water,
Let my penis be a (taut) harpstring,
Let it not slip out of her! (5)

GET UP!

The magician takes control of the woman. Her clothes are to turn into an impromptu bower, her bed a covered spot for a tryst, and, if she is asleep when the spell is wrought, her own couch will unceremoniously awaken her to send her off to the embrace of her admirer.

> I have seized you, I have seized you, I will not let you free! (1)
> As pitch holds fast to boat,
> As Sin to Ur, as Shamash to Larsa,
> As Ishtar to Ekur hold fast,¹
> I have seized you and I will not let you free! (5)
> May the clothes you are wearing be your bower(?),
> May the bed you sleep on be a tent(?),
> May the bed dump you on the ground!
> May the [grou]nd say to you "Get up!"
> [At the com]mand spoken by the Capable Lady, Ishtar. (10)

I HAVE MADE A BED

> Potency, potency! I(?) have made a bed for potency! (1)
> What Ishtar does for Dumuzi,
> What Nanay d[oes] for her lover,
> What Ishara d[oes] for her mate(?),
> Let me do for my lover! (5)
> Let the flesh of so-and-so, son of so-and-so, tingle,
> [Let his penis stand erect]!
> May his ardor not flag, night or day!
> By command of the Capable Lady, Ishtar, Nanay,
>   G[azbaba, Is]hara.²

---

1. Ur was the sacred city of Sin, the moon-god, and Larsa the sacred city of Shamash, the sun-god, but the connection of Ishtar with a temple called Ekur is unknown.
2. Love goddesses.

MAY I NOT MISS MY PREY!

Wind come, mountains [quak]e, (1)
Clouds gather, droplets fall!
Let the (penis of the) ass become stiff, let him mount the jenny,
Let the he-goat have an erection,
    let him mount the she-goat ... time after time.
At the head of my bed a he-goat is tied,[1] (5)
At the foot of my bed a ram is tied.
You at the head of my bed, have an erection, make love to me!
You at the foot of my bed, have an erection, caress me!
My vagina is a bitch's vagina, his penis is a dog's penis.
As the bitch's vagina holds tight the dog's penis, (10)
So may my vagina hold tight his penis!
May your penis grow long as a warclub!
I'm sitting in a web of seduction,
May I not miss my prey!

---

1. Variant has here and in following lines "I have tied ..."

Against Arousal

"Arousal" may refer to onset of sexual desire or anger. The speaker wishes to drive such feelings from his heart.

>   Arousal is coming upon me like a wild bull, (1)
>   It keeps springing at me like a dog,
>   Like a lion it is fierce in coming,
>   Like a wolf it is full of fury. (5)
>   Stay! I pass over you like a threshold,
>   I walk right through you like a flimsy door,
>   I span you like a doorway.
>   I turn back your approach like a hobble,
>   I drive out the fieriness of your heart. (10)

Love Lyrics of Rim-Sin

These love lyrics, partly dialogue and partly the chaffing song of the attendants outside the nuptial chamber, celebrate the springtime new year rite when the king, here Rim-Sin, king of Larsa (ca. 1822-1763 B.C.), has intercourse with a priestess to ensure the fertility of the realm.

(Singers)
[For the new] year pregnant girls took away the ..., (1)
While the slender girl has taken his [fi]ne ...

(He)
The [ras]cal(?) has taken power over me.

(She)
[ ], my delightful partner, prevailed over me ...

(Singers, to Her)
You are too joyful(?), O my beloved, do not rely on him! (5)
You are in too great ecstasy, do not put your trust in him!

(She to Him)
Now, you are the one and only, you listened, my lover,
    you fell silent in my presence,
You accepted my entreaties, may your heart be eased for me.
In the assembly, the city, and among the fine(?) people
    you spoke well of me.
My darling, you made me distinguished, (10)
At a suitable time(?) you [raised] me.

(Singers)
On account of (his) consort's eye ...
    he is thrown into confusion.
Yes! It is springtime, for which we will always bless him,
We are indeed yearning to see him, for so long,
    many days, life forever.

The bearer of happiness to Rim-Sin, (15)
    our Sun-God for the new year,
Gives her wine which sparkles in my right hand.

(She)

"Come here, I want to be embraced,
    as my heart has dictated to me,
"Let us perform lovers' task, never sleep all night,
"Let both of us on the bed be in the joyful mood
    for love-making!"

(She to Him)

Come together with attractiveness and love-making!
    Sustain yourself with life! (20)
Burn out your desire on top of me!

(He to Her)

My love is poured out for you,
    Take as much as you desire in generous measure.

(rest fragmentary)

Love Lyrics of Nabu and Tashmetu

These lines are lovers' talk between Nabu and Tashmetu on the occasion of their marriage rite.

(Singers)

Let whom will trust where he trusts, (1)
As for us, our trust is in Nabu,
We give ourselves over to Tashmetu.
What is ours is ours: Nabu is our lord,
Tashmetu is the mountain we trust in. (5)

(Singers, to Tashmetu)

Say to her, to her of the wall, to her of the wall, to Tashmetu,
..., take your place in the sanctuary,
May the scent of holy juniper fill the dais.

(Tashmetu?)

Shade of cedar, shade of cedar, shade of cedar
    (is) come for the king's shelter,
Shade of cypress is (for) his great ones, (10)
The shade of a juniper branch is shelter for my Nabu,
    for my play.

(Singers)

Tashmetu dangles a gold ornament in my Nabu's lap,
'My lord, put an earring on me,
'That I may give you pleasure in the garden,
'Nabu, my darling,[1] put an earring on me, (15)
'That I may make you happy in the [ ].'

---

1. Literally: "my lord," a term of endearment.

(Nabu)

My [Tashmetu], I put on you bracelets of carnelian,
[   ] you bracelets of carnelian,
I will open [   ]

(gap)

(O Tashmetu), [whose] thighs are a gazelle in the steppe,   (20)
(O Tashmetu), [whose] ankles are a springtime apple,
(O Tashmetu), whose heels are obsidian stone,
(O Tashmetu), whose whole self is a tablet of lapis!

(Singers)

Tashmetu, looking voluptuous, entered the bedroom,
She locked her door, sending home the lapis bolt.   (25)
She washes herself, she climbs into bed.
From (one) lapis cup, from (the other) lapis cup,[1] her tears flow,
He wipes away her tears with a tuft of red wool,
There, ask (her), ask (her), find out, find out!

'Why, why are you so adorned, [my] Tashmetu?'   (30)

'So I can [go] to the garden with you, my Nabu.'
'Let me go to the garden, to the garden and [   ]
'Let me go again to the exquisite garden,
'They would not have me take my place among the wise folk!'[2]

(Singers)

I would see with my own eyes the plucking of your fruit,   (35)
I would hear with my own ears your birdsong.

(Nabu)

There, bind fast, hitch up,
Bind your days to the garden and to the Lord,
Bind your nights to the exquisite garden,

---

1. Her eyes.
2. Literally: "counsellors." This activity is to be private, not for the audience in her throne room.

Let my Tashmetu come with me to the garden, (40)
(Though) among wise folk her place be foremost.

(gap)

May she see with her own eyes the plucking of my fruit,
May she hear with her own ears my birdsong,
May she see with her own eyes,
    may she hear with her own ears!

Love Lyrics of Ishtar of Babylon

Fragmentary collections of enigmatic songs and rituals involving Ishtar of Babylon seem to a modern reader scurrilous, abusive, and bizarre. Scattered excerpts from this collection follow.

(a)

Into your vulva, where you put your trust, (1)
I'll bring in a dog and fasten the door,
Into your vulva, where you put your trust,
As if it were(?) your precious jewel in front of you.
O my girl friend's vulva, why do you keep acting like this? (5)
O my girl friend's vulva, Babylon-town is looking for a rag!
O vulva of two fingers, why do you keep making trouble?

(b)

By night there's no prudish housewife, (1)
By night there's no prudish housewife,
By night no man's wife makes objection!

(c)

Before her was a fieldmouse, (1)
Behind her was a rat.
He girded(?) his hems,
He's a shrew, son of a fieldmouse.
I sent [you?], my girl friend, to Kar-bel-matati,[1] (5)
Why did you break wind and feel mortified?
Why did you stink up her boyfriend's wagon like a wi[ld ox]?
At Kar-bel-matati's crossing point,
I saw my girl friend and was stunned:
You are chalky like a gecko, (10)
Your hide is swart like a cook[ing pot].
You are in full bloom, brought to [bliss].

---

1. Name of a wharf at Babylon.

(d)

O my girl friend's [genitals],
    Babylon-town is looking for a rag, (1)
To swab your vulva, to swab your vagina.
[So] let him say to the women of Babylon,
"Won't they give her a rag,
"To swab her vulva, to swab her vagina?" (5)

Into your vulva, where you put your trust,
I'll bring in a dog and fasten the door,
I'll bring in a watchbird so it can nest.
Whenever I go out or come in,
I'll instruct my little watchbirds, (10)
"Please, my little watchbirds,
"Don't go near the fungus!
"Please, my little watchbird,
"Don't go near the stench of (her) armpits!"

You are mother, O Ishtar of Babylon, (15)
You are mother, O queen of the Babylonians,
You are mother, O palm tree, O carnelian!
The beautiful one, oh so beautiful!
Whose figure is oh so lustrous, oh so beautiful!

Ishtar Will Not Tire

A damaged manuscript preserves part of a hymn to Ishtar. Each line is followed by a refrain: "The city's built on pleasure!"

(seven lines fragmentary)

One comes up to her ...,	(refrain)	
"Come here, give me what I want ..."	(refrain)	
Then another comes up to her,	(refrain)	(10)
"Come here, let me touch your vulva."	(refrain)	
"Since I'm ready to give you all what you want,	(refrain)	
"Get all the young men of your city together,	(refrain)	
"Let's go to the shade of a wall!"	(refrain)	
Seven for her midriff, seven for her loins,	(refrain)	(15)
Sixty then sixty satisfy themselves in turn		
upon her nakedness.	(refrain)	
Young men have tired, Ishtar will not tire.	(refrain)	
"Get on with it, fellows, for my lovely vulva!"	(refrain)	
As the girl demanded,	(refrain)	
The young men heeded, gave her what she asked for.	(refrain)	(20)

(Hymn of praise to Ishtar)

Ishtar at the Tavern

Taverns, besides providing strong drink, could evidently serve as brothels as well. This incantation is part of a ritual designed to enliven traffic in such an establishment.

> O Ishtar of the lands, most valorous of goddesses,
>> this is your bower, rejoice and be glad! (1)
> Come, enter our house!
> Let your sweet bedmate enter with you,
> May your lover and boyfriend [enter] with you.
> May my lips be white honey, may my hands be charm,
> May the lips, my labia(?), be lips of honey! (5)
> As birds flutter around a serpent coming out of his hole,
>> so may these people fight over me!
> Seize him, bring him here, make him feel at home,
>> in the bower of Ishtar, the chamber of Ninlil,
>> the herds(?) of Ningizzida.
> May the far-off come around, may the angry come back,
>> may his heart come back to me as if (to) gold.
> Just as when rain has fecundated the earth,
>> plants become plentiful,
> So too may there be many a basket
>> of (sprouting) malt[1] for me! (10)

---

1. This may refer to a "bumper crop" of excited customers.

The Faithful Lover

This poem deals with the theme of unequal love. A woman is in love with a boor who has taken up with someone else. Despite his selfishness and abuse, she remains true, and eventually wins her prize back, if only through persistence. This Mesopotamian celebration of the power of love, regardless of the merit of its object, is a compassionate forerunner, full of life and humor, to the portrayal of the woman's dilemma in the Song of Songs. One is also reminded of the second elegy of Theocritus on this topic, though there the woman looks more foolish than here.

(He)
Moan on, don't bother to answer, not so much talking! (1)
What I have to say is said,
I haven't changed on your account any opinion that I hold.
He who sprawls next to a woman treasures up empty air!
If he doesn't look out for himself,
 he is no man worthy of the name. (5)

(She)
May my faithfulness stand firm before Ishtar the queen!
May my love prevail,
May she who slanders me come to shame!
Gra[nt that I] charm, seek my darling's favor constantly.
By Nanay's command I am still ... [proud], (10)
Where might my rival be?

(He)
I remember better than you your old tricks,
Give up! Be off with you!
Tell your (divine) counsellor how we've sobered out of it.

(She)
I'll hang on to you, and this very day (15)
I shall make your love harmonize with mine.
I shall keep on praying to Nanay,
I shall have your eternal good will, darling, freely given.

(He)
I shall keep you hemmed in, I shall bank clouds around you,
Let her who supports you take away your ardor. (20)
Put an end to your rash talk, use sane words.

(gap of about 20 lines)

(She)
May the queen Ishtar h[eap] oblivion on
    th(at) woman, who doesn't (really) love you.
May she, like me, [be burdened] with sleeplessness,
The whole night may she doze off [but start awake].

(He)
I despise a woman who can't seduce me, (25)
I have no desire for her charms,
I wouldn't give her [ ].
Talking without [ ],
What does it [ ]?
I'll silence those women who gossip about [me], (30)
I'll not listen [ ]
Wherever [ ]
I have [not] cast off the one I love,
What do you keep prying into me for?

(She)
My omens upset me, (35)
My upper lip grows moi[st], while the lower one trem[bles].
I shall hug him! I shall kiss him!
I shall look and look upon [him]!
I shall get what I want, despite those women
    who gos[sip about me].
And happily, too, I [shall return] to my l[over]. (40)
When our sleep [ ]
We shall reach [ ]

(gap)

(She)
I am running, but I cannot catc[h up with him]:
She has given him away to Ishtar as a g[ift].

(He)
Just as they keep on telling you, (45)
Y[ou] are not the one and only.
Hold off! I have taken my love away, [I shall] not [return].
I have taken it away from your body,
I have [taken] my attractions a million leagues away.

(She)
I am pursuing your attractions, (50)
Darling, I am yearning for [your] love!
Since your smiles are [my ...],
Let them be ..., I hope [they] won't ... [ ]
I will complain day and night [ ]

(He)
Again and a thi[rd] time I'll say it, (55)
Have I not [ ] the beloved [ ] to my mouth?
Do take your place at the window,
Go on, catch up to my love!

(She)
So very tired my eyes are,
I am weary for looking out for him. (60)
I keep thinking he will go through my neighborhood,
The day has gone by, where is [my darling]?

(gap of about 15 lines)

(He)
I ... [   ]
The one and only [   ]
Why [   ] (65)
Come on, let me take [my place],
I shall sit and await if he is on his way to me.

(He)
I swear to you by Nanay and King Hammurabi:
I am telling you the truth about me,
Your love is nothing more to me (70)
Than anxiety and bother.

(She)
They came down on me because I still trust my lover,
The women who gossip about me
    outnumber the stars of heaven.
Let them go hide! Let them be scarce!
Right now let them go hide! (75)
I'll stay right here, ever listening for the voice of my darling.

(He)
My one and only, your face wasn't bad looking before,
When I stood by you and you leaned your [shoul]der
    against me.
Call you "Sweetie," dub you "Smart Lady."
Say the other woman is our ill omen, Ishtar be my witness! (80)

VII
Stories and Humor

At the Cleaners

A sophomoric fop lectures a cleaner in absurd detail as to how to treat his garment. The exasperated cleaner suggests that he lose no time in taking it to the river and doing it himself.

"Come now, Cleaner, let me give you a commission:
    clean my clothes! (1)
"Don't neglect the commission I am giving you!
"Don't do what you usually would!
"You should lay flat the fringe and the border(?),
"You should stitch the front to the inside, (5)
"You should pick out the thread of the border.
"You should soak the thin part in a brew,
"You should strain that with a strainer.
"You should open out the fringes of the ...,
"You should ... with clean water, (10)
"You should ... as if it were (fine, imported?) cloth.
"In the overnight(?) ...
"In the closed container(?) ...
"You should [   ] soap and mix in gypsum,
"You should beat(?) it on a stone, (15)
"You should stir it in a crock and [rinse(?) it],
"You may want to ... the ... and comb it,
"You should [tap it] with a cornel-tree branch,
"You should [fluff out(?)] the flattened nap,
"[You should ...] the woven work with a comb(?), (20)
"You should split the seam and cool it,
"You should dry it in the cool of the evening.
"Lest the weaving get too stiffened by the sun,
"You should put it in a trunk or chest,
    "Make sure it's cool!
"Carry (this) out, I'll make you very happy fast. (25)

"You should deliver it to my home, a measure of barley
    will be poured into your lap!"
The cleaner answers him, "By Ea, lord of the washtub,
    who keeps me alive,
"Lay off! Nobody but a creditor or t[ax collector]
"Would have the gall to talk the way you do,
"Nor could anyone's hands do the job! (30)
"What you ordered me I could not narrate, declaim,
    speak, or repeat.
'Come now'[1] — upstream of town, at the city's edge,
"Let me show you a place to ...,
"The big job you have on your hands
    you can set to yourself, (35)
    'Don't miss your chance, seize the day!'[2]
"Do ease if you please the countless [tangles?] of a cleaner.
"If you can't give yourself more breathing room,
"The cleaner's not yet born who will pay you any mind.
"They'll think you a ninny, so, as they say,
    you'll get all heated up, (40)
"Then you'll get red in the face."

---

1. Here the cleaner mimics the customer, as in line 1.
2. Literally: "The meal must not pass, do come in," perhaps a proverbial expression meaning "*carpe diem.*"

The Poor Man of Nippur

This is a unique example of a Babylonian folktale, in which a poor man takes revenge on a mayor who wronged him.

> There once was a man of Nippur, poor and needy, (1)
> His name was Gimil-Ninurta, a wretched man.
> He dwelt in his city Nippur in abject misery:
> He had no silver, as befits his people,
> He had no gold, as befits mankind, (5)
> His larder wanted for pure grain.
> His insides burned, craving for bread,
> His face was wretched, craving meat and good drink,
> Every day, for want of a meal, he went to sleep hungry.
> He wore a garment for which there was none to change. (10)
> He took counsel with his wretched heart,
> "I'll strip off my garment, for which there is none to change,
> "I'll buy a ram in the market of my city, Nippur."
> He stripped off his garment, for which there was none to change,
> He bought a three-year old[1] nanny goat in the market
>   of his city Nippur. (15)
> He took counsel with his wretched heart,
> "What if I slaughter the nanny-goat in my yard,
> "There won't be a meal, where will be the beer?
> "My friends in my neighborhood will hear of it and be angry,
> "My kith and kin will be furious with me. (20)
> "I'll take the nanny goat and bring it to the mayor's house,
> "I'll work up something good and fine for his pleasure."[2]
> Gimil-Ninurta took [his] nanny-goat by the neck,
> [He went off] to the gate of the mayor of Nippur.
> To Tukulti-Enlil, who minded the gate,
>   he sa[id] (these) words, (25)
> "Say that I wish to enter to see the ma[yor]."
> The doorman said (these) words to his master,

---

1. Note the change of sex and species of the animal.
2. Wordplay on "his stomach" and "his mood" in original.

"My lord, a citizen of Nippur is waiting at your gate,
"And as a greeting gift he has brought you a nanny-goat."
The mayor was ang[ry with Tuk]ulti-Enlil,
"Why is a citizen of Nippur [(kept) waiting] at the gate?" (30)
The doorman [   ] to [   ] ...,
Gimil-Ninurta [came] happily [be]fore the mayor.
When Gimil-Ninurta came before the mayor,
He held his nanny-goat by the neck wi[th] his left hand, (35)
With his right hand he greeted the mayor,
"May Enlil and Nippur bless the mayor,
"May Ninurta and Nusku make his offspring flourish!"
The mayor said (these) words to the citizen of Nippur,
"What is your trouble, that you bring me a gift?" (40)
[Gimil]-Ninurta related his errand to the mayor of Nippur,
"Every [day], for want of a meal, I go to sleep hungry,
"[I stripped off] my garment,
    for which there is none to change,
"I bought a three-year old nanny-goat [in the market]
    of my city Nippur,
"I said to myself [on account] of my wretched heart, (45)
    '[What if] I slaughter the nanny-goat in my yard,
    '[There won't be] a meal, where will be the beer?
    'My friends in my neighborhood [will hear of it]
        and be angry,
    '[My kith and k]in will be furious with me.
    'I'll bring the nanny goat [to the may]or's [house],' (50)
"[That's what I s]aid in the wretchedness(?) of my heart."

(fragmentary lines, then gap)

(The mayor has the goat slaughtered and the meal prepared.)

"Give him, the citizen of Nippur, a bone and gristle,
"Give him third-rate [beer] to drink from your flask,
"Expel him, throw him out the gate!" (60)
He gave him, the citizen of Nippur, a [bone] and gristle,
He gave him [thi]rd-rate [beer] to drink from h[is] flask,
He expelled him, threw [him out] the gate.

As Gimil-Ninurta went out the gate,
He said to the doorman, who minded the gate, (these) words, (65)
"Joy of the gods to your master! Tell him thus,

    'For one disgrace you [laid] upon me,
    'For that one I will requite you three!'"

When the mayor heard that, he laughed all day.
Gimil-Ninurta set out for the king's palace, (70)
"By order of the king!
    Prince and governors give just verdicts."

Gimil-Ninurta came before the king,
He prostrated and did homage before him,
"O noble one, prince of the people,
    king whom a guardian spirit makes glorious, (75)
"Let them give me, at your command, one chariot,
"That, for one day, I can do whatever I wish.
"For my one day my payment shall be a mina of red gold."
The king did not ask him, "What is your desire,
"That you [will parade about] all day in one chariot?" (80)
They gave him a new chariot, f[it for] a nobleman,
They wrapped him in a sash, [ ] his [ ].
He mo[unted] the new chariot, fit for a nobleman,
He set out for [ ] Duranki.¹
Gimil-Ninurta caught two birds, (85)
He stuffed them in a box and sealed it with a seal,
He we[nt off] to the gate of the mayor of Nippur.
The mayor came o[utside] to meet him,
"Who are you, my lord,
    who have traveled so la[te in the day]?"
"The king, your lord, sent me, to [ ], (90)
"I have brought gold for Ekur, temple of Enlil."
The mayor slaughtered a fine sheep to make
    a generous meal for him.
While in his presence the mayor said "Ho-hum, I'm tired!"

---

1. Nippur.

(But) Gimil-Ninurta sat up with the mayor
    one (whole) watch of the night.
From fatigue the mayor was overcome with sleep. (95)
Gimil-Ninurta got up stealthily in the night,
He opened the box lid, the birds flew off to the sky.
"Wake up, mayor! The gold has been taken
    and the box opened!
"The box lid is open, the gold has been taken!"
Gimil-Ninurta rent his clothes in anguish(?), (100)
He set upon the mayor, made him beg for mercy.
He thrashed him from head to toe,
He inflicted pain upon him.
The mayor at his feet cried out, ... pleading,
"My lord, do not destroy a citizen of Nippur! (105)
"The blood of a protected person, sacred to Enlil,
    must not stain your hands!"
They gave him for his present two minas of red gold,
For the clothes he had rent, he gave him others.
As Gimil-Ninurta went out the gate,
He said (these) words to Tukulti-Enlil,
    who minded the gate, (110)
"Joy of the gods to your master! Say thus to him,

    'For one disgrace you [laid upon me],
    'I've requited you one, [two remain].'"

When the mayor heard (that), he [ ] all day.
Gimil-Ninurta [went] to the b[arb]er, (115)
He shaved off all his hair on the le[ft],[1]
He filled a fire-scorched pot [with water?].
He [went off] to the gate of the mayor of Nippur,
He said to the doorman, who minded the gate,
"Say that I want to come in to see [the mayor]." (120)
"Who are you, that you should see [him]?"
"[I am] a physician, a native of Isin, who examines [ ],

---

1. Reading doubtful; a shaved head was perhaps sign of being a physician.

"Where there are disease and emaciation
  [ ] in the body [   ]."
When Gimil-[Ninur]ta came before the mayor,
He showed him his bruises where he had thrashed his body.   (125)
The may[or] said [to] his servants, "This physician is skillful!"
"My lord, my remedies are carried out in the dark,
"In a private place, out of the way."
He brought him into an inaccessible chamber,
Where no friend or companion could take pity on him.   (130)
He threw the pot into the fire,¹
He drove five pegs into the hard-packed floor,
He tied his head, hands, and feet (to them),
Then he thrashed him from head to toe,
  he inflicted pain upon him.
Gimil-Ninurta, as he went out the gate,   (135)
Said (these) words to Tukulti-Enlil, who minded the gate,
"Joy of the gods to your lord!" Say thus to him,

  'For one disgrace you laid upon me,
  'I've requited you two, one remains.'"

Gimil-Ninurta was anxious, pricking up his ears like a dog,   (140)
He looked carefully at the folk (around him),
  he scrutinized all of the people.
He sent(?) a certain man, having recouped his losses(?),
He gave him a nanny goat(?) for [his] present,
"Go to the gate of the mayor [of Nippur?], start shouting,
So all the numerous [people] will crowd around
  at your shouting,   (145)

  'I'm knocking(?) at the mayor's gate,
    I'm the man with the nanny goat!'"

[Gimil-Ninurta] crouched [under] a bridge like a dog.
The mayor came out at the man's shouting,
He brought out the people of his household,
  male and female,
They rushed off, all of them, in pursuit of the man.   (150)

---

1. To extinguish the fire and thus proceed in darkness?

While they, all of them, were in pursuit of the man,
[They left] the mayor outside alone.
Gimil-Ninurta s[prang] out from under the bridge
    and seized the [mayo]r,
He set upon the mayor, made him beg for mercy.
He thrashed him from head to toe, (155)
He inflicted pain upon him.
"[For one disgrace you la]id upon me,
"I've requited you [three]!"
He [left him] and went out in the open country,
The mayor, crawling, went into the city.

Why Do You Curse Me?

This humorous scholastic tale involves a prominent physician from the city Isin, famed as a center for the healing arts, who goes to the city Nippur, a center of Sumerian learning, to collect a promised fee. As he asks directions, he is answered in elementary Sumerian, which, as a scholar, he is supposed to have mastered. Failing to recognize the academic language of the land, which even a vegetable seller in Nippur can speak, he assumes that his interlocutor is abusing him. The text ends with a plea that the school children should run such an ignoramus out of their city. One presumes the discomfited physician never got his fee.

Ninurta-sagentarbi-zaemen, [brother of N]inurta-mizidesh-kiaggani, [nephew] of Enlil-Nibru-kibigi, having been bitten by a dog, went to Isin, city of the Lady of Health, to be cured. Amel-Ba'u, a citizen of Isin, priest to Gula, examined him, recited an incantation for him, and cured him.

"For this your cure of me, may Enlil, lord of Nippur, bless you! If you will come to Nippur, I will put a bib(?) on you, I will feast you on choice viands, and I will give you two massy(?) jugs of fine beer to drink."

"Where should I go in Nippur your city?"

"When you come to Nippur my [city], you should enter by the Grand Gate and leave a street, a boulevard, a square, [Til]lazida Street, and the ways of Nusku and Nininema to your left. You should ask [Nin-lugal]-absu, daughter of Ki'agga-Enbilulu, [daughter-in-law] of Nishu(?)-ana-Ea-takla, a gardening woman of the garden Henun-Enlil, sitting on the ground of Tillazida selling produce, and she will show you."

Amel-[Ba'u], citizen of Isin, priest of Gula, arriving at Nippur, entered by the Grand Gate and left a street, a boulevard, a square, Tillazida Street, [the way of Nusku and] Ninimena to his left. He s[aw Nin-lu]gal-apsu, daughter of Ki'agga-Enbilulu, [daughter-in-law] of Nishu(?)-ana-Ea-takla, a gardening woman of the garden Henun-Enlil, [who was sitting on the gr]ound of Tillazida selling produce.

"Ni[n-lu]gal-apsu?"

"*anni lugalmu.*"
"Why do you curse me?"
"Why would I curse you? I said, 'Yes sir.'"
"May I ask you to show me the way to the house of Nin[urta-sag]entarbi-zaemen, son of Mizidesh-ki'aggani, nephew of Enlil-Nibru-kibigi?"
"*namtushmen.*"
"Why do you curse me?"
"Why would I curse you? I said, 'He is not at home.'"
"Where did he go?"
"*Edingirbi shuzianna sizkur gabari munbala.*"
"Why do you curse me?"
"Why would I curse you? I said,

    'He is making an offering in the temple
       of his personal god Shuzianna.'"

What a [foo]l he is!
The students ought to get together, and chase him out of the Grand Gate with their practice tablets!

The Jester

This text may record the routine of a buffoon or jester. The performer cracks a variety of jokes, some of them presumably of double entendre. In a satire of professions, the jester acts the exorcist by burning down a house to rid it of its haunt. Next an unappetizing religious diet is set forth in prescriptive form. Other portions of the text dealt with a heroic quest and bizarre omens, but these are too fragmentary for connected translation.

    The lion can terrify, (1)
    I can make a roar too!
    The lion can switch his tail,
    I can wag my tail too!
    I'm as trustworthy as a sieve, (5)
    I hold on to my followers like a net.
    I sing like a she-ass.
    I can't stand a thief:
        whatever I see doesn't stay where it was.
    I've gotten large from starvation, enormous from eating,
    I breakfast on ten quarts, I dine on thirty, (10)
    I don't leave off till I've filled the "bushel"[1] to the brim.
    The long, the short of them,
        there's none like me among the girls!
    My limbs are elephantine, my face a hyena's,
    I tower like a tortoise, I have no rival.
    I'm frisky, I'm a lively one: (15)
    So much would my lover be loving me,
    He keeps turning over, front and back, like a snared crab.
    He wouldn't herd his ewes within a league[2]
        of the city gate because of me,
    I've used up all the plants for my [ ]!
    I'm frisky, I'm a lively one! (20)

        (fragmentary lines, then gap)

---

1. His stomach?
2. Text: "400 acres."

"Jester, what can you do?"
[I can ...] and sing laments,
I can squeeze out apple juice and so(?) brew beer.

"Jester, what can you do?"
I can snatch on the run pod-weeds from turnips,
    groats from stink-wort. (25)

"Jester, what can you do?"
Of the whole exorcist's craft, nothing's beyond me.

"Jester, how do you exorcise?"
Here's how: I take over the haunted house,
    I set up the holy water,
I tie up the scape goat, (30)
I skin a donkey and stuff it with straw.
I tie a bundle of reeds, set it on fire, and toss it inside.
I spared the boundaries of the house and its surroundings,
But the haunt of the house, the serpent, the scorpion,
    are not spared.

(gap)

"In October what is your diet?" (35)
Thou shalt dine on spoiled oil in onions,
    and goose pluckings in porridge.

"In November what is your diet?"
Thou shalt dine on pod-weed in turnips,
    and "cleanser-plant" in crowfoot(?)[1]

"In December what is your diet?"
Thou shalt dine on wild donkey dung in bitter garlic, (40)
And emmer chaff in sour milk.

---

1. Or: "asafoetida powder."

"In January what is your diet?"
Thou shalt dine on goose eggs and dung(?) embedded in sand,
And cumin infused with Euphrates water in ghee.

"In February what is your diet?" (45)
Thou shalt dine on hot bread and donkey's ass,
Stuffed with dog turds and fly dirt.

   (fragmentary lines, then gap)

The Gilgamesh Letter

Assyrian school exercises preserve a fictional letter from Gilgamesh to a foreign king, in which he makes gargantuan demands for goods and services. While there are obvious allusions to the epic of Gilgamesh here, one may wonder if a parody on the Assyrian royal style is intended.

Say to Ti[ ], king of [ ]ranunna, thus says [Gilgamesh, k]ing of Ur, the Kullabian, created by Anu, [Enlil], and Ea, favorite of Shamash, beloved of Marduk, who rules all lands from the horizon to the zenith like a cord [ ], whose feet daised monarchs kiss, the king who draws in(?) all lands, from sunrise to sunset, like a cord, this [according to the com]mand of Enlil-of-Victory:

[ ] I wrote to you and sent 600 work-troops ... I wrote to you concerning the great [ ] of obsidian and lapis, overlaid with finest gold, to attach to the [ ] of my friend, Enkidu, but you said, "There are none."

Now I write to once again! As soon as you see this letter, [make re]ady and go to the land of ..., take with you a caravan of horses, send ahead of you [ ] vicious(?) dogs that attack like lions, [ ] white horses with black stripes, 70,000 black horses with white stripes, 100,000 mares whose bodies have markings like wild tree roots, 40,000 continually gamboling miniature calves, 50,000 teams of dappled mules, 50,000 fine calves with well-turned hooves and horns intact, 20,000 jars of ..., 30,000 jars of ghee, 80,000 jugs of wine, 80,000 bundles of crocuses, 90,000 great tabletops of dark applewood, 100,000 donkeys laden with ... and juniper, and then come yourself.

I want to fashion one nugget of gold, its ... should weigh 30 minas, to the chest of my friend Enkidu. I want to fashion [ ] thousand ...-stones, jasper(?)-stones, lapis, every sort of exotic stone into a necklace for it.

40,000 ... of white tin for the treasury of the great lord Marduk, 90,000 talents of iron: pure, excellent, choice, select, scrutinized, precious, ... beaten, that has no ..., the smith will make(?) a stag(?) ...

120,000 talents of good ..., the smith will do work for the temple with it.

Something novel, anything precious, exotic, which I have never seen, look for [ ] troops [to bri]ng them, ready or not(?),[1] and gather them together. Fill big new barges(?) with silver and gold and float them down to the Euphrates with the silver and gold. You should send(?) them to the port of Babylon so I can see for myself and be struck dumb with awe.

If I don't meet you in the gate of my city Ur on the fifteenth day of the month Tashritu, then I swear by the great gods, whose oath cannot be done away with, and I swear by my gods Lugalbanda, Sin, Shamash, Palil, Lugalgirra, Meslamtaea, Zababa, and (my personal?) god that I will send my lord "Attacker-in-My-Vanguard"(?), whose fame you always hear about, and he will wreck your cities, loot your palaces, [cut down] your orchards, and put wickets(?) in your canal mouths. I(?) will enter the ... of your fortified cities, who ... and speak of its ..., and I, Gilgamesh, will occupy them, they must not entrust their(?) ... to me.

[I will] your [ ], your gener[al], your craftsmen(?), your children, your belongings, and your offspring [ ] at the gate of Ur. I will bring you and your family(?) into the [ ]-house and ... talents of copper ... I will inscribe. I will set you up with the (statues of) protective spirits in the thoroughfare, [the citizens] of Ur will lord it over (you) as they go by.

Quickly send me an an[swer to my letter] and come, you will not have to bear anything from me.

Letter of Gilgamesh, the mighty king, who has no rival.

---

1. Unknown expression: "full or empty," here taken to refer to the preparedness of the addressee (having eaten or not).

The Dialogue of Pessimism

This satirical dialogue sets a master proposing various undertakings, for which his servant offers facile encouragements. When the master changes his mind and asserts the opposite, the servant is equally ready with facile discouragements. The master lapses into despair at the futility of life, and, when he finally asks what the best course for him to follow might be, the slave suggests suicide.

I

"[Servant, listen to me]." "Yes, master, yes." "[Quickly, get me the chari]ot and hitch it up for me so I can drive to the palace." "[Drive, master, drive, it will bri]ng you where you want to go; the (others) will be outclassed, [the prince] will pay attention to you." "[No, servant], I will certainly not drive to the palace." "[Do not drive, mas]ter, do not drive. [The pr]ince will send you off on a mission, he will send you on a [journey that] you do not know. He will expose you to discomfort [day and ni]ght."

II

"Ser[vant, list]en to me." "Yes, master, yes." "Quic[kly br]ing me water (to wash) my hands, give it to me so I can dine." "Di[ne], master, dine. Regular dining expands the inner self, [he who eats well] is his own god. Shamash goes with him whose hands are washed." "No, [ser]vant, I will certainly not dine." "Do not dine, master, do not dine. Hunger, (then) eating, thirst, (then) drinking — this is what agrees with a man."

III

"Servant, listen to me." "Yes, master, yes." "Quickly get me the chariot and hitch it up so I can drive to the open country." "Drive, master, drive. The roaming man has a full stomach, the roving dog cracks open the bone, the roaming [bi]rd will find a nesting place, the wandering wild ram has all the [gra]ss he wants." "No, servant, I will certainly not d[rive to the open country]." "Do not drive, master, do n[ot dri]ve. The roaming man loses his reason, the roving dog breaks his [te]eth(?), the roaming bird [puts] his home in the [ ] of a wall, and the wandering wild ass has to live in the open."

IV

"Servant, listen to me." "Yes, master, yes." "I am going to make a [household and have] children." "Do it, master, do it. [The man who makes] a household [ ] ... "No, I will certainly <not> make a household." "Do not make a household. The one who follows such a course has broken up his father's household, [he has gone in] a door called 'the trap'. [The man with a wife and child is one third] robust and two thirds a weakling."

V

"Servant, listen to me." "Yes, master, yes." "I will do something dishonest." "So, do it, master, do it. Unless you do something dishonest, what will [you] have to wear? Who will give you anything so you can fill [your] stomach?" "No, servant, I will certainly not do something dishonest." "<Do not do it, master, do not do it>. The man who does something dishonest is executed or skinned alive or blinded or apprehended or jailed."

VI

"Servant, listen to me." "Yes, master, yes." "I will fall in love with a woman." "[So], fall in love, master, fall in love. The man who falls in love with a woman forgets sorrow and care." "No, servant, I will certainly not fall in love with a woman." "[Do not] fall in love, master, do not fall in love. A woman is a pitfall, a pitfall, a hole, a ditch, a woman is a sharp iron dagger that slashes a man's throat."

VII

"Servant, listen to me." "Yes, master, yes." "Quickly bring me water (to wash) my hands, give it to me so I can sacrifice to my god." "Sacrifice, master, sacrifice. The man who sacrifices to his god makes a satisfying transaction, he makes loan upon loan." "No, servant, I will certainly not sacrifice to my god." "Do not sacrifice, master, do not sacrifice. You will train your god to follow you around like a dog. He will require of you rites or a magic figurine or what have you."

VIII

"Servant, listen to me." "Yes, master, yes." "I will make loans." "So make them, master, [make them]. The man who makes loans, his grain is (still) his grain while his interest is profit." "No, servant, I will certainly not make loans." "Do not make them, master, do not make them. Loaning is [swee]t(?) as falling in love, getting back as pain[ful] as giving birth. They will consume your grain, be always abusing you, and finally they will swindle you out of the interest on your grain."

IX

"Servant, listen to me." "Yes, master, yes." "I will do a good deed for my country." "So do it, master, do it. The man who does a good deed for his country, his good deed rests in Marduk's basket."[1] "No, servant, I will certainly not do a good deed for my country." "Do not do it, master, do not do it. Go up on the ancient ruin heaps and walk around, look at the skulls of the lowly and great. Which was the doer of evil, and which was the doer of good deeds?"

X

"Servant, listen to me." "Yes, master, yes." "What, then, is good?" "To break my neck and your neck and throw (us) in the river is good. Who is so tall as to reach to heaven? Who is so broad as to encompass the netherworld?" "No, servant, I will kill you and let you go first." "Then my master will certainly not outlive me even three days!"

---

1. The meaning of this expression is unclear. The idea may be that if one distributes largesse, the recipient is god himself, so good will thereby accrue to the giver.

Against a Bleating Goat

This parody expresses the murderous rage of a man unable to sleep because of a bleating goat. He claims that Ea, god of wisdom, also disturbed, abruptly sent off the great god Marduk (without the usual consultation), and charged him with silencing the offending animal. Marduk is commanded to insert the goat's own dung into its ear, a sort of "ear-for-an-ear" reprisal in that the goat has filled the sufferer's ears with its plaints. The sleepless one contemplates the goat's demise with relish. He hopes that the gods of livestock will not take this amiss, and expresses confidence that the whole country will erupt with praise and thanksgiving at the awe-inspiring deed.

    When the Ea [   ], (1)
    And Enlil [   ],
    On account of what pertained to the b[easts].
    He caught sight of a goat.
    The goat is sick, it cannot [shut?] its mouth(?)! (5)
    The shepherd is disturbed and cannot sleep,
    It disturbs his herdsman,
    Who must go about, day and night, forever herding.
    When Enki saw it,
    He called the Wise One, sent him off with weighty charge, (10)
    "A goat in pen or fold ... is disturbing me.
    "Go, it must not disturb me!"
    "Take its dung,
    "Stuff it into its left ear,
    "That goat, instead of falling asleep, let it drop dead!" (15)
    May Shamkan, lord of the beasts, hold nothing against me,
    Nor serve me summons for this case.
    Folk and land will sing your praises,
    Even the great gods will praise what you can do!

The Dog's Boast

This excerpt is taken from a large but fragmentary composition dealing with a contest among a wolf, fox, and dog. In this passage, the dog praises his own prowess.

    I am mighty in strength, the talon of Anzu,
        the fury(?) of a lion, (1)
    My legs run faster than birds on the wing,
    At my loud outcry mountains and rivers dry up(?).
    I take my onerous place before the sheep,
    Their lives are entrusted to me,
        instead of to shepherds or herdsmen, (5)
    I am sent off on my regular path in the open country
        and the watering place, I go around the fold.
    At the clash of my fearsome weapons I flush out ...,
    At my baying, panther, tiger, lion, wildcat take to flight,
    The bird can[not] fly away nor go on course.
    No rustler thieves [from] my pens! (10)

Land for the Birds

In this satirical legal document a bird-genie buys a tract of useless land near the entrance to Hell.

> Harhanda, talon-footed genie of the household of [   ], has contracted to buy from Urburu son of Lipugu (as follows):
>
> [Real estate consisting of x hectares of land in] the meadowland ..., adjoining the cemetery, where [there is no] wa[ter], where no barley is brou[ght] forth,
>
> Real estate consisting of two hectares of land in the open country of ..., one cultivates this field with no profit, one [produces] no dried seed therefrom,[1]
>
> Bounded by the River Ulaya at the Gate of Hell, all located in [   ], (as well as) a non-existent field in the duty-free zone[2] at the Gate of Hell, for [seven pounds] of mistletoe and five pounds of birdseed of ..., mother of talon-footed genies.
>
> The money is [paid] in full, he has bought the profitless field, claim and contest shall be invalid.
>
> Whosoever shall raise a claim at any time in the future, be it Urburu or his sons [or grandsons], who shall file [lawsuit] or contest against Harhanda and his sons, [he shall pay] ten talents of [   ], he shall [spend(?) a period of] four months of Augusts and Septembers at the wall of [   ], he shall render up four limestone slabs(?),[3] he shall pay five pounds of birdseed and seven po[unds of mistletoe], he shall contest his (own) lawsuit ....

Witness:	Sa-sidqi, talon-footed genie of [	]
Witness:	Sasallu, deputy of [	]
Witness:	Tab-salame [	]
Witness:	Woo-woo the owl of [	], the same
Witness:	Caw-caw the crow of [	], the same
Witness:	Longlegs the goose of [	], the same

1. That is, birdseed cannot be raised there.
2. Literally, "tax-exempt community."
3. Assyrian palaces were decorated with large limestone slabs, some of which were carved with representations of protective genies.

Witness: At-their-Hymens the wasp of ..., the same whose wife is in charge of the good-time girls(?) of Tur-Abdin
Witness: *(gap)*
Witness: [   ] the express mule [   ]
Witness: [   ], governor of the open country.

(The document is dated, with signatures of the witnesses in the form of claw-shaped marks on the tablet.)

VIII
WISDOM

Numerous texts retail conventional wisdom in the form of apodictic sayings and advice.

Counsels of Wisdom

A learned man [ ] (1)
From [his] wisdom [ ]:
"Come, my son,
"[Pay heed to] the instruction which [I give you],
"Master the counsels [ ] ..." (5)

Don't stop to talk with a frivolous person,
Nor go consult with a [ ] who has nothing to do.
With good intentions you will do their thinking for them,
You will diminish your own accomplishment,
    abandon your own course,
You will play false to your own, wiser, thinking. (10)

Hold your tongue, watch what you say.
A man's pride: the great value on your lips.
Insolence and insult should be abhorrent to you.
Speak nothing slanderous, no untrue report.
The frivolous person is of no account. (15)

Don't go stand where there's a crowd,
Do not linger where there is a dispute.
They will bring evil upon you in the dispute,
Then you will be made their witness,
They will bring you to bolster a case not your own. (20)
When confronted with a dispute, avoid it, pay no heed.
If it is a dispute with you, put out the flame,
A dispute is a wide-open ambush,
    a wall of sticks that smothers its opponents,

It brings to mind what a man forgot and charges him.
Do no evil to the man who disputes with you, (25)
Requite with good the one who does evil to you.
Be fair to your enemy,
Let your mood be cheerful to your opponent.
Be it your ill wisher, tre[at him generous]ly.
Make up your mind to no evil, (30)
Suc[h is not] acceptable [to the] gods,
Evil [ ] is abhorrent to [   ] Marduk.

[ ] the lowly, take pity on him.
Do not despise the miserable and [   ],
Do not wrinkle up your nose haughtily at them. (35)
One's god will be angry with him for that,
It is displeasing to Shamash, he will requite him with evil.

Give food to eat, beer to drink,
Present what is asked for, provide for and honor.
One's god will be happy with him for that, (40)
It is pleasing to Shamash, he will requite him with favor.
Do good deeds and be helpful all the days of your life.

You must not make a slave girl important in your house,
She must not rule your bedroom like a wife
... (45)
Let your people have this to tell you:
"The household that a slave girl rules, she will break up."

Don't marry a prostitute, whose husbands are legion,
Nor a temple harlot, who is dedicated to a goddess,
Nor a courtesan, whose intimates are numerous. (50)
She will not sustain you in your time of trouble,
She will snigger at you when you are embroiled in controversy.
She has neither respect nor obedience in her nature.
Even if she has the run of your house, get rid of her,
She has her ears attuned for another's footfall. (55)

Variant: As to the household she enters, she will break (it) up.
The man who married her will not have a stable home life.

My son, should it be the prince's will that you serve him,
His closely guarded seal should hang (around your neck).
Open his vault and go in, for there is none but you
    (should do so). (60)
You may find countless treasures therein,
You must not covet any of it,
You must not set your mind on stealth.
Later the matter will be [brought out],
And the stealth you attempted will be ex[posed]. (65)
When the prince hears, he will [   ],
His beaming countenance will [darken].
As for you, you will have an explanation [to devise] ...

              (gap)

Do not backbite, speak fair words.
Do not speak of evil things, (70)
Think of something good to say.
As for the backbiter and the speaker of evil,
They will be forced to settle their accounts with Shamash.

Do not speak lightly, guard your speech.
Do not speak your innermost thoughts, (even) when alone. (75)
What you say on the spur of the moment
    you will still have with you later,
So set your mind on restraining your speech.

Bless your god every day,
Sacrifice and prayer are meet with incense.
You should give freewill offerings to your god, (80)
For this is meet for a deity.
Prayer, supplication, and genuflection:

For every grain you render, your profit will be a talent,[1]
So you will proceed at a premium with your god.

Since you are accomplished, read this text: (85)
"Reverence begets benevolence,
"Sacrifice prolongs life,
"And prayer atones for guilt.
"He who reverences the gods is despised by [no one],
"He who favors the Anunna-gods prolongs [his days]. (90)

---

1. A large sum of money, approximately fifty pounds of silver.

Proverbs and Sayings

Marriage Ditty

(He)

My face is a lion's, my figure a guardian angel's, (1)
    my thighs(?) absolute delight!
Who will be the wife for me to adore?

(She)

My heart is discretion, my(!) inmost self is good counsel,
    my emotions are restrained,
    my lips speak delightful words!
Who will be the groom of my choice?

Marrying for Money

Who is wealthy? Who is rich? (5)
For whom shall I reserve my intimacy?

That you fall in love (means) that you bear a yoke.
Plan ahead, you will succeed,
Make no plan ahead, you will not succeed.

The Lord helps them ...

[Gi]rd yourself, your god shall be your help. (10)
[Draw?] your sword! A god shall be your ally.

When you are down, let a friend help.
You did evil to your well-wisher —
    what will you do to your enemy?

Wealth is not your help, but god.
(Be you) great or small, god is your help. (15)

The wise man is clad in finery,
    the fool is dressed in a gory rag.
May the land be destroyed over our enemies' heads,
May the tottering wall collapse on our opponents,
May the land of the foe be wholly awash.

Shamash (=Divine Justice and Truth) will sustain your
    government, even if your king is an ignoramus. (20)
If the plow has turned up evil,
    Shamash could not be the cause(?).
People without a king are (like) sheep without a shepherd.
People without a foreman are (like) a canal without a regulator.
Workers without a supervisor are
    (like) a field without a cultivator.
A household without a master is
    (like) a woman without a husband. (25)

Fear the Nearest?

Have a lord, have a king, (but) respect a governor.

When you have seen for yourself the profit
    of reverencing god,
You will praise god and bless the king.

Refuse a boy's wish, he will make a fuss(?),
Throw a sop to a puppy, he will fawn over you. (30)

The Power of Government

The command of the palace is like the command of Anu,
    it cannot be repudiated.
The king's command is sure as that of Shamash,
    His command cannot be rivalled nor his utterance altered.
The command of the palace is sure as that of Anu.
    Like Shamash, (the king) loves justice and hates evil.

Practical Wisdom

She looked at you, how far will she go with you?
To go, or not to go, to god your lord? (35)
Would you hand a clod to him who throws?

Domestic Wisdom

Linen is laid for fleas, the meat basket(?) is woven for flies,
    the storehouse is constructed for lizards.
He accumulated much but he slaughtered his pig.
He accumulated much but he used up his firewood.

A Woman's Lot

The wife of the tongue-tied talker is a slave girl. (40)
My mouth can make me the rival of men.
My mouth has made me renowned among men.

Life and Labor

Eat no fat, void no blood.
Do no falsehood, fear of [god] will not consume you.
Speak no evil, woe will not work its way into you, (45)
Do no evil, you will undergo no lasting [mis]fortune.
A scorpion stung a man, what did it gain?
An informer caused a man's death, [wh]at did he profit?
The scorpion [ ], informing [ ] ...
[Win]ter is malignant, summer reasonable. (50)
As they say, is she pregnant without intercourse?
    Fat without eating?
Intercourse hinders lactation.
Let me store up, they will rob (me),
Let me squander, who will pay then?

The Unthanked Good Advisor

As its(?) gods returned to its ruins, (55)
Woe has entered the ruined house,
Where the evil man was tenant
(And) the heedful man was not to grow old.
The wise vizier, whose wisdom his master has heeded not,
And anyone valuable whom his master has forgotten, (60)
When the need arises, he will be reinstated.

The shadow which catches me is caught (too).
As they say, did the canebrake turn a profit on its reeds,
    the meadow on its grass?
The strong man lives by the profit of his arm,
The weak by the profit on his children. (65)
My vagina is fine, (though) some of my folks consider
    me a has-been;
It's all fine, and I still (need to) wear a tampon.
Would you slap a moving ox in the face with a pin?
My knees are always on the go, my legs are never tired,
A simpleton dogs me with adversity. (70)
I am a riding steed, yoked to an ass,
I pull the wagon, I bear the lash!
My source of warmth is (only) the garment draped on me,
My carrying basket rests on my neck.
I dwell in a house of brick and mortar, yet a lump of dirt
    falls on my head. (75)
Last year I ate garlic; this year I have heartburn.
The life of yesterday was repeated today.

When you are on the river, the water is putrid,
When you are in a garden, your dates are gall.

If I instruct him, he is only what I begot, (80)
If I polish him, he is only a blockhead.

As they say, the early grain will flourish, how can we know?
The late grain will flourish: how can we know?
Suppose I die, let me consume; suppose I live, let me store up.
They capsized me and I almost died, (85)
I caught no fish and ruined my clothes.

Where the high ground comes down(?), the canal is opened,
The enemy quits not the gate of the city
    where defenses are weak.
You went and plundered the enemy territory,
The enemy came and plundered your territory. (90)

Would you lay out money [for] a pig's squeal?
I make the rounds for an ass's foal.

Prolixity

While the backside was breaking wind,
    the mouth brought forth babble(?).

Who is My Keeper?

I would go to my brother, (but) my brother lives like me.
I would go to my sister, (but) my sister lives like me.   (95)

Wellsprings of Contentment

Long life begets a feeling of satisfaction;
Concealing a matter, sleepless anxiety;
Wealth, respect.

Reflections on Power

When you commit a crime (out of weakness),
The Tigris will bear (it) away.   (100)
When you commit a crime (from a position of power),
Heaven itself will forsake you.
When you get away, you are a wild bull.
When they catch you, you fawn like a dog.
You can't jump a ditch when you're lame.   (105)

Every Man for Himself

When fire consumes the one in front,
The one behind doesn't ask, "Where's the one in front?"

Fat Men and Forked Tongues

Fat is he who, when he goes in the fields,
    his pouch dangles down.

The scoundrel chases after women's intimacy,
The rogue has two sickles.[1]   (110)

---

1. That is, one sickle is enough for an honest man.

One who has not supported a wife,
One who has not supported a son,
Is irresponsible and will not support himself.

Management

I am a manager: hand-picked and brawny of arm.

The foreigner's ox forages, while his own lies hungry. (115)

Candle under a Bushel

When oil is poured inside a stick, no one knows.

Giving is for the king, giving pleasure for the cupbearer.
Giving is for the king, doing a favor for the manager.

Friendship is for a day, association forever.

There is quarreling among associates, (120)
Backbiting among priests.
A resident alien in another city is a slave.

You need not watch a millstone.

The scribal art is mother of the eloquent
    and father of the erudite.

Tempest in a Teapot

Something that has never happened from time out of mind: (125)
A young girl broke wind in her husband's embrace.

Blind Leading the Blind

The unskilled is the cart, the ignorant his road.

Bride, you have made a mother-in-law,
They'll do that to you too (someday).[1]

---

1. That is, by marrying a son, she makes a mother-in-law; she is doomed, in her day, to the same fate.

Favors

As the potter looks at the rain (that might ruin his pots), (130)
May Enlil look at the city whose fate is accursed.

The farmer is one who watches, what (else) can he do?
The day turned dark, but it did not [rain],
It rained but he did not (need) to take off his sandals.
The (very) Tigris by its ... command did not irrigate fields. (135)

The Puniness of Mankind

Can strong warriors withstand a flood?
Or mighty men quiet a conflagration?
The will of god cannot be understood,
The way of god cannot be known:
Anything divine is [impossible] to find out. (140)

Gain and Loss

You find something, it gets lost.
You discard something, it is preserved forever.

The Odds

Who will go out against mighty warriors
    who are one of purpose?

Do the wish of the one present,
Slander the one not present! (145)

One's Deserts

You took out a loan, but will spend it on a trifle.
The mash is bitter, how can the beer be sweet?

Since there is no malt, let him consume,
Since there is no malt, let him squander.

Flesh is flesh, blood is blood. (150)
Alien is alien, foreigner is foreigner.

A Riddle

It came in, (but) is not right,
It goes out, (but) is not used up: The king's property.

From a Cylinder Seal

I have sought after and turned towards
    what pertains to god.
A man whose god chooses him shall lack for nothing. (155)

Proverbs from Letters

The Hasty Bitch
The bitch in her haste gave birth to blind whelps.

Making an Example
When fire consumes a rush, its companions will pay attention.

A Dog's Thanks
When the potter's dog enters the kiln (to keep warm),
    it (still) will bark at the potter.

An Adulteress's Word
In court what the (accused) adulteress says carries more weight
    than the words of her husband.

Brains over Brawn
The man who seized the lion's tail sank in the river.
He who seized the fox's tail escaped.

Servitude
Man is the shadow of god, and slave the shadow of man.

No Hiding Place
Where can the fox go to escape the sun?

The Valorous Ant
When an ant is struck, does it not fight back
    and bite the hand of the man that strikes it?

Silenced Protest

He who has been struck on the back, his mouth may still speak.
He who has been struck on the mouth, how shall he speak from it?

The Dangerous Fool

The ignoramus worries the [jud]ge,
    the inept makes the powerful nervous.

Advice to a Prince

This warning, composed in the casuistic style of omens, lists misdeeds of an unnamed king and their consequences. Most of the misdeeds center around royal abuse of the privileges of the cities Sippar, Nippur, and Babylon. The detailed charges suggest that the writer had a specific king in mind, perhaps Merodach-Baladan, an eighth-century ruler of Babylonia.

(1) If the king has no regard for due process, his people will be thrown into chaos, his land will be devastated. If he has no regard for the due process of his land, Ea, king of destinies, will alter his destiny and misfortune will hound him.

If he has no regard for his nobles, his lifetime will be cut short. (5) If he has no regard for his advisor, his land will rebel against him. If he has regard for a scoundrel, the mentality of his country will alter. If he has regard for a clever trick, the great gods will hound him for the sake of right counsel and the cause of justice.

If he denied due process to a citizen of Sippar, but granted it to an alien, Shamash, judge of heaven and earth, (10) will establish an alien due process in his land and neither princes nor judges will have regard for due process. If citizens of Nippur were brought to him for due process (and) he accepted the (customary) remuneration, (but) denied them due process, Enlil, lord of the world, will raise up against him a foreign enemy that will decimate his army, his commanders and administrators will prowl the streets like vagabonds.

(15) If he took money of citizens of Babylon and appropriated (it) for (his own) property, (or) heard a case involving Babylonians but dismissed (it) for a triviality, Marduk, lord of heaven and earth, will establish his enemies over him and grant his possessions and property to his foe.

If (he) imposed a fine or imprisonment (20) upon a citizen of Nippur, Sippar, or Babylon, the city where that fine was imposed will be razed to its foundations and a foreign foe will enter the place of imprisonment.

If he called up the whole of Sippar, Nippur, and Babylon to impose forced labor on the peoples aforesaid, requiring of them (25) service at the recruiter's cry, Marduk, sage of the gods, deliberative prince, will turn his land over to his foe so that the troops of his land will do forced labor for his foe. Anu, Enlil, and Ea, the great gods (30) who dwell in heaven and earth, have confirmed in their assembly the exemption of these (people from such obligations).

If he granted his steeds forage on the fodder of citizens of Sippar, Nippur, (or) Babylon, the steeds that consumed the fodder will be led off to an enemy's harness. (35) If the citizens aforesaid are conscripted into the king's forces in a time of national conscription, mighty Erra, [van]guard of his army, will shatter his front line and go at his [fo]e's side.

If he absconds with [their] oxen, alters [their] fields, (or) (40) grants (them) to an alien, Adad will come quickly. If he seizes [ ] their sheep, Adad, irrigator of heaven and earth, will decimate his pasturing livestock with hunger and offer them up(?)[1] to the sun.

(45) If an advisor or administrator on the king's service denounces them (the citizens aforesaid) and extorts bribes from them, by the command of Ea, king of the depths, the advisor or administrator will die violently, the place they were will be obliterated to a wasteland, (50) the wind will carry away their remains, their achievements will be reckoned as a puff of air.

If he nullifies their contracts, alters their steles, sends them out on service, or [forces] labor obligations upon them, Nabu, scribe of Esagila, who inspects the whole of heaven and earth, who directs everything, who appoints kingship, will nullify the bonds of his country and ordain misfortune (for it).

(55) If an officer or temple warden or royal administrator who holds wardenship of a temple in Sippar, Nippur, or Babylon, imposes forced labor upon them (the citizens aforesaid) for the temples of the great gods, the great gods will quit their sanctuaries in a fury, they will not enter their shrines.

---

1. Meaning of the verb not clear. I take it to refer to the corpses of the starved beasts lying under the hot sun.

IX
Magic Spells

Birth and Childhood

Numerous Sumerian and Akkadian incantations and rituals were intended for help in pregnancy and delivery.

THE BABY IS STUCK!

The woman in labor is having a difficult labor,	(1)
Her labor is difficult, the baby is stuck,	
The baby is stuck!	
The doorbolt is locked, about to end life,	
The door is fastened against the suckling kid, ...	(5)
The woman giving birth is covered with death's dust,	
She is covered with the dust of battle, like a chariot,	
She is covered with the dust of tuffets, like a plow.	
She sprawls in her own blood, like a struggling warrior,	
Her eyesight is waning, she cannot see,	(10)
Her lips are coated, she cannot open them ...,	
Her eyesight is dim, ... she is alarmed, her ears cannot hear!	
Her breast is not held in, her headbands are askew,	
She is not veiled with ..., she has no shame.	
Stand by me and keep calling out(?), O merciful Marduk,	(15)
"Here is the confusion, I'm surrounded, get to me!"[1]	
Bring out the one sealed up, created by the gods,	
Created by mankind, let him come out and see the light!	

---

1. This line is evidently spoken by the baby.

THE CHILD'S ARMS ARE BOUND

This incantation asks Asalluhi, god of magic, to save a child stuck in the womb and release him to the waiting midwife.

> In the waters of intercourse (1)
> Bone was formed,
> In the flesh of sinews
> Baby was formed.
> In the ocean waters, fearsome, raging, (5)
> In the water of the far-off sea,
> There is the little one, his arms are bound!
> There within, where the sun's eye cannot bring brightness,
> Asalluhi, Enki's son, saw him.
> He loosed his tight-tied bonds, (10)
> He set him on the way,
> He opened him the path.
> "The path is [op]ened to you,
> "The way is [made straight?] for you,
> "The ... physician(?) is waiting for you, (15)
> "She is maker of [bl]ood(?),
> "She is maker of us all."
> She has spoken to the doorbolt, it is released.
> "The lock is [fre]ed,
> "The doors thrown wide, (20)
> "Let him strike [ ],
> "Bring yourself out, there's a dear!"

SIN AND THE COW

The story of Sin, the moon-god, and the cow exists in several widely varying versions from the mid-second millennium on.

> There was once a moon-cow named Geme-Sin, (1)
> Perfect in form, beautiful in limb.
> When Sin saw her, he fell in love with her,
> He set the glory of moonlight ... upon her,
> He set her at the front of the herd, (5)
> The cattle came after her.
> He pastured her in moist grass,
> He would let her drink in a meadow
>   wherein was a watering place.
> Out of sight of the cowherd, the herdsman not seeing,
> A fierce young bull mounted her, raised her tail(?). (10)
> When her days were ended, her months fulfilled,
> The cow knelt down, the cow went into labor.
> Her cowherd's face was downcast,
> All the herd boys with him felt distress for her.
> The herd boys comforted her. (15)
> At her shrieks of anguish, her cries in labor,
>   the radiant one was desperate,
> The moon in heaven heard her cries, he raised his hand.
> Two daughters of Anu came down from heaven.
> One brought a jar of oil,
> The other brought water of labor. (20)
> She rubbed oil from the jar on her brow,
> She sprinkled her whole body with water of labor.
> A second time she rubbed oil from the jar on her brow,
> She sprinkled her whole body with water of labor.
> A third time, as she rubbed oil from the jar on her brow, (25)
> As she sprinkled the front of her body,
> The calf fell like a (running) gazelle to the ground.
> She called the calf's name "Suckling Calf."
> Just as Geme-Sin, the moon-cow, gave birth successfully,

> (So) let th(is) young woman who is having difficult labor
> give birth, (30)
> Let th(is) woman with child give birth successfully.

RUN HITHER TO ME!

This little spell addresses the baby about to be born.

> Run hither to me like a gazelle,
> Slip out to me like a little snake!
> I, Asalluhi, am the midwife,
> I will receive you!

THE BOAT

The mother having a difficult birth tosses like a ship in a storm.

> *(beginning fragmentary)*
>
> May her taut mooring rope be slackened, (1)
> And her battened amidships be opened,
> The mooring rope of the boat for the quay of well-being,
> The mooring rope of the barge for the quay of health.
> May the limbs be relaxed, the sinews loosen, (5)
> May the sealed womb ease, may the creature come forth,
> The separate framework, the human form,
> May it come forth soon and see the sunlight!
> Like rainfall, may it not turn back,
> Like one fallen from a wall, may it not return, (10)
> Like a leaky trough, may its waters not stay behind.
>
> *(Asalluhi carries out the spell.)*

WHY ARE YOU CRYING?

Babylonian parents sometimes tried magic words to calm fretting and crying babies.

> Little one who dwelt in the dark chamber,[1] (1)
> You really did come out here, you have seen the [sunlig]ht.
> Why are you crying? Why are you [fretting]?
> Why did you not cry in there?
> You have disturbed the household god,
>   the bison(-monster) is astir, (saying), (5)
> "Who disturbed me? Who startled me?"
> The little one disturbed you, the little one startled you.
> Like wine tipplers, like a barmaid's child,[2]
> Let sleep fall upon him!
>   (Incantation to calm a little one)

BE PLACID AS A POND

> [Baby, who has aggravated his father], (1)
> [Who has brought tears to his mother's eyes],
> [At whose uproar, at the clamor of whose crying],
> The hairy hero-men were frightened,
> Ishtar got no sleep in her bedchamber, (5)
> May sweet sleep bring you to rest!
> May sleep, life, and release (from care) befall you!
> Burp like a drunkard, wheeze(?) like a barmaid's boy!
> Till your mother comes, touches you, and takes you up,
> Be placid as a pond, (10)
> Be still as a pool!
> May sleep befall you, like an oxherd in repose.
> Listen to me, child, you infant,
> You should be asleep, he who sleeps is released (from care).

1. Probably a metaphor for the womb.
2. Perhaps a reference to the expected alcoholic intake of a child nursed by a woman of bibulous habits, and the child's resulting stupor.

(The spell is not mine, it is a spell of Ningir[imma,
    mistress of spells], (15)
A spell of Gula, mistress of healing,
A spell of Ea and Asalluhi, may it work for you!)

BE STILL AS SWAMP WATER

Dwel[ler] in darkness, who had not seen the sunrise,
You've come out, [you've seen the sunlight].
Be still as swamp[water],
Sleep like a ba[by gazelle].[1]
Like a boundary stone (protected by) the gods,
May there be no one to disturb you!

LET MOTHER GET HER CHORES DONE

This spell was to be recited three times with a piece of bread set by the baby's head. Then the child was to be rubbed all over with the bread and the bread thrown to a dog. After this, the child was supposed to fall silent.

The one who dwelt in darkness, where no light shone, (1)
He has come out and has seen sunlight.
Why does he scream till his mother sobs,
Till, in heaven, Antu herself's in tears?
"Who is this, that makes such a racket on earth? (5)
"If it's a dog, someone give it some food!
"If it's a bird, someone fling a clod at it!
"If it's a human child that's angry,
"Someone cast the spell of Anu and Antu over him!
"Let his father lie down, to get the rest of his sleep, (10)
"Let his mother, who has her chores to do, get her chores done."

---

1. Perhaps proverbial, like Italian *come un ghiro*, or perhaps a misunderstanding of the similar word for "barmaid" (see "Why Are You Crying?"). Babies coming speedily from the womb are also compared to gazelles.

(The spell is not mine, it is a spell of Ea and Asalluhi,
A spell of Damu and Gula, a spell of Ningirimma, master [of spells].
They said it to me, I repeated it.)

AGAINST NURSES HARMFUL TO CHILDREN

O wetnurse! (1)
Wetnurse, whose breast is (too) sweet,
Wetnurse, whose breast is (too) bitter,
Wetnurse, whose breast is infected,
Wetnurse, who died from an infected breast, (5)
Nursemaid, whose armclasp is relaxed,
Nursemaid, whose armclasp is loose,
Nursemaid, whose armclasp is limp,
Nursemaid, whose armclasp is wrong,
Be conjured by heaven! (10)
Be conjured by the netherworld!

Against Lamashtu

Lamashtu was one of the most dreaded figures in Mesopotamian demonology. She attacked young women and small children. The symptoms of her onslaught, according to later medical texts, could be jaundice, fever, fits of insanity, chills, paralysis, and intense thirst. She brought complications in pregnancy and delivery, as well as sudden infant death.

ANU BEGOT HER

The first part of the text fixes upon the culprit by telling of her origins and mode of entry into the house. The magician then orders her out of the house to a tortured wandering in the wilderness.

> Anu begot her, Ea reared her, (1)
> Enlil doomed her a dog's face.
> She is tiny of hands,
> She is long of finger, long(er still) of nail.
> Her forearms(?) are ... (5)
> She came right in the front door,
> Slithering over the (door)post casing!
> She slithered over the (door)post casing,
> She has caught sight of the baby!
> Seven seizures has she done him in his belly! (10)
> Pluck out your nails! Let loose your arms!
> Before he gets to you, Ea, the warrior, as sage for the task.
> The (door)post casing is big enough for you,
>   the doors are open,
> Come then, be gone through the (door)post casing!
> They will fill your mouth with dust, your face with sand, (15)
> With fine-ground mustard seeds they will fill your eyes.[1]
> I exorcise you by Ea's curse: you must be gone!

---

1. That is, to blind her so she cannot find her way back.

SHE IS FIERCE

She is fierce, she is wicked, she is [   ], (1)
She slinks about, she is un[canny].
Though no physician, she bandages,
Though no midwife, she wipes off the babe.
She reckons the month(s) of pregnant women, (5)
She likes to block the dilation of women in labor.
She dogs the livestock's footsteps
She spies out the country with plundering fierceness.
She seizes the young man in the roadway,
The young woman in play, (10)
The little one from the wet nurse's arms.
When the Two Gods saw her,
They made her go out through the window,
They made her slip out the (door) socket,
They tied her up to(?) a t[amarisk], (15)
[   ] in the midst of the sea.
...

SHE IS UNCANNY

She is singular, she is uncanny, (1)
She is a child born late in life(?), she is a will-o'-the-wisp,
She is a haunt, she is malicious,
Offspring of a god, daughter of Anu.
For her malevolent will, her base counsel, (5)
Anu her father dashed her down from heaven to earth,
For her malevolent will, her inflammatory counsel.
Her hair is askew, her loincloth is torn away.
She makes her way straight to the person
      without a (protective) god.
She can benumb the sinews of a lion, (10)
She can ... the sinews of a youngster or infant.

"BRING ME YOUR SONS!"

In this spell the demon is outfitted for a long journey and given farewell presents to encourage her departure.

> She is furious, she is fierce, she is uncanny,
> > she has an awful glamor, and she is a she-wolf,
> > > the daughter of Anu! (1)
> Her feet are those of Anzu, her hands are unclean,
> > the face of a ravening lion is her face.
> She came up from the reed bed, her hair askew,
> > her loincloth torn away.
> She stalks the cattle's tracks, she dogs the sheep's tracks,
> > her hands are gory with flesh and blood.
> She comes in the window, slithering like a serpent, (5)
> She enters a house, she leaves a house (at will).
> "Bring me your sons, that I may suckle (them),
> > and your daughters, that I may nurse (them),
> "Let me put my breast in your daughters' mouths!"
> Ea his father heard her,
> "O daughter of Anu, instead of trying to be the nursemaid
> > of mankind, (10)
> "Instead of your hands being gory with flesh and blood,
> "Instead of entering a house, leaving a house (at will),
> "Accept from the traveling merchant a cloak and provisions,
> "Accept from the smith bracelets as befit your hands and feet,
> "Accept from the jeweler an earring as befits your ears, (15)
> "Accept from the gem cutter a carnelian as befits your neck,
> "Accept from the wood worker a comb, a distaff,
> > and your pectoral."
> I conjure you by Anu your father, Antu your mother,
> I conjure you by Ea, who created your name!

SHE TORTURES BABIES

Great is the daughter of Anu, who tortures babies, (1)
Her hand is a net, her embrace is dea[th].
She is cruel, raging, wrathful, rapacious,
A runner, an abductor is the daughter of Anu.
She touches the bellies of women in labor, (5)
She yanks out the pregnant woman's baby.
She suckles it, she stands it up and it goes about.
Her breasts(?), her belly(?), her muscles are large.
The daughter of Anu is the one of the gods, her brethren,
    with no child of her own.
Her head is the head of a lion, (10)
Her form is the form of a donkey,
Her lips are a rushing wind, they pour out [ ].
She came down from the peaks(?) of the mountains,
She roars like a lion,
She keeps up the howling of a demonic dog. (15)

"I AM THE DAUGHTER OF ANU"

"I am the daughter of Anu, the sky, (1)
"I am a Sutaean,[1] [I have] an awful glamor.
"I enter a house, I leave a house (at will),
    'Bring me your sons that I may suckle (them),
    'Let me put my breast in your daughters' mouths!'" (5)
Anu heard and began to weep,
Aruru, mistress of the gods, shed her tears,
"Why shall we destroy what we have created?
"Shall she carry off what we brought to be?
"Take her and throw her into the ocean ..., (10)
"Tie her to a mountain tamarisk or a solitary reed stalk!
"Like a dead person who has no burial,
"Or a stillborn child who suckles not a mother's milk,

---

1. A bandit folk who were a byword for violence and marauding.

"May the daughter of Anu, like smoke,
   not return to (this) house!"

SHE SEIZED

[She is furious, she is uncanny, she has an awful glamor], (1)
[   ]
She crossed a watercourse and made its water muddy,
She leaned against a wall and smeared it with filth.
She seized an old man, they call her "wipe-out." (5)
She seized a young man, they call her "sunstroke."
She seized a girl, they call her "Lamashtu."
She seized a boy, they call her "Lamashtu."
Because you have come, you seize the form of his features,
You seize the limbs, you destroy the members, (10)
You consume(?) the sinews, you twist the muscles,
You make the face pale, you distort the countenance,
You cause depression, you burn the body like fire!
To remove you, to drive you out so you cannot return,
   so you cannot approach,
So you cannot come near the body of so-and-so,
   son of so-and-so, (15)
I conjure you by Anu, father of the great gods,
I conjure you by Enlil, the great mountain,
I conjure you by Ea, king of the depths,
   creator of everything, lord of all,
I conjure you by Belet-ili, great queen,
   who formed created things,
I conjure you by Sin, lord of the tiara,
   who renders decisions, who discloses signs, (20)
I conjure you by Shamash, light of above and below,
   creator of the universe,
I conjure you by Asalluhi, lord of exorcism,
I conjure you by Ninurta, foremost of the gods his brethren,
I conjure you by Ningirimma, mistress of incantations,

I conjure you by Ninkarrak, housekeeper of Ekur, (25)
I conjure you by Ishtar, mistress of the lands!
Be conjured by Assembly Place of the Gods,[1]
    abode of counsel of the great gods in Ekur,
You will not return to so-and-so, son of so-and-so,
    nor draw near him.

(This incantation is not mine,
    it is an incantation of Ea and Asalluhi,
It is an incantation of Damu and Ninkarrak, (30)
It is an incantation of Ningirimma, mistress of incantations.)

---

1. Ubshu-ukkenna, a cosmic locality.

Against Demons, Phantoms, Ghosts

A DEMON

The magician takes power over the demon.

> I have overpowered(?) you like a [   ], (1)
> I have bound you like a f[og?].
> I have cast you on (your) behind [   ],
> I have taken a string, I have silenced [your] lips,
> I have been pouncing upon you like a wolf, (5)
> I have cast my spittle upon you like a lion.
> Let me give a command, may my command p[revail?]
>   over your command,
> Let me speak, let my speech be stronger than your speech.
> As wild beasts are stronger than cattle,
> So may my command be stronger than your command. (10)
> As heaven is stronger than earth,
> So may my command be stronger than your command.
> You have tied your nose to your anus.
> So there! Have I not slapped you in the face?

I HAVE SEIZED HIM

The magician has caught a firm hold on the oppressor.

> I have seized him — like water
> I have blocked him off, like a watercourse —
> Like a dog by his neck,
> Like a whelp by his scruff.
>   (Incantation)

THE SEVEN EVIL SPIRITS

They are seven, they the seven, (1)
They are seven in the springs of the depths,
They are seven, adorned in heaven.
They grew up in the springs of the depths, in the cella.
They are not male, they are not female, (5)
They are drifting phantoms,
They take no wife, they beget no son.
They know neither sparing of life nor mercy,
They heed no prayers nor entreaties.
They are steeds that grew up in the mountains, (10)
They are the evil ones of Ea,
They are the prefects of the gods.
They loiter in the side streets to make trouble on the highway.
They are evil, they are evil!
They are seven, they are seven, they are twice seven! (15)
Be conjured by heaven, be conjured by the netherworld!

LIFE PASSED THEM BY

Mesopotamian demonology recognized a wraith in the form of a young man or woman (Ardat-lili) that had never known a full or normal life. The excerpts translated below show the nature of this demon and the sometimes fervid descriptions lavished on it by the scribes.

[A young man who] sits stock still in the street, [all al]one, (1)
A young man who groans bitterly in the grip of his fate,
A young man who, on account of his destiny, is aghast,
A young man whose mother, sobbing, bore him in the street,
A young man whose body is seared by woe, (5)
A young man whose (personal) god bound him out of hostility,
A young man whose (personal) goddess forsook him,
A young man who took no wife, raised no child,
A young man who felt no pleasure in his wife's loins,

A young man who did not strip the garment
    from his wife's loins, (10)
A young man expelled from his wedding ...
They (the demons) confront the man who has no god,
They s[et] their hands on his hand,
[They set their] feet on his feet,
[They set their] neck with his neck, (15)
They traded his self [for theirs].
"I am the son of a prince," he said to her,
"I will fill your lap with silver and gold,
"You be the wife,
"I will be your husband," he said to her, (20)
He made himself as alluring to her as the fruit of an orchard.
Ardat-lili wafts through a man's window:
The girl who has no (natural) destiny(?),
The girl who was never impregnated like a woman,
The girl who never lost her virginity like a woman, (25)
The girl who felt no pleasure in her husband's loins,
The girl who never removed her garment
    at her husband's loins,
The girl whose garment pin no fine young man released,
The girl who had no milk in her breasts,
    but only bitter fluid came out,
The girl who felt no pleasure in her husband's loins,
    whose desire was never fulfilled, (30)
The girl without a bedroom,
    who did not call for her mother.
Who made her cheek ugly through unhappiness,
Who did not enjoy herself with (other) girls,
Who never appeared at her city's festival,
Who never wanted anything, (35)
Who was taken away from her husband in the bedchamber,
Who had no husband, bore no son,
Who had no husband, produced no son,
Whose husband was taken away, whose son was taken away,
Who was expelled from her wedding, (40)
Ardat-lili, who was expelled from the window like air,

Ardat-lili, whose spirit was not in her breathing(?),
Ardat-lili, whose misery took her to the grave.
So long as you have not left (this) house,
So long as you have not left (this) city, (45)
You shall eat no food, you shall drink no water,
You shall taste no sea water, fresh water, brackish water,
    Tigris water, Euphrates water, well water, canal water!
If you would fly towards heaven, you shall have no wings,
If you would stay on earth, you shall have no place to sit!

AGAINST A GHOST THAT HAS APPEARED

Mesopotamian magic included spells and rituals against ghosts and restless spirits of the dead.

The ghost which has set upon me, keeps harassing me,
    and [does not quit me] day or [nig]ht, (1)
Be it a stranger ghost,
Be it a forgotten ghost,
Be it a ghost without a name,
Be it a ghost which has no one to provide for it, (5)
Be it a ghost of someone who [has no one to invoke his name],
Be it a ghost of someone killed by a weapon,
Be it a ghost of someone who died for a sin against a god
    or for a crime against a king,
[Place] it [in the care of the ghosts of its family],
May it accept this and let me go free! (10)

Against Disease and Discomfort

Disease and suffering were often treated as consequences of sin or wrongdoing. These spells belong to a collection that seeks release or absolution from illness or other affliction.

THE BRAZIER

I am the master exorcist, I have lit a fire, (1)
I have set up a brazier, I have burned the absolving materials.
I am washed and pure, the clean (agent) of Ea,
    messenger of Asalluhi.
May all the gods I invoked bring about absolution,
By command of Ea and Asalluhi,
    may no god nor goddess be angry. (5)

I have damped [the brazier] I lit,
    I have put out the fire I kindled,
I have smothered the grain I poured (into the fire).
May the grain-goddess, who absolves god and man,
    loose his (the patient's) bond.
Just as I damped the brazier I lit,
Just as I put out the fire I kindled, (10)
Just as I smothered the grain I poured (into the fire),
May the grain-goddess, who absolves god and man, loose his bond,
May the disease, the curse of so-and-so,
    son of so-and-so, be released
    and absolution brought about!

MAY MY SIN RISE UP TO THE SKY!

May my sin [rise up to the sky like smoke],	(1)
May my sin [run off from my body like water],	
May my sin, l[ike a drifting cloud, make rain in another field],	
May my sin [burn out like a flame],	
May my sin [flicker out like a flickering flame],	(5)
May my sin [be peeled off like an onion(skin)],	
[May my sin be stripped off like a date(skin)],	
[May my sin be unraveled like a mat],	
[May my sin, like a shattered potter's vessel,	
never return where it was],	
May my sin [be shattered like a potsherd],	(10)
May my sin, like silver and gold brought from [its] mine,	
[never return where it was],	
May my sin, like ... iron, [never return where it was],	
May my sin, like sweet waters of a river,	
[never return where it was],	
May my sin, like an uprooted tamarisk,	
[never return where it was],	
May a bird take my sin up to the sky,	(15)
[May] a fish [take] my sin [down] to the de[pths]!	

AGAINST TOOTHACHE

This incantation tells how toothache found its place in the world.

After Anu created [heaven],	(1)
Heaven created [earth],	
Earth created rivers,	
Rivers created watercourses,	
Watercourses created marshes,	(5)
Marshes created the worm.	
The worm came crying before Shamash,	
Before Ea his tears flowed down,	
"What will you give me, that I may eat?	

> "What will you give me, that I may suck?" (10)
> "I will give you a ripe fig and an apple."
> "What are a ripe fig and an apple to me?
> "Set me to dwell between teeth and jaw,
> "That I may suck the blood of the jaw,
> "That I may chew on the bits (of food) stuck in the jaw." (15)
> ...
> Because you said this, worm,
> May Ea strike you with the might of his hand!

AGAINST SICKNESS AND PAIN

This excerpt is from a group of short spells that use incineration of garlic, dates, matting, various wools, goat's hair, and flour as a means of symbolically burning the evil besetting a person.

> As this garlic is peeled off and thrown into the fire, (1)
> (And) Girra burns it up with fire,
> Which will not be cultivated in a garden patch,
> Which will not be hard by a ditch or canal,
> Whose roots will not take hold in the ground, (5)
> Whose sprout will not come forth nor see the sun,
> Which will not be used for the repast of god or king,
> (So) may the curse, something evil, revenge, interrogation,
> The sickness of my suffering, wrong-doing, crime, misdeed, sin,
> The sickness which is in my body, flesh, and sinews (10)
> Be peeled off like this garlic,
> May Girra burn it with fire this day,
> May the wicked thing go forth, that I may see light.

AGAINST BILE

Biliousness is here symbolized by a greenish goat browsing in a green world.

> The she-goat is green, its offspring is green, (1)
> Its shepherd is green, its herdsman is green,
> It feeds on green grass in a green plot,
> It drinks green water from a green canal.
> He threw a stick at it, it did not turn around, (5)
> He threw a clod at it, it did not raise its head,
> He threw a wad(?) of thyme and salt at it:
> Bile beset the wasted man like a fog.

(The spell is not mine, it is a spell of Ea, Asalluhi, Damu, and Gula.)

AGAINST EYE DISEASE

Daughters to the Wind

Eye disease was a common problem in Babylonia. The following seven spells seek to cure it.

> Blurred eyes, troubled eyes! (1)
> Eyes, daughters to the wind,
> Eyes, porous blood vessels!
> You have brought upon me a rainfall [of blood?] and fire!
> Let it be extinguished as if with water, (5)
> Let it cease (running) as if with algae.[1]

(This incantation is not mine,
    it is an incantation of Damu and Ninkarrak.
O Ninkarrak, heal, that the specialist receive (his) fee.
Let it not go out above, let it go out below.[2])

---

1. If correctly understood, may refer to clotting of blood or stanching a flow of fluid from the eye.
2. The disease is supposed to be excreted.

Bloodshot Eyes

Cloudy eyes, blurred eyes, bloodshot eyes! (1)
Why do you cloud over, why do you blur?
Why do sand of river, pollen of date palm,
Pollen of fig tree, straw of winnower sting you?
If I called you, come, (5)
If I did not call you, you must not come!
(Be off), before north, south, east, and west wind
      have risen against you!

They are Two

They are two, the daughters of Anu, (1)
Between them bars a barrier,
Never goes sister to her sister!
Whom shall I send to the daughter(s) of Anu of heaven?
Let them bring their pots of chalcedony,
      their pots of pure bright lapis, (5)
Let them draw water and quench the clouded eyes,
      the blurred and troubled eyes.

Mote

In the beginning, before creation,
      the work song came down to the land, (1)
Seeder plow bore furrow, furrow bore sprout,
Sprout root, root node, node ear, ear mote.
Shamash reaped, Sin gleaned.
While Shamash was reaping and Sin was gleaning, (5)
Mote entered the young man's eye.
Shamash and Sin stand by, so the mote will come out!

Wind Blew Down

Wind blew down from heaven and has set a sore in the man's eye, (1)
It has set a sore in the diseased eyes,
This man's eyes are distressed, his eyes are troubled,
This man is weeping bitterly for himself.
Nabu saw this man's disease, (5)
"Take crushed cassia,
"Cast the spell of the Deep,
"Bind the man's eye,
"When the Mother of the gods touches the man's eye
    with her pure hands,
"Let the wind which blew in the man's eye go out of his eye!" (10)

Vessels of Blood

O eyes, porous vessels of blood! (1)
Why do you carry away chaff, thorns, berries, riverweed?
Clods from the streets, litter from the ...,
    why do you carry them away?
Rain down like stars, soar down like sky-fire,
Before flint knife and scalpel of(?) Gula ... get to you! (5)

(A spell of Asalluhi and Marduk,
A spell of Ningirimma, lord of spells, and Gula,
The lord of the physician's art cast it, I bore it up.)

FIRE! FIRE!

This and the following allude to fever.

> Fire, fire! (1)
> Fire seized a lone man.
> It seized (his) insides, (his) temple,
> It spread (to others) the consumption of (his) insides,
> The stock of the human race was diminished. (5)
> Belet-ili went before Ea the king,
> "O Ea, mankind was created by your spell,
> "Second, you pinched off their clay
>   from the sky of the depths.[1]
> "By your great command, you determined their capacities.
> "I cast a spell on the ...-disease, fever, boils, (10)
> "Leprosy(?), jaundice!
> "Rain down like dew,
> "Flow down like tears,
> "Go down to the netherworld!"

(This incantation is an incantation of Belet-ili, the great queen.)

HAS YOUR SMOKE NO SMELL?

> Fire, fire! (1)
> Fire of storm, fire of battle,
> Fire of death, fire of pestilence, consuming fire!
> Has your smoke no smell?
> Has your fire no warmth? (5)
> May Asalluhi drive you away
>   and send you across the Tigris river.
> I conjure you by Anu your father,
> I conjure you by Antu your mother,

---

1. That is, from the ground.

Go out, like a snake from you(r hole in) the foundations,
Like a partridge(?) from your hiding place! (10)
Do not go back towards your prey,
Disperse like mist, rise like dew,
Go up, like smoke, to the heaven of Anu!

AGAINST FLATULENCE

This may be one of the few apotheoses of flatulence in world literature.

> Wind, O wind!
> Wind, you are the fire of the gods.
> You are the wind between turd and urine.
> You have come out and taken your place
> Among the gods, your brethren.

AGAINST HEADACHE

The following three incantations are directed at headache.

It Grants No Rest

[He]adache has come forth from the Ekur, (1)
It has come forth [fr]om the house of Enlil.
A Lamashtu,[1] who wipes out (names),
It grants no rest, makes sleep unpleasant,
It is the sickness of night and day. (5)
Its head is a demon, its body a deluge,
Its appearance is a darkened sky,
Its [fa]ce is the thick(?) shadow of a forest,
Its [ha]nd is a snare, its foot a noose(?),
... it makes the sinews smart ..., (10)
It makes the limbs smart,
It makes the [b]elly(?) tremble, it wastes the body,
It makes [the stomach] rumble like a porous pot,

---

1. A she-demon.

It contorts the tendons, it twists the sinews,
It twists the sinews like a heavy rope, (15)
It contorts [the mus]cles,
It chokes the mouth and nostrils as with pitch,
It crushes the armpit like malt,
It snaps off the [ha]nd like a thread in a tempest,
It destroys the shoulder like an embankment, (20)
It slits open the breast like a (flimsy) basket,
It staves in the ribs like an old boat,
It gets a grip on the colon as if it were intestines,
It flattens the tall like a reed,
It slaughters the great one like an ox. (25)
It struck the ox, it did not pity the ox,
It struck the wild ox, it did not relent to the wild ox,
It struck the ibex, it could not grow its horns full size,
It struck the wild ram, the mountain ram,
    it did not spare their young,
It struck the beasts of the steppe so they butted one another
    like an orchard whose branches are being torn away,[1] (30)
It punctures everything like a ... throw stick.
Asalluhi saw it,

(Cure follows.)

Affliction

Headache, applied in heaven, removed in the netherworld, (1)
Which sapped the strength of the strong young man,
Which has not returned her energy
    to the beautiful young woman,
Which has set upon the sick man.
Ishtar, without whom no one has relaxation or delight,
    made (it) come down from the mountain. (5)
It drew near the limbs of the afflicted man,
The man stands (saying), "Alas!"
Who will remove it, who will cast it out?

1. The comparison may be between the thrashing of branches and the clashing of horns.

Ishtar, daughter of Sin,
Enkum,[1] son of Enlil, (10)
Asalluhi, son of Eridu,
Let them cast it out from the body of the afflicted man!

    (Cure follows.)

Misery

Head disease charges about the steppe, blowing like the wind, (1)
It flashes on and off like lightning, it is poured out,
    above and below.
It cut off, like a reed, the man who did not revere his god,
It slashed his sinews like a (flimsy) basket,
It wastes the flesh of him who has no protective goddess. (5)
It flashes like stars of the sky, it runs like water at night,
It has confronted the afflicted man and paralyzed him,
    as if it were a storm.
It killed that man!
That man writhes like one with intestinal disease,
Like one disemboweled he tosses about. (10)
He burns like one cast in a fire.
(He is) like an onager, whose shrunken eyes are clouded,
He is fed up with his life, he is bound over for death.
Headache, whose course, like a thick fog's, no one knows,
Whose full sign, whose means of restraint no one knows! (15)

    (Cure follows.)

---

1. A servant god to Enki.

AGAINST GAS PAINS

Natural atmospheric wind is, of course, beneficial (see line 3), but wind locked up in the human body is harmful. Thus the wind should come out and go to its natural habitat.

> Go out, wind, Go out, wind! (1)
> Go out, wind, offspring of the gods!
> Go out, wind, abundance of the peoples!
> Go out of the head, wind!
> Go out of the eye, wind! (5)
> Go out of the mouth, wind!
> Go out of the ear, wind!
> Go out of the anus, wind!
> Let the man be released,
> Let him find rest [ ], (10)
> ...

AGAINST CONSTIPATION

This incantation is a common literary form wherein Marduk, son of Ea, learns of the patient's affliction and turns to his father for advice, but his father politely disclaims superior knowledge. In the end Ea provides the remedy anyway (not translated here).

> The insides (are) sick, covered over like a box, (1)
> Like water in a river, they know not where they go,
> Like water in a well, they have no flow,
> They are covered over like a brewing vat,
> Food and water cannot enter them. (5)
> When Marduk has caught sight of them,
> He cries to his father Ea,
> "O My Father, the insides are sick, covered over like a box,
> "Like water in a river, they know not where they go,
> "Like water in a well, they have no flow, (10)
> "They are covered over like a brewing vat,

"Food and water cannot enter them!"
Ea answers Marduk,
"My Son, what could I know that you do not?
"What I know, you too know, (15)
"What you know, I know.
"Be it a human, an ox, or a sheep ..."

        (Cure follows.)

Professional and Business Life

I WILL DISSOLVE YOUR ANGER

Why are you angry, seized (by rage),	(1)
Your eyes bloodshot,	
Your gums spattered with gall,	
The hair of your chest bristling?	
Your (own) son, taking my part,	
is angry at you and seized (by rage),	(5)
My eyes (too) are bloodshot,	
My gums are spattered with gall,	
The hairs of my chest bristle.	
Be it a door, I will open your mouth,	
Be it a bar, I will put a stop to your lips,	(10)
Be it bonding of a wall, I will dissolve your anger!	

ANGER

Spittle was considered to be endowed with magical properties.

I have escaped the spittle of your mouth,	(1)
I have given the word of your father,	
the word of your mother, the word of your sister,	
(As if it were) the word of a trouper, a city whore,	
To the covering earth,	
That does not make ready to speak,	(5)
That does not wag its tongue.	

AGAINST AN ADVERSARY IN A LAWSUIT

To be said "when entering the palace."

> Listen, [ye] of heaven, (1)
> Hear my speech, ye of the netherworld!
> So-and-so, son of so-and-so, my adversary,
> Until I slap his cheek,
> Until I rip out his tongue, (5)
> Until I send his words back into his mouth,
> I will not allow his mouth to speak,
> I will not allow his bottom to break wind.

I AM PROUD

Various spells and rituals were compiled for the use of people about to go to the lawcourt or government buildings. These call for strength, dignity, and protection. Others hope to make a person in authority glad to see the speaker.

> I rub on oil for dignity,
> My hands are full of oil for control.
> I am proud before god, king, lord, prince, great men,
> My lord's face will show (enough) favor for seven maidens!

I'VE PUT MY SHOES ON MY FEET

This spell is to be said three times over a person's shoes when he puts them on, so that, wherever he goes, people will be glad to see him.

> I've put my shoes on my feet. (1)
> I've taken my place before you.
> My laughter is the flowering of my features,
> The winsome charm of my eyes.
> I'm a treat,[1] whatever I say to you will be amusing. (5)

---

1. Text: "I am a festival," meaning a delight for the person who encounters the speaker.

TO RECAPTURE A RUNAWAY SLAVE

O door of the bedroom, you who are so firm,
I have firmed up your support with oil and wine.
Just as you swing out from your position,
But tu[rn back] the other way to where you were,
(So) may so-and-so, a runaway slave, swing out
But turn back the other way to his master's house.

Against Witchcraft and Sorcery

The Mesopotamians attributed many physical, mental, social, and economic problems to the machinations of witches and sorcerers. Some incantations seek to counteract known witches; others confront attacks of unknown origin.

MY MAGIC WORKS

The magician's magic is legitimate because it is controlled; the opponent's not.

> Netherworld, Netherworld, O Netherworld! (1)
> Gilgamesh[1] is master of your curse,
> Whatever you have worked, I know it,
> Whatever I shall work, you know it not,
> Whatever my sorceresses shall work (against me) is confusion, (5)
> With none to sort it out or solve it!

BLOCKADING

The magician cuts off all alien magic to ensure the efficacy of his alone.

> I blocked the ford, I have blocked the quay, (1)
> I blocked the machination of all lands.
> Anu and Antu send me,
> Whom shall I send to Belet-seri (saying),
> "Put muzzles on the mouth of my sorcerer and sorceress, (5)
> "Cast the incantation of Marduk, sage of the gods!"
> Let them call to you — you, (Belet-seri), shall not answer them.
> Let them speak to you, you shall not listen to them.
> Let me call upon you, answer me!
> Let me speak to you, listen to me! (10)
> (This is) according to the command spoken by Anu,
>   Antu, and Belet-seri.

---

1. Here a god of the netherworld.

THEY ARE WORKING AGAINST ME

They worked and keep on working against me, (1)
To roll me up like a mat,
To clamp down on me like a bird trap,
To wreck me like an embankment,
To close over me like a net, (5)
To cord me like cordage,
To climb over me like a rampart,
To fill a foundation ditch with me,
    as if (I were) ditchwater,
To pitch me out at the door like sweepings!
I, by command of Marduk, lord of the evening (rites), (10)
And Asalluhi, lord of exorcism,
Roll up my sorcerer and my sorceress like a mat,
Clamp down on them like a bird trap,
Wreck them like an embankment,
Close over them like a net, (15)
Cord them like cordage,
Fill a foundation ditch with them,
    as if (they were) ditch water,
Pitch them out at the door like sweepings.
[May] the figurines of my sorcerer
    and my sorceress tu[rn to ashes?]!

THE FOOTPAD

The sorceress, she who walks about the streets, (1)
Who intrudes in houses,
Who prowls in alleys,
Who lurks in the square,
She keeps turning around in front and behind, (5)
She stands in the street and turns foot(ways) around,
She has blocked passage on the square.
She robbed the fine young man of his vigor,
She took away the attractiveness of the fine young woman,

With her malignant stare she took away her charms, (10)
She looked at the young man and took away his vigor,
She looked at the young woman
    and took away her attractiveness!
The sorceress saw me, she came up behind me,
She has blocked passage with her poison,
She cut off progress with her spell. (15)
She drove away my (personal) god
    and my (personal) goddess from my person!
I have pinched off my sorceress's clay from potter's clay,
I have fashioned a figurine of the woman
    who bewitched me.
I put tallow in your insides, it harms you!
I implant an ashwood stick in the small of your back
    to burn you! (20)
The ashwood which burns you, may it cut off your poison!
I have kindled a fire above the city,
I have thrown ashes(?) below the city,
I have cast fire towards the house you enter!
(For) what you have done, may Fire consume you, (25)
(For) what you worked, may Fire overcome you,
(For) what you plotted, may Fire kill you,
(For) what you conspired, may Fire burn you up!
May Fire, who harms you,
    send you on the road of no return,
May furious Girra burn your body! (30)

THE EVIL EYE

... Eye, eye! It is hostile, (1)
It is eye of a woman, it is eye of a m[an],
    it is [ey]e of an enemy, it is anyone's(?) eye,
It is eye of a neighbor, it is eye of a neighbor (woman),
    eye of a child minder(?), it is the eye!
O eye, in evil purpose, you have called at the door,
The threshold shook, the beams quaked. (5)

When you enter(ed) a house, O eye, [   ].
You smashed the potter's kiln,
    you scuttled the boatman's boat, (10)
You broke the yoke of the mighty ox,
You broke the shin of the striding donkey,
You broke the loom of the expert weaver,
You deprived the striding horse of its foal(?)
    and the ox of its food(?),
You have scattered the ... of the ignited stove, (15)
You have left the livestock(?) to the maw
    of the murderous storm,
You have cast discord among harmonious brothers.
Smash the eye! Send the eye away!
Make the eye cross seven rivers,
Make the eye cross seven canals, (20)
Make the eye cross seven mountains!
Take the eye and tie its feet to an isolated r[ee]d stalk,
Take the eye and smash it in its owner's face
    like a potter's vessel!

(gap)

The World Around

AGAINST SCORPIONS

It Is Green

The following three spells are directed against venomous scorpions.

> It is green in the thornbush(?),
> It is silent in the sand,
> It is venomous in the brickmold!

Wolf of the Storeroom

The god Enlil encounters a scorpion as he builds a house, and brushes it away with his little finger.

> Wolf of the storeroom, lion of the larder, (1)
> Its pincers stick out, like a wild bull's horns,
> Its tail is curved up, like a mighty lion's.
> Enlil built the house.
> When he mortars the brick stack, (5)
> When he turns over the lapis-blue brick,
> Let Enlil's little finger take (it) away!
> O waters, ... let the libation bear (it) off!
> Let gentle sleep fall upon (this) man.
>
>   (Incantation to relieve a scorpion's sting)

I Poured Over

The speaker exudes vitality, like a river overrunning its banks, against the dread scorpion. Just as the onrush of a flooding river overwhelms stationary objects like dust, clods, and tiny plants, so too the speaker will overwhelm the scorpion, even though the scorpion can move about.

> I poured over myself, I poured over my (own) person,[1] (1)
> As the river poured over its banks.
> Clod in the roadway, dust of the street,
> Furrows(?) in the inundated field, ... of the orchard,
> The scorpion is different. (5)
> It will surely come,
> It will surely strike,
> It will surely not get away!

---

1. Or, "I engender myself."

AGAINST DOGS

These grim descriptions of attacks by rabid dogs, either literally meant or symbolic of the onset of illness, are remarkable for their stark power.

Swift Dog

It is fleet of foot, powerful on the run, (1)
Strong-legged, broad-chested.
The shadow of a wall is where it stands,
The threshold is its lurking place.
It carries its semen in its mouth, (5)
Where it bit, it left its offspring.[1]
    (Incantation to survive a dog['s bite], incantation of Ea)

Dogbite

It is long of leg, it is swift to run,
It is famished for food, scarcely anything has it had to eat!
Its semen dangles from its fangs,
Where it bit, it left behind its offspring.
    (Incantation)

---

1. That is, the dog's bite causes its "offspring" (hydrophobia) to grow in the victim.

AGAINST FLIES

In this spell someone brushes flies away from his head and face. The swarm of flies is ordered to fly away like the rising of a plague of locusts.

>   I have swatted you at the crown,   (1)
>   From crown to brow,
>   From brow to ear,
>   From ear to nostril of the nose!
>   I exorcise you by Ninkarrak: (5)
>   You shall rise a locust's rising
>   From his thrashing.

Glossary of Proper Names

Adad:	God of thunderstorms and rainfall.
Addu:	Another form of Adad.
Agade:	Capital city of the Sargonic empire, located in northern Babylonia. It was noted for its wealth and magnificence during the Sargonic period, but was of little importance thereafter.
Akkad:	Originally northern Babylonia; in later literary texts used anachronistically to refer to Babylonia as a whole.
Amurru:	God of the western nomads whose home was in the region of Jebel Bishri.
Annunitum:	See Ishtar-Annunitum.
Anshar:	Primeval deity, father of Anu the sky god. In late Assyrian texts artificially equated with Assur in order to afford Assur primacy over the Babylonian Marduk.
Antu:	Wife of Anu the sky god.
Anu:	Sky god, head of pantheon. Father of Adad, Enlil, Ishtar (in some traditions), and Nisaba, among others. His principal sanctuary was at Uruk.
Anunna-gods:	A grouping of the gods, originally the great Sumerian gods. In some texts, they may be superior to another group of gods called the Igigi-gods; in other texts the terms are used in parallelism. In some texts it refers to gods of the netherworld.
Anzu:	A monstrous bird, subject of various mythological stories.
Apsu:	A zone of fresh water found under the earth, domain of Ea/Enki, god of wisdom. Personified as husband of Tiamat in the Epic of Creation Epic.
Arbela:	Modern Irbil, important Assyrian city and cult center of Ishtar.
Ardat-lili:	A spirit or demon that haunted and tempted at night.
Asalluhi:	Son of Ea/Enki, god of incantations, often synonymous with Marduk.
Ashgi:	A little-known Sumerian deity.
Assur:	God of the city Assur and of the land of Assyria, after the late

	second millennium a warlike figure. In some texts referred to as "Assyrian Enlil," that is, chief deity of Assyria.
Atrahasis:	"Super-wise," Mesopotamian flood hero.
Aya:	Goddess of dawn; wife of Shamash, the sun-god.
Baltil:	Name for a district of the city Assur sometimes used *pars pro toto* for the city itself.
Bel:	"Lord," often a name for Marduk.
Belet-ili:	"Mistress of the Gods," name for the birth goddess.
Belet-seri:	"Mistress of the Steppe," wife of Amurru and scribe of the netherworld.
Black-headed folk:	A general term for Mesopotamians, as opposed to inhabitants of other lands.
Borsippa:	Important city south of Babylon, cult center of Nabu.
Bunene:	Courier and chariot driver of Shamash the sun god.
Burushhanda:	City in Anatolia famous for its wealth and commerce.
Calah:	Ancient name for the Assyrian capital city Nimrud.
Cutha:	City in Babylonia, cult center of Nergal.
Dagan:	God at home on the Middle and Upper Euphrates.
Damgalnunna:	Another name for Damkina, wife of Ea/Enki.
Damkina:	Wife of Ea/Enki, mother of Marduk.
Damu:	God of healing and healing magic.
Der:	City on the eastern edge of Mesopotamia, cult center of Ishtaran.
Dilmun:	Ancient name for Bahrein, important commercial entrepôt sometimes portrayed in Sumerian tradition as a paradisiacal place.
Dumuzi:	Akkadian Tammuz, shepherd god, lover of Inanna, netherworld deity whose death was annually mourned, vegetation deity, specifically of the spring grass.
Dunnu:	A small city in Babylonia.
Dur-Kurigalzu:	Important Babylonian city of the Kassite period.
Ea:	Sumerian Enki, god of wisdom, father of Marduk, noted in Mesopotamian tradition for his tricks and clever solutions to problems, as well as for his knowledge of magical lore. The "daughters of Ea" were beings who assisted in magical cleansing.

Ebabbar:	Temple of Shamash at Sippar.
E-engurra:	Temple of Enki at Eridu.
Egalmah:	Temple of Gula at Isin.
Ekishnugal:	Temple of Sin at Ur.
Ekur:	Temple of Enlil at Nippur, sometimes used as a general term for "temple."
Elam:	Land in southwestern Iran, usually portrayed in Akkadian literary texts as hostile and threatening to Babylonia.
Emashmash:	Temple of Ishtar at Nineveh.
Emeslam:	Temple of Nergal at Cutha.
Enbilulu:	Sumerian god of irrigation, used as a name of Marduk in the Epic of Creation.
Enki:	See Ea.
Enlil:	Chief god of Sumerian pantheon, whose domain was the earth and whose major cult center was at Nippur, lord of destinies and responsibilities of other gods.
Enmeduranki:	Antediluvian king of Sippar, a city in Babylonia.
Ennugi:	Netherworld deity.
Ereshkigal:	Goddess and queen of the netherworld.
Eridu:	City in Sumer, cult center for Ea/Enki, sometimes portrayed as the primeval city of Mesopotamia.
Erra:	God of scorched earth, of battle, violence, and destruction.
Errakal:	A name for Nergal.
Esagila:	Sanctuary of Marduk in Babylon.
Esharra:	(1) Region in heaven; (2) Temple of Assur in the city Assur; (3) Name for the temple of Enlil in Nippur.
Etemenanki:	Part of Marduk temple complex at Babylon.
Eunir:	Temple of Enki at Eridu.
Ezida:	Temple of Nabu at Borsippa.
Gilgamesh:	Sumerian king of Uruk, subject of epic poem wherein he tries to escape death.
Girra:	God of fire.
Gula:	Goddess of healing.

Gutium/Gutian: In Akkadian literature, a name used anachronistically for barbarian peoples, especially to the north and east of Mesopotamia.
Hana: City and country on the middle Euphrates.
Hanish: Divine servant of Adad the storm god.
Hendursagga: Sumerian deity equated with Ishum, a fire god.
Hubur: River in the netherworld, personified in the Epic of Creation.
Hursagkalamma: Temple of Ishtar at Kish.
Igigi-gods: Generally a group of great gods of heaven.
Inanna: See Ishtar.
Innin(i): Name for Inanna/Ishtar.
Irnina: Name for Ishtar.
Ishara: Name for Ishtar.
Ishtar: Sumerian Inanna, goddess of war, sex, and fertility; astral deity (Venus).
Ishtar-Annunitum: Militant aspect of Ishtar.
Ishtaran: Healing deity, with cult center at Der.
Ishum: Herald and counsellor god, especially to Nergal, fire god, protective of mankind.
Kalkal: Servant god to Enlil.
Kassites: A non-Mesopotamian people who took power in Babylonia and ruled there during the second half of the second millennium B.C.
Kesh: Sanctuary of the birth goddess in Sumer.
Marduk: National god of Babylon, credited in the Epic of Creation with reorganization of the universe with Babylon at the center of the world.
Meslamtaea: Name for Nergal.
Muati: Husband of Nanay, goddess of love.
Mummu: Creative power or intelligence, personified in the Epic of Creation.
Nabu: Son of Marduk, a scholar god, patron of scribal arts.
Namrasit: "Brightly-Rising-God," epithet of Sin, the moon-god.
Namtar: Netherworld deity, god of death by plague.
Nanay: Goddess of love.

Nanna:	See Sin.
Nanshe:	Sumerian goddess, daughter of Enki.
Nergal:	Netherworld deity, king of the netherworld.
Nineveh:	Assyrian capital city, near present-day Mosul.
Ningal:	Wife of Sin, mother of Shamash.
Ningirimma:	Goddess of exorcism.
Ningirsu:	Patron deity of Lagash, a vegetation and warrior god later equated with Ninurta.
Ningizzida:	In Adapa story, a door-keeper in heaven.
Ninhursag:	Mother goddess.
Ninkarrak:	Healing goddess.
Ninlil:	Wife of Enlil.
Ninmah:	Mother goddess.
Ninpanigingarra:	Name for Ninurta.
Ninshiku:	Epithet of Enki of uncertain meaning, here translated "leader."
Ninshubur:	Courier deity.
Nintinugga:	Healing deity.
Nintu:	Birth goddess.
Ninurta:	Warrior and vegetation deity, subject of Sumerian narrative poems dealing with his exploits, most celebrated of which was his defeat of the monstrous bird, Anzu.
Nippur:	Sumerian city sacred to the god Enlil, important cultural and religious center.
Nisaba:	Grain goddess and patron of scribal arts.
Nudimmud:	Name for Ea/Enki.
Nunamnir:	Name for Enlil.
Nusku:	Courier deity.
Palil:	Protective deity.
Pabilsag:	Son of Enlil, equated with Ninurta.
Qingu:	Deity elevated by Tiamat to kingship in the Epic of Creation and slain by Marduk.
Sarpanitu:	Wife of Marduk.

Sealand: Ancient name for marshy regions in the south of Mesopotamia, sometimes seat of a royal dynasty.
Shakkan: God of cattle.
Shala: Wife of Adad or Dagan, mother of Girra.
Shamash: Sun god, patron of truth, justice, and divination.
Shazu: "He-who-knows-the-inside (of things)," a name of Marduk.
Sherua: Goddess of dawn.
Shullat: Servant god of Adad.
Shuzianna: Little-known Sumerian deity.
Sin: Moon-god.
Sippar: City in Babylonia, cult center of Shamash.
Sirish: Goddess of fermentation.
Subartu: Third-millennium term for northern Mesopotamia; in later texts used anachronistically for Assyria.
Sumer: Southern Babylonia.
Sutaeans: Nomadic people portrayed as destructive and barbaric in Akkadian literature.
Tammuz: See Dumuzi.
Tashmetu: Wife of Nabu.
Tiamat: Ocean goddess.
Tutu: In Akkadian literature, used as a name for Marduk in the Epic of Creation.
Umshu: Deified day in Old Akkadian period.
Ur: Sumerian city, cult center of Sin.
Uruk: Sumerian city, cult center of Anu and Ishtar.

www.ingramcontent.com/pod-product-compliance
Lightning Source LLC
Chambersburg PA
CBHW030847170426
43055CB00004B/2